EARTHBOUND CHINA

INTERNATIONAL LIBRARY OF SOCIOLOGY
AND SOCIAL RECONSTRUCTION

Editor : Dr. Karl Mannheim

EARTHBOUND CHINA

A STUDY OF RURAL ECONOMY IN YUNNAN

By

HSIAO-TUNG FEI

PROFESSOR OF SOCIOLOGY, NATIONAL YUNNAN UNIVERSITY

AUTHOR OF *Peasant Life in China*

and

CHIH-I CHANG

LECTURER IN SOCIOLOGY, NATIONAL YUNNAN UNIVERSITY

Revised English Edition Prepared in Collaboration with

PAUL COOPER & MARGARET PARK REDFIELD

Illustrated

LONDON

ROUTLEDGE & KEGAN PAUL LIMITED

BROADWAY HOUSE: 68-74 CARTER LANE, E.C.4

First Published in England 1948

TO OUR MASTERS

PROFESSOR S. M. SHIROKOGOROFF

PROFESSOR ROBERT E. PARK

PROFESSOR BRONISLAW MALINOWSKI

This study was made by the Yenching-Yunnan Station for Sociological Research, National Yunnan University, sponsored at present by the Economic Council of Yunnan Province in co-operation with the Secretariat of the Institute of Pacific Relations.

PRINTED IN GREAT BRITAIN BY
LUND HUMPHRIES
LONDON · BRADFORD

Owing to production delays
this book was not published
until 1949

CONTENTS

FOREWORD

THE present book, a study of three types of rural economy in Yunnan, the southwestern province of China, is a translation of three reports of field investigation of the Yenching-Yunnan Station for Sociological Research, National Yunnan University, made during the war by my colleague, Mr. Chih-i Chang, and myself. It has been prepared for the purpose of supplying some material to social scientists who do not have access to Chinese literature on economic conditions in the interior of China. In a sense, the study represents a background to the traditional economy of China. Since in interior China modern industrial and commercial influence is just beginning to be felt, village folk are still farming with the old techniques, economically more or less self-sufficient, and are imbued with the traditional virtue of contentment. The population is dense, and resources are limited. It is old China in miniature.

The demand for knowledge of the Orient is growing. Because of the rapid development of communications, East and West cannot live alone any longer. Formerly, a man in the New World could live happily in isolation. He could be satisfied by an occasional glance at the antiquities of ancient Cathay in curio shops or could amuse himself by enjoying the exotic and queer manners and customs of a foreign visitor. In the last decade, however, the physical distance that once barred intimate contact and protected local interests has disappeared. Land lying beyond the horizon yesterday is as close as the courtyard today. But close contact without intimate understanding leads inevitably to disaster. The disparity between physical propinquity and cultural distance, the disparity between material expansion and social adjustment—this unhappy situation presents a grave problem to the world today. It has challenged the survival of modern civilization.

To achieve a world community in which all peoples can live peacefully and with mutual respect, there is need of a supreme effort toward establishing mutual trust and co-ordinated action. These require mutual understanding. The basic knowledge of how a people lives and what its problems are is necessary for mutual tolerance, sympathy, and aid. Therefore, the importance of studying actual conditions in Chinese rural economy needs no further comment. But the

introduction in the West of systematic scientific information concerning the East is still inadequate

Some ten years ago Professor R. H. Tawney wrote:

> The scientific study of Chinese society is still in its infancy. Such industrialism as
> exists, being novel, has been frequently described; but the massive and permanent
> background of the traditional economy has received less attention. In spite of ad-
> mirable work by Chinese and foreign scholars many aspects of the economic organiza-
> tion and social structure of China are still but partially known. Nor, even were knowl-
> edge of the normal operations of her economic system more complete than it is, would
> it be easy to allow for the dislocation which it has undergone during a decade of
> disorder.[1]

It may unfortunately be said that with the lapse of more than ten
years the statement stands as true today as it was when it was written,
while the dislocation of which Tawney speaks is even greater, and
the situation more complicated, because of the present war.

To develop the scientific study of social reality is not easy. It requires sound methods of field observation and theoretical analysis,
which, as we shall show, are not yet matured in present-day social
science as a whole and in China in particular. In China this type of
study is in one way a departure from tradition. It is well known that
traditional Chinese scholarship was mainly literary research. Students
believed that all wisdom could be found in books. When Western
social sciences were introduced into modern universities, they did not
change the tradition very much. When we were in college, we were
usually burdened with heavy assignments in textbooks. We learned
from books about Chicago gangs and Russian immigrants in America,
but we knew very little or nothing about the Chinese gentry in the
town and the peasants in the village, because these were not in
books. This situation deeply impressed Professor Tawney, who said:

> The curriculum [in Chinese universities] is based to an excessive extent upon for-
> eign materials. At worst, professors appear to repeat in China the substance of lectures
> heard, or books read, abroad. At best, insufficient attention is paid to the truism that
> the object of a university is not to cram students with information, but to prepare them
> for life in a society, and that, if a university is to aid its members to play a useful part
> in the life of China, it is less important that they should be informed as to the parlia-
> ments and stock exchanges of western nations than that they should understand the
> political and economic conditions of their own. The result is that the whole system has
> the air of a thing exotic and artificial. It is top-heavy, over-intellectualised and, in
> some cases, pretentious. Its atmosphere is that of a hot-house, not of the open air.[2]

[1] *Land and Labour in China* (London: George Allen & Unwin, Ltd., 1932), p. 23.

[2] *Ibid.*, p. 185.

True as are these observations of a distinguished scholar, it is also true that the students stifling in the hothouse were far from satisfied with their lot. Students in China have been trying to free themselves from this unhealthy atmosphere, and the present book is an attempt along this line. It may therefore be interesting to give a short historical account of the development of community analysis in China as a background to this study. It is not my intention to review the entire history of sociological or anthropological studies in China; I shall confine myself to the one institute under whose auspices the present work was done.

It was at the end of the 1920's that China entered a period of political stability and reconstruction. Young students, after having participated in the previous revolution, began to settle down and think about more fundamental issues. It was clear that political enthusiasm by itself would be futile if it were not to be followed by a period of practical reconstruction of the country. But when practical problems arose, most of the responsible leaders were at a loss, not for courage or devotion, but for knowledge of the existing realities. Quite naturally, therefore, students of that period directed their attention to the social realities and demanded a better understanding of the situation about them. It was at this time, in 1931–32, that Professor Robert E. Park, of the University of Chicago, visited Yenching University. He met the need of the students by inspiring them to make direct observations of community life and instructing them in how to carry on field studies. He himself visited the prisons and the Heaven Bridge, the red-light area in Peiping, to demonstrate that useful knowledge can be derived from the life of even the lowliest people. Following his example, and with the able leadership of Professor Wen-tsao Wu, the studer..s of Yenching University started, mostly on their own initiative, a series of community studies in various parts of China. The following is a list of their work completed before the present war.

CHING-KUN YANG. *A North China Local Market Economy.* 1933. A summary in English published by the Institute of Pacific Relations. New York, 1944.

YUNG-SHUN HSU. "Litigation in a Village Community in Hopei." 1933. Unpublished.

SHIH HUANG. "Peasant Custom in Hopei." 1934. Unpublished.

YUEH-HUA LIN. "A Clan Village in Fukien." 1934. Unpublished. In English: *The Golden Wing: A Family Chronicle,* published by Kegan Paul, London, 1948.

TAI-CHUN LIAO. *Chinese Rural Education (in Shangtung) in Change.* Privately printed in Chinese, 1936.

Tung-wei Wang (Mrs. Hsiao-tung Fei). *The Social Organization of Hua Lan Yao, an Aboriginal Tribe in Kwangsi.* Shanghai: Commercial Press, 1936.

Ti Huang. "Ching-ho: A Town-Village Community" (in Chinese), published in *Sociological World* (Yenching University), 1937.

Yu-yi Li. "Land Tenure in Shansi." 1938. Unpublished.

An-lan Cheng. "Emigrant Community in Fukien" (in Chinese), published in *Social Research Weekly*, 1938.

Hsiao-tung Fei. *Peasant Life in China* (in English). London: Kegan Paul, 1939.

This list shows the direction of work in our first stage of endeavor. We explored most of the important aspects of community life: economic, political, family and kinship, educational, and ceremonial. We also approached different types of communities—tribal, village, and town. However, many overenthusiastic young students who daringly explored this vast field, like my wife, who sacrificed her life in an expedition to the Yao Mountains in Kwangsi, were without the benefit of specialized training, systematic theoretical preparation, and co-ordinated group effort. Along with these explorations in the field, attempts at systematization of the research program were made when Professor A. R. Radcliffe-Brown visited the institution in 1936 and when a trip to Europe and America was made by Professor Wen-tsao Wu. But the present war broke out only a few months after Professor Wu returned to China in 1937. Yenching University was first isolated and then captured by the Japanese. The occupation of our base by the enemy temporarily suspended our work. In 1937 Professor An-che Li, a senior member of the research group, was able to get through the Japanese blockade and to come to Free China. He started a research station in northwestern China, studying border communities in that area, near Tibet. Professor Wu entered Free China in 1938 and established his headquarters in the National Yunnan University, with the aim of regrouping the students and carrying on our tradition. This institution now is called the Yenching-Yunnan Station for Sociological Research. The following studies have been completed.

I. On Rural Economics

Hsiao-tung Fei. *Land System in Luts'un.* 1940.
Chih-i Chang. *Rural Industry in Yits'un.* 1941.
———. *Land and Capital in Yuts'un.* 1943.

The first two have been summarized in *Three Types of Rural Economy in Yunnan* (in English), distributed by the Institute of Pacific Relations, 1943. The full texts of these three studies are translated and re-edited in the present book.

II. On Aboriginal Economics

Yu-yi Li. *Economics of a Mixed Community of Lolos and Chinese.* Summarized in *Three Types of Rural Economy in Yunnan.* 1943.

Ju-kong Tien. *Ceremonial Disposition of Wealth in Tai-speaking Tribes in Yunnan.* 1943.

———. *Land System in Yunnan-Burma Border Communities.* 1944.

The above studies will be translated into English in one book, *Primitive Economics in Yunnan.*

III. On Labor and Labor Relations

Kuo-heng Shih. *Industrial Workers in Kunming Defense Industry.* 1942. Summarized (in English) in *Labor and Labor Relations in the New Industries in Western Yunnan,* distributed by the Institute of Pacific Relations (New York, 1943); full text translated in *China Enters the Machine Age* (Harvard University Press, 1944).

Ju-kong Tien. *Female Workers in a Cotton Mill.* 1942. Summarized, inEnglish, in the above pamphlet and reprinted in the above book.

Kuo-heng Shih. "Education and Modern Industry in China: A Study of Apprenticeship" and "Mine Workers in South Yunnan," prepared for publication in Chinese.

IV. On Magic and Religion

Francis L. K. Hsu. *Magic and Science in Western Yunnan: A Study of the Introduction of Modern Medicine in a Rustic Community* (in English). Distributed by the Institute of Pacific Relations, New York, 1943.

———. "Family, Clan and Ancestor Worship in Western Yunnan." In preparation.

V. On Local Government

Pao Kuo. *The Power Structure in a Rural Community in Yunnan.* 1943. English translation in preparation.

The research station started its work in the autumn of 1938 when the Japanese had occupied all the coastal region of China. The front was drawing near to the interior. Conditions were growing steadily worse. In 1940 air raids became a daily routine in Kunming. Academic centers were especially attractive to enemy bombers. One day in October, 1940, our university was bombed and our houses destroyed. So we moved to a village and established our station in a temple. It was called Queike, the tower for worshiping the God of Literature; and later our station was known by that name. By living together in the same village, more or less isolated from the outside, and occupying a common study up in the ancient tower, surrounded by aged pine trees and by rice fields, an informal and intimate atmosphere was created among the small community of research students which encouraged their constant intellectual interaction.

Regular seminars were held in Queike. Fresh ideas developed as new observations were brought back by the field workers. Inspiration came from various sources: from the statue of the monkey-like god; from the purified light through the paper windows, giving the feeling of a reflection from the snow; from the roar of the wind in the pine trees; from the hot tea which was never lacking in the station; from the incense burning on the altar, placed there by devoted old country women; and from the friends from different lands and with different interests who visited us. We kept the research work going in the spirit of individual initiative and personal responsibility—a spirit which was seriously lacking in the pre-war universities.

We began to realize the truth in Tawney's words, "If education is to be alive, it must have its roots in the soil"[3]—the soil here implies a genuine interest in knowledge of the living problems of the day. The poverty of material life; sympathy for the hardships of the masses; the moral enlightenment which comes with the realization of one's part in the community, in the nation, and in the age; the bitterness of facing reality—all these combined to develop intellectual maturity. It is the war which has provided the stimulus long needed by Chinese scholarship. If there is anything of value in the following pages, as well as in the other treatises produced by the research station during the war, perhaps it is due to the adventurous spirit of exploring living problems. If there is anything in the exploration that shows insight and thoughtfulness, it is due to not easily satisfied young minds; the urge for knowing the conditions under which they are living is the incentive for the raising of new problems and the selection of data. To a Western reader the direction of these studies and the problems raised there may be more interesting than the findings themselves.

A few words may be added to describe briefly the material condition of the station. Visitors are surprised by our primitive equipment —a bare temple and a small library, consisting of old books that some of our colleagues accumulated during their student days. Occasionally we have a maid, but frequently we ourselves must cook and fetch water. There are no secretaries, so that we must copy every word and mimeograph every sheet of class material or manuscript. When we go to the field, we usually walk tens of miles and climb mountains day after day. Once we came to a village which was not hospitable. We were put in a supposedly haunted house to share the quarters of dying horses. But we were not in the least discouraged, because in this way we were able to experience the hard bare facts of human existence.

[3] *Ibid.*, p. 186.

The limitation of material facilities and financial support does, indeed, account for some of the weaknesses of the studies. For instance, without any assistance, we were limited to those materials we were able to collect personally while in the field. Although this helped to emphasize the importance of firsthand observations, it did prevent us from collecting data which could profitably have been gathered by assistants, such as the accounts of the villagers' daily expenditures, the enumeration of individuals in the markets, etc. We had no camera. Only by chance were we sometimes able to borrow one from friends. But films were so expensive that we at last gave up the attempt to take pictures. We could not afford to have experts make maps or surveys but had to be content with rough, inaccurate sketches. Moreover, the station could provide only a few full-time research workers. Most of us had to teach in the university. Those who had families were burdened at the same time with housework—shopping for supplies, cooking, and sweeping the floors. Therefore, it was not possible to stay in the field for a whole year. Medical care was lacking entirely. With a diet often inadequate, research workers easily became ill. Once the whole staff was affected by dysentery, and the work was suspended for weeks. Under such conditions the work of the research station has been and is being carried on. It is sustained by one conviction alone, the conviction of the importance of knowledge in reconstructing China as a member of the world community.

Even working in the most economical way possible, under present conditions of wartime inflation, we should not have been able to carry on if encouragement from our government, foundations, banks, and private sponsors had not been vouchsafed us. We are indebted to these sources not only for moral support, such as the prize of the Ministry of Education for the report on Luts'un and that of the Academia Sinica for the report on Yits'un, but also for financial subsidies. The Yenching-Yunnan co-operation program was started with the support of the Rockefeller Foundation. The Farmers' Bank in China, the Ministry of Education, the Ministry of Social Affairs, and Mr. Chin-hsi Li have repeatedly given us grants. In 1944 the Economic Council of Yunnan Province took up the sponsorship. If we have done anything worth while in science, they should share the credit.

All the reports of the research station have been written in Chinese, and a number of them have been published. Realizing the importance of preparing an English edition of our report, we summarized our work, mainly for private circulation, in the pamphlets mentioned above, which were prepared with the co-operation of the International Secretariat of the Institute of Pacific Relations. By various scientific circles in England and America we were then encouraged to translate the full texts of our reports. In 1943–44 I was sent by the National Yunnan University, at the invitation of the Department of State of the United States, to visit America, being instructed at this time to prepare an English edition of our work.

The Institute of Pacific Relations granted me the necessary funds for secretarial work. I am grateful to Professor Ralph Linton for his encouragement and co-operation during the preparation of this book. Part I was prepared at Columbia University with the assistance of Mr. Paul Cooper. The remainder of the book was prepared at the University of Chicago, which provided me with a study bearing the name of Robert E. Park on its door. I mention this not simply to make much of an accident—an accident which, however, through the force of what the Melanesians call *mana*, did actually stimulate me in my work—but, since "door" means "academic entrance" in literary Chinese, to symbolize my intellectual allegiance to this great teacher who initiated our rural studies in China. Could it have been a comfort to him to know before he passed away, only a few months before the completion of this book, that the seeds he had sown on his trip to China had at last borne fruit?

While I was working in the University of Chicago, I profited from daily discussions with the members of the Department of Sociology. Dean Robert Redfield made valuable suggestions in re-writing the material, and Margaret Park Redfield collaborated with me in editing Parts II and III and in arranging the final form of the book.

The title of this book was given by Professor B. Malinowski. When we parted in London in 1938, he assigned to me the duty of investigating the rural community in the interior of China, for he foresaw the possibility and the importance of this work. Before his untimely death he constantly wrote me and suggested many points worthy of special attention. Although a full list of questions was, unfortunately, lost in the mail and never received, the title suggested by him for the book did reach me. I cannot help expressing here my personal feeling of dismay that death has taken from me my three esteemed masters, Professors S. M. Shigorokoroff, R. E. Park, and B. Malinowski. From them I inherited most of my ideas; yet none of them has been able to see the work which has resulted. To them this book is dedicated.

In presenting this English edition I have an additional note to make. This book has been prepared for social scientists, with little consideration for the general reader. Yet I do not underrate the latter. If such a one should come to read this book, I would ask from him the courage to face reality and his sympathy toward an age of transition. There are, at present, certain symptoms of oversensitivity between Americans and Chinese. Most of those who have visited China during this war, as Dr. John K. Fairbank rightly pointed out in a letter to Chinese students in America, "have never studied Chinese history, so that they have no way of knowing how rapidly the Chinese Republic has advanced during the past generation. This makes them often uncomprehending and unreasonable in their criticism. . . . . There is good and bad in China, as everywhere, especially during wartime, and Americans must be made to think about it with understanding, not with emotions of idealistic enthusiasm or disillusioned pessimism." Such an irresponsible emotional reaction which leads to unreasonable criticism, he said, "raises a very great doubt whether the people who have been trying to interpret China or Chinese history to the West have really made any progress." In this sense, the present book will be a test of whether a realistic approach will help to build up friendship between these two peoples. Our success depends on the response of the readers. The encouragement to take up this task, I must not fail to mention, comes to me mainly from Mrs. John K. Fairbank. Through her indefatigable assistance in arranging for me connections with American academic centers, I was able to undertake the present translation. She it is, I believe, who, having lived in China and loving it, sees most clearly the real need of an intelligent understanding as a background to cultural relations. May this book vindicate the correctness of her view.

HSIAO-TUNG FEI

CHICAGO, ILLINOIS

INTRODUCTION

THE present book is a study of the economic aspects of the Chinese rural community. Because the economic life of the Chinese peasant has been deteriorating ever since his first contact with the West, this aspect of the rural community has for a long time attracted the attention of students, both Chinese and foreign. The best book on this subject, in our opinion, is Professor Tawney's *Land and Labour in China*. It is a summary of the Chinese economic situation prior to 1931, based on the data available at that time. All the data are from the work of other investigators. Tawney's conclusions are valuable not so much because of the factual material but because he interprets the data against the background of the general economic changes taking place in China—changes which are comparable to those which occurred in Europe during the Industrial Revolution. The data which sustain Professor Tawney's theoretical deductions were gathered by the social-survey method, of which the work of Dr. J. L. Buck is an example.

Buck's *Chinese Farm Economy* (1930) and *Land Utilization in China* (1937) are still the best-known books in the field of rural economics in China. In the first book, 2,866 farms in seventeen localities and seven provinces, and in the second, 16,786 farms in 168 localities in twenty-two provinces, were studied. The contribution made by these monumental works is great. They not only present a vast amount of information on various topics in the field of rural economics and land utilization but also lay the foundation for the use of the survey method in studying Chinese economic and social problems.

Buck approaches rural problems in China from the technical level, as an agricultural expert whose interest is mainly in increasing the economic return of the land. He defines the situation as follows:

> The technic of crop and animal production is practically the same in both [Chinese and European] civilizations, except for contrasts in the extent of the development of agricultural science. It is rather the type of land utilization, and the success in land use that differentiates the agriculture of the Oriental and the Western civilizations.[1]

[1] *Land Utilization in China* (Shanghai: The Commercial Press, 1937), p. 1.

B

1

He is conscious of a certain one-sidedness in his approach. He adds:

Associated with the type of use, however, are the various agrarian relationships which may facilitate or hinder any particular type of land use. In this study no attempt has been made to appraise in detail the so-called agrarian situation which may be thought of in terms of the political, economic and social relationships between farmers and other classes of society.[2]

The problem of farm ownership and tenancy, which apparently does not interest him, is treated as a side issue. In his first study he remarks that "a special treatment of tenancy was not contemplated in the schedule used for these studies."[3] It is, therefore, unfair to criticize Buck on the ground that his study does not represent a complete picture of the economic life or of the land system in Chinese villages. This is not his purpose, although sometimes he does express an opinion on political, economic, and social problems in the "so-called agrarian situations."

However, it should be asked how far agricultural problems can be studied without taking into account their institutional background? I should like to consider this problem purely from the methodological point of view.

In Buck's study it is clearly demonstrated that types of land use vary among owners and nonowners. A clear analysis of types of land use thus requires an adequate classification of operators, according to the varying categories of social status developed. It is to be expected that these categories will vary from one community to another. Thus, a tenant in one region may have a social status which is somewhat different from that of a tenant in another. Therefore, a study of land utilization requires a study of the whole system of landholding in the particular field being investigated. Buck, however, does not pay any attention to these variations but adopts throughout his study the conventional American classification into owners, part owners, and tenants. The similarity of the Chinese and American land systems is taken for granted; and he draws the conclusion, comparing his figures with those found in America, that "the extent of farm tenancy in China is no greater than in many other countries and, therefore, is not a problem peculiar to China."[4] In a later publication he maintains the same position by saying: "Tenancy is prevalent in Szechwan, 47 per cent of all farmers, but not greatly different than in many countries. In the United States 42 per cent of all farmers are tenants."[5] It is clear that

[2] Ibid., p. 1.   [3] Ibid., p. 145.   [4] Ibid., p. 196.
[5] An Agricultural Survey of Szechwan Province, China (Chunking, 1943), p. 2.

when he makes these conclusions he is not only assuming the similar meaning of tenancy in China and in America but is also isolating the problem of tenancy from other essential facts, such as the size of the farm, amount of rent, standard of living, nutrition, etc., on which he has ample data. This illustrates the danger of the social survey which pays no attention to the interrelation of the separate items, that is, the institutional background.

If Buck had consistently confined himself to compiling "certain elementary information about land utilization, food and population in China,"[6] he would have kept clear of such questionable conclusions. But he seems not to have been content with remaining on the technical level, omitting entirely the vital issues of the agrarian situation. However, when the survey method is applied without proper preparation to the study of social institutions, the weakness of the method becomes even more apparent. An example is the report of the Rural Reconstruction Commission of the Executive Yuan in 1935. This report consists of a number of volumes, one of which deals with rural economics in Yunnan, and is the first extensive study made in that province. A summary in English of this report is found in *Agrarian China*.[7]

In making a social survey, a questionnaire form is usually prepared before the investigator undertakes the work. Items to be observed are determined beforehand. In the questionnaire a classification of status in land system is provided, definitions for each status being given according to some preconceived idea. In this survey, following the American convention, villagers are classified into landowner, part owner, tenant, landless laborers, and nonfarming villagers. The same classification is used in studying various provinces, and the data are assumed to be comparable. Unfortunately, in Yunnan, as we shall see, the social and economic position of the tenants of collective owners, such as clan owners, is essentially different from that of the tenants of private owners. But, since there is no separate category in the questionnaire form, which obviously was prepared by someone who had no knowledge of the conditions in Yunnan, these two different kinds of tenant are thrown into the same category. When figures on the tenant class in Yunnan are compared with those from Kiangsu, still

---

[6] *Land Utilization in China*, p. viii.

[7] *Report on Rural Investigation in Yunnan*, ed. Rural Reconstruction Commission of the Executive Yuan (Shanghai: Commercial Press, 1935); "Land Ownership and Land Cultivation in Yunnan," *Agrarian China* (Institute of Pacific Relations, 1938), pp. 50–56.

more unreliable conclusions emerge, derived because the condition of the tenant of collective owners in Yunnan is not at all comparable with that of tenants renting from absentee landlords in Kiangsu.

Similar defects are found in the figures which deal with the farm laborers. According to the report, there are very few farm laborers in the Yunnan villages. This may be true for some villages. The conclusion that in Yunnan villagers do not depend on hired labor in farming is incorrect, however. Hired labor is a main characteristic of farming economy in most of the Yunnan villages. But, owing to the existence of migratory labor, in some villages there may be little resident landless farm labor, although even this situation is rare, so far as our knowledge goes; and, therefore, the results of the survey do not give a realistic picture of actual conditions. A few examples like this will be sufficient to show that for serious scientific investigation a questionnaire form prepared without full knowledge of the structure of the communities under observation is useless, if not misleading.

Moreover, in a survey of a widespread field it is necessary to hire a team of assistants to collect the basic data for statistical treatment. The work of data-collectors is mechanical and leaves no room for initiative. It does not attract well-trained scientists. Therefore, the most important part of the work is usually intrusted to incompetent hands. Errors, due to dishonesty, negligence, or misunderstanding of the questionnaire, are common. One of the villages we studied had been previously surveyed by the investigators of the Executive Yuan. When we asked the people how the investigators actually worked in the field, they all laughed. One man told us: "He asked me how many eggs I got each day. I answered none. But when he discovered that I had two chickens he thought that I had fooled him. I laughed and told him 'cocks do not give eggs.' " Of course, we should not judge the reliability of the report from the fun poked at it by our friends of the village. However, when we reanalyzed the data published in the report, inconsistencies were so numerous that we were unable to make use of it. This was due to the lack of scientific training of the hired investigators. Competent investigators are rare in China. It seems that Buck's best-known work sometimes suffers from the same weakness. As we shall show later, the amount of rice produced in Yunnan villages appears so high in Buck's book that we can only suspect that the investigator took the unhusked rice to be husked rice. These errors are difficult to avoid so long as the basic data are collected by students who are not interested in the work and do not share due credit for the study.

It is a common belief among those who advocate the social-survey method that data collected in this way can be used by others. As Buck writes in the Preface of his first book: "It is hoped the technician will find the tables useful as source material for additional interpretation, since it has been impossible in this one volume to interpret all aspects of their contents."[8] It is, therefore, interesting to see to what extent data collected in such a raw and unconnected form can be used reliably by other technicians or even by such a learned scholar as Professor Tawney.

Professor Tawney does not set himself up as an agricultural expert, and from his wisdom and experience he realizes fully that the problem of land and labor in China should be defined on a broader basis than that of "types of land utilization." He has outlined the essential problems that demand careful analysis if the agrarian situation in China is to be studied.

Natural conditions, varying widely from region to region; the diversities of cropping and cultivation which these conditions produce; cultural traditions and social habits of a half-legendary antiquity; a technique which in the past—and not unjustly—was the admiration of Europe, but which still has to make its own the fruits of the scientific revolution that has transformed Western agriculture in the course of the last century; economic organization and political institutions—all these, and other factors demand consideration.[9]

Information on most of the factors essential for presenting a complete picture of the agrarian situation is singularly lacking in the existing material. To construct a synthesis from the isolated data of social surveys, Tawney had to resort to conjectures based on his wealth of knowledge of the economic history of Europe. The parallel between the Industrial Revolution in the West and that which is likely to take place in the East is clear. One who reads Chinese material against the background of medieval Europe certainly will gain illuminating insights. Tawney's admirable summary of the Chinese economic situation, *Land and Labour in China*, remains the best treatise on China. But, as Tawney himself recognizes, the analogy between the medieval West and present-day China may sometimes be misleading. To illustrate this point, we may quote at length a passage from Tawney on the problem of tenancy. We quote this at length because it is also the starting-point of our study in the present book, which is mainly a re-examination of Tawney's statement.

[8] *Chinese Farm Economy*, p. v.
[9] *Agrarian China*, p. xii.

The distribution of different forms of tenure is influenced by the past history, soil conditions, types of farming and general economic environment of different parts of China. Occupying ownership is least prevalent in the proximity of great cities where urban capital flows into agriculture—in the Canton delta 85 per cent of farmers, and in the neighbourhood of Shanghai 95 per cent, are said to be tenants—and most general in the regions but little affected by modern economic developments. The provinces of Shensi, Shansi, Hopei, Shantung and Honan, where some two-thirds of the farmers are stated to be owners, are the original home of Chinese agriculture. They have been little touched as yet by commerce and industry. The yield of the soil is too low to make it an attractive investment to the capitalist, while the farmer has not the resources to rent additional land. In the south, where the soil is more productive, agriculture yields a surplus; the commercialization of economic relations has proceeded further; and both the inducement and the ability to invest capital in land are accordingly greater. It is reasonable to expect that, with the expansion of modern industrial and financial methods into regions as yet unaffected by them, similar conditions will tend to establish themselves in other parts of the country. In that case, the struggle which has so often taken place in Europe between the customary rights of the peasant, farming largely for subsistence, and the interest of absentee owner in making the most of his speculation is likely, it may be anticipated, to be repeated in China. In parts of the country, it is being repeated already.[10]

This statement is essentially true and is confirmed by our observations in rural areas around Lake Tai, where the soil is good and modern industrial and commercial influence is strong. The absentee system of tenancy is, accordingly, most developed.[11] But the link between good soil and the concentration of landownership under the influence of industrial and commercial development is not direct. It works as Tawney mentioned at the beginning through past history, through types of farming and general economic environment. It is, therefore, necessary to examine the ways in which the land system varies with differences in the institutional conditions.

In our study of rural economy in the area around Lake Tai we have seen that the development of absenteeism in land tenure was closely related to the decline of rural industry. Since the peasants were dependent on the silk industry, which is a household industry, its decline led to financial crisis. The peasants could only sell their land to avoid starvation. It is clear that, had economic conditions in the village been better, the peasants would not have given up their land to which they are so strongly attached. So it seems that the main cause of the concentration of landownership in the hands of town-dwellers lies primarily in the decline of rural industry. It is true that if the land were so

[10] *Land and Labour in China* (London: George Allen & Unwin, Ltd.), pp. 37–38.

[11] Hsiao-tung Fei, *Peasant Life in China* (1939), pp. 181–91.

poor that it could only maintain the cultivators on a subsistence level and that no rent could be exacted from it, the noncultivators in the town would not buy it. But in this case the fertility of the soil is only a condition making the development of tenancy possible, not the immediate cause of it.

It is clear that the process of concentration of landownership which gives rise to absenteeism should not be explained mainly by the relative fertility of the soil. An adequate study should start from the institutional background for buying and selling of land. This leads to an investigation of land utilization, of the labor situation, of the distribution of ownership, of farming profits, of economic attitudes, of inheritance, and of various channels for the accumulation of wealth—in short, to a community analysis. This kind of study is exactly what Tawney hoped for from scholars who were interested in the Chinese agrarian situation.

YUNNAN—A LABORATORY FOR COMMUNITY ANALYSIS

The three villages studied in this book are all in Yunnan; so a brief description of this province may be given in this connection. Yunnan is China's southwestern frontier province; its name, "South of the Cloud," carries with it a sense of distance. Far removed from the center of China, it hangs on the ridge of the continent, separated from the basins of the great rivers by chains of mountain ranges. It is not very accessible from the central provinces; and, since distance breeds suspicion, only yesterday the age-old belief was still current that Yunnan was a wild region overrun with beastlike aborigines, in early times held in subjection only by the resourceful godlike hero, Chu-ke of the Three Kingdoms, and later by the fearless Mongols. It was also believed that the air of this mountainous country was filled with a lethal vapor which would attack strangers in a mysterious way.

These tales were, of course, groundless; but, screened by its mystery, this frontier land had been visited by few travelers. Real knowledge of the land is not easily gained by outsiders. The best account of the province is Davies' *Yunnan: The Link between India and Yangtze*, written more as a travel sketch promoting a railway project than as a scientific account. Only during the present war has Yunnan become one of the most important bases of Free China. With large numbers of refugees pouring into the interior from occupied China, universities have moved in and modern factories have been established. Motor roads stretch into hitherto isolated regions, and railways are being built. The rapid tempo of social change in this region is unprecedented in any part of the world.

The influence of modern civilization on ancient cities like Kunming can be seen from day to day and from week to week, but the peculiar topography of the country prevents this influence from spreading easily. Cressey describes the region, which he calls the "southwestern tableland," as "high and rugged surfaces, cut by deep valleys and crossed by towering mountains. . . . . Scattered throughout the tableland are high plains, small in area and separated by mountains."[12] Settlements are found in the small scattered valleys. Like separate cells, they are connected only by narrow, rough, winding mountain trails, except for the Yunnan Indo-China Railway, the Burma Road, and other newly constructed highways. However, the latter are of little service in intervillage communication. Walking is the most common way for human movement, horses being used for transportation of goods. The difficulty in communication is best illustrated by our own experience. When we took our journey from the nearest station on the Burma Road to Yits'un, a distance of about 27 miles, we spent ten days getting there. This included frequent stops on the way for various reasons, such as the lack of pack horses or the necessity of waiting for an armed guide. It is not surprising to find people in the interior villages who have never been out of their own valley.

The topography of the land gives rise to the complicated ethnic composition of the people. "The south-western tableland is the most diverse region in all China in its human make-up," says Cressey.

Only about half of the population consists of real Chinese and the remainder is made up of a great variety of primitive peoples. The Chinese themselves are all immigrants from other provinces and are chiefly found in the plains and in more accessible valleys from which they have driven away the original inhabitants. Perhaps few parts of the world contain such a complicated racial mixture or offer such a fertile field for the study of anthropology as this region and the adjoining mountains.[13]

Successive migratory waves from different parts of the continent, during the last ten centuries, have pushed the less strong ethnic groups farther into the interior and higher up the mountains. Different peoples with diverse cultures can in these isolated valleys as easily ignore each other as do lodgers in an apartment house in any metropolis. Each of them can, more or less, pursue an almost independent line of

[12] G. B. Cressey, *China's Geographic Foundation* (New York: McGraw-Hill Book Co., Inc., 1934), p. 369.

[13] *Ibid.*, p. 371.

d evelopment under given cultural and geographical conditions. Modern industrial civilization adds to the already complicated scene another type of community; but, like the others, it is limited to restricted areas.

If the course of economic development can be read from human geography, Yunnan should serve as one of the best fields for study. The whole process of cultural development—from the primitive headhunters to the sophisticated and individualized city-dwellers—can be seen in concrete form. Take Kunming as a starting-point. Modern concrete buildings fill the center of the city. When night falls, neon lights illuminate an intensified activity. On the north side of the city thousands of aspiring students swoop into the barrack-like temporarily built classrooms, libraries, and laboratories. Talk of Einstein's theory of relativity or of Plato's Utopia can be overheard in the discussions in the teashops in the "cultural quarter." A few miles outside the city, modern machines are operating in the electric, machine, and munition factories. In the evening the near-by village centers are crowded with proud industrial workers speaking in unmistakable Shanghai accents. When we go farther, we find airfields lined with Flying Tigers, Liberators, and C-34's and see jeeps dashing headlong through partly bombed-out villages. The bright lights of the city shade off quickly as one goes farther on. At the outskirts of Kunming Valley, villagers are still not much disturbed by the strange and confusing goings-on of the city. Housewives are worrying about the bad temper of their husbands. Ceremonies are being seriously performed for warding off enemy airplanes or for suppressing the evil spirits of epidemics. Here the old order is still dominant. On market day we meet hundreds of womenfolk, in colorful and exotic costumes, coming down from the mountains where aboriginal communities live peacefully. If we follow them back to their own villages, we can be entertained in the "bachelor house," a place reminiscent of that described by Malinowski in his Trobriand material; and we will find tabooed quarters where the ancestors' ashes are kept. In a single day we will have traveled from Polynesia to New York. If one is a sociologist, one cannot fail to be excited by the opportunity for a comparative study of cultural types and for analyzing the process of cultural change. Here is a cultural laboratory par excellence.

This inviting field of social investigation presents another and more gloomy aspect. The relentless impact of modern civilization, especially emphasizing material power, the roaring of airplanes through the sky,

B*

and the gigantic plants generating the power to move enormous machines and light the city cannot hide the persistence of deep-rooted traditions of the past. But the bridge between the two is not well established. Even men of vision are not sure how much we must pay for our entry into the machine age. In this laboratory we may glimpse the processes of change which are taking place throughout the entire East. The traditional background, long neglected by students, still lives more or less untouched beside the more recently introduced customs of modern civilization. It is here we will see in flesh and blood how the process of modernization is working out. As it happens, we are living in the laboratory itself, and the most exciting incidents are our daily experience. This explains why we can somehow forget the tremendous difficulties of our material life and keep our work going under the most adverse conditions. This also explains why we have broadened the scope of our studies without regard for our own capacities. Our work may, indeed, suffer from superficiality because of our haste, but we should feel guilty if we missed the opportunity to leave a record of this most interesting epoch.

THE FIELD

The three villages studied are spoken of in this book not by their own names but by type names assigned to them by us. However, since they are concrete villages, a brief description of their locality and appearance can be given here. Luts'un is about 100 kilometers west of Kunming, the capital of Yunnan province, in an oval plain which is the center of Lufon district. The Burma Road passes the plain at the south end. It takes about half an hour from the station to the village by foot. Yits'un is found in a gorge on the Luyi River about 50 km. south of Luts'un. The river is not navigable. If the river bed is followed when the water is low, it takes about an entire day, with no stops, to reach Yits'un from Luts'un. But the ordinary route is much longer. The mountains are high and the trails steep. We took ten days by a roundabout route for the trip. Yuts'un is a village beside a town in the Yuchi plain about 100 km. south of Kunming and connected with it by a motor road. Yuchi is an important commercial center in Yunnan. Before the building of the Kunming Indo-China Railway and of the Burma Road, the main trading route to Indo-China, Thailand, and Burma started in this town.

In the above paragraph we have shown the general topography of Yunnan. All these villages are set in oval plains surrounded by mountains. The crowded villages of these plains present a scene which always reminds us of the land around Lake Tai in Kiangsu, although on the mountainside of Yunnan few houses are found and the inhabitants are usually aborigines. In the plains there is a dense population. According to some estimates, the average density of population around Kunming, including a part of the uninhabited mountain regions, is 400 persons per square mile. If we take the plain alone, I believe, the congestion of population is not much lower than that found in Kiangsu, which is 896 per square mile. For many centuries immigrants from various parts of China have flowed into the frontier provinces and settled themselves in the fertile plains. They carried with them the traditional ideology of filial prosperity—of having many sons—which, in Yunnan, must have been as effective as elsewhere in China in bringing the size of the population up to the saturation-point in a short time. The average land for each household is only 5.7 *mow*, about 1 acre, in Luts'un, while the average in China is about 30 *mow*, or 5 acres. This indicates that the man-land ratio is more unfavorable in Yunnan than, on the average, in the rest of China. A comparison with America will be even more striking. A farm of 150 acres is quite common in America; but in Yunnan, on the same amount of land there will be more than 100 landowners, besides the landless laborers. This amounts in size to a village. It will not be too much of an exaggeration to say that the resources of a Yunnan village are more or less similar to those of one normal American farm family. But in population a village of a hundred houses will have about 500–600 people, about one hundred times as many people as found in a small farm family in America. Of course, this is a rough comparison. However, it is the basic fact that we must always keep in mind as we proceed to the following detailed analysis.

The social structure in Yunnan villages with regard to both neighborhood and family is, on the whole, similar to that observed in villages of Kiangsu as described in *Peasant Life in China*. The household is the social and economic unit, holding property in common, living together in the same house except for temporary absences, and working under the system of the division of labor to keep life going. Clan organization is stronger in Yunnan than in other parts of China. Here the clan possesses common property. The form of the village is similar to that seen in Kiangsu. Houses are close together in a compact residential area, separated from other similar units by a considerable distance. Surrounding the residential area are farms which sometimes may be quite far from the houses of the operators. One essential difference between Yunnan villages and Kiangsu villages is that the former have not the advantage of water transportation. Most of the rivers and streams in Yunnan are not navigable. Transportation is entirely dependent on roads. Roads connecting villages are often badly paved or not paved at all and unsuitable for vehicles, although occasionally some buffalo carts may be seen dragging along the muddy trails. Loads are carried either on human backs or on horseback. The former seems more common. Owing to the difficulties in communication, especially in interdistrict relations, modern industrial and commercial influence is not very strong in most of the interior villages. Villagers may remain in one small region for life.

The field work of this study was carried out during the period 1939–43. Luts'un was studied mainly by Hsiao-tung Fei, who was assisted by his colleagues Yu-yi Li, Tse-yi Chang, and Chung-yin Chang. The study was started in November, 1939. The first stay in the village lasted two months. In August, 1940, he and his colleagues revisited the village and stayed about another three months. The study of Yits'un followed immediately after the study in Luts'un was completed. It was made in October, 1940. Tse-yi Chang stayed there until the end of the year. Because of the difficulty in communication, it has not been revisited. In August, 1941, Tse-yi Chang started his study in Yuts'un. The first stay lasted three months, and he was able to repeat his visit several times in 1941–42 and again in June, 1943.

Various methods of introduction were used in approaching the people. In Luts'un we established our connection with the villagers through the personal introduction of Miss Chi-wei Yang, Fei's aunt, who was a missionary and had spent a year in that locality previous to our visit, and Mr. Wu-kou Wang, Fei's classmate in Yenching University and a native of the village. In Yits'un we had no private introduction but only official credentials from our university. We became acquainted with the villagers through direct contact. In Yuts'un an introduction was given us by the president of the agricultural school in Yuchi. Except for the first week in Yits'un, we had no difficulties in being accepted. This was due chiefly to the help of the above-mentioned friends and to the traditional prestige of scholars. We also had the advantage of being familiar with the proper way of behaving among our own people. We have become good friends with many of the villagers. The village head of Luts'un, Chao, always calls on us whenever he comes to Kunming. Uncle Chang, a perfect example of the old Chinese gentry class, with his amiable personality and hospitable spirit, keeps up our friendship through his son, who comes to us quite often. Our landlord, Fong, of Yuts'un, paid us frequent visits even after we had moved from Kunming to our village station. Our relations with these people extended far beyond the mere giving and receiving of information. We have become, to a large extent, their personal advisers even in family affairs. In the beginning we made clear to them the nature of our work. We hid nothing from them. As a result, we were able to jot down figures and memoranda as necessary in front of them. They often suggested to us that we write down information they had given us, so that we might not forget it. We were invited to arbitrate the village disputes and to act as go-between for them in dealing with the district government. The district governments were also exceedingly courteous to us and supplied any document that we asked for. It was only through the assistance of all those mentioned that we were able to collect the material of this study.

METHOD OF COMMUNITY ANALYSIS

Analysis of peasant communities is a new development in anthropological studies. Originally the field of anthropology was confined to so-called "primitive communities." But as the demarcation between savagery and civilization, a justification of the white man's burden, has gradually become meaningless in the evolution of a world community, certain anthropologists, working on sociological principles, have refused to be bound by nineteenth-century conventions and have claimed the right to study human communities of all descriptions. During the last hundred years, moreover, they have had the opportunity of developing a technique of community analysis which in some respects differs from those employed by the other social sciences. Having begun by studying more isolated and integrated communities of so-called "primitive" peoples, social anthropologists have come to realize the importance of studying the total life of the inhabitants. The interrelation of different aspects of life—political, economic, religious, educational, etc.—which has been neglected by other departmentalized social sciences, must be recognized in a less specialized or differentiated community. Again, owing to the fact that social anthropologists often study communities with cultures different from their own, they must present the full cultural context in order to make their observations understandable to others, while other social scientists who study their problems within their own culture can omit most of the cultural setting of their field of study. Social anthropologists have played the role of cultural interpreters. With this background, they have developed the method of intensive field study and the consciousness of cultural differences. It is common sense in social anthropology that an established concept in one culture should not be automatically applied to another culture—a consideration not always recognized by the social-survey worker. Anthropologists will assume, for instance, that the meaning of tenancy in America may be different from that in China. Thus, when social anthropologists extended their field of study to modern communities, they were particularly well equipped to deal with intercultural comparative studies.

Nevertheless, the early stages of a community study of this sort are not very different from those of a social survey. The aim is to describe the community life; and, so far as there is a difference in method, it is a difference of degree. Social anthropologists attempt to gain a complete picture, while social-survey workers are satisfied with unconnected quantitative data. However, so far as descriptions are concerned, they approach the community in the same way. On the other hand, as social anthropologists develop their intensive studies, they do so at the expense of the extension of their field. To study community life in full, the investigator must limit his field of observation to a small area, so that he himself can participate in full. The question then arises: How is it possible to study every community intensively? Moreover, there is no limit to intensity in observation. It would take a whole lifetime—to put it extemely—to make a complete record of the behavior of any single individual. Even on the descriptive level, the social anthropologist must find certain criteria for what is to be considered an adequate description. On this point, it seems, no agreement can be reached.

It must be recognized, however, that, with respect to intensive research, anthropologists have made great advances in the techniques of observation. Emphasis is now laid on the direct interview in the native language, on participation in native activities, and on extensive uses of genealogical, ecological, and quantitative methods. In recent publications, detailed records of minute details of behavior often run to great lengths, sometimes with the result that the broad outlines of the culture are obscured.

With all these technical improvements in intensive observation, however, the descriptive study of any particular community not only must fail of absolute completeness but also will lack significance unless it is related to concepts established on a broader basis. A community study is fully scientific only when the community is reported with reference to questions of some general significance. We cannot study every community any more than we can report everything in any one community. Out of this fact, and out of the impulse to have general rather than special knowledge, arises the problem of "cultural taxonomy"—the recognition of types and the identification of single communities as examples of these types. Once types are established, the single intensive study becomes representative of a category, a class of communities.

A description of a community type may be said to be sufficient when the characteristics that differentiate the type are established. But what shall be the characteristics of the type? Some students have endeavored to identify the more subtle and comprehensive aspects of culture—the covert culture, the basic configurations, or even the "national genius"—a synthesis of all cultural elements into one dominating impression. But we have no established techniques for studying this "highest level of cultural synthesis." It seems that attempts to classify cultures in such terms are premature. It may be better to start cultural taxonomy on a lower level. The characteristics identifying the types will, instead, be chosen with reference to the special problems and interests with which the study is undertaken. Thus, in an economic study, types will be differentiated on the basis of different economic institutions, as a dominating concern with problems of familial relationships may look to social organization as the basis for the typology. Out of such beginnings a higher synthesis may one day come.

It needs further to be emphasized that, in a cultural taxonomy so developed, the classification is guided by an interest in some general problem of functional interrelationship or of social change. If the science of biology can be our guide in studying human communities, we may learn that taxonomy does not develop if it remains on a purely descriptive level. It is the explanation of variation among species—for instance, the theory of evolution—that, in fact, leads to the development of anatomical analysis. Differences become meaningful only when they are related to a general principle, which may be of a purely hypothetical nature. Earlier social anthropology profited by the theory of evolution. But since the theory was too crude and those who were called "evolutionists" were too narrow-minded, a reaction set in and an opposing school of thought developed. However, this school offers no theory of culture and even goes so far as to deny the possibility of general study. It thus becomes a nonconstructive force in the development of anthropology. If one is not satisfied to make anthropology a hodgepodge of separate museum specimens, some effort must be made to organize anthropological material in a more systematic way. That is why Professor Radcliffe-Brown repeatedly reminds his students that a field worker should, first of all, be equipped with a theory in his own mind. The field work is then to test the theory. This type of field study has been demonstrated by Redfield's work in Yucatan.[14] His work is more than a description of the four communities he studies merely to show how different they are and to find Latin or Greek terms to name them; he endeavors to explain their differences by a theory of cultural change from folk culture to civilization. His definition of the process of change is based on concrete observations in these communities and is expressed in general terms which can be applied and tested in other fields. Of course, there is room to criticize the content of the theory, which, like any theory, is a working hypothesis for further study. But the method employed in his study is significant in modern social anthropology.

The present book, on the whole, follows the same method, although the problem is more restricted. As we have said above, our study is an attempt to form a bridge between social survey and world-wide generalizations.

We will connect the various aspects of the economic life of the villagers by showing their interrelations in the land system. By comparing the land systems in four types of rural community, we shall be able to formulate a general statement of the way in which the concentration of landownership and the development of tenancy is effected by the decline in income of the peasants as a result of the Industrial Revolution. This is a result of an examination of Tawney's theory, as we have mentioned above. Under the influence of the classical theory of rent, he emphasized the productivity of land, and thus insufficient attention is paid to the general economic conditions and institutional context.

In order to study landownership, four types of community were selected. They were selected to represent different degrees of concentration. In one community, Luts'un, most of the landowners are occupants and their farms are small. In another community, Yits'un, there are several large landowners who possess land in other villages; the others are small, occupying owners. There are no tenants in the

---

[14] Robert Redfield, *The Folk Culture of Yucatan* (Chicago: University of Chicago Press, 1941).

community. The third community, Yuts'un, is the reverse of the second type. Tenants are found in numbers, and the big owners live in the near-by town. These three communities are all in Yunnan. A fourth community, not described in this book but which may also be used for comparison, is that studied in Kiangsu, described in a previous publication, *Peasant Life in China*. It is a community of tenants whose landlords are absentee owners in big towns, a further development of tenancy than that in the third type.

In making this study, we have proceeded on two levels. The first, on the taxonomic level, defines the character of the community with special reference to its land system. Taking into account all the fundamental characteristics expressed by general factors, such as high population pressure, low differentiation of occupation, development of labor-employment handicraft, the rise of capitalistic enterprise, etc., we are able to define community types which will serve as a basis for the classification of Chinese rural communities.

When the factors affecting the different types of land system are clarified by being compared, we reach the second level, the interpretation level. The factors accountable for the resemblances and differences of these types are brought forth to interpret the differences in degree of concentration in landownership. In this way the present study finds its unity as a treatise studying the important processes of change in the Chinese land system. It is found that the concentration of landownership and the development of a durable system of absenteeism arises only when certain mechanisms for the continuous accumulation of wealth exist in the community. The wealth thus accumulated will enter into land when it cannot be effectively reinvested in the same mechanism—industry or commerce—which is limited by the general economic condition. Concentration of landownership becomes effective when the general standard of living of the small owners is lowered by individual crisis or by general deterioration of the rural economy.

The comparative method in community studies on the basis of certain hypotheses is particularly to be recommended for China because it stimulates the further exploration of new fields. An investigation in one community opens up more problems than it settles. The ramifications of inquiry and the continuous refinement and ever more detailed definition of conditions nourish a science still in its infancy in a new field like China. It is needless to say that the four types of rural community represented in the present and previous books are only a beginning of a more extensive program of similar studies. The value of theoretical guidance in making the selection of a field can be seen from a study of this sort. For instance, we selected the above villages not mainly for convenience or by chance. The problem which was posed by Tawney's study and also by *Peasant Life in China* led us to seek a village where there was no absentee landlordism. With this in mind, we took up the study of Luts'un. From the study of Luts'un, we realized the importance of the effect of rural industry on the land system. So we traveled ten days to find a place where rural industry should be developed. Such a spot was Yits'un. In Yits'un we became interested in the financial influence of centers of industry and commerce upon near-by villages. We came to Yuts'un because it was located near a commercial center of Yunnan. Each study was an introduction to the next, and all were connected by a common problem—the gradual concentration of landownership.

No claim will be made for a complete treatment of the agrarian situation in China in this book. But, following this method of establishing and analyzing the essential types of land system, we believe that such work may eventually be accomplished. It will not require an exhaustive study of every village in China, because most of the villages can be placed in known types.

PART I

LUTS'UN: A COMMUNITY OF PETTY LANDOWNERS

LUTS'UN is located in a fertile valley, about 100 km. west of Kunming, close to the Burma Road. We started our study with this village because we found here a simple form of economy in which neither commerce nor industry plays an important part. The main occupation of the people is the management and cultivation of farms, and the villagers are either petty landowners or landless laborers. Landlords with large holdings are lacking, and absentee owners are few and insignificant. It seems to us that this village represents a basic type of farming community in interior China. The life of the peasants is characterized by the use of traditional farming techniques on rather fertile land and under a strong pressure of population. In these fundamental ways Luts'un represents, in miniature, traditional China. It is also logically a prototype of the types of villages described later, where the development of handicraft industries and the commercial influence of the town complicate the structure.

Luts'un is a village of 122 households, with 611 individuals—about the average size for the region. The total area of farms owned by the villagers, privately or collectively, is about 920 *mow*, or about 140 acres.[1] Owing to the fertility of the soil, the yield from a unit of farm land is higher even than that of the area around Lake Tai, the well-known rice-producing area in eastern China. However, the distribution of land among the villagers is unequal. Most of them either have no land or have too little land for their maintenance. These must seek employment on the land of others, since there is little opportunity for gaining a livelihood in occupations other than agriculture, and they form a large supply of hired labor. The petty owners, on the other hand, are able to manage their small estates by employing cheap labor to work for them and themselves to enjoy leisure. The dichotomy of work and leisure among the villagers is characteristic of this type of village economy.

The average size of a holding is small—less than 1 acre. It tends to

[1] The standard adopted by the Chinese government in 1915 was 6.59 *mow* to 1 acre.

diminish gradually under the increasing pressure of population, because, according to custom, brothers have equal rights of succession to land. Since there is no open and easy source of income other than in agriculture, most of the small landowners must eventually become landless laborers. Some of them will remain single all their lives and then die out completely. Occasionally rural families may, through hazardous ventures in the outside world, suddenly rise to wealth; but such families are soon leveled down by the merciless pressure of population. One or two generations is quite enough to reduce the holdings of a rich family to petty units. The movement upward on the economic ladder is slow, but the movement downward is rapid. The supply of landless laborers is maintained by a constant increase in the population and a constant decrease in the size of landholdings. The traditional structure of the village is thus dependent upon the existence of two groups of people: the petty owners, who form a leisure class; and the landless laborers. This is the type of rural economy that we shall analyze in the following pages.

CHAPTER I

FARM CALENDAR

I T WOULD, perhaps, seem desirable to preface a study of the land
system by an analysis of the problem of land utilization; but,
because of the limitations of our technical knowledge of agriculture, we must confine ourselves to a description of the fundamental
data which are necessary as a basis for the later discussions. These data,
which constitute the agricultural calendar, are arranged in the form
of a table (Table 1) for ready reference. This table will serve the purpose of showing graphically the co-ordination of climate, crop growth,
and agricultural activities. The following pages will be devoted to an
explanation of the various columns in the calendar.

Three important categories of information appear in the calendar:
climatic changes (Column B); the growth process of the crops (Col.
C); and the activities, the amount of labor, and the tools required of the
farmer in the cultivation of the crops (Col. D). Because these factors
are co-ordinated in time by virtue of the nature of agriculture, the
calendar appears as a system of vertical and horizontal co-ordinates.
The process of growth, determined by the physiology of the plants
and by the climate, is not subject to the desires of man. The human
effort expended on the farm simply provides the plants with an opportunity to grow. As Mencius said: "It is foolish to pull the shoots to
help them grow." Since different crops differ physiologically and in
their response to the climate, an understanding of the agricultural
activities of a people requires a knowledge of the kind of crops grown
and the climatic conditions to which they are subject. Hence our
discussion begins with Column C.

I. CROPS AND CLIMATE

Only two crops—rice and broad beans—are listed, since these serve
as the basis of the agricultural economy of the village. From the surrounding higher lands the valley appears to be covered by a solid
carpet of green, furnished in early summer by the rice plants and in
late fall by the beans. A walk through the fields, however, reveals the
presence of additional crops. Corn grows on the sandy land bordering
the stream, various vegetables are raised in the gardens back of most

TABLE 1

THE CALENDAR OF WORK

A		B		C	D
Western Solar System	Traditional Solar System	Climate (in Kunming) Temp. (° C.)	Rain (Mm.)	Crop	Farm Work and Labor Required, for 1 *Kung* (M = Male; F = Female; MF = Mixed Labor)
Feb.	Li Ch'un	10.9	20.5	About 60 days — Picking season of broad bean	
	Yu Shui				
Mar.	Ching Che	14.2	23.1		30 days' allowance — Sowing seeds for rice MF (hand)
	Ch'un Fen			About 60 days — Young rice shoot in nursery farm	30 days' allowance — Collecting and threshing broad bean 3 F (sickle and beater)
Apr.	Ch'ing Ming	17.5	33.1		
	Ku Yu				45 days' allowance — Breaking soil 4 M (hoe) / Irrigating / Mending dikes } ⅓ M (hand and hoe)
May	Li Hsia	19.3	111.0		30 days' allowance — Adding fertilizer 1 MF / Leveling the farm ⅔ M / Plowing ¼ M + animal labor (plow) / Transplantation 1 F (hand) / Transport 1 M (carrying pole)
	Hsiao Man			About 75 days — Young rice in main farm	
June	Mang Chung	19.4	207.5		
	Hsia Chih				
July	Hsiao Shu	20.0	261.4		75 days' allowance — Weeding (three times) 4½ F (hand)
	Ta Shu				
Aug.	Li Ch'iu	19.9	246.9		
	Ch'u Shu			About 45 days — Rice in blossom and bears fruit	
Sept.	Pai Lu	18.1	158.3		
	Ch'iu Fen				30 days' allowance — Reaping 1 F (sickle) / Threshing 1 M (threshing box) / Transportation ½ M (carrying pole)
Oct.	Han Lu	15.8	75.6		
	Shuang Chiang			About 80 days — Growing and blossom periods of broad bean	30 days' allowance — Digging trenches for broad bean ½ M (hoe) / Sowing seed for broad bean 1 F (hand and dibble)
Nov.	Li Tung	12.7	41.2		
	Hsiao Hsueh				Transportation of straw storage ½ MF (carrying pole)
Dec.	Ta Hsueh	9.9	7.2		
	Tung Chih				
Jan.	Hsiao Han	9.2	5.0		Total labor required 10.3 F 1.5 MF 8.5 M
	Ta Han				

of the houses, wheat is planted in scattered squares among the fields of broad beans, and the trailing vines of green beans impede the walker as he traverses the paths between the rice paddies. There are many secondary crops in addition to these, but they are produced in relatively small quantities. Since all of these secondary crops are raised in small quantities and almost exclusively for consumption by the farmers themselves, they do not constitute an important part of the economy and are therefore omitted from the calendar.

Although rice and broad beans are often grown alternately on the same plots of land, the acreage devoted to rice is much greater than that sown with beans. In the absence of actual statistics, our estimate that the bean acreage is approximately 70 per cent of the rice acreage is probably not greatly in error. The explanation for this fact lies in two factors: soil and terrain. Owing to the narrowness of the valley and the rocky deforested nature of the mountains surrounding it, the small tributary streams carry a considerable load of sand. The flooding of these streams results in small areas with sandy soil, which are not suitable for rice cultivation but must be devoted to corn and other crops. The land farther away from the streams is of two types, both of which are suitable for rice. On the higher slopes at the east side of the village, the loose, well-drained soil is excellent for broad beans, though it does not produce abundant crops of rice. Farms in this area are invariably double-cropped. On the lower slopes, nearer the main stream, on the other hand, since the sticky, poorly drained soil is ideal for rice but unsatisfactory for beans, the fields usually lie idle during the autumn and winter.

Column B of the calendar provides data on two significant climatic factors—temperature and rainfall. Before discussing the significance of the climate in the agriculture of the village, a few notes relative to the validity of the data given are in order. The first is in regard to the source of the figures. Since there are no recording instruments in or near the village, it has been necessary to utilize the records taken in Kunming, which is about 100 km. east of Luts'un. If other factors were uniform, this distance would not be important climatically; but there is a difference in altitude which is reflected in the respective climates of the two localities. Luts'un, with an elevation of only about 1,650 meters above sea-level, is more than 200 meters lower than Kunming, at 1,890 meters, and is consequently warmer. The degree to which the climate of the village varies from that in the provincial capital has not been directly measured, but it may be observed indirectly in the agriculture. The variety of rice grown in Luts'un (a type with grains which drop readily from the stalk when ripe, thus requiring a short harvest period) is not raised in the Kunming area. Furthermore, the harvest is earlier at the lower altitude—a fact the importance of which in the labor situation will be discussed later. In 1939, on our return from Luts'un, where the gathering of the rice crop had been completed before October 15, we found the harvest just begun in Kunming. There is, thus, a discrepancy of approximately one month in the agricultural calendars of the two regions.

A second characteristic of the temperature and rainfall figures should be noted—namely, that they represent an average for the years 1929–36 and lack validity for any specific year. That there is actually considerable variation from year to year is demonstrated by the situation in 1939, when the spring was unusually late. According to the custom of previous years, the farmers of the village sowed their rice seed in the nurseries shortly after Ching Che (the middle of March). But seven days after Ch'un Fen, i.e., on March 28, the germinated seeds were killed by frost, and the final sowing was not accomplished until the eleventh day after Ch'ing Ming, twenty days later. In other words, in that year the actual agricultural calendar lagged one month behind the traditional calendar based on the climatic average. Therefore, it is obvious that the figures given have value only for general reference purposes.

Two outstanding characteristics of the climate are revealed by the figures appearing in Column B. The first is the relatively slight annual variation in temperature. The difference between July (the hottest month), with an average temperature of 20° C. (68° F.), and January (the coldest month), with an average of 9.2° C. (48.5° F.), is only 10.8° C. (19.5° F.). The second characteristic is the high variation in precipitation, which amounts to 261.4 millimeters in July but totals only 5 mm. in January. The monsoon season, which begins suddenly in May, extends through September and is followed by the dry season, which terminates at the end of April. These two peculiarities, taken together, constitute a climatic complex to which the agricultural complex here is admirably adapted. The lack of severe cold permits a perpetual growing season, and thus the double-cropping of the land, with only brief intervening periods for the preparation of the soil. Rice and broad bean make the ideal combination for complete utilization of the land, since the former requires warmth and a constant water supply, while the latter needs dry weather and lower temperatures.

II. FARMING ACTIVITIES

Although the growth of the crop, which is a continuous process, governs the farming activities, the latter are discontinuous. Before the crop is planted, there is a period of preparation of the soil; but after the planting, only weeding and irrigation are necessary until harvest time, when the work is again heavy. The concentration of well-defined types of farming activities in definite periods, with intervening seasons of relative idleness, justifies the use of the concept of sections of work. In Column D are listed the various sections of work, together with the amount of labor required for each.

The ideal method of collecting the data for this column would be direct observation by the investigator for a full year, with a complete day-by-day record of the actual work of the observed individuals. Since we were unable to remain in the village for a year, this method was impossible, and we had to resort to the use of informants, checking the information so obtained against the direct observations we were able to make during our investigations. The key to the problem of securing accurate information by this method is, of course, the selection of the proper informants, which we did not find difficult after a period of residence with the villagers. Dishonest and evasive answers are relatively easily detected by posing the same questions to several individuals and by asking related questions of a single person. Perhaps the most essential requirement for the investigator is a constant awareness that the information and experience of the individuals in a community are not uniform. It is impossible to acquire complete and satisfactory knowledge of the conditions in the school by questioning a shopkeeper. Although it would seem that this requisite for sound field work is so self-evident that it need not even be mentioned, there have been instances in which investigators have reached absurd conclusions as a result of averaging equally weighted answers from indiscriminately selected informants. Hence, it is vital that the necessity for selecting the proper informants for the specific inquiry be steadfastly borne in mind.

The securing of good informants presents no difficulty as far as some of the items in the agricultural calendar are concerned; examples of these are the process of crop growth and the sequence of farming activities. Anyone connected with agriculture, whether he be an actual worker on the farm or one who employs others to manage his land, can give, without hesitation, the number of days which elapse between the germination of the grain and the harvest or the succession of tasks involved in cultivation. As a matter of fact, similar information can be obtained from almost anyone in the village. A fourteen-year-old boy living near my house once recited to me the complete annual agricultural cycle without omission or deviation from the proper order.

My original assumption that such problems as the dates of the beginning and the completion of each section of work would be readily solved by the simple expedient of asking anyone engaged in agriculture was quickly demolished by the variety of answers to my questions given by different individuals. Some responded with the actual dates for the current year; others, with dates from the standardized calendar. Every year each household sets its own dates for each type of work. In 1939, for example, some households sowed their rice seed as early as the eighth day of the second moon, while the rest selected dates as much as ten days later. The standard calendar prescribes, not the dates for each activity, but the period within whose limits the activity must be accomplished. It sets the date before which the work in question should not be done and the date by which it should be completed. A villager expressed this in describing to us the schedule for rice cultivation: "After Ching Che the seeds may be germinated. After remaining in the nursery farms for sixty days, the rice should be transplanted to the main fields, but this should not be done later than Hsia Chih. The weeding may start not earlier than fifteen days after transplantation and should not continue beyond Li Ch'iu." It is apparent that the standard calendar consists of a set of terminal dates within which the individual calendars may vary. It is a system of reference based on the accumulated experience of the people and may, like other rules derived from experience, fail to meet a specific situation. As mentioned in the preceding section, the villagers attempted to adjust their activities to the standard calendar in 1939, with the result that the seed they sowed was wasted. Contrary to the general rule that all sowing must be completed before Ch'ing Ming, only the seed sown after that date in 1939 was successfully germinated. The villagers considered this an exceptional circumstance and said that "something was wrong with the heavens." Despite the 1939 failure, it is clear that, given the lack of better means for predicting temperatures and the need for a system of reference to make advance planning possible, the preponderance of past experience must be accepted as a guide.

While the standard calendar can be repeated in its entirety by everyone, this is not true of the individual calendars of work. These are different for different households, who usually do not remember even their own. The only effective method for collecting them would be the maintenance of a diary for each household, a difficult task under the conditions of our investigation. In 1939 we attempted, by direct observation, to enumerate the hired laborers in the fields; but, after a full day of work, we found that we had missed a number of them. In view of the impracticability of maintaining detailed daily records of the activities of several households, we did not attempt to collect individual calendars but are, instead, presenting the standard calendar as an adequate exposition of the agricultural cycle.

III. TIME RECKONING

In Column A appear the divisions of the Western and of the traditional Chinese solar calendars. It will be noted that the climate column is co-ordinated with the Western system, while the other two columns are subdivided vertically to correspond with the Chinese calendar. This is necessary because of the different sources of data for the various columns. The climatic record is taken from the *Chinese Yearbook*, where it is organized according to the Western system. Although we are aware of no precedent for this in the literature on Chinese economic problems, we are using the traditional system as our primary frame of reference because it is the system by which the farmers themselves regulate their farming activities. It seems to us that, for the best understanding of the life of a people, their activities should be studied, as far as possible, in terms of their own systems of reference. The local system may then be correlated with the system familiar to the reader. Time reckoning is a basic part of the life of a community; and, being man-made, it is adapted to the needs of that community. It is a functioning element in the culture and cannot be understood without reference to the experiences of the people. Since time itself is continuous, its division into units is a cultural phenomenon, which means that it is designed to serve human purposes. This is why we believe that the imposition of the time system of one group upon the study of another is a real obstacle to an investigation.

The Chinese peasants use two calendrical systems—a lunar and a solar—both of which have been described in a previous book.[1] We need restate here only a few salient features of these systems in order to indicate the reasons for the fact that the solar calendar prevails as the system of reference in agriculture. Since the lunar cycle is 29.53 days, the months are either 29 or 30 days long. The discrepancy between the lunar calendar and the solar calendar resulting from the fact that

[1] Fei, *Peasant Life in China*, pp. 144–53.

twelve lunar months amount to only about 354 days, necessitates the insertion of an intercalary month every few years. But even with this correction, the differences between the two calendars may amount to more than 10 days. Since agricultural activities must be adjusted to the growth processes of the crops, and these are dependent on climatic conditions, it is evident that the lunar calendar would be a poor guide for the farmer's work schedule. An illustration will suffice to make this clear. In one year the people of Luts'un will find that the twenty-eighth day of the second moon is the proper time for sowing rice; but the next year, after the intercalation of a month, the weather on the same lunar date will be too cold, for the solar equivalent of that date in this year will be the ninth day of the third moon.

It is understandable, then, that it is the solar calendar by which the peasants regulate their farm work. Because the twenty-four sections of which it is composed are delimited accurately in terms of the position of the earth in its orbit, they are co-ordinated with the seasonal changes. Consequently, it is not surprising that, though the city-dwellers may not even know the names of the sections, this calendar is a living system among the agriculturalists. As documented in *Peasant Life in China*, expressions of time in connection with agriculture in the daily conversations, letters, and in folk songs of the peasant are mostly in terms of the solar calendar. The section, however, is not further subdivided; so the lunar calendar must be used in conjunction with it as a system of dating. The peasants must remember the lunar dates for the beginning of each section; and they will tell you, for example: "This year Ch'un Fen will fall on the first day of the second moon and Ch'ing Ming on the sixteenth day of the second moon."

IV. THE FARM UNIT

A people's space-reckoning system, like their calendar, is a functioning part of their culture and should therefore be expected to meet their particular needs. The functional basis for the determination of the farm unit is different in different regions of China. In Kiangts'un,[2] the village described in *Peasant Life in China*, the *mow*, a unit whose function is mainly to serve as a basis for taxation, is an expression partly of the productivity of the land and partly of the ability of the owners to evade taxation. In Hunan, according to our information, the unit *tai* represents the amount of land which, according to one theory, will produce 10 *piculs*[3] of rice or, according to a second theory,

---

[2] The village of Kaihsienkung is referred to throughout this study as Kiangts'un,, *i.e.*, village of Kiangsu.

will require 10 *piculs* of seed. The land unit in Lunan, a district in Yunnan 150 km. south of Kunming, is the *chia* (literally, a cart), the area which a buffalo can plow in a day. As in these other regions, the inhabitants of Luts'un are concerned primarily with a unit of measurement which reflects their specific needs rather than absolute area. Here the size of a farm is expressed in terms of the *kung*,[3] which is described as the amount of land which can be worked by one laborer in one day. There is a considerable amount of variation in the *kung*, not because of inability to measure accurately, but by virtue of differences in the soil, location, and other factors determining the amount of labor required for different farms. Since the labor required for different sections of work and the efficiency of individuals vary widely, the definition of the *kung*, as given, is not clear; and it is not possible to determine with certainty what types of laborer and of work serve as the basis for determining the unit. The villagers themselves, however, are not concerned with the problem, for each plot of land consists of a traditional number of *kung*, the enumeration of which will not be altered to conform to changes in the efficiency of the laborers. As to the question of how, in the past, the size of a farm was established, our informants were vague, though a few ventured the opinion that a *kung* is the amount of land a laborer can transplant with young rice shoots in a day. Whether or not this was the criterion used when the traditional values were assigned to the various plots of land, it is true that today the man who can complete a *kung* in a day during the transplanting season is considered an acceptable worker. As we will explain later, the landowners figure on this basis when they estimate the amount of labor they must employ on their farms. The logic of the system of land measurement developed here will become apparent when we see how important to the whole structure of the village is the institution of hired labor. Although the functional unit of measurement is as described, the peasants do not lack the concept of absolute size. They often pointed to two fields and told us that in one the *kung* were larger or smaller than in the other. In some villages, they said, the *kung* was twice the size of the average *kung* here. They were unable, however, to supply us

[3] [According to the *China Handbook for 1937–1943*, the Chinese *picul*, which is a measure of weight rather than of volume, may vary locally; but that now chiefly in use is equivalent to 100 Chinese catties, or 110.231 pounds. According to the Louisiana State Rice Milling Company of Abbeville, Louisiana, the weight of 1 bushel of unhusked rice is 45 pounds.]

[4] Our informants insisted that the word *kung* meant labor; and, though we at first suspected that it was the word for "bow," which is a traditional unit of land measurement in some parts of China, a study of land documents confirmed their interpretation. The characters for "bow" and "labor," although different, are pronounced in the same way.

with exact figures; so, in order to gain some idea of the average size of the *kung* and its variations, we were compelled to make our own measurements. Since we lacked surveying instruments, it was necessary to resort to more primitive methods, which consisted of selecting rectangular plots for chaining or pacing. The division of our results for each plot by the reported number of *kung* contained in it gave us a range of from 240 to 300 square meters per *kung*. According to the 1935 report of the Rural Reconstruction Commission of the Executive Yuan, the local *mow* contains 701 square meters and is equivalent to 3 *kung*. On this basis the size of a *kung* would be about 230 square meters. In view of this figure and the results of our measurements, an estimated average of 250 square meters per *kung* would seem reasonable. The standard *mow* of 666 square meters is roughly the equivalent of 2.6 *kung*.

<h3 style="text-align:center">V. THE LABOR UNIT</h3>

The local unit of labor is also called *kung*, which in this connection is defined as the amount of work one individual performs in a day. It is obvious that for several reasons such a unit is not very satisfactory for comparative purposes. In the first place, there are wide variations in the age, sex, and energy of laborers and in conditions of work; secondly, different types of work vary greatly; and, thirdly, a day is a flexible period, from the standpoint of work measurement. Because no standard unit of energy can be established, we will describe some of the typical activities of the workers in the hope of imparting to the reader a general understanding of the local unit.

There is a very clear division of labor between the sexes. In general, the men do the heavier work, that which requires more strength and energy. During the transplantation of rice the men pull the shoots from the nursery beds and transport them to the main fields, where the women plant them. In the rice harvest the women cut the grain, tie it, and transport it to the threshing box. The men do the threshing and carry the threshed grain to the storehouse. The work in connection with the broad bean crop is performed mainly by the women. At planting time the men dig the trenches for the placing of the seeds by the women; but the latter do all the work connected with the harvest, including the cutting, the threshing, and the beating of the vines, while the men devote themselves to the preparation of the fields for the new rice crop. This division is reflected in the tools used by the two sexes: the most important for the men is the hoe; for the women the sickle and the beater are most characteristic. The distinction between the sexes is carried over into the matter of remuneration for hired labor: women are paid at only one-half the rate received by the men. Children from the age of twelve years on are commonly employed on the farms, usually to perform the tasks which require relatively little strength. For example, at threshing time they may be used to carry the grain from the cutter to the threshing box, a duty they can perform as well as can an adult. The work of children is regarded by the villagers as the equivalent of female labor and is paid for accordingly. Since the various farm tasks are strictly divided between the sexes we have retained the distinction in the agricultural calendar. The work of the men is designated by the letter "M"; that of the women, by the letter "F." The symbol "MF" indicates labor of both sexes where it was not feasible to make a further breakdown. The tools used in the different types of work appear in parentheses.

When an employer estimates the number of units of labor required for certain work, he must, of course, base his calculations on the efficiency and industry of the workers he can expect to hire rather than on the quantity of work of which unusual employees are capable. The piecework laborer who, by reason of his superior skill and his willingness to work long hours, can accomplish three times as much as the average worker hired by the day is exceptional. An illustration will give some idea of the normal efficiency of the average laborer. During our stay in the village our landlord employed a man to plow his field. The worker arrived at nine-thirty in the morning and, after asking for water to wash his face, squatted in the sun beside the house to smoke his pipe while the woman of the house prepared his breakfast. After a leisurely breakfast, prolonged by conversation with the people about the house, he waited a few minutes for the maidservant to get the buffalo from the stable and then followed her to the field with the plow on his shoulder. By the time he had started work, it was ten-thirty. His lunch was sent to the field between one and two o'clock, and at five-thirty he returned to the house for dinner, his working day ended. Even without the deduction of time spent in eating lunch, smoking, and making a trip to his home to care for his children, his working time did not exceed seven hours.

During the harvest, which is the heaviest period in the agricultural cycle, we were able to observe directly the schedules of many of the workers. For example, we frequently went in the morning to the village gate, where the girls with their sickles waited to be hired. About nine o'clock they left for the fields, but they returned to their employers' houses at one o'clock for a heavy lunch and an hour's rest. Their work was completed some time before dark, after a working day of eight to nine hours. Rest periods were frequent and rather prolonged, their frequency and duration largely depending on whether or not the employer was in the field. Additional periods of idleness occurred after the cutting of a plot had been completed and the men were finishing the threshing.

If the employer wants his work done in the fewest days possible, he may start his workers before breakfast at six or seven o'clock, by paying an additional wage. If he provides lodging and good entertainment, the employees may do this extra morning work without charge. Such long hours are, however, the exception; and the unit of labor, the *kung*, seldom exceeds seven or eight hours a day for either male or female.

VI. ESTIMATES ON FARM LABOR

Before we can proceed to an analysis of the relationship between labor supply and demand, we must form an estimate of the labor required for the cultivation of the farm unit. Here we encounter the problem of finding satisfactory informants. The hired laborers immediately proved unsatisfactory for this purpose, since they had no reason for maintaining records of their work. Except for the busy periods, the work is of a part-time nature, which makes it almost impossible for a person to provide information relative to the time he has spent on an individual farm. During the busy periods several people usually work together, and no individual worker could supply the necessary figures. But there are villagers to whom this problem is of immediate concern. They are the landowners who hire others to cultivate their farms and who must know how much labor is required for the various phases of cultivation. It is necessary for them to plan in advance; and, moreover, they remember later how much they have spent for wages. Consequently, we went through the calendar with two different landowners of this class—our landlord and Chou, who is known as a man skilled in computation. Both were able to tell us how much labor was required for each section of work, how much wages were paid, and the total costs of cultivation per *kung*.

The figures obtained through these discussions were checked by two methods: first, by asking from as many competent persons as possible their estimates for each section of work and, second, by direct observation. During the rice harvest about one hundred households were interviewed to determine the amount of work which was accomplished during a day and the number of workers being used. A few corrections were made as a result of this check; but, on the whole, the original estimates proved to be reliable.

On the basis of all the data it was possible to collect, it was found that on a double-cropped farm, which is in use throughout the year, each *kung* of land requires 10.3 units of female labor, 8.5 units of male labor, and 1.5 units of mixed labor—a total of 20.3 units.[5] It should be borne in mind that these figures represent the requirements in terms of hired labor and that the picture would be altered if the owner cultivated his own land.

[5] It is interesting to compare these figures with those given by J. L. Buck. On the basis of his survey of 2,866 farms in northern China and eastern and central China, he concluded that "man labor on grain crops is greatest for rice, amounting to 117 man-work units per hectare for ordinary rice; 122 for glutinous rice" (*Chinese Farm Economy* [1930], p. 227). In four localities he recorded the amount of labor required for growing the broad bean: 91.14, 108.52, 73.81, and 89.06 man-work units per hectare (*ibid.*, p. 229). The average is 90.63 units. He defined a man-work unit as "the amount of work the average farmer accomplishes in a ten-hour day" (*ibid.*, p. 20). In his more extensive survey of 16,786 farms, in 1929–33, he gives 137 days of work per acre in the Southwestern Rice Area, including Yunnan (*Land Utilization in China* [1938], p. 302). In the latter book he expresses the man-work unit in terms of days without further definition in terms of hours. Presumably, he is following the definition given in his previous book. Now, if we reduce all these figures to a comparable basis, with a ten-hour day of work as the labor unit and 100 square meters as the farm unit, the results are as follows:

	Buck (1930)	Buck (1938)	Luts'un
Rice (ordinary)............	1.67	3.38	4.40
Broad bean...............	0.90	1.26	1.24

It will be noted that our estimate for rice is higher than that of Buck's. In a footnote in Buck's table (*ibid.*) we read: "The high amount for the Southwestern Rice Area has been omitted from the average." It appears that what has been excluded must be near to our estimate. We checked our estimate with material from other villages in Yunnan and found them even higher than those from Luts'un. It is unfortunate that Buck does not give the reasons for this exclusion.

CHAPTER II

AGRICULTURAL EMPLOYMENT

I. AGRICULTURAL LABOR REQUIREMENT

NOW that we have derived the time sequence of the various farming activities of the village from the agricultural calendar and have estimated the amount of labor required for each section of work, we may proceed to analyze the agricultural employment of the villagers. We have already seen that labor requirements are discontinuous and unevenly distributed over the year. The intense activity in the period from Ch'ing Ming (middle of April) to Mang Chung (middle of June) and the virtual lack of essential farm work in the period from Li Tung (middle of November) to Ching Che (middle of March) give rise to the peasants' division of the year into two periods—the busy and the slack.

This differentiation is inherent in the nature of the agriculture practiced. The farmer, unlike those engaged in handicrafts, to a large extent lacks freedom of choice as to the amount of work he will perform and when he will perform it. The weaver can stop his work for a time or can increase his output by working long hours, without affecting his product. This is not true of the farmer, whose product dictates his activities. Each step in agricultural work has time limits which cannot be altered by any effort of the individual, who must adapt himself to the schedule determined by the growth processes of the crops he raises.

The busy period extends from the sowing of the rice to its harvest. As I have already mentioned, the period during which rice may be sown is strictly delimited by the climate, and the young shoots must have reached a certain stage of development before they can be transplanted from the nursery to the main fields. In Luts'un the elapsed time between sowing and transplantation is approximately 60 days. Transplantation must be preceded by preparation of the field, which includes turning over the soil, fertilizing, and letting in water. On a double-cropped farm this work can be started only after the harvest of broad beans has been completed. The ripening of this crop, which, of course, regulates the time of the harvest, occurs in Luts'un about

34

Ch'ing Ming. Consequently, on these farms there is a period of not more than 40 days during which the preparation of the fields for the rice shoots must be accomplished. Although from 120 to 140 days elapse between transplanting and harvest, weeding of the rice fields is confined to a period of approximately 75 days, for it may not begin until a half-month after transplanting, and it must terminate when the rice is in blossom and the grains begin to form, about Li Ch'iu. The rice must be harvested at the proper stage in its ripening if waste is to be avoided, for failure to do so may result in its being threshed by the wind and rain. In the fall of 1939, while we were in the village, there was a full week of rain, which delayed the harvest; an inspection of the fields revealed that the plants had been beaten to the ground and that about one-tenth of the grain was lost.

Inasmuch as the growth period for rice is only 180–200 days, there will be about a half-year of idleness for land and farmer in the case of a single-cropped farm. The double-cropped farm will be occupied throughout the year; but this is not true of the farmer, who will enjoy a long period of relative idleness during the growth of the broad bean. This is true because after the trenching and planting no care is required except occasional draining, which involves little time and effort.

We still have to consider the question whether a farmer will be fully employed even during the busy half of the year. Let us suppose that a man and a woman cultivate 1 *kung* of land. After the sowing of the rice the woman must spend 1 day collecting the broad beans and 2 days threshing them, while the man is preparing the fields to receive the rice shoots, a task which demands 4 days' work. Between transplanting and harvest there is a long period during which the woman does some weeding. Then harvesting the rice and planting the broad beans occupy 2 days. It is immediately apparent that the extent of the couple's employment will depend on the size of the farm they cultivate. We may ask, then, how many *kung* will provide maximum employment during the agricultural period. Since the sections of work vary in the amounts of labor they require, the size of the farm of a couple who do all their own work and have no help from others will be limited by the area they can care for during the busiest season (Table 2). This season extends from the collecting of the broad beans to the transplanting of the rice and is from 35 to 60 days long. During this time a couple can manage only 10 *kung*, since each *kung* demands 5.5 units of male labor, 3 units of female labor, and 1 unit of mixed labor. A farm of this size would, of course, allow a considerable amount of leisure during the remaining period.

As will be demonstrated later, because a farm of 10 *kung* will not support a family, some more lucrative schedule of employment must be developed. This is commonly achieved by the cultivation of larger farms, which necessitate the use of additional labor at peak work periods. Furthermore, the farmer may work on the farms of others when his own land does not demand his attention. The farmer may either hire laborers and hire himself out or may exchange services

TABLE 2*

SIZE OF FARM AN INDIVIDUAL CAN CARE FOR IN
DIFFERENT SECTIONS OF WORK

Section of Work	Labor Units Required for each *Kung*	Time Limit for the Work (Days)	Maximum Number of *Kungs* a couple can work
Reaping and threshing of broad bean.............	3 F	30	10
Preparation of farm for rice..	{6 M†} {0.5 F }	45	7.5
Transplantation...........	{1 M } {1 F }	30	30
Weeding................	4.3 F	75	17.5
Reaping and threshing of rice	{1.5 M } {1 F }	30	20
Preparation of farm for, and planting of, broad bean...	{0.5 M } {1 F }	30	30

* Unimportant tasks are omitted from the table.

† It is assumed that the work of fertilizing the fields is shared equally by the males and females.

with his neighbors. A count made during the harvest in 1939 revealed that one-half of the workers in the fields were working on an exchange basis rather than for wages. Exchange of labor is possible only because the farmers stagger the dates of their planting so that the crops do not reach the same stages of development simultaneously. If this were not done, the busy periods and the slack periods would coincide on all the farms. Groups of farmers commonly co-operate in this fashion to produce an alternation of busy periods, enabling each to obtain assistance when his work is heavy and to help others when his time is free. There is, however, a limit to the latitude permissible in setting the time for planting. The climatically defined limits within which each act of operations must be performed are given in Table 1 (p. 22).

II. LOCAL LABOR SUPPLY AND DEMAND

Having developed an estimate of the labor requirements for the agriculture of this locality, we may proceed to establish the total farming area and the labor supply in order to learn the relationship between the supply of and demand for labor in the village. The total farm land may be arrived at on the basis of three different criteria: (1) the land lying within the boundaries of the village, (2) the land owned by the villagers, or (3) the land cultivated by the villagers. The total farm land within the village boundaries consists, according to the official land survey, of 594 *mow;* but a part of this is owned and cultivated by outsiders. The inhabitants of the village, on the other hand, own 690 *mow* privately and 237 *mow* collectively, part of which is obviously outside the village area. The significant figure for our present purpose, however, is clearly the quantity of land under cultivation by the villagers; and this figure is 1,080 *mow*, or 2,800 *kung*. Thirty per cent of this land grows rice only; the remainder is double-cropped.

For the labor supply, we must rely on the population statistics from the official census taken in the spring of 1938. The enumeration was taken by the headman of the *shang*,[1] who knows the village well and is even personally acquainted with all the adult inhabitants. Since conscription had not yet been put into effect in 1938, there was no incentive for falsifying the number of individuals. The purpose of the census was understood by the villagers to be the securing of information for the organization of the administrative unit and for taxation. Neither a *de jure* nor a *de facto* principle was adopted as a basis for the census, but those absentees whose families remained in the village were enumerated, while absentees holding membership in the village but absent with their families were omitted. Because this principle did not yield ideal results for our purpose, we contemplated making a new count ourselves but gave up the idea to avoid creating the suspicion that we were agents sent by the government. We were, therefore, compelled to accept the 1938 report as the basis for our analysis. At the time of our second visit we obtained information from the headman and other elders relative to deaths, births, emigration, and immigration subsequent to the census. These house-by-house vital statistics are probably not completely reliable, especially for the children.

The census figures for individuals, as reflected in Table 3, are probably fairly reliable; but this cannot be said for its inventory of house-

[1] *Shang* is an administrative unit, occupying a place between *hsien* (county) and *pao* (about 100 households).

holds. Because it was understood by the villagers that taxes would be levied on households, families tended to combine for the census, so that this official count enumerated only 95 households, whereas our count showed 122. The total population in the spring of 1938 was 694, of which 359 were males and 335 were females; and in the autumn of 1939 it was 611, of which 293 were male and 318 were female. Table 3 classifies the individuals by age and sex and shows the changes re-

TABLE 3

POPULATION CHANGES IN LUTS'UN, MARCH, 1938—OCTOBER, 1939

AGE	1938		BIRTHS		DEATHS		IMMI-GRATION		EMI-GRATION		LOSS		TO-TAL LOSS	1939		AGE
	M	F	M	F	M	F	M	F	M	F	M	F		M	F	
Under 6..	46	43	3	7	4	6	...	...	2	2	3	1	4	43	42	Under 7
6–10....	46	36	...	...	...	...	...	...	1	1	1	1	2	45	35	7–11
11–15....	30	23	...	...	1	...	...	...	2	1	3	1	4	27	22	12–16
16–20....	35	27	...	...	...	...	1	4	12	4	11	...	11	24	27	17–21
21–25....	35	29	...	...	...	...	1	...	9	...	8	...	8	27	29	22–26
26–30....	37	23	...	...	2	1	...	1	8	3	10	3	13	27	20	27–31
31–35....	20	20	...	...	...	...	...	...	5	1	5	1	6	15	19	32–36
36–40....	34	37	...	...	1	2	...	...	9	3	10	5	15	24	32	37–41
41–45....	17	13	...	...	4	1	...	...	5	1	9	2	11	8	11	42–46
46–50....	16	24	...	...	...	...	...	...	1	2	1	2	3	15	22	47–51
51–55....	16	20	...	...	1	...	...	...	1	1	2	1	3	14	19	52–56
56–60....	12	22	...	...	1	...	...	...	...	...	1	...	1	11	22	57–61
61–65....	9	9	...	...	2	...	...	...	...	...	2	...	2	7	9	62–66
66–70....	4	5	...	...	...	...	...	...	...	...	...	...		4	5	67–71
Over 70..	2	4	...	...	...	...	...	...	...	...	...	...		2	4	Over 71
Total..	359	335	3	7	16	10	2	5	55	19	66	17	83	293	318	....
Grand total.	694		10		26		7		74		83		83	611		....

sulting in the population in the autumn of 1939. To obtain an inventory of the potential labor force, a different classification of the population is necessary (Table 4). Children from twelve to fifteen years of age are regularly employed for the lighter work, comparable to that performed by the women. Individuals between the ages of sixteen and fifty years fall into the adult-work category. Many continue to work between their fiftieth and sixtieth years, but after that most of them retire.

Table 5 presents an analysis of the relationship between the potential labor supply of the village (from Table 4) and the labor requirements of the land cultivated by the villagers (based on Table 2).[2] For

[2] In calculating the amount of labor required in cultivating beans, only 70 per cent of the land is considered, because 30 per cent of the land grows rice only.

the purposes of this table we are placing all the individuals of the twelve- to fifteen-year-age group in the female category and are assuming that half of those between fifty and sixty years of age are still

TABLE 4
AGE AND SEX DISTRIBUTION OF THE POPULATION IN LUTS'UN

AGE	1938 (SPRING)		1939 (AUTUMN)	
	Male	Female	Male	Female
Under 11	98	87	88	77
12–15	24	15	22	17
16–50	194	173	142	161
51–60	28	42	24	34
Above 70	15	18	17	29
Total	359	335	293	318

TABLE 5
CONDITIONS OF FARM-LABOR SUPPLY IN LUTS'UN

SECTION OF WORK	LABOR REQUIRED	DEFICIENCY (−) OR SURPLUS (+)			
		1938		1939	
		Male	Female	Male	Female
Reaping and threshing of broad bean	200 F	−	+ 33	−	+ 17
Preparation of farm for rice	386 M / 32 F	−178	+201	−232	+185
Transplantation	97 M / 97 F	+111	+136	+ 57	+120
Weeding	166 F	−	+ 67	−	+ 51
Reaping and threshing of rice	145 M / 97 F	+ 63	+136	+ 9	+120
Preparation of farm for, and planting of, broad bean	39 M / 68 F	+173	+165	+119	+149

potential workers. The result is a potential supply of 208 male and 233 female workers during the spring of 1938 and of 154 male and 217 female workers in the autumn of 1939, showing a sharp loss of males during the intervening period.

According to Table 5, the only section of work for which the potential labor supply is insufficient is the preparation of the farm for rice; actually, the deficiency here is less serious than is apparent, because the single-cropped farms can be prepared during the slack winter-time. It is difficult to estimate how much preparation is done on these farms before that on the double-cropped land is begun; but if we assume a figure of 50 per cent, the number of units of labor required for the regular 45-day period would drop to 328, thus bringing the deficiency down to 120 in 1938 and 174 in 1939. If the work of adding fertilizer to the fields were entirely assumed by the women, the deficiency would be decreased to 88 in 1938 and to 142 in 1939. Except for this one short period, there would appear to be a surplus of labor in Luts'un.

Table 5 is not a real inventory of the labor supply but assumes that everyone is able-bodied and will work and that the full time allowable for the different farming operations will be utilized. Actually, many are unable to work in agriculture because of illness or other duties, while many who could work do not. Furthermore, the planting period is not always arranged in the most efficient manner. Nevertheless, the figures given will serve as a rough approximation of the manpower potentiality of the village. In the light of this evidence, the large number of outside workers who are employed by the villagers is surprising. To understand this apparently paradoxical phenomenon, we must seek to gain some insight into the social structure within which it occurs.

III. THE LEISURE CLASS

We first arrived in Luts'un on November 16, 1938, during the period of winter inactivity. Walking from the district town, we were impressed by the absence of workers in the fields of luxuriant broad-bean plants. As we entered the village, we observed many men idling about, some talking in groups, others squatting at the door of their houses, puffing their pipes. Catching sight of strangers in city garb, they immediately gathered around to ask questions. They welcomed us cordially when it was learned we were from the university, and the master of the primary school immediately invited us to lunch. Their hospitality and the warm, leisurely atmosphere of the village brought to my mind the old Chinese poem:

> The harvest's wealth this plenteous year
> Has gladdened us, for we may share
> With welcome guests who travel from afar.

But this mood was quickly dispelled when we saw, stumbling along the roughly paved paths of the village, lines of heavily laden coolies with lean, hungry faces and in worn, ragged clothing. On their backs they carried huge blocks of salt, burdens beneath which their bodies were bent almost double. Inquiries directed to our new friends elicited the information that these people were salt-carriers, whose job it was to transport salt on their backs from the well to the district town—more than a full day's walk. For this they were paid a wage of twenty cents a day. So, almost at the moment of entering the village, we were introduced to the startling contrast between the two classes who inhabit it: those who do not need to work during the slack agricultural period and those who must work continuously.

It was not long, however, before we learned that those who talk and smoke during the period when there is no farm work to be done spend their time in the same way during the busy periods on the farm. The salt-carriers, on the other hand, transfer their energies to the farm when the work is ready there. The individuals who enjoy their leisure are idle, not because they are not able-bodied or cannot find employment, but simply because they are landowners. As such, they receive the greater part of the produce of the land. The landless, on the contrary, must labor on the land, whether or not they are really able to work. The line of demarcation between the leisure class and the worker class coincides roughly with the line separating the haves and the have-nots. This situation is rather shocking, in the light of the avowed national policy that "those who work on the land shall possess the land."

The cases which follow serve to illustrate the characteristics and attitudes of individuals belonging to the leisure class.

Wang the Christian, our landlord, during our first visit to the village, was about forty years of age and able-bodied, although, because of a former addiction to opium, not strong. He spent fully half of his time in bed; rarely retiring later than nine o'clock in the evening and rising shortly before breakfast, at nine o'clock in the morning. He attended church regularly; and on market days he spent all his time in the tea-shop, where he sometimes painted pictures for his admiring friends. He was the owner of 35 *kung* of land but rarely performed any farm work himself. During the winter of 1938 the laborer he employed to plow his single-cropped farm left the village, after being accused of theft, leaving his task uncompleted. Wang answered our suggestion, that he himself finish the work, with the statement that it would not be necessary because other laborers would be available. The result was that the

C·

rest of the farm was not plowed until the next year, but my landlord was not much perturbed. Despite this fact, he is regarded by the villagers as an industrious man, and this judgment is probably deserved; for when the labor supply proved insufficient during the 1939 harvest, he did join the crew on the farm. But this was an exceptional case, as proved by his statement that he had not touched agricultural tools for many years.

Others, with equivalent amounts of land, are even less industrious. Sze, the schoolmaster, and the former officials Wang and Chang, all opium-smokers, were usually in bed when we called on them. When we asked them bluntly why they did not work on their land, they were amused by our ignorance of the tradition that manual work was not for men like them.

Wang's nephew, a young man of twenty-five, was regarded as one of the exemplary young men of the village because he indulged neither in smoking opium nor in gambling and because he possessed an estate of 50 *kung*. After failing in several attempts to see him, we found him one evening with a number of village notables in a near-by temple, whither we had been led by strains of music. He was participating as a musician in a big ceremony, organized by his father for the purpose of "warding off enemy bombing planes." He had been free to spend all his days and nights in the temple during the two months the ceremony had been in progress because it was not necessary for him to work on the farm.

Young Wei, a middle-school graduate and formerly a tax-collector in a neighboring district, often called on us in order to impress our guests with his wide knowledge of the outside world. He once expressed his opinion on economic reform in the village in these words: "The educated young men should go down to the farms themselves to spread their new knowledge of agriculture among the farmers. This is the only way to promote progressive reforms." When we commended him for his worthy sentiment, he continued with the vehement declaration that he would see this program carried out. However, the following year, when labor was scarce, he flatly refused his father's request that he participate in the farm work, on the ground that the family was not so poor as to reduce him to the status of a farm hand.

At a dinner to which he had invited me, old Wang, a member of a secret religious society, told me something of the history of his family. "My father had five sons, and we were a large family. Happy were those days when we had an estate of 200 *kung* and were rich and prosperous. Laborers were hired to do the farm work; and we, the sons, had nothing to worry about but were able to smoke and gamble to our heart's content. None of us acquired any vocational training. But the penalties of our sins are upon us now. Our estate has been divided, and each portion has dwindled in size. What shall we leave to our sons?" When I called to see him the next year, he was away at a society meeting, but I learned that his son had been sent to work as an apprentice to a shop in the city.

Many similar instances could be cited to illustrate the lives of members of the leisure class who are able to live in idleness owing to special economic conditions in the village. Since agriculture is the only industry, there are practically no opportunities for employment other than in farming. Therefore, the landless and those with little land constitute an abundant and, consequently, a cheap labor supply which permits the landowners to free themselves from toil on the land. The latter are thus forced up into a distinct social class by the army of laborers beneath them.

CHAPTER III

SOURCES OF FAMILY INCOMES

THE agrarian problem in China, although it may seem complex and confusing, is, in reality, extremely simple and obvious. Tawney has summarized it well in a few words: "The fundamental fact, it is urged, is of a terrible simplicity. It is that the population of China is too large to be supported by existing resources."[1] The analysis presented in this book is in large measure merely a concrete illustration of this conclusion. The reader will see in the village described here a picture of one type of rural economy staggering under the heavy pressure of overpopulation, with the land system, the most vulnerable point in the structure, suffering the first impact. In a village like Luts'un, where even simple handicraft industry is not developed, almost the entire burden of the population, both landed and landless, must be supported by the land. Before proceeding to a discussion of the distribution of the limited land resources, let us test the validity of this statement by an inventory of the various enterprises other than farming which produce income for the villagers.

I. OCCUPATIONAL DIFFERENTIATION

Table 6 is a list of all occupations, other than farming, engaged in by inhabitants of Luts'un. The compilation of this was not an easy task, for various reasons; for example, several of the occupations noted therein are not characterized by an easily observed stock-in-trade like that of the grocer. Perhaps more important is the fact that in most instances the family combines farming with another occupation and does not maintain regular hours for the latter. One of our neighbors, for example, works in the field most of the time and is to be found at his forge for brief periods only when hoes are brought to him for sharpening. Chao, from whom we rented a room during our second visit in the village, is a druggist and doctor; but the windows of his store are always closed. Even were they open, his place would look more like a church than a drug store, because his cases are concealed by a large screen, covered with hymns. I have never seen him sell drugs in the store; but, as a doctor, he carries drugs to his patients. A prominent

[1] *Land and Labour in China*, p. 103.

Christian, his treatment of patients is really a practice of his religion rather than a professional service. In the course of friendly calls, he gives medicine to those he finds to be ill, without any formulated policy regarding payment. In fact, whether he or the village's other "doctor" (who is able to compound only two or three prescriptions but calls himself a professional doctor) receive compensation for their services is not an important consideration, since each has his own land for his support.

Most of the villagers have sufficient skill and simple tools to enable them to function as carpenters and masons. When a household needs its furniture or house repaired, the neighbors are invariably willing to give assistance without pay. Brother Liu, who lived next door to us,

TABLE 6*

TABLE OF OCCUPATIONS OTHER THAN AGRICULTURE

Innkeeper	9	Witch	1
Grocer	3	Taoist priest	1
Bean-curd-maker	3	Fortuneteller	1
Carpenter	3	Butcher	1
Cold-jelly-peddler	2	Wine-maker	1
Blacksmith	2	Schoolteacher	1
Druggist and medicine man	1	Cotton-comber	1
Medicine man	1	Total	32
Mason	1		

* Twenty-seven per cent of total households in village.

has a reputation in the village for being very handy with tools and for always being ready to help anyone who needs assistance. Temperamentally incapable of idleness, he built his own kitchen and stable and made baskets for himself and his friends. When my cot was broken, he appeared with his tools to repair it and was hurt when I offered him payment. Such people do not appear in Table 6, which included only those whose services can be obtained for a fee. Informants were used for part of the list because we never saw at work some of those said to engage in part-time occupations.

Thirty-two households (27 per cent of the total households of the village) are engaged in occupations other than farming. Of these, however, only four do not also gain part of their livelihood from farming, either as owners or as laborers on the farms of others. For the rest, the occupations other than farming are purely supplementary and are relatively insignificant. These four include a grocer, who is also an opium-dealer; a bean-curd-maker; the seeress; and the blind fortuneteller.

All the grocery stores in the village are very small and hardly deserve the name, for their merchandise consists chiefly of cigarettes, tobacco, bean oil, and paper. The complete stock of the largest has an estimated value of $300,[2] while the smallest has a stock worth about $10. The owner of the latter, a widow, buys fruit and cigarettes at the village market and retails them. She asks exorbitant prices, and people buy from her only for charitable reasons. As I shall explain in the next section, because of the existence of the periodic market there is little need for retail grocery stores. The only grocer who makes his entire living from his shop uses it also as an opium den, which is a source of considerable profit to him. We found it an excellent place to visit when we wished to talk with the villagers, for it was always occupied. How much of his gross income of approximately $20 a day is profit it is impossible to say, since this is an illegal business about which it is difficult to acquire reliable information.

The one bean-curd-maker who does not work on a farm finds it necessary to supplement his income by transporting merchandise from one market to another. He is a poor man.

The top profession, from the standpoint of income, is that followed by the seeress, who is a diviner and serves as a medium between her clients and the dead. She is so popular that it is frequently necessary to make an appointment in order to see her. It is said that a high official in Kunming once sent a car for her but that she refused to visit him. Unlike the carpenter, she has a large measure of control over her market. Likewise, although there is a fixed price for each service, she may at any time exact money from a client by making her demands in the name of a spirit. She need never be unemployed, for she may, at will, inform a villager that a certain spirit is calling for him. She supports her husband as well as herself, and both are able to smoke opium lavishly.

The blind fortuneteller, on the other hand, is a destitute bachelor. He is rarely consulted, and he finds it necessary to travel all over the valley to make a few pennies. When I first saw him on the road, I assumed he was a beggar, and only later learned that he was a professional man.

The reason for the large number of innkeepers in the list is that the village is located a day's journey by horse from the salt well, so that

[2] ["Dollars" (or $) as used throughout the text refers to the Chinese dollar, which before wartime inflation varied in exchange value from four to twenty to the American dollar.—EDITOR.]

each evening the street is crowded with horses and their drivers arriving for a night's lodging. The innkeepers provide beds for the drivers
and feed for their herds of pack horses. During a normal month an
average of about 200 horses will be cared for in the stables of each of
the inns. During 1939 the traffic was greatly increased because of the
war, and late-comers often were compelled to travel on to the next village for accommodations. We estimated that the average income for
each inn at that time was approximately $200 per month.

Except for the inns, there are no important businesses in Luts'un.
The reason for the lack of differentiation in the economic structure is,
we think, the existence of the marketing system, which we shall describe in the following section.

II. MARKETING

Marketing is a subject which could be made the basis of a special
investigation, but for our present purpose a brief discussion showing
how it provides income to the villagers will suffice. The system for the
exchange of commodities existing in most of rural Yunnan is characterized by markets which are periodic and temporary. This system is
called *kai-tzu* (literally, "street"). Transactions which take place in
these markets are mainly between the producers and the ultimate consumers, although a certain number of the sellers are peddlers. Such
markets are a convenient means of merchandising for producers who,
like those in this village, are not able to set up permanent shops because they do not have a constant supply of goods to sell. The Luts'un
market, which is held every six days, is small because of its proximity to
the district town, where a market is held two days earlier than the one
in Luts'un. Here in the town market there are usually more than a
thousand buyers and sellers, and almost anything needed by the peasants can be obtained. Consequently, most of the Luts'un people do
almost all of their buying and selling in the town. A count of the sellers
in the village market during the most crowded period showed a total
of only 51, of whom 13 were inhabitants of the village, 11 were from
the district town, and 13 were tribesmen from the mountains, the rest
being from neighboring villages. The most important commodities
sold in the village market are firewood, brought in by the tribesmen,
and clothing and foreign goods, mostly for the household, which are
sold by peddlers from the city. The villagers sell salt, tobacco, cold
jelly, and wine, the last two items being consumed on the spot for re-
freshment. Actually, the town is the center of almost all the marketing

activities of the villagers, and nearly every household sends a representative there every market day to sell produce and to buy needed commodities.

As a means of supplementing their incomes, the residents of Luts'un commonly employ their free time in visiting the markets in different villages and towns, buying where the prices are low and selling where they are higher. About a half-day's journey to the north is a village market as large as the one in the district town, but here the prices are much lower. For example, pigs may be purchased for about three-quarters of the price paid in the town, while the cost of firewood is only one-half of the town-market price. When villagers have free time, they buy here and sell in the district town. Some of them even travel as much as two days to other districts in order to find lower prices. Since very little capital is required, it is possible for anyone, no matter how poor, to carry on such activities in at least a small way. Even a poor laborer may obtain a small quantity of produce on credit from his relatives to transport to the markets for sale. In most instances, these ventures amount to nothing more then a selling of the individual's labor for transporting the commodity. On the other hand, there is some speculation. The old lady in our landlord's house kept a bag of grain bought at a previous market for sale when the price should rise, and the wife of our landlord once bought four chickens and sold them for a profit in the same market.

III. TRANSPORTATION

An occupation engaged in by many of the poor laborers is the transportation of salt. The neighboring district produces large quantities of salt and supplies a large area, including Kunming. Since motor transport is available only on the public highway, human and animal carriers must be used between it and the wells. In November, 1938, a carrier was paid 80 cents for transporting a 130-pound load. Deducting the cost of his food and lodging for the three days required for the round trip, his wage would be about 20 cents a day. Although this was, at that time, double the pay for farm labor, the task is so strenuous that only extreme poverty and the lack of any other work would induce the villagers to undertake it. It is impossible to work at it continuously. In fact, even a strong, healthy man can make no more than four trips a month. Kong, who was both poor and industrious, had made only six trips the year before; and he then gave up this work completely because he could get enough farm work. Owing to the reluctance of the villagers to serve as carriers, except when circumstances forced them to it, the wage was increased in 1939 to three times the farm wage. According to information I obtained in 1938, approximately 40 people in the village, including even women and children, constantly carried salt during the slack agricultural period. In 1939, despite the increase in the rate of pay, the number had been reduced to about 20, owing to the better opportunities for other employment which the war had created.

Four of the wealthier families raise horses to use in the transportation of salt. A horse carries a load of approximately 200 pounds and requires only two days for the round trip. The income of the owner, after the cost of stabling the horse and the wages of the driver have been deducted, is $1.40 a day for each horse. Inasmuch as a driver can handle 5 horses, a working force of this size will earn $7.00 a day. But the horses must rest between trips, so only 4 out of the 5 horses can be in service at any time; and, furthermore, inclement weather reduces the working time to nine months out of the year. Allowing for these factors, we find that the owner of 5 horses will receive an average of $4.00 a day. Since a horse is worth $100, an investment of $500 is necessary to set up in business on this scale. The high mortality among the draft animals is revealed by the fact that in 1939 there were only 34 horses, 7 mules, and 3 donkeys in the village, while during 1938, 23 horses and 15 mules died. Among those that had died were 15 animals belonging to a single owner. This high death rate is at least partly attributable to the lack of any veterinarian other than a quack, who is trusted by no one. The animals are permitted to die and are thrown into the wasteland, where they become food for the dogs. We felt it a pity that such callous treatment should be their reward for faithful service, but this feeling paled into insignificance beside that which we experienced when we learned that the same treatment was accorded the poorest of the human laborers.

IV. LIVESTOCK-RAISING

Not everyone in the village is engaged in transport and marketing. In fact, the most popular subsidiary occupation is the raising of poultry and animals. Almost every house has 2 or 3 pigs, which are fed the outer layer of the rice grain and the pulverized stalks of the broad bean, mixed with rice water. Thus the pigs get the most nutritive parts of the rice, which would otherwise be wasted. The price of a small pig is $2.50; and feed for a year—consisting of rice hulls worth $40, bean-

stalks worth $24, and broken rice valued at $15—brings the total cost
of raising the animal to $81.50, more than the selling price of about
$80. This would seem, then, to be an unprofitable venture, but it
should be pointed out that the costs cited are largely theoretical. The
materials used for feed need not be purchased, and there is little market for them, since pigs are not raised with purchased feed. The price
we have used is that which is charged for the very small supply which
is purchased only when there is an emergency need for it. Even a poor
laborer may raise a pig by purchasing the whole rice grain for his own
use and feeding the pigs the hulls, together with some purchased
chopped bean straw.

A few families raise other animals as well. Two of them keep a total
of 70 sheep. Since the village is not near the mountains and hence
lacks good grassland, this number has remained stable for years. Three
households raise a total of 900 ducks during a short season of the year.
This season begins with the rice harvest, when the single crop field is
used for range. In 1938, 100 ducklings cost $8.60 and were fed $4.20
worth of grain during their forty-day growing period. Allowing for the
number that die, the selling price of 50–60 cents apiece will give a man
who raises 100 ducks a profit of approximately 90 cents a day.

V. THE IMPORTANCE OF FARMING IN THE VILLAGE ECONOMY

From the above description of the subsidiary occupations of the village it is apparent that there is not a single important household handicraft or profession, and no important commerce, in the village. Those
activities described bring in some income, but they are very limited.
We are forced to the conclusion that it is the land which provides the
livelihood of the people and employs the labor.

We may now anticipate our later, more detailed discussion to survey briefly the relation of the land's productivity to the food and other
needs of the villagers. In Luts'un there are three grades of land, as defined in the official survey. There are 1,140 plots of first-grade land,
producing 9.6 *piculs*[3] of grain per *kung;* 530 plots of second-grade land,
producing 7.7 *piculs;* and 80 plots of third-grade land, producing 4.8
piculs. This is a ratio of 65:31:4. The total land under the management of the villagers is about 2,800 *kung,* of which 400 are rented from
other villages. The total produce of the 2,400 owned *kung,* on the basis

[3] According to the *China Handbook, 1937–43,* compiled by the Chinese Ministry of Information (New York: Macmillan Co., 1943), the Chinese *picul,* which is a measure of weight
rather than of volume, may vary locally, but that chiefly in use at the present time is equivalent to 100 Chinese *catties,* or 110.231 pounds. According to the Louisiana State Rice
Milling Company of Abbeville, Louisiana, the weight of 1 bushel of unhusked rice is 45
pounds.

of the established ratio, is about 21,000 *piculs* of grain, while the 400 rented *kung*, after the payment of rent, yield an income of 1,700 *piculs*. Therefore, the net produce under the control of the villagers is 22,700 *piculs* of grain. Since husking reduces 10 *piculs* of grain to 4 *piculs* of rice, the net rice yield is about 9,000 *piculs*.

In order to estimate the amount of food needed for the whole village, we have first attempted to determine the consumption of an average adult individual. The average villager having two meals a day in ordinary times will consume from 6.4 *piculs* of husked rice a year. But during busy periods the working laborer will have three meals a day. Assuming that the adult works one-half of the days during the working season, we have to add a hundred meals to the number, giv-

TABLE 7

ANALYSIS OF RICE NEEDS OF LUTS'UN VILLAGERS

Age Group	Equivalence to Adult Male	Population, 1938	Equivalent Adult-Male Units
Under 6......	MF 0.35	89	31
6–10........	MF 0.50	82	41
11–15........	M 0.70 F 0.60	M 30 F 23	35
16–20........	M 0.95 F 0.80	M 35 F 27	55
21–60........	M 1.00 F 0.80	M 187 F 188	337
Above 60.....	M 0.80 F 0.70	M 15 F 18	25

Total equivalent adult-male units...................... 524
Total rice requirement (*piculs*)........................ 3,668

ing a total of about 7 *piculs*, or 470 pounds, a year on the average. To arrive at the total need for rice as food, it is necessary to make adjustments on the basis of the factor of sex. In this we have followed mainly Atwater's scale for changing individuals of different ages and sex to adult-male units, with modifications determined by our own observations in the village. Table 7 presents this analysis.

According to our estimate, the village needs about 40 per cent of the total yield of rice for food, leaving 60 per cent for the purchase of other necessities. Hence it would seem that the standard of living of the Luts'un peasants must be well above the average, since in the average Chinese village about 60 per cent of the income is spent for food, of which rice comprises 80 to 90 per cent. But this is actually not the case, because the income from the land is not equal among the villagers.

Since the economy of this type of village is based mainly on the land, which determines the standard of living of the people, it is fitting that we turn now to a study of its distribution.

CHAPTER IV

DISTRIBUTION OF LANDOWNERSHIP

I. SOURCES OF DATA

A S A source of information relative to the distribution of landownership among the villagers, the government land survey made in 1933 would seem to be dependable. The owners of all land were registered by this survey, which was intended to be used as a basis for taxation. An examination of the records, however, immediately revealed a number of difficulties. The first of these stems from the fact that the unit for the survey was the village, so that the lands within the administrative boundaries of each village are recorded in a single book. The name of an individual who owns land in different villages will appear in as many different books, while, on the other hand, a single book will include the names of owners from various other villages. Since the information desired for this study was a description of the land owned by the inhabitants of Luts'un, it was necessary to pore through the registry books for all the villages in the surrounding area. To miss some of the names proved exceedingly easy.

Another difficulty encountered was the frequent discrepancy between the names of the registered owners and the names of the people who, we knew, actually owned the land. Upon inquiry we found that many of those whose names appeared in the books had died and that the record had not been altered when the ownership changed through inheritance, since the government is interested only in the collection of taxes and does not make inquiries concerning ownership so long as the levy on a piece of land continues to reach the treasury. Furthermore, some of the estates had been divided among brothers, who are still paying taxes jointly. Some genealogical work was thus necessary for the identification of owners. A somewhat similar difficulty was that some of the collectively owned lands were registered under the names of individuals.

After more than a week of work on the land maps and the registry books we had what we thought was a complete record of the village landownership, but we later found several omissions and other errors. It was decided that this record should be checked by making inquiries of the villagers.

Gleaning information from the owners relative to their land holdings presented substantial difficulties. The 1933 land survey was remembered as a disaster comparable to a bandit incursion, because of the enormous increase in taxes it brought about. Previously, taxation had been based on the reported size of farms. According to the report of the Rural Reconstruction Commission, the amount of cultivable land in the ten districts surveyed increased 290.9 per cent in 1933! The memory of this calamitous event, still vivid in the people's minds, conduces to a hostile, suspicious attitude toward anyone who evinces an interest in the extent of their property holdings. Even our ventures in questioning the families in whom we had inspired a measure of confidence were met with courteous evasion. One day we asked Grandfather Wang how many *kung* of land he owned; he was visibly perturbed when his grandson, eager to display his intelligence, broke in and answered my query. While it would doubtless be possible, after long residence, to break down the reserve of the owners, a method of acquiring the needed information in a short time was imperative. We soon discovered that everyone was exceedingly well informed in regard to his neighbor's business and was willing and eager to talk about it. A man who was apparently ignorant of the size of his own farm proved himself capable of providing an accurate figure for almost every other piece of land in his neighborhood. By this information we were able to check our original data.

For information on the ownership of land by clans, temples, and other groups, on the other hand, the records of the survey were found to be quite satisfactory, because these owners are fewer in number, are more easily identifiable, and have greater continuity than the individual owners. Questioning of representatives of these groups was, on the other hand, of little avail, since the fact that the land was a source of profit seemed to make them reluctant to divulge the extent of their holdings.

II. FAMILY HOLDINGS

Table 8 gives the distribution of family ownership of land in Luts'un. The *kung*, instead of the *mow* (in terms of which the land survey records appear), is used as the unit, because, as we have demonstrated, it alone is significant in the lives of the owners.

The total land owned by individual families comprises about 1,800 *kung*, or 690 *mow*, which is an average of 5.7 *mow*, or 0.87 acre, per family. Thirty-one per cent of the households in the village, however, are landless. The 1,800 *kung* are owned as follows: 446 (25 per cent) by 35 per cent of the households with less than 16 *kung* each; 614 (34 per cent) by 19 per cent with 16–30 *kung* each; and 740 (41 per cent) by 15 per cent with 31–65 *kung* each. In other words, a minority of the population holds most of the land, and the majority is landless or has insufficient land for its support. But it is noteworthy that there are only petty owners here, for the largest estate comprises only 65 *kung*, about 25 *mow* or about 4 acres.

III. COLLECTIVE HOLDINGS

A substantial amount of land is owned by social groups, such as clans, clubs, and temples. It comprises, in fact, 27 per cent of all the land owned by members of the village. The largest such holding comprises 135 *kung*, or more than 52 *mow*, which is more than double the

TABLE 8

SIZE OF FARMS IN LUTS'UN

Size of Farm (in *Kung*)	No. of Households	Size of Farm (in *Kung*)	No. of Households
0	38	31–35	1
1– 5	14	36–40	7
6–10	21	41–45	0
11–15	8	46–50	6
16–20	5	51–55	0
21–25	3	56–60	3
26–30	15	61–65	1

largest private holding. Table 9 presents a complete list of the groups, together with an inventory of their respective properties.

The largest property-holder of the village is the Temple of the Lord of the Earth, an institution which is found in almost every village in the region. Possessed of all the appurtenances of a place of worship, it is yet more than that; it is, in fact, the material embodiment of the community organization. Its property, acquired mainly by the reversion of the land of many villagers who perished during the Moslem rebellion of 1855–73, is considered the possession of all the inhabitants of the village, for whose benefit the income is disbursed. Specifically, its funds are spent for (1) the maintenance of the village temple, (2) part of the maintenance of the village school, (3) emergency restoration of the dam, (4) entertainment of soldiers passing through the village, (5) gifts at the marriages and burials of villagers, and (6) partial subsidization of the village government.

Although the resources of the temple are supposed to be administered for the welfare of the population as a whole, their management is not subject to the will of all the people. The treasurer is not a part of the formal administrative system of the village but is charged with the duty of representing the people in bargaining with the headman.

TABLE 9
COLLECTIVE HOLDINGS

	No. of Mow
1. Land owned by groups in Luts'un:	
Temple to the Lord of Earth	52.671
Wei clan	28.407
Family shrine of Wang Wen Yi Kong	27.268
Pine Garden of Wang clan	26.748
Another branch of Wang clan	23.732
Tien Sen dam	15.608
Taoist Music Society	14.109
Fraternity of Honesty and Righteousness	12.756
Imperial Teaching Society	9.803
Older Fraternity	7.004
Confucius Club	6.749
Temple (Hong Chiao Kong)	5.084
Chang clan	3.085
Chou clan	2.201
Dam for the new ditch	2.085
Total	237.310
2. Land within the village owned by groups outside the village:	
Temple of the God of Literature	7.067
White-Robe Nunnery	5.950
Chia No. 1 of the district town	4.285
Congregation of God of the Military	3.118
Educational bureau of the district	2.784
Total	23.204
Grand total	260.514

He is theoretically selected by common consent; in practice, the position is held in rotation by the influential men of the village by their common consent. The invariable practice of ignoring the poor in questions of administration is justified by the statement that their poverty disqualifies them, since they could not reimburse the public coffers were they to make mistakes. It is impossible to say how much profit accrues to the treasurer, for, since the only concern of the people is that the traditional functions be performed, there is no system of auditing or making public his accounts.

There are a number of landowning clubs, differing widely in their purposes and activities. The Confucius Club is now inactive, and the rent from its properties is assigned to the school. The Taoist Music Club, with a voluntary membership, performs ceremonies in honor of various gods on the first and fifteenth days of each month and is also invited to participate in village funeral ceremonies. Its income, derived both from its property and from fees paid by individuals for whom it performs services, is used to defray the expenses of its meetings. The Imperial Teaching Society, which is supposed to have been organized during the Ching Dynasty for the purpose of reading and interpreting the book of moral teachings promulgated by the imperial palace, holds meetings on the first and fifteenth of each month. It still fulfils its original function of teaching morality; but it is, in addition, a charitable organization which assists the poor in meeting burial expenses.

Ownership of land by the clan may arise through agreement by a group of brothers to leave a portion of their inheritance in a common pool to avoid the necessity of constant sharing of their own produce for the general clan welfare or through donation of land by wealthy members for the care of needy ones. The gift of Wang Wen Yi Kong, a well-known official, was an example of the latter sort. The income from the clan lands is used to finance sacrifices to the ancestors and clan feasts and to provide scholarships for the college education of its members and general assistance to poor members. The treasurer who manages the clan land is selected on the basis of ability and prestige, factors which also determine his tenure. Since the office may be profitable, there is keen competition for it, and all the aspirants watch the incumbent closely, at the same time seeking to reduce his personal profit by making constant demands for expenditures of the funds. The treasurer of Wang's clan told me that there was never a peaceful clan feast and that many ended in violent disputes. At the feast of the Pine Garden branch in 1939, after solemn sacrifice to the ancestors, someone demanded that the treasurer open his accounts to inspection. The latter refused but was forced to give another feast to pacify his fellow-clansmen.

Other owner groups are the monks of the Temple of the God of the Military and of the Temple of the God of Literature; the irrigation organization, which devotes its income to the maintenance of the irrigation dams and ditches; and the educational bureau, whose land provides the revenue to pay part of the expenses of the village school.

CHAPTER V

FARM LABORERS

I. LANDLESS HOUSEHOLDS

OF THE thirty-eight landless households in the village, only four are able to make a living from nonagricultural occupations; all the rest are dependent for at least part of their livelihood on farm employment and constitute a large proportion of the total labor supply. The members of nineteen of these households are called "new settlers" by the villagers. Table 10 gives the origins of these immigrants. Of these nineteen families, one operates a farm which it possesses temporarily on the basis of a loan; seven rent land; and the remaining eleven work only as laborers on the farms of others.

TABLE 10

NATIVE PLACES OF THE NEW SETTLERS

Other villages of Lu-fon	4	Yu-chi	1
Lo-tsu	2	Chu-ching	1
Yen-ching	1	Hei-ching	1
Chiang-ch'uan	1	Szechwan province	8

This labeling of certain of the villagers as "new settlers" piqued our curiosity, especially since we knew that at least some of them had been inhabitants of Luts'un for many years and since we were aware of the fact that the village itself did not have a long history. The old residents declared that the village had grown up during their lifetimes, asserting that in their youth only a few houses marked the site. Until the war, immigration had been an important factor in the growth of the population, for the fertile land and the system of hiring workers for the cultivation of the land had constantly attracted labor from outside. Our inquiries first elicited the statement that new settlers are those who have come to the village in recent years, but it was obvious that the factor of recency alone was not actually very important. The laborer Kon Wen, for example, though the son of an immigrant, had been born in the village; but he was still considered a "new settler." It soon became evident that the real criterion was the possession of land. Those immigrants who acquire land are then, and not until then, accepted as members of the community, while those who remain landless continue to be regarded as outsiders. In this agricultural village, as in other similar sections of China,[1] ownership of land is a necessary qualification for complete integration into the community. The acquisition of land by immigrants is, however, not generally easy. The individual who moves into an area whose land is already fully utilized must, if the economy is strictly agricultural, support himself as an employee or as a tenant unless he has the power to deprive the earlier residents of their land. The latter usually have a potent advantage in such a struggle because they are intrenched in their holdings by law and custom, both of which militate against the landless intruder, who has to work against well-organized resistance in his struggle for land of his own. In a later section we shall describe the restrictions imposed on the disposition of land in Luts'un, where clan members always have a prior right to acquire land which is being sold.[2]

Even in the absence of restrictive laws or customs, the acquisition of land by newcomers in a community is unusual, inasmuch as individuals with the capital required for purchase of property rarely emigrate. It seems to be pretty generally true here that most immigrants who leave their homes do so under the pressure of poverty and that they cannot hope to save enough from their wages to buy farms.

II. WANDERING SOULS

The villagers we described in the preceding section are those who, although they have not founded estates and are not wholly accepted by the old residents, have been able to establish themselves permanently in the community and intend to become full members of it. They usually marry and, though they commonly rent only one or two rooms in someone's house, raise families. Some of them (like Kang, whose children are the third generation of the family in Luts'un) are natives of the village. These "new settlers" are well-established villagers, in comparison with the class of laborers to be discussed in this section, who may be called "wandering souls"—individuals of either

[1] For the characteristics of "outsiders" in another area, see Fei, *Peasant Life in China*, p. 23.

[2] In a village with which I am familiar near Kunming, purchase of land by immigrants is effectively prevented by special, insupportable duties for water. In the country of the Yao tribesmen in Kwangsi the earliest settlers occupied the land and constituted an organized front against those who later infiltrated into the area. The servile status forced upon the latter has been maintained by laws prohibiting ownership of land by new settlers. See Tung-wei Wang, *Social Organization of Hua Lan Yao*.

sex who are landless and without special skills and who have no roots in Luts'un or elsewhere. They are often drifters, who appear suddenly in the village, work for a while, and then disappear again, though some of them have indeed resided for a long time in the village, alone and outside the stream of community life. They live in the homes of their employers on a hand-to-mouth, day-to-day basis. There were approximately thirty such individuals in the village in 1938, but by 1939 this number had been reduced about one-half.

Old Lao Tsung, who became well known to us because he was always on hand to carry our baggage, is a typical wandering soul. Born in the village, he left at the age of ten with his father, an itinerant laborer, to go to Tali. After more than twenty years he suddenly reappeared, explaining his presence with the story that he had been impressed into labor by the soldiers and had finally been released near Luts'un. Having no ties elsehere, he remained in the village, where he was employed as a casual laborer by villagers who had known his father. Once, rebelling against the hopelessness of his lot as a laborer, he left the village and, impersonating a monk, solicited funds, allegedly for a temple. An encounter with someone who understood the professional vocabulary of the monks, however, led to his exposure, and he was forced to return to his unhappy life in the village. He is now a foolish, babbling old man, worn out by years of unrewarding toil, the laughing-stock of the community. Too old to work regularly, without a family, and ignored or ridiculed by the villagers, he is living out his last days as a wretched derelict whose only diversion is attendance at the Christian church, where he can get a free cup of tea and join in the singing. One of these days his futile, pathetic life will end; but there will be no one to mourn or even to notice his passing.

In Uncle Chang's house lives Lao Wang, a man thirty years of age who had come to Luts'un from a neighboring village ten years earlier. Deprived of his inheritance by an uncle when his parents died during his childhood, he is possessed of a stubborn independence which prevents his attempting to recover his property and impels him to seek security by his own effort. A steady, conscientious worker, he hires himself out to the farmers when agricultural work is available and at other times collects firewood in the mountains. The only relief from the drabness of his life of drudgery comes in the evening, when he returns to his little room in Chang's house to find solace in a few cups of wine. We were especially smitten by the pathos of this homeless, unattached man when we saw him among the guests at the celebration of the harvest moon, to which Chang had invited us. Surrounded, as he was, by those who had families and occupied secure, comfortable positions in the community, his lack of stable ties and sense of belonging were most striking. Those around him represented the personification of the goals he strove for, but the expression in his eyes betrayed his feeling of hopelessness. When he presented us with a piece of moon cake, which symbolizes the fulness of family life, and we responded with a toast wishing him the joy of a family before the coming of the next harvest festival, he acknowledged to us his sense of the futility of the struggle to achieve such a desirable state. The attitude of the more fortunate villagers was expressed in the warning of the host's wife to the young man: "Beware, Lao Wang, that some unscrupulous woman doesn't come along and make you lose the little savings you have. The earnings of ten years' work with the hands are not enough to let you dream of getting a wife who will settle down and stay with you." There is little prospect for Lao Wang other than the prolongation of his present kind of life until the end of his days.

Many of the workers of this class remain in the village for much briefer periods than the two already described. During our first stay in the village, our landlord had as a maid a poor girl from a neighboring village, who worked for food, clothing, and shelter only. When we inquired about her the next year, we found that no one knew where she was. Once, after we had been in Luts'un for some time, a boy of about seventeen years, whom we had never seen before, appeared suddenly in our room to ask for medicine for an injured foot. We were surprised when he told us he lived in a near-by house, for we thought we knew all the faces in the village; but he explained that he had just recently arrived from Kweichow, after having been lost from the army. We were struck by his lack of attachment to any community and by his ability to adapt himself to any place and situation in which he might find himself.

III. MIGRATORY LABORERS

Having described in the previous sections the labor supply in the village, let us turn to the question of the availability of workers resident in other places. Outside labor is necessary because, as we have seen, during certain seasons even the total potential local supply of labor is insufficient, and, moreover, many of this number never work. Since this shortage is seasonal and there is a surplus of workers during much of the year, access to a reservoir of migratory labor is essential. According to our informants, outside workers are very numerous during the bean harvest and are used, though to a lesser extent, even in the weeding and harvesting of the rice crop. Before about 1930, these outsiders were mainly aborigines from the mountains, but in recent years many of them have been Chinese from neighboring districts. Formerly two out of every three workers were nonresidents, but now the proportion has been reduced to approximately 50 per cent. Being skeptical of this information, because our analysis had indicated a relatively minor deficiency in the local labor supply, we took a census during the rice harvest of 1939 to determine the relative proportions of local and nonlocal employees. The results of our enumeration are summarized in Table 11.

These figures indicate in a striking fashion the importance of migratory labor in the local economy, especially when they are viewed in

TABLE 11

EMPLOYEES: LOCAL AND NONLOCAL

	No. of House-holds	Male Labor	Female Labor	Outsiders		Per-cent-age of Out-siders
				Male	Female	
First day........	5	35	30	9	0	14
Second day......	10	66	42	16	4	18
Third day.......	7	72	52	24	9	27

the light of the fact that the local labor supply is theoretically adequate for the rice harvest, that at this period there are fewer outsiders than during the spring, and that in 1939 it was difficult to get outside workers because of the increased labor demand for construction of railroads and public highways. Despite these factors, approximately 20 per cent of the workers in the fields at the beginning of the harvest period were from outside Luts'un. It is evident that the economic structure as it exists in the village is dependent upon the availability of this seasonal supply of workers.

An examination of the provenances of the nonresident workers reveals that a rather large area is involved. They come from the Yenching, Wu-ting, Lo-tsu, and Kwang-tung districts around Luts'un; but some are from as far as Tali, a journey of two days by motorbus. Most of them proved to be, not mere laborers, but owners of land which, owing to climatic differences, requires no attention during this period. Although these same climatic variations would permit the inhabitants of Luts'un to seek employment in other localities, there are actually very few of them who leave the village for this purpose. This one-sided relationship is undoubtedly attributable to differences in standards of living, for, although I have not investigated the conditions in the places from which laborers come to Luts'un, the dress of these individuals betokens a condition of much greater poverty than that of the natives.

On the other hand, the flow of labor from poorer areas to a more fertile region affects the standard of living of the latter. With a limited demand for labor, on the one hand, and a large number of migratory workers available, on the other, the wage will inevitably be reduced both for local workers and for those from outside. This abundance of cheap labor, in turn, causes the landowners to assume the role of a leisure class. But the economic structure which has developed on the basis of the past abundance of manpower is now threatened by the siphoning-off process resulting from the war.

IV. THE DECLINING LABOR SUPPLY

Two factors are responsible for the present rapid decline in the population in Luts'un: emigration and the unfavorable ratio between births and deaths. The reader may consult Table 3 for a picture of this trend in the period from the spring of 1938 to the autumn of 1939. During that time there were twenty-six deaths but only ten births. The ten births were balanced by a like number of infant deaths. Of the remaining deaths, only two were of persons over sixty years of age, so that fourteen of the deaths, or only two less than the net loss, were of individuals of working age. This ratio of births to deaths, it appears, is abnormal, for the villagers are acutely aware of the declining birth rate. That latter is, however, not likely to increase soon if, as seems likely, it is a consequence of the exodus of adult males because of the war.

The loss of population through death, however, is insignificant in comparison with that brought about by emigration. During the twenty months covered by Table 3, seventy-four individuals (10.7 per cent of the original population) moved away, while only seven moved in; and, since sixty-five of the emigrants were of working age, there was a net loss of fifty-eight in the labor supply. The importance of conscription as a factor in this movement of population is substantiated by the large loss in the sixteen- to thirty-year age group. Not only were nineteen men taken in the nine calls for conscripts up to October, 1939, but, because deferments from military service were granted students and those with jobs in industry and the government, many others left. There was not a single son of the more wealthy families in this age group remaining in Luts'un.

The demand for labor on public construction connected with the war had a further effect on the supply of help for farm work. In the autumn of 1939 twenty-seven villagers were working regularly, and thirty to forty were working part time, on the construction of the Yunnan-Burma railroad, while during the rainy season approximately twenty would expect to be called out for about a week of work on the Burma Road after each flood.

The growing demand for workers of various sorts was largely met by members of the hired-labor class, since they were more likely to be without families or other ties which would prevent them from moving to the places where the highest wages were being paid. The higher wages paid for railroad construction and other public works also affected the supply of migratory workers.

As a consequence of this situation, the landowners were fearful in the fall of 1939 that they would be unable to get their rice harvested. My landlord, who normally employed five immigrants from Szechwan for five days to collect his rice, made frantic but unsuccessful efforts to find help. I was present when he called on a poor settler in the outskirts and appealed to him on the basis of the fact that they were fellow-Christians. He was refused, even though he offered a substantial bonus, because the man's full time had been engaged. Uncle Chang's normal practice was to refuse to bargain with prospective employees because of his confidence that plenty of men would appear to work for him on his own terms, but this year not a single worker approached him. Consequently, he was forced to call on other landowners to assist him on an exchange basis, although on the second day of harvest he was able to persuade two salt-carriers of his acquaintance to take over the job.

Notwithstanding the drastic change in the labor situation, the owners are striving to perpetuate the traditional type of management. The magistrate voiced the sentiments of all when he told me worriedly: "It will be very difficult to enforce the conscription laws here, for the district suffers from a shortage of labor now." This concern about labor supply while there are many able-bodied men who pass their days in idleness admittedly seems absurd, but it is the tradition of leisure for the landed and of sale of services by the landless which is the cornerstone of the economic structure of Luts'un.

CHAPTER VI

FARM MANAGEMENT BY PETTY OWNERS

I. LABOR EXCHANGE

THE first important problem faced by the managing owner is the mobilization of manpower for the cultivation of his farm. For the poor owner the most direct solution of this problem, namely, the utilization of his own and his family's services, raises the question of the labor resources of the average family. In Luts'un the average family (excluding the single adults) had 5.4 members in the spring of 1938 and 4.9 members in the autumn of 1939. Counting only the adults (sixteen to sixty years of age), the average was 1.8 males and 1.8 females per family in 1938 and 1.3 males and 1.8 females in 1939. If each family confined its labor to its own farm and employed no additional help, the average family could manage but 18 *kung* of land in 1938 and only 13 *kung* in 1939, assuming the average efficiency for each member. The management of a farm larger than these figures would require the utilization of outside labor. One of the commonest methods of securing help is by exchange, a method by which the small owner gets additional employment for himself while he is able, at the same time, to muster the assistance he needs without cash expenditure.

An important factor making for the popularity of labor exchange in Luts'un is the advantage derived from teamwork on the farm, especially for certain activities. During the rice harvest, for example, the most efficient crew consists of ten individuals—four on the threshing floor, four reaping, and two transporting the grain from the reapers to the threshers. In transplanting rice shoots, a team of six or seven women who co-ordinate their work on adjacent rows is essential for greatest efficiency. Another factor in stimulating this practice is the need felt to complete planting within a brief period in order that the whole crop on a farm may grow uniformly.

Prior to 1938 the abundance of labor had made advance arrangements for workers unnecessary. In 1939 many of the owners were still relying on the old methods of calling on people the evening before the work was to start or of going in the morning to the village gate, where those who wished to work were wont to gather. The village headman was one of those who clung to this practice. When he was asked the evening before the rice harvest if he had organized his working crew, he responded: "No, tomorrow will do." On the morrow, finding no one available, he postponed work until the following day, again making no advance arrangements. When again there was no one to be hired, he was forced to go into the fields with only his wife and daughter, and he was finally convinced that under the changed conditions planning was necessary. In contrast to this man, our neighbor Liu this year formulated in advance a detailed schedule for exchange labor with other villagers, with the result that his farm work was done without difficulty. His experience attests to the importance of a planned adjustment of the individual work calendars of the whole village to permit the most efficient utilization of the reduced labor supply.

Far from being confined to the village, the exchange of labor is commonly practiced among different localities. Since such transactions, based as they are on reciprocity, really constitute a credit system, some form of security is needed, and this is provided by the ties of kinship. Thus we find that exchange of services among relatives is considered most desirable. The headman, whose troubles were described in the preceding paragraph, called on his married daughter to come from her home to help in the harvest, and later he sent his wife to his daughter's household as repayment. The harvest team on Wang's farm was an example of ordinary mutual assistance in the village. It consisted of himself, his wife, a son and his wife, and a niece—all from the village—and two nephews from another village. Because the successful functioning of this exchange system depends upon service equivalent to that received always being repaid, a household which for any reason is unable to supply sufficient members must hire workers for the return work. Failure to discharge such an obligation fully affects the relations between relatives and friends and tends to disrupt the whole system of labor exchange.

II. FEMALE LABOR

The statement made previously that there is a tendency for landowners to avoid working on their farms might seem to be contradicted by the fact that the women of all families, even of those with large landholdings, are invariably active in agriculture. During the harvest period almost every woman in the village, except those occupied in cooking for the workers, is to be found toiling in the fields, while the little girls who are too young for farm work care for the babies. Chang, the former official, who, lying on his opium bed, laughed at

D

my suggestion that he might go to work on his farm, had a pretty young daughter who could be found working in the fields, either on her father's or on some other farm, almost any day in the busy season. This situation, however, does not invalidate the generalization that those who do not own the land are the ones who expend their labor on it, for women are not considered as participating in ownership.

Although it is popularly said that land belongs to the family group, this is true only in the sense that the group is entitled to enjoy its products. As will be demonstrated more fully in chapter ix, the principle of patrilineal inheritance excludes the females from the privilege of land ownership. Women never bring land to their husbands' families, and inheritance by the sons from the father is so absolute that a widow who holds custody for a young son is prohibited from making any disposition of the property. Even the woman who contracts a matrilocal marriage is considered only a temporary link in the chain of patrilineal inheritance.

Since women have no rights in the land, their right to share in its products must be validated by the contribution of their labor. Our expectation that this principle will be reflected in the attitudes relative to marriage is amply confirmed by the criteria employed in the selection of a daughter-in-law. Health and industry are the primary qualifications for a girl who is being considered as a potential bride for a son, and a seventeen- or eighteen-year-old girl is frequently selected to marry a son of twelve or thirteen years. The acquisition of a daughter-in-law is in many respects equivalent to the securing of a long-term laborer.

III. LABOR HIRING

Inasmuch as even the full utilization of the female members of the family in work exchange will not provide sufficient labor for the exploitation of a farm large enough to support the family, additional workers must be employed. In Luts'un there are three categories of hired labor: long-term employees, workers paid by the day, and workers paid on a piecework basis.

A long-term employee lives in the house of his employer and is available for any task assigned to him at any time. He may be sent to work on neighbors' farms on an exchange basis or to trade from market to market. A woman hired on this basis will be expected to do housework as well as to work in the fields. Workers of this type are normally hired on an annual basis and are paid, in addition to food and lodging, a certain wage per year. For men this wage was $40 in 1938, but for

women the amount was always much smaller and was less standardized, ranging down to nothing more than food and lodging. The standard yearly rate of $40 for male workers was well in excess of the amount
an individual could earn on a daily basis, at the standard rate of 10
cents a day, even if he were able to find employment every day in the
year instead of the average of two hundred days. While this class of employment is advantageous to the employee, because of the relatively
high wage and the security it affords, it is not economical for employers other than those whose farms are so large that outside help is needed during the slack periods. The average farmer employs workers only
during the busy seasons. In 1938, according to the census, there were
six female long-term employees; at this time there were not more than
fifteen male workers of this type. In 1939 there were only seven of the
latter, almost half having left because the annual wage had not been
raised while the daily rate increased considerably.

The daily wage in cash was 10 cents for males and 5 cents for females in 1938, but the rate had increased to 20 and 10 cents in 1939,
with a further advance to 30 and 15 cents, respectively, during the
harvest of that year. The actual wage, including cash and subsistence,
was, of course, greater and rather flexible. Owing to the difficulty of
obtaining workers under the new conditions, many of the employers,
under the guise of paternalism, made unusual concessions in the way
of improved food and other nonmonetary rewards, as a substitute for
further cash increases, which were repugnant to them. Past favors, too,
were used as weapons in securing help, as in the case of Uncle Chang,
who said that he had been convinced that hospitality was the best policy because he was able to get two salt-carriers to work for him in consequence of his having given them free lodging on their trips through
the village.

Many of the workers in the fields were found to be working not for
cash but as payment for debts. In 1939 fourteen men and six women
came from outside Luts'un to harvest rice for the schoolmaster to repay him for rice which they had previously borrowed. Another case
was that of Kang, who worked out, at the wage prevailing during the
harvest, his debt of 2 *piculs* of rice to one of the Changs, according to
the price at the time of the loan. No interest was charged on this transaction, since the lender profited in that his labor supply was insured.
Another individual exchanged a month's service for a pig.

Inasmuch as they are paid for their time rather than for the amount
they accomplish, the daily workers are prone to work in a leisurely

fashion and to indulge in frequent, prolonged rest periods. While this circumstance is fortunate for the investigator, in that he experiences no difficulty in finding people in the field willing to talk with him, it is not so satisfactory from the standpoint of the employer. Hence, many of the owners who themselves do not work follow the practice of employing labor on a piecework basis.

In general, the owners who avoid spending time on their farms prefer to have their work done and paid for by the job, for this involves very little effort on their part. The wife of Uncle Chang told us, when we accompanied her to a neighboring village, where she was trying to make arrangements with some Szechwan immigrants for the harvest work on the farm, that this procedure, which relieved the family of all concern for the farm work except for making arrangements with the workers, was customary in her family. Li, who was ill at harvest time and whose wife had just died, resorted to this method of getting his work done. He contracted with five men from a neighboring district to harvest his farm of 20 *kung* for $14, a bottle of wine, and $1\frac{1}{4}$ pounds of tobacco. The cost to him was considerably less than the amount of 60 cents per *kung* plus subsistence, which employment of workers by the day would have required. From the employees' point of view, also, this arrangement was eminently satisfactory, for, by working from early morning until dark, they were able to finish the job in approximately three days. In this way each man earned about a dollar a day. Efficient as this type of employment is from the standpoint of labor utilization, it is conducive to careless work and a consequent wastage of grain—facts which tend to deter some of the owners from operating their farms in this fashion.

IV. FARM PROFIT FOR THE MANAGING OWNERS

The management of land by the use of hired labor, as in Luts'un, is in sharp contrast to the situation in Kiangts'un[1] (the village described in *Peasant Life in China*), where most of the villagers are tenants and there are almost no hired laborers, because the extremely few resident owners work their own farms. This difference leads us to inquire as to the economic factors which are responsible for the development of the system practiced in Luts'un. Both the renting-out of land and the hiring of labor are the results of the owner's desire not to assume himself the burden of the farm work. Assuming that the decision to shift this burden to others has been made, the owner is faced with the necessity of making a choice between the two methods. The answer to the two questions which are important in influencing his choice, namely, whether it is possible for him to assume active management and whether renting out his land or hiring labor will bring him the larger profit, will depend upon the particular conditions prevailing in a locality.

A comparison between the villages of Luts'un and Kiangts'un will illustrate certain conditions which determine whether or not management by the owners is possible. For present purposes, management is defined as consisting of three functions: formulating the schedule of farm activities, providing the tools and other farm capital, and supervision of the farm work. It is obvious that owners who do not live near their farms are incapable of performing at least the last of these functions, so that only residents can be managers in the true sense. In Kiangts'un, where most of the land is held by individuals who live in the city and who may not even know the exact locations of their properties, owner management is impossible, whereas it is almost inevitable in Luts'un, where the holdings are so small that the income would not support life in the city. Luts'un owners, living as they do in the vicinity of their farms and in a region where neither commerce nor industry is well developed, must either perform the functions of management or have nothing on which to expend their time and energy.

Notwithstanding the fact that management by resident owners is convenient, it would not be practiced were it not more profitable than renting out the land. If the earnings of a self-managed farm, after payment of wages and other expenses of cultivation, were less than the rent which could be commanded, the land would inevitably be rented. Table 12 represents a composite balance sheet reflecting expenditures and receipts for farms in Luts'un.

It must be confessed that the task of compiling accurate data relative to farming is beset by many difficulties. Table 12 is admittedly a very general and rather rough approximation of the average farm finances of the village, but it was formulated as carefully as possible on the basis of lengthy consultations with the farmers. In the following paragraphs the various items in the table and some of the difficulties encountered will be described to enable the reader to evaluate the material.

Let us consider first the several problems encountered in estimating the receipts from the farm. One of these is the establishment of prices for the produce, much of which never appears upon the market. A large part of the rice, for instance, will be polished for the consumption of the household and its employees, while the hulls and straw are fed to the horses and cattle or are used for fuel and the residue from

TABLE 12

ESTIMATED RECEIPTS AND EXPENSES PER *Kung* OF A DOUBLE-CROPPED FARM IN LUTS'UN *

	High Grade		Medium Grade		Low Grade	
	Quantity	Value (in Dollars)	Quantity	Value (in Dollars)	Quantity	Value (in Dollars)
I. Farm receipts:						
Rice (grain).........	9:6 *pic.*	8.00	7.7 *pic.*	6.40	4.8 *pic.*	4.00
By-products of rice (straw)...........	80 bundles	0.30	50 bundles	0.17	40 bundles	0.15
Broad bean...........	2.6 *pic.*	1.00	1.5 *pic.*	0.60	0.5 *pic.*	0.20
By-products of broad bean.............	5.2 *pic.*	0.30	3.1 *pic.*	0.19	1.6 *pic.*	0.09
Green bean..........	1.0 *pic.*	0.50	0.8 *pic.*	0.40	0.5 *pic.*	0.25
Total money value		10.10		7.76		4.69
II. Farm expenses (money value in dollars):						
Labor:						
Male, 8.5 units at 0.10...........				0.85		
Mixed, 1.5 units at 0.075...........				0.11		
Female, 10.3 units at 0.05...........				0.52	1.48	
Food for laborers at 0.08 per unit.......					1.62	
Animal hire (including fodder)...........					0.20	
Seeds:						
Rice, 0.01 *pic.* ($0.08).........,						
Broad bean, 0.015 *pic.* ($0.27)......					0.35	
Fertilizer (bartered for straw)............					0.24	
Depreciation of farming implements.........					0.10	
Taxes..............					0.18	
Total money value					4.17	

* Money values are expressed according to 1938 prices.

the polishing is eaten by the pigs. Nevertheless, some unit of value must be fixed in order to measure the self-sufficient part of the farm economy as well as the cash income. In the case of rice, the unhusked product has been selected as a basis for computing value, because this is the form in which it almost always appears on the market. There remains the question of the price level to be adopted for the present purpose. During a period of inflation, such as the present, prices are subject to rapid changes. If the farmers sold all their produce, it would theoretically be desirable to use the actual prices received; but since this is not the case, the level of November, 1938, was arbitrarily chosen as a base for all commodities as well as for labor. The choice of this date, which antedated the beginning of the inflationary trend, obviates the difficulties which would arise if we attempted to use a date during the later period of unstable prices.

It hardly need be stated that the picture of the crop yield as given in the table is much simplified, for no two pieces of land will produce equally. Moreover, the same plot will vary in its yield from year to year, depending upon the efficiency of the soil preparation, fertilization, and weeding. A count of the grains on sample rice stalks from two farms considered to be of equal quality gave an average of between 170 and 200, with a maximum of 300 for one and an average of 110 for the other. The highest-grade land may, under extremely bad management, produce as little as the poorest. Under the circumstances, the only possible procedure was to accept the three categories of quality established by the land survey and the yield which is generally anticipated for each grade by the farmers.

If we convert our estimate of the yield per *kung* to an acreage basis, we arrive at figures of about 165 *piculs* of unhusked grain per acre of high-grade land and about 130 *piculs* per medium-grade acre. Inasmuch as a *picul* of unhusked rice will produce 0.4 *picul* of polished rice, the yield of the latter is 68 *piculs* an acre for the best land and 52 *piculs* for the medium. These figures are considerably higher than the average of 40 *piculs* for Kiangts'un, which is considered a fertile rice area.[2]

Our figures for the yield of broad beans were even more difficult to compile than those for rice. The soil which grows the greatest quantities of the one may not be well adapted to the other. In addition, the variation in bean production is rather great from year to year. The farmers were nearly unanimous in their explanation of variations in the rice crop, but they were vague in their attempts to give reasons for changes in the yield of beans.

Now we may be permitted to make a few observations regarding farm expenses. The portrayal of these expenses in the table as identical

[2] Fei, *Peasant Life in China*, p. 201.

for all three grades of land is not strictly correct, for there are certain variations. For example, high-grade land requires less fertilizer and seed. But the differences are so slight as to be insignificant in arriving at what is, after all, but an approximation. As in the case of receipts, we are using for all prices the level of November, 1938.

The expenditures for labor are computed as though all workers were hired, but it should be remembered that, in reality, a large part of the female labor is recruited from the owner's household and does not require payment. Mixed labor is assumed to be divided equally between the sexes.

The estimate given of the cost of food for workers represents the result of our effort to achieve an average of the variations by sex and sections of work. There are customary rules for the types of food to be provided employees during the different agricultural seasons. For example, harvest hands must be given meat, while those engaged in preparing the fields and transplanting the rice are provided with both meat and wine and frequently with tobacco, depending upon the generosity of the employer and the habits of the employees.

Inasmuch as only nineteen households own the village's twenty-six buffaloes, most of the farmers must hire animals for plowing their fields. The fee normally paid for the buffalo and driver is 15 cents per *kung* plus fodder and subsistence. These last two items, which consist of beans, rice hulls, and fresh grass for the animal, and food, wine, and tobacco for the man, amount to about 20 cents a day. Since 8 *kung* can be plowed in one day and the farm must be plowed twice, their cost is 5 cents per *kung*, bringing the total expense of plowing a *kung* to 20 cents.

The item of fertilizer in Table 12 was especially difficult to estimate, mainly for two reasons. In the first place, much of it is human, or pig, cattle, and other manure from the farm, which represents no expenditure. In cases of deficiency the boys gather manure left by passing horses on the roads and small amounts may also be procured from the innkeeper in exchange for straw. In the past, however, although there were nominal prices of 4 cents a load for manure and about 0.4 cent for a bundle of straw, there was, in reality, an extremely small volume of trade in them, for there was an enormous surplus of straw and a limited supply of manure. Since there were few animals to consume the straw, of which about 80 bundles were produced per *kung*, the bulk of it was ordinarily left in the fields. But in 1939 much of the straw which had been stored rotted, and the price advanced to as much as 5 cents a

bundle. At the same time, an increase in traffic on the roads augment-
ed the innkeeper's supply of horse manure, so that the hitherto dormant market in these commodities was opened up.

Further, the amount of fertilizer required varies for different pieces
of land. For example, certain farms close to the village do not require
any because they receive the drainage from the streets. The average,
however, is about 6 loads of manure per *kung* yearly. It has been demonstrated that production on much of the poorer land would be increased 20 per cent by the application of 4 additional loads of fertilizer,
thus creating an additional income of $1.60 for an extra investment of
only 40 cents. This fact and the expanded market for manure in 1939
clearly indicate that the soil of Luts'un is chronically underfertilized
and point to a means of greatly expanding its production.

Reference to the list given in Table 1 will convince the reader that
the tools employed by the Luts'un farmers are very simple. The ordinary household, which does not possess buffaloes and so hires others to
do its plowing, usually has three hoes and three sickles, each costing
approximately 50 cents and lasting more than ten years. The rest of
the implements, such as rakes, threshing boxes, bean-beaters, planting
sticks, and carrying frames, are all of wood. The total value of the
average farmer's inventory of those tools, which last seven or eight
years, is roughly $20. According to the estimates given me by the vil-
lagers, the sum of $1.50 a year will cover the cost of replacing all tools
and sharpening the metal ones. This represents a depreciation of 10
cents a *kung* for the owner of a farm of 15 *kung*. The owner of a buffalo
will be subject to the additional expense of a plow and a rake (the
combined value of which is $10), a stable, and fodder; but these will
be counterbalanced by the income derived from contracting for plowing the land of others.

From the above comments on the table, the difficulty in estimating
farm receipts and expenses will be apparent. However, from lengthy
discussions with the villagers, we reached certain approximate figures.
The net profit from high-grade land is about $6.00 per *kung;* from
medium-grade land, $3.50; and from low-grade land, $0.50. Since the
proportion of low-grade land in Luts'un is small and the ratio of the
high- and medium-grade is about 2:1, the average profit is about
$5.00.

In this connection we may raise the question: How many landowners of Luts'un can obtain an adequate livelihood entirely from the
land? As a minimum requirement for a modest living, we propose the

D*

following estimate. In Luts'un the value of food consumed, either grown on the farm or purchased, is about $20 per year for each adult. With an average of five and four-tenths members, equivalent to four adults, the yearly expenditure for food per household comes to about $80. In general, in Chinese villages, food costs account for 60 per cent of the total expenditures. Thus, the annual expenditure of such a household would be around $135. On the average, therefore, it will take the net earnings of a 27-*kung* farm to cover the total domestic expenditure of a household farming its land entirely with hired labor. According to this, in Luts'un there are only about thirty-three households, or 27 per cent of the total (see Table 8), in which the owners need not work— always provided they are willing to accept a relatively low standard of living. But, in fact, idle males far exceed the above estimate. This is made possible through the cutting-down of labor costs on the smaller farms by means of work performed by the women of the family. Having their own female workers at command, farm owners can hire less labor and consequently realize greater profit; thus in 1938 the highest net return from a single *kung* was $7.50. In other words, the qualifications for the enjoyment of leisure may be met even by those owning 18 *kung* of land. Moreover, farm receipts can also be increased by selling hulled rice and by utilizing the hulls to raise pigs. Therefore, it is not surprising that in Luts'un idle men can be found in one out of every three houses.

CHAPTER VII

TENANCY

I. RENT

UNLIKE the hired laborer, who is paid solely on the basis of time or of production, a tenant has an interest in the productivity of the land. With his payment of annual rent, he takes over from the owner all responsibility for the exploitation of the farm, and it is he who must accept the risk and provide the working capital. He may work the farm himself or hire laborers instead, whichever he chooses, for all income in excess of the sum he pays the landlord is his to dispose of in any way he sees fit.

The nominal rental is approximately 60 per cent of the rice yield. In practice, however, this rate rarely prevails. A typical example of the deviations from the theoretical standard is the case of Chen, who leased one farm, of 10 *kung*, for half the yield of rice; another, of 5 *kung*, from the Wang clan for 10 *piculs* (33 per cent of the 30-*picul* production); and a third, of 25 *kung*, of the common land of a neighboring village, which yielded 180 *piculs* and for which he paid 100 *piculs*, or 55 per cent. The high rental of 60 per cent (15 *piculs* out of a yield of 25 *piculs*) paid by Kang Wen in 1937 on a farm of 4 *kung* rented from Chou was the result of an increase demanded of him because of an exceptional harvest the preceding year; for ten years he had been paying only 12 *piculs*. Brother Wang, on the other hand, rented a piece of land from the son of his father's brother for only 4 of the 10 *piculs* it produced. These instances show that, under ordinary circumstances, the nominal rate of 60 per cent is in reality the maximum and is seldom in effect. Even at this high rate, an owner of high-grade land would receive a rent of only $4.80 a *kung*, which is approximately $1.00 less than the income he could enjoy by retaining the management of his farm and employing others to work it. Land rented at the more usual figure of 50 per cent would bring $1.50 less. These figures confirm the villagers' observation that an owner will find managing his farm much more profitable than renting it out. In the light of these financial considerations, a scrutiny of the circumstances under which a proprietor would be willing to rent his land seems pertinent.

75

As might be anticipated, a very limited number of the 1,800 *kung* owned by the individual households of Luts'un are rented, and there are special reasons to account for the few exceptions to the general rule. Most of the 140 rented *kung* are located so far from the village that the owners are not able to manage them. A few others belong to widows, as in the case of a sister-in-law of Chao, the village headman, who has no adult males in her house and rents her farm to her nephews. Still other land is leased at low rates by wealthier families to their poorer relatives as a form of assistance. The case of Wang, mentioned previously, is of this nature.

Although the households of Luts'un rent out very little of the land they own, they do rent, for their own use, a considerable quantity from

TABLE 13

Size of Farm Managed by the Villagers

Size of Farm (in *Kung*)	No. of Households	Percent-age	Size of Farm (in *Kung*)	No. of Households	Percent-age
0...............	18	15	31–35..........	7⎫	
1– 5..........	6⎫		36–40..........	9	
6–10..........	8⎬	16	41–45..........	2	
11–15..........	6⎭		46–50..........	5⎬	21
			51–55..........	0	
16–20..........	14⎫		56–60..........	1	
21–25........,....	19⎬	48	61–65..........	2⎭	
26–30..........	25⎭				

others, as indicated by the discrepancy of 1,000 *kung* between the 1,800 they own and the 2,800 they manage. The ownership of the about 1,000 *kung* rented by the villagers may be analyzed as follows: 624 *kung* owned by groups in Luts'un, 60 *kung* located within the village but owned by outside groups, 100 *kung* in the village owned by outside individuals, and 200 *kung* lying outside the village and belonging to individuals and groups of other villages.

The distribution of the land managed by the households of Luts'un, regardless of ownership, is presented in Table 13. A comparison of these figures with those in Table 8 will disclose that management of land is much more evenly distributed among the villagers than is ownership. Although there are thirty-eight households which hold title to no land, there are only eighteen with none under their management. Forty-three households (35 per cent) own, but only twenty (16 per cent) manage, less than 16 *kung*, while almost half of them farm from 16 to 30 *kung* of their own or rented land, in contrast to the 19 per cent who are the actual proprietors of such estates. Again, the number of farmers managing large amounts of land is greater than the number of owners of large farms.

These figures demonstrate that the holders of relatively large properties, as well as the landless and the small owners, tend to expand the amount of land under their management through renting rather than through purchasing land. Table 14 gives the distribution of ownership by those households which cultivate rented farms. This table shows clearly that those who rent land are not necessarily landless or even poor people; the rich rent land too. This is because tenants can enjoy a profit even if they operate their rented land by hired labor. Moreover, as we shall show in the next section, the rent on the collectively

TABLE 14

SIZE OF UNIT OWNED BY TENANTS

Size of Unit (in *Kung*)	No. of Households	Size of Unit (in *Kung*)	No. of Households
0	19	21–25	1
1– 5	13	26–30	2
6–10	17	31–35	1
11–15	7		—
16–20	1	Total	61

owned land is usually much lower than the normal rate. To be tenants of the collective owners is, in fact, a privilege. Those who are able to rent a piece of land from their clan are not far from acquiring a piece of land of their own. Since the largest owners who rent out land are collective owners, it is easy to see why the tenants are not limited to the poor. This fact should be borne in mind when we come to the discussion of the problems of tenancy in interior China—problems which should be understood as different from those in coastal China, which have been studied heretofore. In coastal China, tenancy is inevitably a system of exploitation of the peasants, while in the interior this is not necessarily true.

II. RELATIONS BETWEEN OWNERS AND TENANTS

The fact that the landlords of Luts'un are mainly collective owners whose properties are managed by selected individuals is important in explaining the relations existing between owners and tenants. Because he is rarely compelled to account for his administration of the group's affairs, which includes the selection of tenants and the fixing and collection of rents, the treasurer of a landholding organization is a key figure in the tenancy system of Lųts'un. It is an open secret in the village that the average treasurer is motivated primarily by self-interest and that he will make concessions to tenants in the form of low rentals if social and economic advantages accrue to him thereby. As a consequence, the necessity for retaining the good will of the tenants, to insure the perpetuation of such benefits, tends to secure the tenure of the tenants, even when they are lax in their payments. This is especially true if the treasurer has been guilty of gross irregularity in his conduct of the group's business and is fearful of exposure.

The renters of clan lands are in a particularly fortunate situation, for, inasmuch as they are members of the owning group, it is virtually impossible to alienate them from their farms. The poorer households have a traditional right of occupancy and, though they are theoretically bound to pay the fees fixed for that privilege, the treasurer will have difficulty in dispossessing them for delinquency in payment or for any other reason. His freedom of action is limited both by the sanctity of kinship ties and by his fear that incurring the hostility of members of his clan will result in the loss of his job. An incident we witnessed in the house of our landlord, who was the treasurer of his clan, will serve to illustrate some of the attitudes of both parties in the landlord-tenant relationship.

One morning two tenants, both of them members of my landlord's clan and one of them his senior, came to the house to pay their rent and proceeded directly toward the storeroom to empty their containers of rice. When the treasurer halted them with the suggestion that the rice should be measured, the old man was obviously furious and the young man protested vehemently; but our landlord, although very embarrassed, firmly explained: "This rice is not my own. It belongs to the clan, and I can't afford to make good any deficiencies myself." After the two had grudgingly measured the grain and left with the promise that they would return with the amount of the shortage, our landlord turned to us and exclaimed: "You see how difficult it is to have to deal with your own relatives. If they were outsiders, it would be much easier to insist on full payment." We learned from him that many treasurers never know how much rent is paid because they are afraid to insist on measurement of the rice brought by the tenants.

When we discussed this problem with the treasurer of Wang's clan, he told us: "In effect, the clan land is divided among the members, and the clan as such receives very little income. Formerly, not a penny was paid in rent, and the tenants had come to feel that they owned the land they were occupying. This possessive attitude was so strong, in fact, that I was brought into court on the charge that I refused to turn the deeds over to them. But I produced every deed to show the court that I was honestly administering the clan's property and pleaded that it was my duty to retain them. Otherwise, the individuals might have disposed of the land, if they had wished, and the clan would then have been without property. The magistrate ruled that the occupants of the land were renters, not owners, and that henceforth they should pay rent, which was to be used for the benefit of clan members. Since then the situation has been better, but it is still far from easy to collect the rent." When we asked him why he did not enforce the court order with a firmer hand, he replied: "After all, we are fellow clan members. If they are poor, we must support them. How can you deal harshly with members of your kinship group?"

It is evident that, though the changing of tenants is theoretically a prerogative of the landlord, the freedom of the representative of an owning group to evict members is definitely circumscribed and that, as a consequence, tenants of this class will, in general, enjoy permanent occupancy of their farms, often without payment for the privilege. On the other hand, the relations between the landlord and the tenant in cases where kinship ties are not involved are likely to be characterized by aggressive self-interest on the part of both participants in the transaction, though even here the scales are weighted somewhat in favor of the tenant. The following excerpts from two cases of disputes between owners and renters were taken from court documents.

The first extract, the complaint of an individual owner, reads:

I am the owner of a piece of land in ———. A resident of this village, named ———, and his brother wished to rent that land, and the brother took possession. My request that a contract be drawn up was refused, and, after four years, there is still no contract. I have been paid 10 *piculs* some years and 20 *piculs* other years, according to the whim of the tenant; and I tolerated this situation, to avoid a dispute, until last year. Then I went to him and asked for a rent of 30 *piculs* but received only 20, although the yield from the farm was very good. I informed him courteously that I would accept his payment then, but that to continue occupying the farm he must thereafter pay an annual rental of 40 *piculs* and sign an agreement. To this he gave no reply, but he has sent me no contract and has continued to cultivate my land. He has again this year paid me only 20 *piculs*. When I demanded that he meet the terms I had outlined, he threatened me, so I am asking redress of the court.

The second excerpt from the court records is a petition from the Pine Garden branch of Wang's clan.

We are the owners of a plot of land of 12 *kung* in ———, which was rented in 1923 to ———. It was agreed in the presence of a witness named ———, who guaranteed payment, that the tenant would pay rent at the rate of 6 *piculs* of rice per *kung*. In 1937, only 32 *piculs* were paid, leaving a balance of 28 *piculs* due.[1] The tenant rejected our demand for payment of this balance.

In the first case, the court ruled:

The tenant shall pay 10 *piculs* of rice or $50 in settlement of past claims within two weeks and shall in the future pay an annual rent of 30 *piculs*, a figure which has been declared equitable by a relative of the tenant. A three-year contract embodying these terms shall be executed. If this contract is not acceptable to the tenant, he shall vacate the property of the complainant.

The judgment in the second case was simply: "The tenant shall pay an additional 15 *piculs;* the difference between this amount and the 28 *piculs* claimed is canceled."

These examples confirm the impression that the tenants here are far from being helpless victims of the landlords. In the first case the deficiencies in the 1936 and 1937 payments were canceled and the 1938 rent was set at 30 *piculs*, although the claimant asked for 40. In the second case the landlord received only half of the amount claimed. The effect of these judgments was actually to sanction, in the first case, the fixing of the rent by the tenant and, in the second case, the laxity by the tenant in carrying out the terms of a contract. Furthermore, it appears that landlords are unable to exercise their theoretical right of eviction but must resort to legal action.

The protected position of the tenant in Luts'un is in striking contrast to the situation in coastal China, where he is almost entirely at the mercy of the landlord. The reasons are found in the small number of individual landlords, who are, moreover, small owners and hence not powerful, and in those factors described above which serve as checks on the power of the group owners. The traditional pattern of favoring the tenant, in turn, effectively deters the individual owners from renting out their land and is responsible for the focusing of emphasis on the employer-employee, rather than the landlord-tenant, relationship in this village.

[1] Error in original document: The unpaid due should amount to 40 *piculs*. This might be the claim of the landowner, who had accepted certain deductions from the amount of default.

CHAPTER VIII

FAMILY BUDGETS

I. TRADITIONAL ECONOMIC ATTITUDE

IN THE foregoing pages we have outlined the basic structure of the rural economy as it exists in Luts'un. In the course of this survey there have been revealed certain phenomena that may be puzzling to an observer who is not familiar with the traditional attitudes of the villagers. Such an observer would almost inevitably ask: "Why should the landowners be content with a small income and a low standard of living when these could be increased by working the farm themselves instead of hiring laborers for that purpose?" It is clear that, if it is at all possible, the owner refuses to perform any labor on his farm and solves the problem of cultivation either by hiring workers or by renting his land to tenants. By so doing, he renounces some income which he might otherwise enjoy, unless the time thus freed is employed in other productive activities. But in Luts'un, as we have seen, the owners devote their time to noneconomic activities in opium dens, at gambling tables, or in the teashops. It is apparent that they are not concerned with securing the maximum material return for the energy they expend. They are interested in improving their family fortunes but, ordinarily, only within certain limitations. These limitations are of a sort which it is difficult for an observer from an acquisitive world to understand, and they result from a deeply rooted and pervasive attitude which characterizes the outlook of the villagers.

The traditional outlook of any group is an outgrowth of the total situation within which the social structure operates and, in turn, plays an important part in the integration of the various institutions and activities into a system and in the perpetuation of that system. Human behavior is always motivated by certain purposes, and these purposes grow out of sets of assumptions which are not usually recognized by those who hold them. The basic premises of a particular culture are unconsciously accepted by the individual through his constant and exclusive participation in that culture. It is these assumptions—the essence of all the culturally conditioned purposes, motives, and principles—which determine the behavior of a people, underlie all the in-

stitutions of a community, and give them unity. And it is these un-
articulated assumptions which prevent the participants in different
cultures from mutual understanding. They are the roots of what
Sumner has called "ethnocentricity" and are responsible for feelings
of abhorrence toward an alien ethics—feelings which are essential to
maintaining intact the integrity of a culture. This, unfortunately, is the
most elusive aspect of culture. Since it is taken for granted by the people, the student will not find it formulated verbally. On the contrary, it
must usually be inferred from concrete behavior, a process which requires a certain insight on the part of the observer. The danger of sub-
jective speculation in such a process is apparent; but if this aspect of
the culture is ignored, our knowledge of an institution must remain
incomplete and superficial. We should like to discuss briefly the traditional economic attitude before we come to the problems of consumption and standard of living.

The traditional economic attitude prevailing among the Chinese
can be summarized in one word—contentment, which means, in this
case, an acceptance of a low standard of material comfort. Nearly
without exception, traditional teachings of different schools and doc-
trines agree on that point. Simplicity is the necessary virtue for leading
a good life. Recognition of human limits in material expansion is a
starting-point for classical thought. It is widely accepted by the people as the wisdom of life. "Contentment leads to happiness" is a very
popular motto often found on the front doors of village houses. To a
large extent, the people live up to it.

We have seen in the above analysis that the real incentive to work is
a striving not for material gain but merely for subsistence. When subsistence is secured, the peasants relax and even retire from active work.
They are satisfied at the level at which a comfortable living is maintained, "comfort" being defined by the absence of strenuous effort
rather than by the satisfaction of numerous material wants. They will
accept small rewards if to increase their gain involves painful effort.
An incident which we observed in Luts'un illustrates very well the
dominant reaction in such a situation. During the harvest of 1939,
when labor was scarce, Wei, one of the landowners, told his son:
"Tomorrow you had better not go to the market, but stay and help us
with the farm work." The son replied: "If I work in the field it will
save us only 30 cents. If I don't smoke tomorrow, we shall save that
amount. So I shall not go to the farm." Accordingly, he was absent
and his father had to employ a worker to take his place. Although we

do not know whether he gave up smoking that day or not, it is clear that the family's consumption had to be reduced somehow. To the peasants, the avoidance of toil by the reduction of consumption is a natural and justifiable course to follow.

Is this behavior irrational? If we were to accept their premises, we might make the same choice. Refraining from smoking is painful, but working on the farm is no less so. Were two such alternatives presented to us, we, too, should select the less painful. To arrive at a different choice would require the definition of smoking as a pleasure and of work on the farm as a necessary means to the achievement of this pleasure. On the basis of the villagers' logic, the young man's choice is quite intelligible. We should remember that in a community where the implements of production are so simple, the suffering involved in working is not inconsiderable. We have already pointed out that in Luts'un most of the farm work is done by hand. The Chinese describe labor as "sweat and blood." That this is literally true we can testify, for we were constantly being called upon to give first aid to the workers. The people who work on the farms, being made of flesh and blood, would be difficult to convince that greater happiness would be achieved by more work. The avoidance of painful experiences, which are necessarily involved in work, is their immediate concern.

This attitude may be difficult for the West to understand, because in the West desire for material gain has come to be regarded as a natural incentive for strenuous efforts directed toward economic ends. But it must be remembered that the emphasis on material gain in economic activities is a comparatively recent phenomenon. Before the Industrial Revolution most of the European peasants were, in fact, similar to those we find in interior China. They were far from realizing the ideal of "economic man" in the modern world. The change from contentment to acquisitiveness took place when the old forms of landed society were yielding before the rise of modern industry and commerce in an expanding universe. In this transformation, says Professor Whitehead, "the history of Europe shows a slow swing away from social structure in which great emphasis was placed on the individual's responsibility to his society or community, and a move towards a type of organization permitting greater individual initiative and freedom of action." In this new world, he continues,

personal initiative was commonly understood to be a panacea for all social ills. Biological generalizations were pressed into its support; "the survival of the fittest" was the slogan of the period. "Free competition" was a short description of Heaven, and the "Laws of Economics" were taken by the average man to be in part a moral creed and in part a statement of immutable fact.[1]

Both attitudes—contentment and acquisitiveness—have their own social context. Contentment is adopted in a closed economy; acquisitiveness in an expanding economy. Without economic opportunities the striving for material gain is a disturbance to the existing order, since it means the plunder of wealth from others. Whatever form this plunder may take, it is a curse to the common man. Therefore, to accept and be satisfied with the social role and material rewards given by the society is essential. But when economic opportunity develops through the development of technology and when wealth can be acquired through the exploitation of nature instead of through the exploitation of man, the doctrine of contentment becomes reactionary because it restricts individual initiative.

The modern capitalistic spirit marks a fundamental departure from the traditional view of the world. Its unscrupulousness and ruthlessness in material exploitation is completely uncongenial to an agricultural society. The conquest of nature by science removes the former economic restrictions on human desire, but whether the chain has been loosed forever or whether we are seeing only the beginning of another cycle, at the end of which men must again place a limit on exploitation, it is too early to say. If such a cycle does run its course, the revival of the traditional economic attitude on a higher level is quite possible.

Now that we have looked at the economic attitude which reinforces the traditional rural economy, we may proceed to see on what level the villagers are more or less contentedly living. This will involve an examination of the prevailing standard of living in the village.

II. SAMPLES OF FAMILY BUDGETS

By accepting a lowered standard of living, approximately 30 per cent of the Luts'un landowners are able to free themselves from physical labor. These men demonstrate how deeply rooted is the economic attitude described in the preceding section. We may now attempt to define roughly the standard which represents the line below or above which work is considered the lesser or the greater evil. This will necessitate an examination of the standards of living of village families of both the leisure and the working classes. If our generalization is valid, then those who work will be found to have a living standard below the

[1] A. North Whitehead, "Social Motives in Economic Activities," *Occupational Psychology*, XII (autumn, 1938), 14–15.

line of satisfaction and those who do not work will have a standard above that line.

The measurement of a family's consumption of goods and services is not an easy task, especially in a community such as Luts'un, where virtually no one maintains written records and where the economy is, to a large extent, self-sufficient. In a society where all commodities were purchased, the expenditures of a family would reflect its living standards. Although this situation may be approximated among city-dwellers, it does not exist in rural areas, where labor and important goods are provided by the family itself and seldom appear in cash transactions. Hence a complete budget will include, in addition to those items for which payment is made, an evaluation of this self-sufficient portion of the household economy. Since the villagers do not maintain records and the maintenance of daily records by the investigator was impossible, it was necessary to select as informants a few families representing different economic levels. They were asked to give in detail their consumption for the past year, and the resultant quantities were translated into monetary terms.

In Table 15 we have listed the budgets of five different Luts'un households, of which the first three were worked out in October, 1938, and two were developed in August, 1939. In order that all might be comparable, they were converted in terms of a single price level, that of October, 1938. A brief analysis of each of these households follows.

Households A and B represent the landowning class. Household A owns 40 *kung*, of which it cultivates 36 *kung*, yielding 350 *piculs* of unhusked rice, and rents 4 *kung* to a clan brother for 16 *piculs* of rice. Approximately 130 *piculs* of polished rice are available for use or sale after refining (which reduces the husked rice to 146 *piculs*) and the deduction of 10 per cent for spoilage and shrinkage. This represents a surplus of roughly 100 *piculs* over the 28 *piculs* needed in the family's diet, with a cash value of $250 at the price level of October, 1938. The income from rice alone would thus more than cover the family's normal living expenses, which, excluding the cost of a son's education, wholly paid for by the clan, amount to $120. Other income (e.g., the income·from beans alone amounts to one-fourth that of rice, or about $80) increases the amount available for extraordinary expenses to more than $100.

Household B owns a farm of 14 *kung* and holds an additional plot of 13 *kung* through temporary transference. Its farm of 27 *kung* yields 240 *piculs* of unhusked rice or, after refining, 96 *piculs* of polished rice. After the reduction of 40 *piculs* for home consumption and allowing for storage losses, 50 *piculs* will be available for sale and will bring $125. This

HOUSEHOLD A

Source of income: Farming; farm operated by hired labor
Land under cultivation: 36 *kung* of land owned is cultivated by family; 4 *kung* rented out; 3 *kung* temporarily transferred

Members of household (and ages):

Head of house	40 years	First son (at school)	17 years
Wife	38	Daughter	13
Mother	60	Second son	3

HOUSEHOLD B

Source of income: Farming; farm operated by hired labor
Land under cultivation: 14 *kung* owned; 13 *kung* held through temporary transference

Members of household (and ages):

Head of house	51 years	Second son's wife	25 years
Wife	49	Third son (absent)	17
First son (deceased)		Daughter	15
Second son (absent)	25	First son's child	9

HOUSEHOLD C

Source of income: Farming; land cultivated by family; only necessary labor employed
Land under cultivation: 7 *kung* owned; 30 *kung* rented

Members of household (and ages):

Head of house	59 years	First daughter	17 years
Wife	49	Second daughter	10
Son	21		

HOUSEHOLD D

Source of income: Labor of members
Land under cultivation: None

Members of household (and ages):

Head of house	41 years	Daughter	12 years
Wife	40		

HOUSEHOLD E

Source of income: Labor of members
Land under cultivation: None

Members of household (and ages):

Head of house	47 years	Wife	39 years

sum, added to $60 for the bean crop, little more than covers the family's annual cash expenditures of $160. The head of this family, however, supplements his income by buying and selling in the markets. In 1939, for example, he made a profit of $100 by purchasing oxen and trans-

TABLE 15

FAMILY BUDGETS OF FIVE HOUSEHOLDS

LIVING EXPENSES	HOUSEHOLD A			HOUSEHOLD B			HOUSEHOLD C			HOUSEHOLD D			HOUSEHOLD E		
	Supplied by Household	Purchased	Total	Supplied by Household	Purchased	Total	Supplied by Household	Purchased	Total	Supplied by Household	Purchased	Total	Supplied by Household	Purchased	Total
Food:															
Rice	$ 56.00	.....	$ 56.00	$ 80.00	.....	$ 80.00	$ 32.00	$ 56.00	$ 88.00	.....	$45.00	$45.00	.....	$22.50	$22.50
Beans	3.00	.....	3.00	9.00	.....	9.00	9.00	.....	9.00	.....	.....	.....	.....	.....	.....
Corn	0.50	.....	0.50	.....	$ 0.50	0.50	0.50	.....	0.50	.....	.....	.....	.....	.....	.....
Wheat	.....	$ 2.50	2.50	.....	1.25	1.25	1.25	.....	1.25	.....	.....	.....	.....	.....	.....
Meat	.....	27.00	27.00	12.00	6.00	18.00	.....	3.60	3.60	.....	5.00	5.00	.....	2.50	2.50
Vegetables	6.00	.....	6.00	6.00	.....	6.00	6.00	.....	6.00	.....	3.60	3.60	.....	6.00	6.00
Salt	.....	7.20	7.20	.....	7.20	7.20	.....	6.00	6.00	.....	1.80	1.80	.....	0.60	0.60
Wine	.....	1.70	1.70	.....	1.40	1.40	.....	2.80	2.80	.....	0.42	0.42	.....	.....	.....
Miscellaneous	.....	1.00	1.00	.....	1.00	1.00	.....	1.00	1.00	.....	.....	.....	.....	.....	.....
Total	$ 65.50	$ 39.40	$104.90	$107.00	$ 17.35	$124.35	$ 48.75	$ 69.40	$118.50	.....	$55.82	$55.82	.....	$31.60	$31.60
Clothing:															
Dresses	.....	$ 20.00	$ 20.00	.....	$ 20.00	$ 20.00	.....	$ 14.00	$ 14.00	.....	$ 1.50	$ 1.50	.....	$ 0.70	$ 0.70
Shoes	.....	2.50	2.50	.....	3.00	3.00	.....	1.00	1.00	.....	0.70	0.70	.....	0.70	0.70
Hosiery	.....	3.00	3.00	.....	4.00	4.00	.....	.....	.....	.....	.....	.....	.....	.....	.....
Hats	.....	2.00	2.00	.....	5.00	5.00	.....	1.80	1.80	.....	.....	.....	.....	.....	.....
Ornaments	.....	6.00	6.00	.....	2.00	2.00	.....	.....	.....	.....	.....	.....	.....	.....	.....
Total	.....	$ 33.50	$ 33.50	.....	$ 34.00	$ 34.00	.....	$ 16.80	$ 16.80	.....	$ 2.20	$ 2.20	.....	$ 1.40	$ 1.40

TABLE 15—Continued

HOUSEHOLD

LIVING EXPENSES	A Supplied by Household	A Purchased	A Total	B Supplied by Household	B Purchased	B Total	C Supplied by Household	C Purchased	C Total	D Supplied by Household	D Purchased	D Total	E Supplied by Household	E Purchased	E Total
Housing:															
Rent		$ 3.00	$ 3.00								$ 2.50	$ 2.50		$ 3.00	$ 3.00
Repairs		15.00	15.00		$ 1.80	$ 1.80		$ 0.80	$ 0.80						
Charcoal		15.00	15.00		3.00	3.00									
Firewood					12.00	12.00	$ 10.00		10.00	$10.00		10.00	$10.00		10.00
Oil		4.48	4.48		4.48	4.48		4.48	4.48		1.20	1.20		0.25	0.25
Furniture		5.00	5.00		5.00	5.00		2.00	2.00		0.45	0.45		1.80	1.80
Total		$ 42.48	$ 42.48		$ 26.28	$ 26.28	$ 10.00	$ 7.28	$ 17.28	$10.00	$ 4.15	$14.15	$10.00	$ 5.05	$15.05
Recreation:															
Toys		$ 1.00	$ 1.00												
Sweets		5.00	5.00		$ 8.00	$ 8.00									
Tea		1.50	1.50		1.00	1.00									
Tobacco		2.00	2.00		4.00	4.00		$ 1.00	$ 1.00						
Total		$ 9.50	$ 9.50		$ 13.00	$ 13.00		$ 1.00	$ 1.00						
Gifts:															
Funeral		$ 5.00	$ 5.00												
Marriage		5.00	5.00		$ 15.00	$ 15.00									
Ordinary		3.00	3.00					$ 3.00	$ 3.00						
Total		$ 13.00	$ 13.00		$ 15.00	$ 15.00		$ 3.00	$ 3.00						

TABLE 15—*Continued*

	HOUSEHOLD														
	A			B			C			D			E		
LIVING EXPENSES	Supplied by House-hold	Pur-chased	Total	Supplied by House-hold	Pur-chased	Total	Supplied by House-hold	Pur-chased	Total	Supplied by House-hold	Pur-chased	Total	Supplied by House-hold	Pur-chased	Total
Religion:															
Sacrifices					$ 6.00	$ 6.00									
Christian contributions		$ 3.00	$ 3.00					$ 0.20	$ 0.20					$ 0.20	$ 0.20
Total		$ 3.00	$ 3.00		$ 6.00	$ 6.00		$ 0.20	$ 0.20					$ 0.20	$ 0.20
Medicine		$ 5.00	$ 5.00		$ 6.00	$ 6.00		$ 0.80	$ 0.80						
Education	120.00		120.00												
Taxes:															
Household tax		2.52	2.52		2.52	2.52		2.16	2.16		$ 1.80	$ 1.80		$ 1.80	$ 1.80
Special tax		1.00	1.00		1.00	1.00		1.00	1.00						
Common granary	$ 1.60		1.60	$ 1.60		1.60	1.20		1.20		0.80	0.80		0.80	0.80
Conscripted labor	5.00		5.00	5.00		5.00	5.00		5.00	$ 5.00		5.00	$ 5.00		5.00
Total	$ 1.60	$ 8.52	$ 10.12	$ 1.60	$ 8.52	$ 10.12	$ 6.20	$ 3.16	$ 9.36	$ 5.00	$ 2.60	$ 7.60	$ 5.00	$ 2.50	$ 7.60
Grand total	67.10	274.40	341.50	108.60	126.15	234.75	64.95	101.64	166.59	15.00	64.77	79.77	15.00	40.85	55.85
Percentage			60.6			58.9			42.7			98.3			97.70

TABLE 15—Continued

HOUSEHOLD

CAPITAL EXPENSES	A			B			C			D			E		
	Supplied by Household	Purchased	Total	Supplied by Household	Purchased	Total	Supplied by Household	Purchased	Total	Supplied by Household	Purchased	Total	Supplied by Household	Purchased	Total
Current investment:															
Wages	$ 1.84	$ 50.00	$ 51.84	$ 8.88	$ 30.00	$ 38.88	$ 40.28	$ 13.00	$ 53.28						
Rice seed	2.88		2.88	2.16		2.16	2.96		2.96						
Bean seed	9.45		9.45	7.10		7.10	9.45		9.45						
Fertilizer	3.20		3.20	2.40		2.40	3.20		3.20						
Tools		4.00	4.00		3.00	3.00		4.00	4.00		$ 1.40	$ 1.40		$ 1.30	$ 1.30
Tax		5.00	5.00		1.50	1.50		1.00	4.00						
Labor on ditch		1.50	1.50		1.00	1.00	1.50		1.50						
Total	$ 17.37	$ 60.50	$ 77.87	$ 20.54	$ 35.50	$ 56.04	$ 57.39	$ 18.00	$ 75.39		$ 1.40	$ 1.40		$ 1.30	$ 1.30
Rent	$144.00		$144.00	$108.00		$108.00	$148.00		$148.00						
Total investment	$161.37	$ 60.50	$221.87	$128.54	$ 35.50	$164.04	$205.39	$18.00	$223.39		$ 1.40	$ 1.40		$ 1.30	$ 1.30
Percentage			39.4			41.1			57.3			1.7			2.3
Grand total	$228.47	$334.90	$563.37	$237.14	$161.65	$398.79	$270.34	$119.64	$389.98	$15.00	$66.17	$81.17	$15.00	$42.15	$57.15

90

porting them to Kunming for sale and a profit of $50 through the sale in Luts'un of paper which he purchased in the distant village where it was manufactured.

Although neither of these households is considered to be the wealthiest in the village, the standards of living of both are representative of the upper stratum. Each owns a two-story house with three rooms on the ground floor and a large porch extending the length of the front wall. The porch is the locus for eating and most other domestic activities, while a central room, containing the best furniture and the ancestral tablets, is reserved for more formal occasions. The remaining two rooms are partitioned to make three or four sleeping compartments, one of which we occupied in Household A during our first visit in the village. It proved to be very light, airy, and comfortable. The second story does not serve for living quarters but is used entirely as a storeroom. At one side of the front yard is a kitchen, at the other a pig pen—both separate from the house. There is a vegetable garden at the side of the house, with a privy in one corner. The arrangement of buildings and grounds outlined here is representative of the homes of the higher-income groups in the village. These houses are appreciably superior in quality and cleanliness to those we have observed in coastal China. This high standard of housing seems to be characteristic of the province of Yunnan, where even in the small villages exceptionally fine houses are not at all uncommon.

The members of Households A and B wear excellent clothing. The heads of the families have long robes for formal occasions, as well as hip-length jackets for ordinary wear, some made of silk or other expensive materials. The women likewise are provided with good wardrobes, which include silver earrings and hair ornaments. In Household A the boy wore a student uniform with leather shoes and European shirts, and the three-year-old child wore knitted jackets and caps of foreign style. Since the best clothing of these families is purchased for special occasions, such as marriages or funerals, its cost does not appear as part of the normal living expenses.

These families also maintain a high standard for the food they consume. The household's average daily consumption of meat, which is obtained both from the pigs they slaughter and by purchase in the market, is more than $\frac{1}{2}$ pound. Their diet includes an abundance of vegetables, raised in their own garden, and wine, which they make themselves; and every evening a dessert of wheat or rice-flour cakes and honey is served. During the time we boarded with Household A, the wife, an excellent cook, whose skill is abetted by the quality of the ingredients she uses (e.g., she is able to afford lard instead of vegetable oils), never failed to produce a delectable meal. Similarly, the food we frequently shared with Household B was always very good, even when special dishes were not prepared for us. It is otherwise in the poorer homes. The food in the house in which we boarded during our second visit was so inadequate that we were compelled to supplement it by traveling to the district town for additional meals.

It is commonly conceded that these two families (Households A and B) enjoy the highest standard of housing, clothing, and food in the village. While their budgets show that the food they purchase constitutes only 14 per cent of their total cash expenditures, the inclusion of the items they produce themselves shows that food makes up about 31 per cent of the total living cost for Household A and about 53 per cent for Household B. But these figures present a distorted picture because that for Household A is computed on the basis of a total which includes an educational item which actually is not paid by the family. If this item is excluded from the computation, food comprises 47 per cent of the real living cost. Household B spends less for housing than does Household A because its newer house requires fewer repairs and less fuel. On the whole, however, the scale of living of these two families is almost identical.

Household C belongs in the owner-tenant class. It is closely similar to Household A in the amount of land cultivated and in the size of the family; but it differs greatly in its income, by virtue of the necessity for paying rent. The payment of 150 *piculs* of grain for rent and polishing and the deduction of 10 per cent for spoilage reduce the amount of refined rice available for use or sale to 65 *piculs*. After the family's requirement of 42 *piculs* for food has been satisfied, there remain only 23 *piculs*, which can be sold for $55. To this amount may be added $80, the income from the broad-bean crop. The cash income will thus barely cover the cash expenditures of $120. Because of the lack of a reserve, it is often necessary to sell the rice intended for the table to meet unusual expenditures and then to buy rice when it is needed for food. This is a financial handicap, since it is frequently necessary to sell at low prices and to buy at high prices.

Expenditures for food occupy a prominent place in Household C's budget, accounting for approximately 71 per cent of the total living costs. Of the total cost of food, meat comprises only 3 per cent, in contrast to 25 and 34 per cent for Households A and B, respectively. The poverty of this family is manifested most conspicuously in the clothing of its members. Their garments are worn and patched, and even the head of the family lacks socks and is often without shoes.

Since its original house was torn down, to make the materials available for sale, and replaced by a small, two-story building with no windows in the second floor and with only two rooms on the ground floor, the family has suffered from overcrowding. All the members slept in one room until the marriage of the son, when the living-room was converted into a bedroom. As a result of this overcrowding, the whole family was suffering from malaria at the time of our second visit to the village. The family head was so changed by the ravages of the disease that I failed to recognize him in the pale, feeble old man who came tottering toward me with the aid of a stick. He attributed his misfortunes—the death of his wife a few months earlier and the illness of his two daughters and son—to the unlucky influence of his son's new wife, who was also ill. He bitterly lamented the marriage of his son to this girl, who was, he insisted, "a vehicle of ill fortune." The small expenditure for medicine by a family so stricken by disease is attributable to the fact that prayer is substituted for more material remedies. It is said that the daughter-in-law had died but was restored to life by the prayers of a Christian. So the Christian God, who, according to their belief, demands no pecuniary reward, is relied upon for the physical well-being of the family.

Households D and E are representative of the landless families. They do not own their own homes but rent ramshackle, one-room huts outside the gates of the village. While we were visiting Household E one day, following a period of rainy weather, part of the saturated earth walls of the dark, windowless house suddenly collapsed, letting in a flood of unaccustomed light. We were appalled by this catastrophe; but the family accepted it calmly, for, as we learned, it was a frequent occurrence. The wife simply remarked that once more they would have a poor night's sleep. Then we discovered that the water was still trickling through the poor thatching of the roof into the attic where the family slept. The building in which Household D lived was equally unsatisfactory. Because the floor is lower than the garden at the back, it was flooded whenever there was rain, until at the suggestion of a neighbor a ditch was dug through the house to carry off the water. Both houses are almost constantly filled with smoke, since, by reason of the inadequate clothing of the occupants, a fire is essential for warmth in chilly weather and since poverty necessitates the burning of grass and wood rather than charcoal. The smoke was so heavy that we, unaccustomed to it, were unable to open our eyes and were convinced that the equipment of an investigator should include a gas mask. Inasmuch as the activities of almost all the occupants are carried on within the walls of these wet, smoky hovels, it is not suprising that, although each family had produced six or seven children, only one was alive at the time we were in the village. The last death had occurred during the year before our visit. The living members all suffer from trachoma, and the head of Household D is nearly blind.

Both of these families depend entirely upon wages for their livelihood. Even though they are employed most of the time, with food pro-

TABLE 16

PERCENTAGE BREAKDOWN OF FAMILY LIVING EXPENSES BY CATEGORIES

ITEM OF EXPENDITURE	HOUSEHOLD				
	A	B	C	D	E
Food..........	30.7	53.0	70.9	70.0	56.6
Clothing........	9.8	14.5	10.1	2.8	2.5
Housing........	12.4	11.2	10.4	17.7	26.9
Recreation......	2.8	5.5	0.6	0.0	0.0
Gifts...........	3.8	6.4	1.8	0.0	0.0
Religion........	0.9	2.6	0.1	0.0	0.4
Medicine.......	1.5	2.5	0.5	0.0	0.0
Education......	35.1	0.0	0.0	0.0	0.0
Taxes..........	3.0	4.3	5.6	9.5	13.6

vided by their employers, their food costs are as much as 60 or 70 per cent of their total budgets, or up to 80 per cent of their cash expenditures. If the amount provided by employers is taken into account, food will be found to constitute a much larger proportion of their total living requirements.

Mr. Chang, coauthor of this book, became a close friend of the members of Household E and so was able to secure accurate information as to their income. The husband was employed for about 350 days during the year and earned approximately $35. The wife worked 10 days a month in December and January, 30 days a month in August and September, and 15 days a month during the rest of the year; her wages for the 200 days she worked during the year were $10. In addition, the man carried salt six times for $6.00, and there was some subsidiary income from other activities, such as dealing in the market. The total cash income was thus only slightly greater than the cash expenditures for current needs.

Table 16, which breaks the total living cost of each family down in terms of the percentages represented by each category, reveals several significant relationships between income and living standards. Food consumption varies widely among the villagers; the poorer people eat only two meals a day except during the time they work on the farm, while the more prosperous are distinguished by the fact that they always eat three times daily. Yet it is apparent that food consumption is the least elastic of all the categories, for, according to our figures, its percentage in the budget drops rapidly with increase of income. The clothing percentage, on the contrary, rises with income, suggesting that the poorer peasants are very inadequately clothed. Our findings in this respect correspond with observations made in India, among Shanghai workers, and among the peasants of Wuhsing, Chekiang.[2] Although actual expenditures for housing by the wealtheir families, who own their own homes, represent a smaller proportion of the living expenses than do the rents paid by the poorer families, the assignment of rental values to these structures would reverse the situation. This again reflects the extremely low standard of the housing facilities for the poorer villagers. With the exception of taxes, which fall proportionately more heavily upon the poor, the percentage of the expenditures for other, more flexible, goods and services increase with the income.

III. DEGREE OF SELF-SUFFICIENCY

In Table 15 the items provided directly by the family's own efforts and those which are purchased were presented separately. Table 17 shows the degrees to which the economies of the different families are self-sufficient. This is a significant problem, especially in relation to the effects of inflation on the standard of living. Household C is most self-sufficient, with 67 per cent of its needs met other than by cash expenditure. Households A and D seem to be the least self-sufficient; but if the cost of educating the son and the money received for this purpose is eliminated from the calculation, A appears at the top of the list (69.7 per cent self-sufficient). Households A and B, unlike C, pay cash for everything except part of their food and taxes. They buy their fuel and hire others to perform their public works, while C has to carry his own

[2] These data are given in *A Study of the Rural Economy of Wuhsing, Chekiang*, ed. Director of Institute (Shanghai: China Institute of Economic and Statistical Research, March, 1939), p. 47.

firewood and work on the public projects himself. Households D and E have only their labor to provide for their needs. Most of these needs cannot be supplied directly by their labor and so appear as cash expenses, since they have no land on which to raise food and no houses on which to make repairs. Only Household C uses both land and labor for the direct satisfaction of its needs. If this family had sufficient reserve to withhold from the market all the rice needed for its own consumption, the cash-expenditure figure would be still smaller.

TABLE 17*

ANALYSIS OF FAMILY EXPENSES SHOWING DEGREES OF SELF-SUFFICIENCY

(In Percentage)

ITEM OF EXPENDITURE	HOUSEHOLD									
	A		B		C		D		E	
	SS	CP	SS	CP	SS	CP	SS	CP	SS	CP
Food.........	97.6	14.3	98.5	14.3	75.2	68.3	0.0	86.2	0.0	77.4
Clothing.....	0.0	12.2	0.0	26.8	0.0	16.5	0.0	3.4	0.0	3.4
Housing......	0.0	15.5	0.0	20.7	15.4	7.2	66.7	6.4	66.7	2.4
Recreation....	0.0	3.5	0.0	10.3	0.0	1.0	0.0	0.0	0.0	0.0
Gifts.........	0.0	4.7	0.0	11.8	0.0	3.0	0.0	0.0	0.0	0.0
Religion......	0.0	1.1	0.0	4.7	0.0	0.2	0.0	0.0	0.0	0.5
Medicine.....	0.0	1.8	0.0	4.7	0.0	0.8	0.0	0.0	0.0	0.0
Education....	0.0	43.8	0.0	0.0	0.0	0.0	0.0	0.0	0.0	0.0
Taxes........	2.4	3.1	1.5	6.7	9.4	3.0	33.3	4.0	33.3	6.3
Totals....	20.1	79.9	54.3	55.7	67.0	33.0	18.7	81.3	25.8	74.2

* SS = Self-sufficiency; CP = cash payment.

IV. PRODUCTIVE EXPENSES IN FARMING

The investment required for each unit of land has already been discussed, so that here we need consider only the relation of farm investment to the family budget. The five households whose budgets we are examining are of three types, from the standpoint of the means by which they secure their livelihood. Households A and B are landowners, who manage their farms with hired labor, while C is an owner-tenant, who also employs hired labor. Households D and E are landless laborers. Farm capital is almost wholly provided by the manager, either owner or tenant; and laborers are required to provide only a few hand tools, such as the hoe and the sickle. The plow, the threshing box, and other more expensive items of equipment are provided by the managers. Consequently, only a small proportion of the expenditures of Households D and E is for tools.

A comparison of the figures for Households A, B, and C, all of which operate farms, reveals that, as the income increases, the proportion required for cultivating the land decreases. These ratios reflect the inelasticity of farm investment and the relatively fixed cost of farming a piece of land. Although there are a few exceptions, like the fifth brother of Chou, whose high-grade land has a poor yield because he will not hire sufficient labor to keep it free of weeds, the farmers almost never economize by reducing expenditures on the farm. They will drastically reduce their consumption rather than endanger the productivity of the land, the source of their livelihood. On the other hand, there is an

TABLE 18

ANALYSIS OF TOTAL FAMILY EXPENDITURES BY CATEGORIES
(In Percentage)

EXPENDITURES	HOUSEHOLD				
	A	B	C	D	E
Daily living expenses....	60.6	58.9	42.7	98.3	97.7
Farm investment........	13.8	14.0	19.3	1.7	2.3
Rent.................	25.6	27.1	38.0	0.0	0.0

upper limit to the amount that can be spent on the land, primarily because the bulk of the cost of cultivation consists of wages.

If the cost of operating the farm in terms of money expended is considered, greater differences among the three households are revealed. The costs of farming account for 77.7 per cent of Household A's total cash expenditures, 63.2 per cent of B's, and 22.8 per cent of C's. The great discrepancy between the figures for A and B, on the one hand, and C, on the other, reflects the fact that the poorer farmers must rely on the labor resources within the family, while the wealthier ones are able to pay wages for the services of outsiders.

V. TAXES AND DUES

This section will be devoted to a discussion of the taxes paid by the villagers, a discussion which will be more meaningful if we first sketch briefly the framework of the local political organization. The ninety-five officially recognized households of Luts'un (as we have explained,

E

since the household is the unit for allotment of taxes, some of them were combined in the census) comprise 9 *chia* of the fifth *pao* of the Sui-Fong *shang* of the district. Two other villages—one of 3 *chia* and the other, populated by eighteen households of recent immigrants from Szechwan, of 1 *chia*—are included in this *pao*. As might be expected, the political dominance of the villages varies with their numerical dominance. The headman of the *pao* is always selected from Luts'un, and the village of 3 *chia* provides the vice-head, while the immigrant village has only a *chia* head, with no representation in the *pao* government.

This *pao-chia* system is a part of the normal governmental organization and has as part of its function the execution of orders of the district government. Actually, many of the strictly local affairs are carried on by village organizations which have no place in this formal structure. Among these are the Temple of the Lord of Earth, the income from whose properties is disbursed for various public services, and a society for the maintenance and regulation of the water system. Although each of these organizations controls essential community activities, neither has any relationship to the formal government.

The regular taxes fall into three categories, all of which are collected by the *pao* government. They are: (1) a household tax, (2) a special tax, and (3) a collection of rice for the public granary. The household tax, which is used to defray the costs of the *shang* government and to pay the salaries of the head and vice-head of the *pao*, is assessed on the basis of which of three categories a household is assigned to. In 1938 the assessment was on a monthly basis and was 21 cents for first-grade, 18 cents for second-grade, and 15 cents for third-grade houses. In 1939 the district government decreed that collections should be made annually and increased the assessments to $3.60, $3.00, and $2.30, respectively. Theoretically, the grading of the households is on the basis of the amount of property they own; but, actually, it is at the discretion of the headman of the *pao*. The Szechwan immigrants complained to us that, because of their lack of representation in the *pao* government, they were all classified as first-grade households, while the rich families in Luts'un paid taxes as second-grade households. We did not investigate this complaint.

The expenses of the *pao* government, except for the salaries paid from the *shang* treasury, are met by the special tax and by contributions from the collective owners. This tax is not fixed but is collected at times and in amounts dictated by the needs of the *pao*. This assessment is the same for all households, regardless of grade. Among the expenses of the *pao* are wages for the night guard, war-bond payments, food for conscripts before they report to the army, the maintenance of the home guard, the repair of culverts, maintenance of the village school, and the taking of the census. During the twenty-two months from September, 1937, to the end of July, 1939, the total cost of the *pao* government was $922, of which $250 came from the special tax and the remainder from the collective owners. According to the tax records, $150, or about $1.20 per household, were collected from the families of Luts'un. But, since there seem also to be collections which are not recorded, the figure of $1.00 a year given by informants and recorded in Table 15 is probably not far from the correct one.

The public granary is an institution which has existed for many years. At harvest time each household contributes a set quantity of rice to the common store, from which it may, in turn, borrow in case of need. Before 1937 this contribution was exacted only from landowners, and its size was governed by the size of the holdings. It varied from year to year and ranged between 3 and 5 per cent of the total yield. Since 1937 every household, including those without land, has been required to contribute. Since every household makes its payment every year and loans are repaid the second year at 2 per cent interest, the total amount in storage increases from year to year. In 1938 there were 10,000 *piculs* accumulated in the granaries of the district. These stores, which the magistrate of the district has the right to sell in case of necessity, have proved of great value in solving the food problems created by the war.   87812

Loans are secured through application to the *pao* head, to whom is allotted a certain quantity of rice for distribution as he sees fit. While it is true that occasionally those not in need are able to obtain loans, the system works, on the whole, as genuine public relief for the poor. In 1938 seventy-seven households in the village borrowed 5 *piculs* each and three borrowed 10 *piculs* each. In 1939, after half of the stores were sent to Kunming at government order to supply the needs of the increasing wartime population, only thirty households were able to get loans.

Another form of tax is the conscription of labor for public works. The construction of the Burma Road, which was accomplished entirely by workers so obtained, had, according to the estimate given by the villagers, required 800 man-days from each household in the period from 1929, when the work was begun, to 1938. After the road was completed, each household still had to provide 25 man-days a year for

maintenance. It was only after the central government took over the
road that wages were paid for this work. Although the sacrifice of the
people has been justified by the opening of this outlet, so vital to
China's continuation in the war, the villagers have been left with a
deep-rooted resentment. When we remarked on the poor quality of
the grain an old woman was drying, she explained: "It is the road
which brings in an unlucky wind. We have not gotten good grain
since its opening." Although we may question the supernatural terms
in which she discusses the situation, it may well be true that the heavy
burden placed upon the people by the construction of the road has
deeply affected the economy of the villagers.

The direct taxes we have discussed (we have made no attempt at an
estimate of indirect taxes) do not exceed 10 per cent of the total budgets
of the families. Lack of comparative data prevents our knowing
whether this is high or low in relation to other areas; but if it is low, as
is likely, this is because the larger part of the cost of government is
paid for by the collective owners. It seems to us that the public lands,
if better managed, could easily be made to bear the whole burden.
The total yield of the group-owned land exceeds 3,000 *piculs* of unhusked rice, worth $2,400 in 1938, while the total expenditure of the
shang and *pao* in that year was only $1,200. If a system of management
of the collectively owned lands by village councils of representatives of
the owners, with technical assistance from the government, were in-
stituted, sufficient funds would be available for a much-improved program of community welfare. These funds exist now, but they are di-
verted by individual treasurers and are used for unnecessary expenditures.

VI. CEREMONIAL EXPENSES

Our discussion thus far has been confined to items of current expense—those necessary for day-to-day living. Another important
category of expense is that connected with the ceremonies which are
necessary at life-crises, such as birth, marriage, and death. We shall not
discuss the importance of the ceremonies in meeting the crises or the
justification of the expenditures, for we are concerned here only with
the economic aspects of the social structure as it exists. This section
will be devoted to expenses involved in five types of ceremonial occasions—namely, marriage, funeral, and birth ceremonies, the ceremony for general good fortune, and the ceremony in celebration of
long life.

The funeral ceremony for the father of the schoolteacher took place while we were in the village. During the six days it lasted, a feast was provided twice a day. On the first day, 21 tables of six guests each were served. On the succeeding days the guests were much more numerous: on the second day, 38 tables were served; on the third day, 45 tables; on the fourth day, 70 tables; on the fifth day, 98 tables in the morning and 105 in the evening; on the sixth day, 60 tables. These figures represent a total of 4,026 individual meals; the entire village was fed by the family for several days and, in addition, there were visitors from other villages. The number of guests would have been still larger except for the fact that the magistrate of the district was giving a funeral feast for his father on these same days. Yet the schoolteacher was apologetic about the limited number of guests, explaining, "I did not send out announcements, because I did not want to bother people. So only those who have wanted voluntarily to console me have come." With my statement that the cost of such a lengthy ceremony must be a heavy burden, he disagreed vehemently: "Only by spending as much as I am able to can I pay honor to my deceased father. That is my obligation. I would feel only shame if I could not spend the money in his honor."

The tenant-farmer of Household C was arranging a marriage ceremony for his son while we were in the village. When we offered to shop for him on a visit we were about to make to Kunming, he gave us, after consulting with his wife, a long list of merchandise, which included three types of cloth and a woolen blanket. The old woman in our landlord's house reprimanded him for his extravagance, admonishing him against the spending of so much money during these hard times and urging that some native cloth would be quite sufficient for the son. After conferring again with his wife, the man eliminated the blanket from the list, but the remaining items still cost him well in excess of $10. When we were about to make a second trip to the city, he asked us to buy him a quantity of a certain tea which I had served him, replying to my protest that it was very expensive with the simple statement that he must have only the best. On another occasion he asked that I obtain for him a special type of red card for invitations. I was repeatedly amazed by his insistence on obtaining nothing but the best for the ceremony and his utter disregard of the cost, since I knew, and the reader will find this confirmed in Table 15, that he is normally extremely thrifty and has a low standard of living. He works on the farm himself, does not smoke or drink, is usually barefooted, and wears patched clothing. Ordinarily, he buys nothing which is not essential, but in the case of this ceremony he threw all financial discretion to the winds and seemed to acquire a completely different personality. Despite the fact that, as a consequence of the marriage of his son, he was in debt for several tens of dollars and his store of rice had been sold, the smile on his worn face revealed an inner peace which made us feel that his life's goal had been attained. The old woman in our landlord's household explained: "We don't experience real happiness in our own marriage, we achieve it when we accomplish our son's marriage."

TABLE 19

SAMPLE CEREMONIAL EXPENDITURES

Ceremony	Household or Individual Concerned	Date	Expenses Involved
Marriage.............	Son of school inspector	1938	$ 85.00 (engagement) 74.00 (announcement) 227.00 (wedding) $386.00 (total)
Funeral and burial.....	Schoolmaster's father	1938	$200.00 (placing body in coffin) 301.00 (funeral ceremony) 100.00 (burial) $601.00 (total)
Birth.................	School inspector's grandson	1939	$ 99.90
General good fortune...	Chou household	1939	$477.20
Long life..............	Liu household	1939	$483.15

On the other hand, there are those for whom it is impossible to raise money for marriage ceremonies and who are thus doomed to lifelong bachelorhood.

The conventional expenditure for funeral ceremonies is more variable than that for marriages, since a marriage can be delayed and planned and accumulated for, while the time for a funeral is determined by death alone. During our second stay in the village a man who lived across the street from us died. The family was so poor that it was necessary to borrow money even for a coffin; and on the day of burial there was but one table of guests, those who had come in to assist with the funeral. In cases of extreme poverty the corpse may even be left at the side of the road for days until it is buried by some philanthropic organization.

Samples of expenses for other ceremonies, as well as for those of marriage and death, are given in Table 19. One of these is held a month after the birth of a child; this observance is usually elaborate for the first child, but for subsequent children it consists merely of a simple dinner to which the maternal uncle and a few other guests are invited. The ceremony celebrating long life is given only by the wealthy. In 1939 we attended such a ceremony given by the family of Liu in honor of his old mother—a wealthy, dominating personality, notorious for her interest in, and influence on, the private affairs of all the villagers. The sons arranged the celebration at her own insistence. The ceremony for general good fortune is held when there is a disturbance in the normal life of the household. After he had lost half his horses and suffered from frequent disputes in his house, Chou, the wealthiest man in the village, arranged such a ceremony in 1939 in the hope of improving his lot.

These large occasional expenses, each of which may exceed the total current living expenses of the year in which it occurs, may easily exhaust the financial resources of a family and may even be responsible for hopeless indebtedness. Thus they have significant consequences from the standpoint of the possibility of accumulating capital and achieving security for the family. We shall have the opportunity to discuss this problem later.

VII. OPIUM-SMOKING

Although the members of the five households whose budgets we studied in the last chapter happened not to be addicted to opium, the importance of this habit in the economic life of the village makes a discussion of its cost necessary. In 1938, according to the estimates given me by the villagers, the monthly consumption of opium for the village was 200 ounces. At the price of $4.00 an ounce, then current, the annual expenditure for this drug would be $10,000. Because this figure seemed incredibly high, we recorded the names of all the addicts, i.e., those who had to smoke daily, during our second visit in 1939. Despite the fact that the number was said to have been much reduced, owing to the price increase and the effectiveness of the government's prohibition, our census revealed thirty-eight addicts. Since the minimum per capita daily consumption would be 0.03 ounce, which in September, 1939, cost $0.50, the annal minimum cost of opium for these thirty-eight individuals would be $7,000.

Since the government now prohibits the raising of the poppy plant, all these smokers, except those wealthy ones who have opium left from previous years, must rely on outside sources. Although governmental regulations specify that addicts must register and that they shall be given a supply for a tapering-off period, only eight of the villagers have complied; the rest depend on smuggled supplies and are responsible for the heavy drainage of money out of the village. We were told that, if this situation continues, all the rice in excess of that actually consumed by the villagers will be required to pay the opium bill. This statement is not far from the truth, for, on the basis of 1939 prices, $5,000 spent for opium would require the export of 8,750 *piculs* of rice grain. The significance of this figure will be apparent when we recall that the total yield of the village, according to our estimate, is only about 21,000 *piculs*, of which about 9,000 are needed locally for food. It is obvious that such a large proportion of income cannot be dissipated without seriously curtailing other consumption and depressing the standard of living.

It is true that the number of addicts has decreased during recent years, for the middle-aged man who has not at some time smoked opium is extremely rare. Yet, despite severe regulation by the government, about half of the addicts have not completely rid themselves of the habit. Since Luts'un produced opium of an exceptionally good quality before its cultivation was made illegal, the use of the drug required no expenditure of money. At one time, even the women and the children smoked, and at the present time almost anyone who feels unwell will resort to a pipe for relief.

The elimination of poppy raising was relatively easy, and not a flower is to be seen in Luts'un; but the eradication of the opium habit is another matter. Without medical assistance the termination of smoking is accompanied by almost intolerable torture. Moreover, although the price increase will exert a pressure which must inevitably reduce still more the amount of opium consumed and the number of addicts, failure to take positive action on the problem will result in serious economic consequences. There is no doubt that the price factor will be effective only after many families have been financially ruined. It is evident that, unless the prohibition on smoking is accompanied by a sound medical policy, impetus will be given to the collapse of the village economy and to administrative corruption.

When the villagers, in accordance with the traditional economic attitude, have attained an adequate standard of living and have renounced the painful experience of work, they are faced with the problem of whiling away their many leisure hours. For my landlord, who neither works nor uses opium, this is a burdensome problem, which he can solve only by sleeping long hours and by loitering about the church and the teashops. To the smokers, however, there is no such problem. We have always felt that the spread of opium over China in the last one hundred years was not accidental but that there must have been some factor in the social environment which gave it its imeptus. We are now inclined to believe that the existence of this leisure class must have been in some degree responsible, for lying contentedly on an opium bed, gossiping with one's fellow-addicts, would seem to be an adequate solution to the problem of passing that time for which there is no constructive use. Smoking has become integrated into the social system and is a link in a vicious circle: the man who has leisure smokes; the man who smokes will have a profound distaste for work.

VIII. INFLATION AND THE VILLAGERS' LIVELIHOOD

The effects of inflation, as expressed in rapid price increases, first became apparent in Luts'un in 1939. At the time of our first visit in 1938 there had been no noticeable change in prices. When we went to the village, we carried a large supply of 10-cent notes, since we had been informed that the $1.00 bill of the Central Bank was still not popular. When we inquired about wages and prices, the amounts were given without hesitation, as though they had remained constant for a long time; and the figures of 10 cents a day as the wage for a male worker and of $8.00 for 10 *piculs* of rice grain were given to us without any time reference.[3] However, at the time of our second visit, seven months later, we found that the price of rice had doubled. During our stay there was no noticeable change; but a few days after our departure the price began to rise rapidly and had soon doubled several times. In 1939 we recorded prices every six days (on market days) from the beginning of October and had certain villagers maintain a record for us from the time we left until the end of November. The price index given in Table 20 was computed by assigning the value 100 to prices of October 10, 1939. The three categories of commodities are: (1) those which are usually sold by the peasants, including rice, beans, by-products of the refining of rice and the threshing of beans, and wheat; (2) those which the peasants may either buy or sell, including wages, land, pork, chickens, eggs, vegetables, oxen, buffaloes, horses,

---

[3] There had, of course, always been fluctuations in the price of rice; but the changes never exceeded 5 cents a *picul*.

E*

and mules; and (3) those usually bought by the peasants, including bean curds, salt, wine, sugar, young pigs, firewood, charcoal, vegetable oils, tobacco, opium, and clothing.

An understanding of the Luts'un peasant's relation to the market is essential to an analysis of the effects of inflation on the local rural economy. It should be constantly borne in mind that a large part of the farmer's consumption is of products he supplies himself and that commercial transactions involving farm products are, in general, a minor part of the peasant's economic activities. Only those who are wage-earners and those who have not enough rice depend on the market for

TABLE 20

PRICE CHANGES IN LUTS'UN

DATES	CATEGORY		
	1	2	3
November, 1938........	31.3	45.2	33.4
July, 1939.............	92.0	80.9	98.7
October 10, 1939.......	100.0	100.0	100.0
October 16, 1939.......	126.6	112.1	124.9
October 22, 1939.......	125.1	130.9	136.4
October 28, 1939.......	132.1	123.8	128.4
November 3, 1939......	169.1	132.6	135.7
November 9, 1939......	178.6	132.8	144.1
November 15, 1939.....	193.6	130.7	153.3
November 21, 1939.....	195.2	139.2	157.6

their food supplies. On the other hand, the producer will not sell his rice unless he has a specific need for cash or for a commodity, in which case he will sell or exchange only the required amount of his product. Thus the supply of rural produce on the market is determined, not by prices, but solely by the need of the producers. Instead of selling the rice and saving the money received, the farmers commonly save the grain itself. Since it is obviously impossible to keep their stores intact and they must, even unwillingly, sell them as their needs arise, the rate of consumption regulates the flow of rice to the market. Although there is a tendency for some families to hold their rice stores even at the expense of having to borrow money to meet their needs, this attitude merely retards the movement of grain to the market; it cannot effectively block it, for even those who normally have a surplus will ultimately be faced with expenses which will force its liquidation. This traditional attitude was quite consistent with conditions prevailing in the pre-inflation period, when, because the poorer farmers were compelled to sell to meet their obligations, prices were low immediately after harvest and then gradually increased until the next harvest. Owing to the traditional attitude, a rise in the price of rice, if it outstrips the prices of other commodities, will result in an actual decrease in the supply, because less rice need be taken to market in exchange for other commodities. Hence, inflation, with its encouragement of rice storage, fits well into the traditional pattern.

Contrary to the expectations that the lagging of other prices behind that of the villagers' product would stimulate increased buying, the mere fact that commodities are more expensive than in the past restrains the thrifty peasant from increasing or even maintaining his accustomed level of consumption. Although the consciousness of increased wealth is present, the habitual, deeply ingrained habits of thrift prevent increased purchasing. Our landlord, much impressed by a watch of ours and inspired by an awareness of his sudden prosperity, went so far as to ask us the price, but then he abruptly terminated the negotiation, as though he had suddenly realized the enormity of the thing he had contemplated doing. The surplus money resulting from increased wages for public works and the curtailment of consumption encourages speculation. The rich ex-headman of the *pao* organized a group of his friends to store more than 50,000 pounds of salt, and even the poor laborers bought pigs for later sale in the rising market.

The increase in the price of rural products is definitely favorable to those farmers who raise produce in excess of their needs, but such producers are extremely few. The effect of inflation on the laborers depends on whether the wage increases keep pace with the price of rice. During the harvest of 1939, wages had increased to 30 cents for the male and 15 cents for the female per day (triple the 1938 rate), but at the same time the price of rice was seven times the 1938 price; even at the end of November, when they had increased to 50 cents (male wage), they were still disproportionately low. So, during the early period of inflation, the laborers suffered from a drop in real wages. Later, however, as the labor shortage became more acute, wages outstripped the price of rice. Although we are not informed of the later situation in Luts'un, in some villages in 1942 wages rose, at times of special labor shortage, to fantastic levels, and reached as high as $100 a day. The average, however, was $30–$40, which is three hundred to four hundred times the pre-war level. In view of the fact that rice was selling at only two hundred and fifty to three hundred times its pre-war price, the laborers benefited not so much by inflation as by the wartime shortage of labor.

It might be supposed that during the period when wages lagged behind the price of rice the owners would have been encouraged to employ more labor, but this was not the case. Actually, they were inclined to insist on hiring at the old, pre-inflation rate, which the workers would, naturally enough, not accept. Thus the exit of labor from the village was hastened, and the shortage forced wages so high that the owners have been compelled to go to work themselves.

Since the effects of inflation appear only in cash transactions, many of the economic activities of the villagers will not be directly affected by the new trend. For example, since rent is paid in kind, the relation between the landlord and tenant is not altered. It will be interesting to see whether the sphere of transactions in kind will contract and money economy will expand under the influence of inflation. Presumably, this will depend on which system is more advantageous to the most influential group in the community. The owners may prefer to abandon the practice of providing food as part of the wage in favor of a strictly cash wage, while the moneylenders may insist on the payment of interest in kind.

CHAPTER IX

INHERITANCE OF LAND

THE preceding chapters have revealed the importance of land in the life of the villagers. The possession or lack of land is the decisive factor in determining an individual's standard of living and in determining whether or not he shall enjoy the privilege of leisure. This fact is so well understood by the villagers that it is the driving force behind much of their activities. Those who suffer from lack of adequate land strive constantly to acquire it, while those who possess land do everything in their power to hold it. Given the limited supply of land, these conflicting forces have introduced a dramatic element into what might otherwise be a dull and static rural economy. The following chapters will deal with the dynamic aspects of the land system through an analysis of the ways in which the villagers acquire their land and the ways in which they lose it. The rise and fall of peasant households constitutes an ever repeating cycle and stabilizes the traditional system in a dynamic equilibrium.

I. UNILATERAL INHERITANCE

By far the commonest means of acquiring land here is inheritance, through which ownership passes from father to son. Since the period during which land can be utilized far exceeds the life-span of any of its human exploiters, some principle of inheritance to determine the succession of holders is necessary. In Luts'un this principle is based upon the kinship system. Although kinship, which is created by birth and marriage, is bilateral in nature, the principle of inheritance in Luts'un, as in most human communities, is unilateral. Unilaterality means that the property of the parents is not divided among their offspring of both sexes but goes either to the sons (patrilineal) or to the daughters (matrilineal). In Luts'un patrilineal inheritance is the normal practice, and the daughters have no right of inheritance. They take no land with them when they marry, but throughout their lives they dwell on the land of their fathers, husbands, or sons.

It is commonly recognized that the property-possessing units in the Chinese traditional community are the family and the clan, but this statement is true only in a limited sense. Strictly speaking, the family would be better considered an economic unit, the members of which work together as a team and share the income thus derived. As against the outside, the family is the holder of its common property; but if we examine the situation from the inside, we find that individual rights over property are far from being submerged. When viewed from this point of view, it is readily apparent that the land belongs to the man.

The lack of right over land by the women of the family, which undoubtedly has been instrumental in making their position in the family low and inferior, does not mean that they are completely deprived of property ownership. The wife makes her contribution to the formation of the new family through the dowry which her parents provide. This includes such articles as bedding, a charcoal-burner, a washbasin, trunks, wardrobes, and other furniture, as well as her clothing and presents for her new relatives. It is true that a part of a dowry is purchased with the money sent by the bridegroom's family as a marriage gift, which also includes clothing and ornaments. But in Luts'un the bride's parents will usually add an equal sum, in order that there may be a respectable dowry, since the prestige of the daughter in her husband's house will depend, to a large extent, upon the wealth she has brought with her. In 1938 the cost to the bride's parents was from $30 to $60. The fact that the bride's dowry is largely used for furnishing the room for the new couple, so that the furniture of the house is thus renewed, generation after generation, explains the very small amount which, as we have seen, is spent on that item in housing. Such costs are concealed among the ceremonial expenditures.

The property which is contributed by the bride belongs to her, and she may protest when her husband infringes upon her right to it. Family disputes over the husband's confiscation of his wife's precious ornaments are not rare; but in such cases public opinion is always on the side of the wife, as against the husband, although the sanction will not necessarily be strong. The main significance of such disputes is that they indicate quite clearly that individual ownership does exist within the family organization. Personal ownership of income earned by the individual through his own efforts is also recognized. Our landlord's wife makes money through buying and selling on the market. When her husband scolded her one day for bringing home a second-hand shirt of unknown origin, which he felt she should not wear, she retorted that it was not his concern, since she had bought it with her own money. The daughter of the house was constantly busy making children's hats. In response to our question, she informed us that she sold them on the market and thus got some money for herself. The old woman in the house also has her own savings. We once read for her a letter from her grandson, who was boarding in a middle school, in which he asked her for some money to buy a new pair of shoes. When we asked why he should ask her rather than his father for the money, the old woman laughed and replied that he had been instructed to do so by the father, who knew that she had money. We know of one instance in which this man had to borrow money from somebody outside the family while his mother and his wife were both lending money to others. I wondered, at the time, why the women should keep their purses so tightly closed, but the reason is probably that they are so completely excluded from any control over matters concerned with land. Here the man holds full sway. A mother or wife may exert her influence upon her son or husband to prevent him from disposing of the land on which the livelihood of the household depends; but if he is adamant in his determination to sell it, there is nothing she can do to prevent him from doing so. The dissatisfaction felt by the wife may lead to tension within the family but never to an outburst such as that which may result from the husband's sale of her earrings. The villagers explained that the land is no concern of the women because they bring none into the household.

Providing the daily living for the family is the man's burden. The women retain whatever income they may have themselves and ask their husbands for funds to run the household. This feminine privilege is balanced by the feminine duty of rearing children, on the one hand, and supplying labor for the farm, on the other. In the earlier discussion on farm labor I emphasized the fact that even in the very wealthy houses the women and girls work regularly in the fields. Although it may not seem fair that the weaker sex, with their bound feet, should toil in the mud while the men spend their days in idleness, an examination of the property structure of the family makes it appear that there is a kind of balance and reciprocity in the household economy.

In a community where land is the main foundation of the economic structure, the dominance of the landowning sex is to be expected. The females have a definitely inferior social position and may be said to suffer exploitation by the male sex. The unilateral principle of inheritance, which seems to be responsible for the inequality of the sexes and which has been a long-standing grievance of the feminine movement, has been so effectively attacked that a new law bestowing the right of

inheritance upon the females, as well as on the males, has been en-
acted. There is, however, strong reason to doubt that the bilateral
principle of inheritance is workable in the present rural economy. The
results of the present field study have not enabled us to modify our
earlier conclusion on this subject: "But so far as this village is concerned, I have yet found no indication of any actual change pointing
in this direction [i.e., toward the actual adoption of the bilateral prin-
ciple], although the new law has existed for seven years."[1]

Let us consider, for a moment, some of the problems that might be
expected to arise if the bilateral principle of inheritance were put into
practice. According to this principle, both the sons and daughters will
have the right to inherit from their parents. The establishment of a
new family will mean the combination of two geographically separated shares of land acquired by the husband and the wife from their
respective parents, so that ecological factors will, of necessity, enter
into the selection of mates. Since the married couple must live together and since effective management requires that the manager live
not too far from his farm, there is obviously introduced a new limitation on the number of possible marriage combinations. The result of
such a practice would naturally be strict local endogamy. The achievement of sex equality would thus require a reduction of the social
sphere, which would otherwise be constantly expanding through the
creation of new kinship relations. This limitation on marriageability
would be unfortunate also in that it would narrow the field for the selection of mates. To retain local exogamy (that is, selecting mates from
outside the villages) under the bilateral principle of inheritance would
lead to confusion in farm management. Of course, it may be argued
that the farm acquired by one of the spouses could be rented to tenants, while the couple lived together and managed the other. However, it is doubtful whether the encouragement of tenancy is wise. It
is definitely contrary to the present policy of the government, which
is based on what may be called the owner-cultivator principle, that is,
"those who cultivate the land should own the land." It is probably
these difficulties inherent in bilateral inheritance which have caused
the practical-minded peasant to let the new legislation lie dormant
while the high tide of feminine emancipation sweeps the cities.

II. MATRILINEAL PRINCIPLE

There are exceptions to the patrilineal principle in the actual practice of the villagers in Luts'un. Instances of the matrilineal principle in

---

[1] Fei, *Peasant Life in China*, p. 82.

marriage and in inheritance can be found anywhere in China, but it is normally operative only as a temporary solution when the deceased owner has no male successor. In such a situation the daughter will take a husband into her father's house, so that she may have children to perpetuate the family line. This is the case in Luts'un, but here a daughter who has brothers may also remain in her father's house after marriage and share her brothers' privileges. Yet such an act will certainly be regarded as contrary to the traditional spirit of patriliny, and the brothers will be loath to tolerate such an encroachment by their sisters upon their full rights of succession. The existence of this exceptional pattern may be the result of influence by the aboriginal inhabitants, of the important role played by women in farming, or of the existence of the large number of landless immigrants, who, by reason of their hunger for land, are willing to accept a servile position in the household.

Uncle Chang, whom we have mentioned several times before, carries the surname of his mother, who was the eldest child of a wealthy family with three sons. She was a very capable person, who gave her parents much assistance in the management of their farm. A bachelor named Soong, who had brought some money with him from Tali when he came to the village to live, was taken into the Chang house and married to the eldest daughter. The daughter was given a share of Chang's land, and the couple later acquired more than 10 *kung* by themselves. As long as they lived, they enjoyed fairly amicable relations with all the members of Chang's house; but when they died, the brothers demanded that the land be returned. Uncle Chang, who is still unhappy about this unfriendly action, told me that he could have refused them, since he had never taken his father's name. Bearing the name Chang, he was entitled to inherit the land from his mother's line. However, he felt that the maintenance of good relations with his uncles and cousins, who were influential persons in the community, was worth more than the land; so he yielded to their demand. The matrilineal inheritance was thus discontinued.

According to custom, the man who enters into a matrilineal marriage changes his surname and retains the name he receives from his father as the last word of his personal name. For instance, a man whose original name is Soong Pai-sen will become Chang Pai-soong if he marries a woman whose surname is Chang and joins her house. He will work on the piece of land which his wife inherits from her father. Their first son will take his mother's surname, but subsequent children are free to choose their father's original surname. If they do so, however, they will not be entitled to inherit land from their mother's line. The status of the man who contracts a matrilineal marriage is definitely low, both in his house and in the community. He is, in actuality, a laborer on his wife's land and in her household. On the other hand, he has security; and he may, with the advantage his wife's land gives him, be able to acquire some land through his own effort and thus become a landowner in a real sense. Such good fortune is rare, of course, but it does occur frequently enough to permit the poor bachelor some hope for the future. If he does not succeed in establishing himself fairly well, he may, upon the death of his wife, be forced to return his land to her brothers and again assume his own name. Household C is an example of this. The resentment of the man, who had taken back his original name and had married again, when he is called by his first wife's name, reveals how strong must be the motive to force men into such distasteful arrangements. The principal motive for the acceptance of a matrilineal marriage is the acquisition of land as a means of achieving security of employment. Those laborers to whom such marriages are not open have very little hope of acquiring land and are likely to pass their lives as bachelors, since they are not able to assume the heavy burden of a family. So the institution of matrilineal marriage is an opportunity for the landless immigrant who lives in some landowners' house and may, if he proves to be industrious and dependable, be allowed to marry a daughter. Especially if the girl is the only daughter or is, for some other reason, important in the household, the parents may prefer accepting a husband into the house to letting her leave. The presence of numerous young male immigrants is mainly responsible for the practice of matrilineal marriage.

III. DIVISION OF HOUSE

Another principle in the local system of inheritance is the sharing of the father's estate by all the brothers. Although their shares may be unequal, all the sons have a rightful claim on the father's land. This principle has a disintegrating effect on landholdings, for, however large the original estate may be, it will be broken up into small tracts as the male descendants multiply. Moreover, such a division of the family estate is not necessarily delayed until the time of the father's death. An adult son may, when he marries, demand a share of the family property to establish his own house. The large-family system, which has been often overemphasized as the dominant type in China, is certainly not the prevailing form in this village. On the contrary, the division of the household into small families during the lifetime of the father is a common practice, even though it is opposed by the father and by the traditional ethical teachings of the scholar class. The forces resisting the division of the house are strong. It is natural that the father should fight against the disruption of the unity of the group of which he is head, for it has both economic and emotional consequences. The division of the house challenges his power to control the family and diminishes the land under his command. Ethical ideas and even the supernatural are mobilized in the fight to maintain the rule of the old. In a book of poems written by spirits through a medium, we found many passages expressing disapproval of division of the house. The following is a translation of a poem written under the name of a deceased father:

> You brothers should be friendly to each other. Don't quarrel over trifling differences. My eldest and third sons: with your wives and children, be nice to your neighbors. Arrange a marriage for your second brother. You older brothers should behave like parents toward your younger brothers. This will make your parent in heaven glad. Your father will help you to clear up your debt. Do not divide my house within ten years.

Whether or not we accept the authenticity of the voice of the spirit, this passage does reveal the moral teaching which has at least a certain amount of control over the behavior of the villagers.

The forces working for the maintenance of the family unit are counterbalanced by forces working toward its breakdown. One such force is the conflict likely when an outsider marries into the family. When a new daughter-in-law is introduced into the house, the old unit becomes unstable, for the new member, having had no previous relations with the group, will not easily adjust to the older members. Such an economic unit can be maintained only by an equal sharing of duties and privileges among the members who are no longer united entirely on the basis of intimacy and altruism. Into the group whose solidarity has heretofore been maintained by the self-sacrificing kinship relation is introduced a new individual who does not fit into any of the established patterns of interaction. New relationships which develop must, almost of necessity, be based upon self-interest and will be incompatible with these pre-existing patterns. To build a smoothly functioning economic unit on such a basis is a difficult, if not impossible, task. This is especially true when the family is actually a working team, as in Luts'un, rather than a group of parasites living on the rent from land, as among the big families of absentee landowners.

A case in point is that of Wang, our neighbor during our first visit to the village. The old man has two sons. The elder, who is married and has several children, is an opium addict and has a wife who is also lazy and worthless. But the younger son is industrious and energetic. Originally, the whole family lived together on the same farm and shared a common kitchen, with the result that the younger brother was actually supporting the family of his elder brother as well as his father. Furthermore, the elder brother tried to prevent the younger brother's marriage, so that he could continue to live on the latter's labor. This situation, together with the constant discord between the mother and her daughter-in-law, led the father to effect the division of his estate in order to protect the younger son and to free himself of responsibility for the elder. The old man was much saddened by the necessity of breaking up his household but realized the inevitability of it. A general breaking-down of the old unit is just as inevitable as it was in Wang's case. The traditional moral ideas can, at best, only delay the process; and in the meantime they are the means of torturing the minds of both the old and the young when division is necessary.

Although brothers may not necessarily share equally in their father's estate, the principle of equality is recognized as equitable. In the case of Wang, 6 *kung* were reserved by the father and each son received 9 *kung*. Since the father is too old to work, his share is combined with that of the younger son, who rents, in addition, a farm of 16 *kung*. Thus the latter has under his management a farm of 31 *kung*, which gives him a sufficient return to maintain his parents and himself. The elder son, on the other hand, is rapidly losing his property. He is a slave to his opium pipe, and it is an accepted fact in the village that he will soon become a landless pauper. It is said that, when the father dies, he may ask for a share of the residual estate, but his younger brother is entitled to all of it by virtue of the fact that he alone has supported his parents. Moreover, if the older brother is not able to make contributions to his father's funeral ceremony, he will have no grounds for a claim on an additional share of his father's property. The final settlement is an open question, however, and has caused much speculation among the villagers, who are interested because a dispute among the brothers may give them an opportunity to acquire the 6 *kung* of land left by the old man.

Our landlord's deceased father was a brother of the old man. He died very early, leaving a widow and a son with a farm of 30 *kung*. The widow, an exemplification of the traditional virtues, worked hard and had, through careful management and thrift, enlarged her estate to 36 *kung* by the time her son came of age.

Although the Wang brothers received equal shares at the division of their father's house, this is not always the case. In the house of Liu there are three brothers. While their father was living, the family had a large farm of 90 *kung*. The father gave 30 *kung* of land to the eldest son when he married and asked for an independent household, but he died before the marriage of the second son. When the latter asked for his share, his mother, the old woman whose celebration of long life has been mentioned previously, gave him only 15 *kung*, because of her favoritism for her youngest son. As long as the old woman lives, the second son has no recourse but can only hope that he will get another 15 *kung* when she dies. However, the youngest son is an opium addict and has begun to sell his land. Since, according to our landlord, the second son is a gentle man and avoids disputes, he may as well renounce this hope. Another case is that of Chao, the present village head, who received 3 *kung* of land from his father while his brother, the Christian doctor, received 8 *kung*. In consideration of the inequity of this arrangement, the latter was persuaded to give his younger brother a sum of money equal to the price of a *kung* of land.

The principle of sharing of land among brothers may seem equitable, but it has had the effect of bringing population pressure to bear directly on the land. As the population increases, the farm holdings become smaller and smaller. Owing to this division, wealthy houses cannot be perpetuated. In this regard, let us compare the grandsons of the common grandfather in the house of Wang. Our landlord is one of the wealthy men in the village, while the elder son of the family next door will soon belong in the poor laboring class. The children of these two men will find themselves in two entirely different strata in the community. The son of our landlord is a student in the middle school, while the sons of the opium addict are illiterate and had to begin working on the farm in early childhood. When they grow up, the latter will inherit no land from their father, so that, unless they move away from the village, they will be dependent on their labor for a meager living. The former, on the other hand, will be the second most highly educated in the village, even if he does not continue beyond the middle school, and will be able to enter the government. The enormous difference in the prospects for these children is due not to any differences in intelligence or morality but mainly to the amount of land possessed by their fathers. Even were the father, who is an opium addict, as industrious as his clan brother next door, he would not be able to attain the same position because of the small size of his farm. If his industrious brother marries and has several children, he, too, will be unable to leave them sufficient land for their support, and they will be forced to sell their labor on the farms of others. The difference between these cases is, in the last analysis, a matter of population pressure. My land-lord is wealthy because his father died early and he is an only child, who can inherit an estate which he need share with no one. How tragic it is that the blessing of economic security in this rural economy should require the premature death of a father.

A generation ago, several of the houses in Luts'un possessed large landholdings, some of them comprising more than 200 *kung*. In con-trast, the largest present holding is slightly over 60 *kung* as a result of the division of houses. The average holding is only 5.7 *mow*. It is not necessary to dwell at length here on the disadvantages of small farm-ing—how it prevents the introduction of mechanical implements and makes the introduction of improved techniques difficult. But it is difficult to see any alternative to this situation. Since there are few opportunities for employment outside of agriculture, the adoption of primogeniture or ultimogeniture would simply result in the elimina-tion of those who inherited no land. Such a procedure would not fit in with the traditional ideas of fairness and filial prosperity; so the most humane course would seem to be to permit a certain amount of crowding on the limited quantity of land and to let the brothers share equally in the sacrifice.

It should be pointed out, however, that what makes the division of ownership a really divisive force is the combination of farm manage-ment and farm ownership, which are two different things and need not necessarily be combined. When the unit of management is sy-nonymous with the unit of ownership, a division of the house will mean a division of the farm. Perhaps the situation would be ameliorated if the individual owners were to participate in a co-operative system of farming, for it is small managing units, not small owning units,which constitute an obstacle to the introduction of new farm techniques. The possibility of a development along these lines certainly deserves our more detailed consideration, but this must be left for another occasion.

CHAPTER X

FAMILY FINANCE

THE second method of acquiring land is by purchase. But the land market is greatly restricted by the traditional disapproval of selling this source of family security and symbol of family solidarity. Only as a last resort will the land be sold. So, let us first examine the alternative means of weathering financial crises.

I. MUTUAL HELP

Considerable financial assistance is generally needed only when the resources of a family are insufficient to meet ceremonial expenses. As we have already seen, the needs of the villagers are relatively elastic. If income decreases, expenditures will be reduced. If there is a temporary shortage, small sums can always be obtained from friends and relatives. During our residence in the village many people came to our landlord's house to ask for money to buy rice and beans and even to hire labor. This sort of mutual help, for which no interest is charged and no definite time for repayment is set, is governed by sentiments of friendship and kinship. It is, however, generally limited to assistance in cases of small and temporary deficiencies. The most that can be obtained in this way is a few days' work, a few bowls of rice, or a few dollars. If the need is greater, this sort of assistance is normally not available.

The most inelastic of the daily expenses is that of opium. Under the pressure of their craving, addicts cannot resist borrowing money when they are without funds to buy the drug. But the largest number of loans are secured to cover the expenses of ceremonial occasions, when large sums are needed. Even here the principle of mutual help exists, and relatives and friends make contributions, mainly in cash. For the marriage ceremony of the son of the school inspector, $128, or 33 per cent of the total expenses, were received from friends and relatives. Gifts for the funeral ceremony of the schoolteacher amounted to $203, or 34 per cent of the total expenses. Since such assistance meets but a portion of the need, if there are inadequate savings for the bulk of the expense, those who give the ceremonies must fall back on the organization of credit societies, the securing of loans, the temporary transference of land, or, as a last resort, the sale of their land.

II. CREDIT SOCIETIES

The organization of the credit society in Luts'un is similar to that described in *Peasant Life in China*.[1] This society is a sort of savings system, into which each member pays a certain amount at certain intervals and from which he is paid a certain sum on a specified date. The size of the payment to be made by each participant and the time at which he will be paid are prearranged. Anyone in need of money may organize a society by enlisting ten other members. Each will pay a predetermined proportion of the $100 which the organizer receives, as shown in Table 21. Thereafter the society meets every six months,

TABLE 21

TABLE OF PAYMENTS AND RECEIPTS OF MEMBERS OF CREDIT SOCIETY*

(In Dollars)

SUBSCRIBER	PERIOD										
	1	2	3	4	5	6	7	8	9	10	11
Organizer	(100)	14.50	13.50	12.50	11.50	10.50	9.50	8.50	7.50	6.50	5.50
Subscriber I	14.50	(100)	14.50	14.50	14.50	14.50	14.50	14.50	14.50	14.50	14.50
Subscriber II.....	13.50	13.50	(100)	13.50	13.50	13.50	13.50	13.50	13.50	13.50	13.50
Subscriber III....	12.50	12.50	12.50	(100)	12.50	12.50	12.50	12.50	12.50	12.50	12.50
Subscriber IV....	11.50	11.50	11.50	11.50	(100)	11.50	11.50	11.50	11.50	11.50	11.50
Subscriber V.....	10.50	10.50	10.50	10.50	10.50	(100)	10.50	10.50	10.50	10.50	10.50
Subscriber VI....	9.50	9.50	9.50	9.50	9.50	9.50	(100)	9.50	9.50	9.50	9.50
Subscriber VII...	8.50	8.50	8.50	8.50	8.50	8.50	8.50	(100)	8.50	8.50	8.50
Subscriber VIII..	7.50	7.50	7.50	7.50	7.50	7.50	7.50	7.50	(100)	7.50	7.50
Subscriber IX....	6.50	6.50	6.50	6.50	6.50	6.50	6.50	6.50	6.50	(100)	6.50
Subscriber X.....	5.50	5.50	5.50	5.50	5.50	5.50	5.50	5.50	5.50	5.50	(100)

* Figures in parentheses represent amount received by member; other figures are payments made.

usually in March and September, at which time one member receives $100 and the rest make their payments. Members other than the organizer pay sums directly proportionate to the order in which they are paid, so that, in effect, the first five are paying interest for loans they have received, while the last five are receiving interest for money they have deposited. The organizer, on the other hand, repays just $100 during the five-year life of the society and has thus secured a loan without interest. But he is obliged to offer a feast at each meeting and has the responsibility of collecting the money. Furthermore, in case of default by any of the subscribers, he is held accountable. The functioning of this system depends on the invariable discharge of their obliga-

[1] Pp. 267 ff.

tions by the subscribers, and this is secured only by existing ties of friendship and kinship. We were able to obtain lists of societies joined by three individuals. One belonged to ten societies; the organizers of five of these were neighbors, one was a son-in-law, three were other affinal relatives, and one a friend in another village. A second subscribed to two—one organized by a friend, the other by a maternal uncle. The seven societies to which the third belonged were organized as follows: one by himself, four by friends, and two by his cousin. When we asked why the villagers tended to join societies organized by friends and affinal relatives rather than those organized by clan members, we were informed that there is no special preference but that clan members should assist each other without such special devices. Moreover, there may be certain difficulties in attempting to maintain an organizer-subscriber relationship with a close relative. For example, it is difficult for the organizer, who must make good any default by the members, to enforce payment by a member of his clan. We were acquainted with a man who complained bitterly because his uncle was insisting that he pay his assessment on time. Kinship ties are built on the principle of mutual help, and it is not well to attempt to exploit them in ordinary business transactions.

III. LOANS

The need for a large sum of money is commonly met by the negotiation of a loan, and it is said that all but thirty households in the village are in debt. Being in debt does not, of course, necessarily mean that a family is desperately poor, for in some instances money is borrowed to finance productive enterprises. For instance, the $100 which our landlord owed a creditor was loaned out by him to someone else at a higher rate of interest, so that his debt was really a reflection of our landlord's business acumen. Most of the families, however, are in debt because of poverty. Their financial difficulties arise most commonly from the habit of opium-smoking or from the need for large expenditures on ceremonial occasions.

It was impossible to record all the debts of the villagers; but we can give here a sample case, that of a laborer who carries a burden of perpetual indebtedness. Table 22 shows the nature of his creditors, the amounts of his loans, and the rates of interest he pays. Before 1939, interest was paid in terms of grain, commonly at the rate of 4 *piculs* of unhusked rice on a loan of $10. Since 4 *piculs* were worth $3.20, the rate was 32 per cent. In 1939, 4 *piculs* were worth $11.20, bringing the interest rate to 112 per cent—an exorbitant amount. At that time, on the other hand, the debtors hastened to clear up their old debts at their face value, so that much of the burden of inflation fell upon the creditors. Those who have extra money are now hesitant to make any new loans on the old terms. Table 22 shows that the debtor had recourse to the co-operative society and to a friend who let him have money without interest. In other cases, cash interest of 32 per cent is demanded.

Although 32 per cent is recognized in the village as a fair rate, there are moneylenders who ask higher figures. The debtor of Table 22 was

TABLE 22

Debts of a Luts'un Laborer

Creditor (His Relation to the Debtor)	Amount of Loan	Interest	Rate of Interest in 1938 (When 10 Piculs of Grain Was Worth $8.00)	Rate of Interest in 1939 (When 10 Piculs of Grain Was Worth $28.00)
Husband of the debtor's sister	$50.00	20 pic. of grain yearly	32%	112%
A friend, Li	$70.00	28 pic. of grain yearly	32	112
A friend, Yao	$35.00	18 pic. of grain yearly	41	144
Co-operative society	$30.00	$4.22		14
A friend	$10.00	No interest		
Public granary	10 pic. of grain	2 pic. of grain yearly	20	20

compelled to pay Yao at an annual rate of 41 per cent, and we have known our Christian landlord to demand as much as 50 per cent. Our conversation with the latter one morning was interrupted by the arrival of a member of his clan, who brought a deed for a mow of land as security for a loan. The debtor was handed $20, among which we saw a banknote with which we had that morning paid our rent. Our landlord told his fellow clan member that he had arranged the loan for him with a man named Chang, who asked that he sign a contract providing for the payment of 50 per cent interest. But we learned that the name Chang appeared nowhere in the contract, and there is every reason to suspect that the money actually belonged to our landlord. The fact that he felt impelled to lie to protect himself against the charge of improper treatment of a clan brother suggests a strong community sanction against the exploitation of debtors through exorbitant interest rates.

Only the wealthy families of the village are able to lend money; so most loans are secured in the town. A well-known moneylender in the town, an old woman, told me that those with money to invest are anxious to lend it because the profits are greater than would be the rent if they were to invest in land.

We have already stated that in the fall of 1939 we observed many outsiders helping the village landowners harvest the rice. Most of them had previously secured loans from the owners and were paying off their debts with their labor. We were informed that no interest was charged in these cases, since the primary motive of the lender was to insure an adequate supply of labor during the busy period.

In order to secure a relatively large loan, the borrower must offer the lender some collateral, which is usually in the form of a deed to land, as in the case mentioned above, where our landlord received a deed for 3 *kung* of land as security for a loan of $20. Thus, for those who have no land, a large loan is almost impossible to obtain. They are, in general, restricted to borrowing small amounts which they can repay with their labor.

In Table 22 the lowest rate of interest (excluding the one case which involved no interest) was on the loan extended by the credit co-operative. This organization was established by the government in 1939 to make credit available to the farmers. According to its regulations, each member is entitled to borrow $4.00 on each *mow* of land he cultivates, up to a total of $60 in provincial currency ($30 in national currency). Thus, anyone who manages land may receive help from the co-operative, whether or not he is an owner. The capital for this organization is loaned by the government banks. The rate of interest is 1.3 per cent monthly, which is about half the local rate; so this is a government measure for relieving the peasants from exploitation through high-interest loans. Low as the co-operative rate is, in comparison with the prevailing local rate, it is still too high for investment in agriculture. The farmer who must borrow money to invest in his land will not realize a sufficient return to leave him any profit after paying interest; so he will be compensated only for his labor. On the other hand, the government has already experienced difficulty in the financing of this policy, since the rate of interest in the city market is much higher, especially during the period of inflation. Economic factors will prevent the government from further expanding this program; but, limited as it is, it constitutes a good beginning for the government's agrarian policy.

IV. TEMPORARY TRANSFERENCE OF LAND

The use of land deeds as collateral for loans does not affect the ownership or the management of the land involved. It means only that in case the debtor proves incapable of clearing his obligation—either interest or capital—the creditor is protected. So long as the debtor continues to pay the interest on his indebtedness, he retains possession of and manages his land as usual. The system of temporary transference of land works differently. In return for a loan the debtor delivers his land to the creditor, who manages it until the debt has been cleared. The creditor receives the income from the land, while the debtor need pay no interest, although he must pay the land tax. Our landlord has 3 *kung* of land transferred for a loan of $70. After paying the cost of farming out of the annual gross income of $30, the creditor will make a net profit of $21, which amounts to an interest of 30 per cent—approximately the normal rate on loans.

An ordinary loan has no fixed duration. If the interest is paid monthly, the debtor may clear his debt at any time in the year; if it is paid annually, the debtor may clear his debt at the conclusion of any year. But in the case of temporary transference, a minimum term must be agreed upon in advance. For instance, the contract between my landlord and his creditor is to run at least three years. After that time, the loan may be settled after the harvest in any year. According to our information, the total amount of land transferred under this system in the village is about 86 *kung*—a rather small fraction of the total land. Since the owner who secures a loan by this method thereby forfeits his opportunity for employment, only those who do not cultivate their own land—that is, the members of the leisure class—resort to this system of credit. In some cases it serves as a means of assisting relatives who have not sufficient land for cultivation. Further discussion of this system will be found in Part III.

CHAPTER XI

LAND TRANSACTIONS

I. RESTRICTED MARKET FOR LAND

THE residents of Luts'un attach an extremely high value to the land they possess because it is the main source of the income upon which their material comfort and social prestige depend and because it is the symbol of the family's continuity. The individual is only the temporary custodian of the family land; and he accepts, when he inherits it from his ancestors, the obligation to transmit it intact to his descendants. If he is not able to retain it, he will stand condemned in the eyes of the community. So the financially pressed peasant will exhaust every possible means of raising money before he considers giving up his land. In the previous chapter we have shown how the villagers may solve their immediate financial difficulties through the existing credit system. But it is clear that, in view of the high rate of interest (twice as high as the rate of farm profit), this system does not offer a lasting solution to the villagers' financial problems. Once a peasant is enmeshed in debts, his only hope of freeing himself is through a reduction of his standard of living. But where this is already very low, it may be impossible to accumulate enough to repay his creditors. Thus the existing system in most cases serves only to delay the inevitable loss of the land. In spite of the resistance of the villagers to this final extreme step, there are always some limited offerings on the land market.

A fairly common occasion for the sale of land is the death of the head of the family. In the chapter on inheritance we stated that, when the father of a family divides his estate among his sons, he usually retains a part of it for his own support. At his death this residue may be divided among the sons. But if they are not able to finance his funeral ceremony, they may sell it, since a decent ceremony for the dead ancestor is considered more important than the prosperity of the living descendants.

The feeling that the need to sell the land is an unmistakable indication of the unworthiness of the seller prevents any direct negotiating between him and possible purchasers. The transactions are, instead,

conducted in a roundabout manner. When the mother of our landlord urged us to acquire some land in the village, we seized the opportunity to learn from her how this should be accomplished. We inquired: "Could we ask anybody whether he would like to sell us some
land?" "No," she warned us. "That would be an insult. It would be
like asking him whether he would like to ruin his family or asking him
if he is a bad man." She explained that the usual procedure was to
wait until somebody approached us. At least theoretically, the initiative should be taken by the seller. He, being financially distressed,
must find some middleman to go and talk the matter over with those
who have money and who might be willing to buy land. Of course, she
added, if we really intended to buy, she was in a position to help us,
because she knew of some families that were ready to put their land on
the market. In a community in which everybody knows so much about
others' affairs, such a devious procedure is no more than a face-saving
mechanism. It reflects a psychology which makes owners unwilling to
throw their land on the market, and so helps to restrict the market.

Even more effective restrictions surround the transaction itself. The
landholder is not free to choose his buyer. Because the land is mainly
inherited from the ancestors and it is the duty of the descendants to
keep it within the clan, custom decrees that the clan members shall
have a preferential right to buy it. Only if the clan members are unable to buy the land or to lend him money to extricate him from his
financial difficulty, may the individual sell to an outsider. In this case
the buyer must secure the signatures of all the near members of the
seller's clan; if the transaction takes place without their permission, the
contract is both customarily and legally invalid. Our neighbor Liu's
younger brother, an opium addict, once attempted to sell a piece of
his land secretly; but when Liu learned about it, he announced that
he would refuse to place his signature on the contract and that he was
willing to help his brother or to buy his land at any time. The prospective buyer immediately withdrew from the transaction.

The demand for, as well as the available supply of, land is limited,
for more attractive investment opportunities are open to those who
have money on hand. In 1938 high-grade land was worth $80 a *kung;*
medium grade, $50; and low grade, $30. In 1939 the value of high-
grade land had risen to $100 and that of medium-grade land to $60;
the value of low-grade land remained the same. The low-grade land is
too poor to attract any buyers and thus remains outside of the market.
The net profit from land cultivated by hired laborers in 1938 was

$5.93 for the high grade, $3.59 for the medium grade, and $0.52 for the low grade. On the basis of 1938 land prices the rate of profit on the investment would thus be 7 per cent for the high and the medium grade and 1 per cent for the low grade. It is clear that the income from the low-grade land would be just about sufficient to cover the wages of the workers.

Hence, farm profit is less than one-fourth that which may be realized from money loaned at the prevailing interest rate. It would seem that those who have money would prefer to lend it rather than to invest it in land. However, opportunities for moneylending are not unlimited, and it is recognized that loans are often risky. Furthermore, the interest rate is too high to permit the borrowing of money for use as agricultural

TABLE 23

LAND TRANSACTION IN LUTS'UN IN 1938

Amount of Land Involved in Transaction (in *Kung*)	Number of Transactions	Total Amount of Land Involved in Transaction (in *Kung*)
3	2	6
6	3	18
9	1	9
12	1	12
Total 30	7	45

capital, and loans are normally secured to meet financial crises due to misfortune or to cover the expense of ceremonial occasions. Having spent the money without increasing his earning capacity, the borrower will usually find himself quite unable to clear the debt and in the end will very probably have to let his land go to the creditor himself. Thus the lender's investment proves, after all, to be in land.

The limited land market is reflected in Table 23, which is an analysis of all the land transactions in Luts'un during the year 1938. It is clear that there was no noticeable trend toward concentration of land in that year, for there were only seven transactions and only 45 *kung*, or about 2.5 per cent of the total land owned by individual households, changed hands.

II. ACCUMULATION OF WEALTH

The small amount of land in circulation may be explained partly on the basis of the limited financial capacity of the ordinary villagers.

It must be recognized that, tempted, as they may be, by the high returns on loans, wealthy people are drawn by the prospect of acquiring land, which they feel much more secure and permanent. Their attitude was epitomized by the old woman's arguments when she attempted to persuade us to buy land. She explained that land is the foundation of a family, that it secures not only one's own living but also the living of future generations. The experiences of the villagers, who have repeatedly suffered from the depredations of bandits and the destruction of fires, have taught them that everything else can be destroyed and that land alone is permanent. So, in the final analysis, lack of funds of the ordinary villagers is also an important factor in limiting their acquisition of this desirable possession.

We may ask whether it is possible for the ordinary peasant to accumulate the considerable funds required for the purchase of land. The largest owner in Luts'un, who possesses about 65 *kung*, would derive an annual income of $650 from his farm if he worked it himself. If he hired workers, however, his net income would be only about $390 a year. With his family's living costing about $350 (see Household A in Table 15), he may save from $40 to $300 a year, which he may use for the purchase of land. At the 1938 price of $80 a *kung*, he could acquire from ½ to 4 *kung* of high-grade land each year.

But the cost of living cited above includes only the current expenses of the household and fails to account for the costs of ceremonial occasions. These average, according to the estimate we have given above: $400 for a marriage, $600 for a funeral, $100 for a birth, $500 for a ceremony of blessing, and $500 for a celebration of longevity. It is manifestly impossible to establish the frequency of such ceremonial occasions in a household, but we shall not be much wide of the mark if we assume it to be once every five years. If our large owner manages his farm with hired labor, as is the case in Luts'un, his savings will not be adequate to meet the requirements of these periodic ceremonies. It should be emphasized, moreover, that this estimate is based upon the income of the wealthiest owner in the village, and the situation will obviously be no better for the smaller owners. It is, therefore, clearly apparent that income from farming alone will not enable farmers to enlarge their holdings.

While we were in the village in 1938, three families acquired some land. Among them was one none of whose members engaged in any occupation other than farming. The suspicions of the villagers were aroused, and I heard it rumored that the head of this family had received a mysterious revelation which led him to unearth a hoard of gold on his farm. While the rumor was undoubtedly false, it serves to illustrate the common disbelief in the possibility of accumulating wealth from farming alone.

Land breeds no land. But is there any way of satisfying the powerful craving of the ambitious peasants for possession of more of it? We have already seen how, under the pressure of population, the rich peasants may lose their estates and how the repeated division of houses prevents the perpetuation of the leisure class. If there were no way by which the landless could acquire land or by which the small owners could become large owners, the traditional structure could not survive, since ultimately there would be no sizable farms in existence. Hence it is pertinent to ask what makes possible the upward movement on the agricultural ladder, a movement necessary to maintain that cycle which is characterized by the rise and fall of the village families.

The way to wealth lies outside the occupation of farming, and ambitious villagers must leave the land to seek their fortunes by other means. If they are fortunate enough to achieve their goal, they return, buy land, and become large owners. But how can they get rich outside of farming, since neither industry nor commerce is developed in the region?

In 1938 there were about twenty young men who were engaged in some activity outside the village. Among these were a college graduate working for the government, a tax-collector in the neighboring district, a chauffeur, an apprentice to a scissors-maker, a shoemaker's apprentice, a middle-school student, a student in a nursing school, and a commissioned officer in the army. The rest were soldiers. These individuals represented approximately 20 per cent of the males in the sixteen- to thirty-year age group. The number of men outside the village increased to twenty-nine in 1939. Two of the seven new emigrants were working in the co-operatives, and the rest had joined the army. This list shows that the majority of the young men who had left the village entered the army. There were few who were engaged in or were preparing for careers as skilled laborers, and still fewer were in the civil service. This phenomenon can be understood only in terms of their economic backgrounds.

It is the hope of all the parents that their children will enjoy a living better than their own, and they are aware that this hope can be realized only if the children are so prepared that they can secure better jobs in the town or city. Such preparation, however, requires financial sacri-

F

fice. It is true that primary education is free in the village; but sending a child to school is an economic burden on the parents, since, as we have shown, children contribute useful services in the house or on the farm. When we suggested that our landlord's twelve-year-old daughter, who was completely illiterate, should be sent to school, her mother explained that she would not be able to keep the house going without her daughter's help. The children in poorer homes have still less opportunity to attend school.

The village provides only a lower primary school with four grades. For the education available in the higher grades, it is necessary to go to the district town, which is a twenty-minute walk. Although this distance would not seem to constitute a serious obstacle, we know of only two children from the village who attend the school in the town. There is one middle-school student, the son of our landlord, who is studying in a neighboring district. For his support his father sent him a hundred dollars, in addition to clothing and other provisions and a subsidy he got for his son from his clan. In other words, the income from more than 10 *kung* of land is required for the support of a middle-school student. It is, therefore, not surprising that so few can obtain a higher education. The village's only college graduate is an exception, for he was subsidized by his clan and the church. Had he not received scholarships, his family would have been ruined by the expense involved in his acquisition of a higher education. Under present economic conditions the villagers cannot afford to give their children even a middle-school education.

It is difficult to see how promising jobs can be open to these only partially literate boys. It is quite clear that professions better than those we have listed above will not be open to them. But how can a soldier, a subordinate officer in the army or in civil service, a chauffeur, a scissors-maker, or a shoemaker become rich? Yet, incredible though it may seem, such jobs do lead to wealth. The traditional saying, "To be promoted in political rank is to become richer and richer," appears still be to true.

A family which we knew to have been in debt for several hundred dollars cleared up all its obligations and acquired more than 10 *kung* of land in one year after a son had entered the army. The richest family in the village has a son who is the commander of a regiment. We might also mention the cases of the principal of the public school (who is an official in the eyes of the people), the head of the local government, the tax-collector, and others, to prove the pecuniary value of political position. In a community where industry and commerce are not developed, where land has already been exploited to the full, and where population pressure is increasing, wealth can apparently be accumulated only by noneconomic means. To those who may view with indignation the choice of such disreputable paths to wealth, we say: "It is up to you to help create better outlets for the hard-pressed peasants, so that their security may be guaranteed without the necessity of committing criminal acts."

Those newly wealthy individuals who return to the village and become big landowners become immediately subject to the pressure of population, which, after a few generations, will break their estates down into a number of petty holdings. As gentlemen farmers with abundant cheap labor at their command, they lead their idle lives, heedless of the fact that their sons may be degraded to the bottom level of the community. Unless some opportunities other than farming are available to them, the small owners will eventually become landless laborers. Some of them will not be able to marry and perpetuate their families' names. The movement upward on the agricultural ladder is limited, but the movement downward is rapid. As an inevitable consequence, the size of the average farm remains at a minimum.

PART II

YITS'UN: RURAL INDUSTRY AND THE LAND

WHILE we were in Luts'un we became great friends with a villager whom we called Uncle Chang. He was a talkative old man. One day he suggested that we should go to a village called Yits'un and make an investigation of the paper industry there. From his standpoint, our investigation in Luts'un would prove futile because there was nothing in particular which would make us rich. But Yits'un, he suggested, would be worth an adventure. It seems, from the inaccurate and exaggerated narration of Uncle Chang, that at the end of the river which passes by Luts'un there is a place quite similar to our ancient poet Tao Yuen-ming's imaginary resort for hermits. Among the mountains of red stone, which are believed to have once been burned by a heavenly fire, a village is found along the great river, locally called Luyi River—the greatest river that Uncle Chang had every seen and one he could never forget. Thriving bamboos grow everywhere in the valley. The villagers all live on papermaking. Uncle Chang said with great enthusiasm: "Every house in the village makes paper. Go and open a big, big factory, and we all will be rich." His eloquence was persuasive. However, instead of looking for a hidden fortune, we were attracted by the opportunity to investigate a village where a traditional rural industry is highly developed. We made our trip.

Yits'un is about 50 km. south of Luts'un. The river is not navigable. When the water level is low, one can reach the place from Luts'un in one day by following the river bed. But in the rainy season travelers have to take a roundabout route. We traveled by the latter and spent ten days on horseback. The trip was not all pleasant. The village is situated in a narrow valley—perhaps better called a "gorge"—at a sharp turning of the river, which is about 150 meters in width.

Yits'un is a small village, consisting of 54 households, which form one clan, and having a population of 236. There are 9 paper mills, owned by 20 households. There are 35 households which are engaged in papermaking. Although Uncle Chang's statement was exaggerated, the importance of the paper industry in the village is obvious. Side by side with the paper industry, we find another popular craft among the people: this is basketry. There are 23 households engaged in the latter craft. Roughly speaking, the village can be divided into two groups: the papermakers and the basketmakers. There are overlapping cases, but the dividing-line is significant. It separates the rich from the poor. The papermakers fall on one side of the line; among them we find the village magnates, who possess most of the village land. On the other side of the line are the poor peasants, whose landholdings are too small to provide them with even enough food. It is this structure that we shall analyze in the following pages.

CHAPTER XII

LAND UTILIZATION

I. IRRIGATION

ALTHOUGH the Luyi River, which comes from the north, has become a large stream by the time it enters the village, the gorge is so deep that the cultivated land does not easily profit by its water. The rainy season lasts from May to August. When it rains, the whole valley is filled with water; but when it stops raining, the water level goes down again. This kind of flood and recession occurs several times a year. In August, 1939, there was a big flood. The water level came up even to the village site and destroyed nearly all the crops, both rice and vegetables. We arrived there in October of that year and found no vegetables whatever obtainable in the village. We saw heaps of uprooted rice, which had dried out and was good only for feeding pigs. The entire crop was destroyed. At this time there was a heavy deposit of sand in the fields. Part of the bamboos were laid flat. Debris still clung to the bamboos, showing that the water had come up about 30 feet above the lower level of land. This is why the villagers build their homesites high up above the river. Otherwise, even their houses might be flooded. When we were walking along the river, we met some villagers. They warned us: "Don't go to that side of the river in the evening!" Later they told us many stories of how women had drowned in crossing the river. From their accounts we had a vivid impression of their dread and dislike of the river. The river is felt to be not a source of livelihood but a threat. However, the villagers are always trying to utilize the water. In 1938 they tried to construct an irrigation ditch—from a point about 7 miles up the river, in order to make it run on a level with their fields. Shortly before they started their work, the Irrigation Committee of the province sent a surveyor to make a plan for them, and they discovered that the place they had chosen for their ditch was not far enough up the stream. In order to reach a place in the river channel from which the water would run, they would be compelled to go much farther up still. This would have been very expensive; so at last they gave up the plan entirely.

The only possible way to utilize the water in the river, under present circumstances, is to draw it up by means of water wheels. The wheel is of wood, is about 30 feet in diameter, and is run by water power. The water pours over a dam and fills the buckets attached to the wheel. As the wheel goes up, the water empties into a ditch and runs into the fields. Each wheel can irrigate from 30 to 40 *kung* of land. When the river water reaches a higher level, a wheel may irrigate from 50 to 60 *kung*. But land lying more than 30 feet above the water level cannot be irrigated by this method. In 1939 the cost, according to the price level of October, 1939, of building a dam was $1,000; and a wheel cost $100. Every year the dam must be repaired, at a cost of $100; and the wheel also, at a cost of $50. Around the village there are six dams and eleven wheels which work. Only three of these six dams are owned jointly by people of the village. The other three belong to other villages. The cost of the dam and the wheel is shared among the land-owners proportionately, according to the amount of land owned and irrigated. When we arrived, four of the wheels had been partly demolished by the flood. Only two wheels were working.

The lands that can be irrigated by these wheels are limited to those on the lower level, as stated above. Those located a little above depend on rain water alone. Every year, before the rainy season comes, the people are busy digging ditches and dikes to direct the streams coming from the top of the mountain onto their land. If the rain is not sufficient, the upper land will be too dry to cultivate. We were told that, a few years ago, they gave up planting on this higher land because during May and June it did not rain.

This type of irrigation shows clearly the limitations of agriculture in this region and the influences which force the people to extend their efforts beyond farming.

II. THE SOIL AND THE CROP

Agriculture in this village is restricted not only by the amount of water available but also by the topography. The village is located on a sharp turn of the Luyi River. The slope is very steep, while the valley is very narrow. After long erosion sandstone becomes broken into small pieces, so that it easily crumbles away. On this sandstone land, dark red in color, nothing can be grown—not a single blade of grass. When it rains, the water does not soak in; it runs off quickly and washes the sandy fragments down onto the valley. Thus the lower level is always covered with a deposit of sand. Only in the places which

are both near the river and somewhat removed from the moun-
taintop is the quality of the soil a little better. The village fields are
differentiated into four types, according to the position of each up or
down the slope. The first type, at the highest level, is called "dry land";
the second is "dry field"; the third type, land which can be irrigated,
is the "wheel-field"; and the fourth is the "sandy land." They use
two terms to distinguish land according to the use to which it is put:
"field" is used for land which will grow rice; "land" for soil which will
not grow rice.

In this connection we shall define what a unit of land is here, since it
will be useful for our later discussions. The unit is called a *kung*, which
is, as we have seen in Luts'un, not a unit of actual size but a functional
unit, determined by the amount of labor needed in cultivation. For
the sake of comparison, we measured roughly the actual size of each
kung and found it to be, on the average, about 320 square meters—
larger than the amount denoted by the same term in Luts'un. In
Yits'un about 2 *kung* will cover 1 *mow*.

Now we may discuss the local classification of land. First, the "dry
land." "Dry land" is the top level of the mountain. Cactus and
boughs are used to make fences around the individual plots here. The
hill is dark red in color. It is loose and infertile and is only a little better than sand. The value of this land is very low: in 1939 it was only
about $30 a *kung*. Peanuts, soybeans, potatoes, cotton, and tobacco
may be grown here; but the amounts produced are very limited—
insufficient to supply even the villagers themselves. Some of this dry
land, once cleared, is now no longer used, because it is not worth the
effort. The cultivated portion is to be found mainly near the small
mountain streams. But when the rains come, this land often washes
out, since the momentum of the water is very great. In the deserted
plots there are sometimes bamboos, but these are very small. Only one
kind of tree, the tree cotton, suits this type of land, and it has been
introduced only recently. The villagers told us: "It is true, it is very
easy to grow in this land. One seed will grow into one tree. When you
chop it down, it grows again. In about one year you get a tree an inch
in diameter and about five feet high. In three or four years it will
flower and give cotton." From an economic viewpoint, this tree is very
profitable. The wood can be used for making washbasins, buckets, and
steamers for cooking rice. Each tree, a foot and a half in diameter, will
fetch a price of $20; a smaller one, about a half a foot in diameter,
brings $5.00. The flower can be used in medicine and also to feed pigs,

F*

and the fibers from the seed pods, which bring a price of 25–30 cents a pound, can be used in pillows. Moreover, experiments are being made on the use of these fibers in textiles, and there is some promise that they may be useful industrially.

The next level is the "dry field." The soil here is yellow and whitish in color and is clayey. This land produces only a single crop of rice. During April and May, at the beginning of the rainy season, the villagers collect the water in streams and build small irrigation ditches, which must be cleared and repaired every year. Before the land can be plowed, water must remain on it some time, in order to allow it to become thoroughly saturated, for the dry season has rendered it so hard and dry that nothing will grow upon it. The land value here is about $50 a *kung*.

Next to this "dry field," somewhat lower in level, is the double-cropped land which is planted in broad bean and rice. This is called the "irrigated field," or "wheel-field," because the water for it is carried in by water wheels. This land is brownish black in color and is fertile. The land value varies from $70 to $130. These fields are not easily flooded, as are those located lower down. They do not, therefore, receive a heavy deposit of sand every year. However, in 1939 they were flooded and covered with sand. Unless the sand could be removed, the land could not be used efficiently for growing rice. The villagers were worried about the labor of removing this sand, but they felt it necessary to remove it.

The lowest level has the "sandy land" lying along the river. There is plenty of water for this land, which is yellowish black in color and is very fertile. The sand is deposited when the river floods in June and July. The land is too loose for growing rice; but here may be grown corn, broad beans, rapeseed, peas, wheat, barley, and all sorts of vegetables. The value of the sandy land is $140, even higher than that of the wheel-field.

If we compare the value of the sandy land with that of the wheel-field, we find that of the sandy land is even higher. In other words, the crops grown on the sandy land are more profitable than the rice grown on the wheel-field. After the big flood, this wheel-field turned into sandy land. We might have expected the peasants to change their crops instead of carrying away the sand, but a self-sufficient economy of land utilization is not dependent so much upon actual profit as upon the produce needed for consumption. In Yits'un, at least, they to some extent still preserve the economy of production for direct consumption.

The vegetables and the wheat grown on the sandy soil are as important as the rice on the wheel-field: they are all used directly for family consumption in the village.

Villages like Yits'un, given better facilities for marketing and for transportation, should be able to specialize in handicrafts. Theoretically, from an economic standpoint, it should be very advantageous for them even to give up their efforts to grow foodstuffs. But, in fact, the market for their handicrafts is limited, and transportation facilities are extremely difficult. The nearest market center is located 10 miles away: the second one is 17 miles away; and another market center is 120 miles away. This is mountainous country, so that a round trip of 20 miles takes at least one day; and the cost in transportation is high. Moreover, there are no near-by villages which produce a large amount of foodstuffs that can supply their needs. If the people of Yits'un depended upon having their foodstuffs brought from outside, they would have to pay very high costs for transporting them from distant places. Under these circumstances, there is no way for them to specialize. Since they needed rice, they were forced to move away the sand in order to grow the rice.

From the sandy land, walking toward the river side, we face the flourishing bamboo, forming a high green wall. Under this green shade, looking back to the dry and barren land behind, we feel a real contrast. In an economic sense the bamboos represent a different line of development. We have said that the land behind the bamboos is used mainly for maintenance. But even though the people work very hard on the land, owing to the limitations on size, they cannot get enough to live on; so they have to depend on the bamboos to supplement their needs. From these bamboos they manufacture paper and make baskets, and they export their products in exchange for all those necessities they cannot produce by themselves. The contrast between the products grown for home use and those grown for export is vividly indicated even in the color of these two lands—the vivid green bamboos and the dark-red soil. The belt of land near the river has, for a long time, been used for producing raw materials used as a basis for commercial products. We were told that formerly sugar cane was grown in these lands. From this they made brown sugar, which was sold in the markets in the form of cakes. But now it is difficult to find a trace of that product. The only remnant of the industry is found in one of the temples, where a bamboo sugar-cane press lies in the dust, the only remaining reminder of this phase of economic history in the village. At that time no one thought of using bamboo for industrial purposes. Bamboos were grown only to prevent the sugar-cane field from eroding. Later some Szechwan people used these bamboos for manufacturing paper. A short time after the manufacturing of paper was introduced, sugar cane gave way entirely to bamboo.

On the one hand, we see the villagers trying to remove the sand in order to recover their rice field. On the other hand, we also see that they have no special attachment to their sugar cane, without hesitation substituting bamboo for cane when it seems more profitable to do so. This seems to be a contradiction; but if we examine closely the reason for recovering the rice field and that for substituting bamboo, we may see the difference in motive. The land used for sugar cane was employed in growing export materials which enter into an exchange economy. In an exchange economy, that which determines the product is the profit to be gained. This is different from the principle which determines the growth of produce for use. The purpose of growing commercial products is profit. Once it was demonstrated that papermaking and basketry were more profitable than sugar production, the people were willing to change their crop.

In the economy of this village there are two interrelated parts—self-sufficiency and exchange. Thus, although the main purpose of this section of the report will be an analysis of rural industry, because industry itself is so closely related to agriculture, we must start with an analysis of agriculture.

CHAPTER XIII

FARM LABOR

I. FARMING ACTIVITIES

ONE of the factors which encourage the development of handicrafts in Yits'un is the fact that agriculture cannot utilize fully the labor supply of the village. But if we try to explain why there is a surplus of labor, we have to describe the farming activities themselves.

Farming activities are not entirely controlled by the peasants themselves. Every crop has its own cycle of growth, and those who tend them follow the cycle. In Yits'un the main crops are rice, broad bean, corn, peanuts, and cotton. The time of growth varies for each crop. Table 24 shows how these crops are co-ordinated on the farm. Rice grows from Ku Yu (i.e., from late April to early May) up to Ch'iu Fen (i.e., late September and early October)—about 150 days. The broad bean grows from Shuang Chiang (late October and early November) up to Ch'un Fen (late March and early April)—about 160 days. Corn grows from Li Hsia (in early May) to Pai Lu (in September)—about 120 days. Peanuts grow from Mang Chung (the middle of June) to Han Lu (in October)—about 135 days. Cotton grows from Mang Chung to Shuang Chiang—about 145 days. From this table we can see that rice, corn, peanuts, and cotton are all grown from summer to autumn. Rice is about one or two periods earlier than corn. Peanuts and cotton start at about the same time. Only the broad bean grows in winter and spring; so it follows the others in completing the cycle, for those crops which grow at the same time cannot occupy the same land. For instance, the dry land, if used to grow peanuts, cannot be used to grow cotton, since peanuts and cotton are mutually exclusive in land utilization. The broad bean and rice or corn are complementary crops, which succeed one another and can occupy the same land. On the wheel-field and sandy land there can be double crops. In farming, the work can be divided into several types, according to its nature. For instance, rice can be roughly divided into four types of work: sowing of seeds, transplanting, weeding, and harvest. Around Ku Yu, "if the time is right" (meaning weather is normal), the seeds can be germi-

TABLE 24
FARMING CALENDAR

CROP	RICE			BROAD BEAN			CORN			COTTON			PEANUT		
SOIL	Wheat- or Dry Field			Wheat-Field or Sandy Land			Sandy Land			Dry Land			Dry Land		
	Process of Growth	Farming Activity	Period for Work	Process of Growth	Farming Activity	Period for Work	Process of Growth	Farming Activity	Period for Work	Process of Growth	Farming Activity	Period for Work	Process of Growth	Farming Activity	Period for Work
	About 150 days	Trans-planting, Sowing, Weed-ing, Har-vesting	About 45 days, About 30 days, About 45 days, About 45 days	About 160 days	Harvesting, Planting	About 20 days, About 30 days	About 120 days	Planting, Harvesting	About 45 days, About 40 days	About 145 days	Planting, Harvesting	About 15 days, About 55 days	About 135 days	Planting, Harvesting	About 15 days, About 70 days

Li Ch'un
Yu Shui
Ching Che
Ch'un Fen
Ch'ing Ming
Ku Yu
Li Hsia
Hsiao Man
Mang Chung
Hsia Chih
Hsiao Shu
Ta Shu
Li Ch'iu
Ch'u Shu
Pai Lu
Chiu Fen
Han Lu
Shuang Chiang
Li Tung
Hsiao Hsueh
Ta Hsueh
Tung Chih
Hsiao Han
Ta Han

nated and sown in a nursery bed. It takes forty days for the growth of the young shoots. During these forty days there is very little work on the farm—just the labor of keeping water on the plants. When the young shoots are matured, they will be transplanted into the main field. When the transplanting is done, there will be another forty-five days of slack labor. Then the weeding is begun. The weeding should not be started too early, because the roots of the young plants might be loosened. But, if weeded too late, the rice will not grow well. After weeding, there is another slack period of forty to forty-five days. Then comes the harvest. All these periods of work should be performed at definite times. They cannot be hurried, and they cannot be delayed. The same is true of the broad bean and of the corn, but these can be handled with less strictness.

Since most of the crops are in the ground during summer and autumn, the peasants are busy during these two periods, and work slacks off the rest of the time. But, even in the busy time, work is discontinuous; and there are periods when time off is taken.

For the various families, farming activities are not simultaneous. Some of the households will begin earlier than others. In agriculture there is no strict rule as to the date of beginning. For instance, we know that one family sowed rice three days after Li Hsia and harvested and reaped eight days after Ch'iu Fen—that is, 150 days after sowing. Another family sowed one day before Hsiao Man, and their harvest occurred at Han Lu—about 147 days after sowing. There was a difference of 11 days in sowing, but in the harvest a difference of only 8 days; and in the entire period of growth a difference of only 3 days. With a difference in starting-points, these two houses had worked on different days throughout the period. However, there is a limit to this elasticity. For instance, rice is normally sown at Ku Yu, but it could not be sown earlier than Ch'ing Ming or later than Li Hsia. The period during which a choice of time can be made amounts to 30 days. This shifting of time may be used for the adjustment of the labor supply.

II. ADJUSTMENT OF LABOR

In the above section we mentioned that each crop has its own cycle of growth and that for each part of the cycle which requires a different type of work there is a definite period for completion. Therefore, the same amount of labor may be insufficient for one section or too much for another. In this way the problem arises of how best to utilize each individual's labor in farming.

Let us take a concrete instance. A household with three members needs about 19 *piculs* of rice. In the best wheel-field each *kung* will produce 1.5 *piculs* of unhusked rice. Thus, 13 *kung* of land will be needed to supply food for the household. If we assume that, for the harvest, two adults work on the farm and leave a girl to take care of the household, each *kung* of land requires 1.5 female laborers and 1.5 male laborers to do the threshing; added to this, workers must bind the bundles of rice straw and carry them home. Thus, for the whole farm of 13 *kung* of land, one man and one woman should work nineteen and one-half days to complete the harvest. But it is desirable that the work be completed one week after the rice has ripened. Otherwise, owing to rain or wind, there will be waste. If the householders are going to be able to complete their task in a period so short, they must have some help. If they hire help, they have to pay $25 for wages and food for two women and two men for that work. If they don't wish to spend this amount and also wish to avoid waste in the field, they can resort to a system of exchange labor. This is a common practice in the village. Since individual households may start their farm work at different dates, one household may harvest while another has not yet begun; and, as a result, one neighbor can help another. This is how labor is adjusted to the situation. In fact, this system enables the people to shorten the period of unemployment and to give more opportunities for work on the farm. But even with this system they still have a long period of unemployment in the field. From Hsaio Hsueh to Ch'un Fen there is, in the whole village, practically no work on the farms; and during this long period, if the people are not otherwise employed, labor is wasted. How to utilize this time becomes an important problem for the peasants.

III. ESTIMATE OF THE LABOR REQUIRED ON A UNIT OF LAND

Now we may ask how much labor is needed for all the farms of this village; and we shall ask, too, whether during the busiest period of farming the village has enough labor supply? Have they still a surplus? To answer these problems we must estimate the total labor requirements for a unit of land.

It is difficult to speak of labor units in farming. Usually a unit of labor means a peasant's work for one day. But, because of the difficult physical conditions each individual will not supply the same amount of labor in one day. "One day" is also somewhat vague. There is no definite amount of work done on each day, nor is a check kept on the amount of time spent. Once, when we were walking in the village, we saw an old man bringing a hired aboriginal laborer to the field when it was already ten o'clock in the morning. If this laborer were to work until dusk, the time spent would total only about seven hours. This was not a regular procedure in the village; the aboriginals are recognized as lazy. But even for those who work energetically, one day's work will not be over eight hours. Moreover, farming work is usually irregular. We once saw a woman take a hoe and go out to dig up the soil of her field in late afternoon. In the busy time, however, they do as much work as they can manage. But following our observations in Luts'un, we are convinced that the peasants' real work day rarely exceeds nine hours, including frequent time off; and so it seems to us that the unit of labor given by J. L. Buck[1] as ten hours daily is unjustified. Nor does Buck explain why he takes ten hours as his unit.

The labor required for each crop is again different. Let us take the dry field and the double-cropped wheel-field for rice cultivation first. The different quality of soil demands a different amount of labor. So, for the wheel-field we shall classify work according to the two grades of land—high and low. Table 25 gives the amount of work for these three types of fields: dry fields and the two grades of wheel-field. The figures in this table are the results of long discussions with many people. Each informant gave slightly different answers; what is given in this table is a rough estimate. We differentiated female and male labor. However, unlike the practice in Luts'un, the sex differentiation in work is not very strict here. We ourselves have seen women digging the soil.

The problem of estimating the amount of labor needed for other crops is much more complicated. There are many different crops growing in the land, and each one has different labor requirements. Moreover, the work put on these crops is not regular but intermittent. The total area of this kind of land consists of about only 28.6 per cent of the total, and for the better sandy land it is only of about 16.5 per cent. On this area there are about twenty different types of crop; and since each crop occupies only a small area, it is not important to make this inquiry. The difficulties of estimating the labor required on the land for these crops can be seen; but without an estimate of some sort, we should not be able to figure out the total amount of labor required in the village. As a result, we could only work indirectly by finding out the proportion of labor required on the land and in the field. For

[1] *Chinese Farming Economy*, p. 20.

EARTHBOUND CHINA

TABLE 25

LABOR REQUIREMENTS

OCCUPATION	DRY FIELD		WHEEL-FIELD			
			High Grade		Low Grade	
	Male	Female	Male	Female	Male	Female
Sowing seeds*	0.03	....	0.03	....	0.03	....
Repairing ditches†	4.0	....	....	....	....	....
Repairing farm dikes	1.0	....	1.0	....	1.0	....
Fertilizing‡	1.0	....	1.0	....	1.0	....
Ploughing§	0.3	....	0.3	....	0.3	....
Transplanting:						
Bringing young shoots from nursery to the field	....	....	....	....	....	....
Planting young shoots	....	1.0	....	1.0	....	1.0
Weeding, first‖	....	1.5	....	1.5	....	1.5
Weeding, second	....	1.5	....	1.5	....	1.5
Cutting weeds	....	0.5	....	0.5	....	0.5
Collecting ripened rice	....	1.5	....	1.5	....	1.5
Thrashing	1.5	....	1.5	....	1.5	....
Stacking the straw	0.3	....	0.3	....	0.3	....
Digging ditches for broad beans¶	....	....	1.0	....	1.0	....
Planting broad beans	....	....	....	2.0	....	2.0
Pounding the soil	....	....	1.0	....	1.0	....
Adding fertilizer**	....	....	1.0	....	1.0	....
Collecting broad beans††	....	....	....	3.0	....	1.0
Beating broad beans	....	....	....	4.0	....	2.0
Digging soil‡‡	....	....	4.0	....	6.0	....
Preparing nursery field	0.6	....	0.6	....	....	....
Preparing single-crop field§§	4.0	....	....	....	....	....
Total	15.73	6.0	14.73	15.0	16.73	11.0

* One man can sow 6 *kung* a day. Each *kung* of young shoots transplanted is enough for 5 *kung* of field.

† The dry field depends on rain water brought in by irrigation ditches. The wheel-field does not require labor of this kind.

‡ The work of fertilizing consists mainly in the transportation of the fertilizer. Thus, the further the farm, the more labor is needed. A distant farm needs 4 units of labor.

§ Buffaloes are used in ploughing. One man (with buffalo) can plough 3 *kung* of land in a day.

‖ Some farms are weeded only once.

¶ The dry field is single-cropped.

** Sometimes no fertilizer is added during this time.

†† Beans are abundant on the high-grade farms, and this makes more labor in harvesting.

‡‡ Better land requires less labor in digging.

§§ On the dry field, sometimes 7–8 units are needed when the soil is too dry.

this ratio we had to depend on Buck—that is, for the ratio between rice and other crops. According to Buck, except for cotton and rapeseed, the amount of labor required for other crops is approximately only one-half that required for the rice field.[2] Elsewhere in Buck's work he has estimated that, except for tobacco, all the other minor crops require less labor than rice. Some of them, like peas, require only one-fourth; wheat, one-half; and rapeseed, five-eighths, the labor needed for rice.[3] On the average, it will not be far from true to say that one-half of the labor needed for rice will be sufficient for the other crops. We got the impression from talking to the peasants that, except for tobacco and vegetables, which require intensive farming, the rest are all cultivated by extensive farming, which means that much less labor is needed. In our estimate, according to that ratio, the labor required for all other crops besides rice amounts, in the whole village, to one-half the labor needed for rice.

IV. AREA OF CULTIVATED LAND AND LABOR SUPPLY

If we wish to know whether there is a surplus of labor in agriculture in the village, we must have two other figures—the total area of cultivated land and the population—from which we may estimate the total amount of labor supply. How did we get these figures? The government had not yet completed the census, and the official reports of the land survey, if we had been able to obtain them, would have been far from reliable.

Under the circumstances, we could not obtain the population data by direct enumeration. The village had been visited by outsiders like us only twice before in its history. The first visitors were the men who came to measure the water level; the second, the surveyors sent by the government to survey the land. Our party made the third group of visitors. The village persisted in regarding us as in some way connected with the government and in calling us officials. If these "officials" should be too inquisitive in regard to the population, the people would become very suspicious. The following incident occurred. The headman of the village was actually keeping some of the names of householders off the village records in order to exempt them from taxation. As a result, when his superior attempted to send us these records through him, he did not deliver them to us. We pretended ignorance of this, however. Actually, we did not need the document, be-

---

[2] *Ibid.*, p. 228.

[3] Buck, *Land Utilization in China*, p. 302, Table 14.

cause in a small village of this sort everyone knows everyone else. In time we found those who trusted us; these people gave us a complete report on each household.

Since the village consists of only fifty-four households and the households belong to one clan, the villagers knew very clearly who usually worked on the fields and who did not. We questioned our informants on each house and marked down the number of people living there and also the numbers of those who occupied themselves with farm work. Later on, when we became more familiar with the households, we checked our data. Our only difficulty lay in getting information on the age of the people. People did not even know their own ages.

We had not obtained the report of the land surveyor, and after our experience in Luts'un we felt it would not be wise to ask the owners directly how much land they had. We worked it out very well in Luts'un by the method of asking others. But in the case of Yits'un it was more complicated, for many owners had land in distant places and the plots were scattered. Few knew exactly the place and the amount of land owned by their neighbors. But they did know the amount of rent collected for this distant land. Practically all this distant land was rented out, and from this rent we could estimate the amount of land owned.

According to our estimate, the actual numbers of people who take part in farm work are 51 men and 61 women, who vary in age from fifteen to sixty-four (total population is 236). The total amount of rice land owned by the villagers of Yits'un is 1,177.5 *kung*. Of this amount, 382 *kung* are rented to outsiders and an additional 20 *kung* are rented from outsiders; so the total amount under cultivation by the villagers is 815.5 *kung*. Besides this, there are 472 *kung* for other crops.

According to the above analysis, the busiest periods in farming are, as one can see from Table 25, the time of transplanting and the time of harvest. Is this village self-sufficient in labor for these two periods of work? Let us first look at the transplanting. This activity takes forty-five days. If the 51 men and 61 women all work every day during that period, we will have 2,295 units of male labor and 2,745 units of female labor. Each *kung* of land requires 3 male laborers and 1 female laborer. All the fields under cultivation require 2,146.5 units of male labor and 815.5 units of female labor. There is, accordingly, a shortage of 151.5 units of male labor but a surplus of 1,929.5 units of female labor. Since in this village the sex division of work is not so strict, the shortage can be easily made up by the female laborers. There is, therefore, a net surplus of 1,778 units of labor. But at the same time there is work on the corn, peanuts, and cotton crops. If all the land not used for rice (472 *kung*) were used to grow these crops (and, according to the above, each *kung* of land requires 2 units of labor daily during the growing season), then the total requirement would be 944 units, still leaving a surplus of 834 units.

The harvest covers a period of work lasting from thirty to forty-five days. If thirty days is taken as our basis of calculation, the total supply of labor is 1,830 units of female labor and 1,530 units of male labor. Each *kung* of land requires 1.8 male labor units and 1.5 female labor units. The total requirements on the fields of this village are 1,467.9 units of male labor and 1,223.3 units of female labor. Thus there is a surplus of 62 units of male labor and 607.7 units of female labor—669 units surplus in all. During the harvest period, moreover, there is no work on other crops. Thus, according to the above estimate, in this village, even during the busy periods, there is always a certain amount of surplus labor. And this estimate is based on actual labor supply only. If we include the potential labor supply, such as the mill-owners, some of the basketmakers and the wealthier women, and some hired labor, the amount of surplus will be much larger. During the remainder of the year the villagers are mostly unengaged, and it is now clear that agriculture in this village cannot fully utilize the labor supply. Land is limited, and the village is overpopulated. The villagers cannot depend on land for full employment, and this gives rise to industry.

CHAPTER XIV

INVESTMENTS IN AGRICULTURE

I. FARMING PROFITS

YITS'UN is located in the interior in mountainous country—a village limited in land and overpopulated. These factors give rise to a surplus of agricultural labor. On these reddish, sandy slopes grow few green trees and little grass; in the valley the lands are very poor. In order to cultivate this soil much energy must be spent, and little profit is gained. The margin of cultivation is easily reached. Owing to the diminishing returns on land, on this marginal land no profit can be gained. If the people wish to invest further in land, they must spread out. Their lands extend far beyond the village, but this extension is also limited by present farming techniques and by bad transportation. Since the land cannot absorb the increase in capital, surplus capital, wherever it exists, will go outside agriculture. This encourages the development of handicrafts in village life.

Now we shall examine outlay and income from the land in order to discover what the profits are from farming. I shall confine my discussion to the rice field, since there are only small amounts of other crops, and these are difficult to assess. These other crops are merely supplementary to the village economy; they are not the staple food. The people do not try to solve deficiencies in their family budgets by developing these subsidiary crops. They are, therefore, not important in discussing profit in agriculture.

From the estimates in the last chapter on the amount of labor required in farming we can calculate the cost of labor, which includes wages and food. To this we may add the cost of fertilizer, seed, rent for the buffalo and fodder for it, the depreciation of tools, and the land tax, as listed in Table 26. In this table we take the price level for November, 1939.

It is difficult to estimate the item for fertilizer because there is no sale of fertilizer and therefore no price. It is supplied by the manure of pigs and buffaloes which are owned by the various households. (These farmers do not use human manure but only that of animals. We did not see any pits for human manure anywhere.) For supplying the need for fertilizer each household has some animals. No money is made on pigs, only barely enough to pay for their upkeep; but use is made of the manure. In order to calculate the cost of manure, we shall have to make use of the estimate we worked out in Luts'un. This estimate, we may add, has been corrected by multiplying it by four, in accordance with the rise in the price level. According to this, fertilizing each *kung* of land once costs $1.00. The dry field is only fertilized once; the double-cropped wheat-land, twice. The expenses for labor of fertilizing are included under labor costs.

TABLE 26

INVESTMENT

(Per *Kung*, or ½ *Mow*)

	Dry Field	First-Grade Wheat-Field	Second-Grade Wheat-Field
Fertilizer..................	$ 1.00	$ 2.00	$ 2.00
Seed:			
Rice, *sheng*.............	1.68	1.68	1.68
Broad bean, 3 *sheng*......	....	2.40	2.40
Wage.....................	9.67	11.87	11.67
Food for laborers..........	8.70	11.89	11.09
Rent for buffalo...........	0.17	0.17	0.17
Fodder for buffalo.........	0.07	0.07	0.07
Depreciation of tools.......	0.40	1.40	1.40
Land tax.................	0.04	0.16	0.08
Total.................	$21.73	$31.64	$30.56

* A common Chinese unit of measure roughly equal to 1 liter.

The daily wage at the time we were in Yits'un was 50 cents for a male, and 30 cents for a female, worker. Food was provided by the employer, and the average consumption of food by four laborers daily amounted to 7 pounds of husked rice. The rent for the buffalo which is used for plowing was 50 cents a day, and the cost of fodder was 20 cents. Each buffalo can plow 3 *kung* of land each day. The depreciation in tools follows the estimate given for Luts'un, corrected for the price level, and amounted to about 40 cents for each *kung*. But for the wheelland of Yits'un we included the repairing of the water wheels and the dams; so we added $1.00 to the costs.

From Table 27 we can see that, in farming, labor costs are the most expensive item. They make up 84.7 per cent of the total expenses for the dry field, 75 per cent for the high-grade wheat-field, and 74.5 per cent for the second-grade. This indicates the primitiveness of the farming techniques. Most of the work is done by manual labor, a fact which makes the increasing of investments difficult. To get the price of rice and beans, we faced another problem. In this village there is no market and no store. Before the harvest many of the villagers who have not enough rice for themselves must go out and buy rice elsewhere. The market to which they go is 17 miles northwest of the village. This is a place where rice is produced in quantity and where the price of rice is lower. After the harvest, some of the villagers who need money will sell their reserve rice in a market 10 miles to the southeast, where rice prices are high. Thus, they buy rice from the rice-producing areas where rice is cheaper, and they sell where prices are higher. The same is true with beans. In Table 27 we have used the higher price—that is,

TABLE 27

INCOME

(Per *Kung*, or ½ *Mow*)

	DRY FIELD		FIRST-GRADE WHEEL-FIELD		SECOND-GRADE WHEEL-FIELD	
	Quantity	Value	Quantity	Value	Quantity	Value
Rice	10 *piculs*	$28.00	15 *piculs*	$42.00	10 *piculs*	$28.00
Straw	400 bundles	1.20	400 bundles	1.20	400 bundles	1.20
Beans	....	....	8 *shen*	6.40	5 *shen*	4.00
Total.....	....	$29.20	....	$49.60	....	$33.20

the price at which the villagers sell. The rice straw is used ordinarily to feed the buffaloes and horses. If the villagers do not have sufficient straw for this purpose, they will buy some from a neighbor, at the cost of 3 cents a bundle.

In Table 28 are listed the land values and the amount of current capital invested in a year. From these two tables (27 and 28) we get the total amount of investment and the rate of profit.

II. FARM MANAGEMENT

From Table 28 we can see the low rate of profit. It hardly exceeds 12 per cent, and the lowest is only 3 per cent. This shows that the villagers have already come to the margin of cultivation of the land. From this poor land the cultivators will get nothing except their wage. They take up the land, not for profit, but to give themselves employment. They do not employ labor but work for themselves; and in this respect Yits'un is markedly different from Luts'un, where the system of hired labor is common.

The system of hired labor developed in Luts'un, as compared with Yits'un, as we can see now very clearly, is based upon the fertility of the soil in the latter community. That is, after paying the cost of production, the owners in Luts'un can still enjoy a certain amount of profit. The productivity of the land there is high, and the amount of labor which has to be spent there is smaller than in Yits'un. On a double-cropped farm on 320 square meters in Yits'un there will be produced only 220 pounds of rice, but 347 pounds will be produced in Luts'un. For this, 29 units of labor will be required in Yits'un and only 26 units of labor in Luts'un. This shows the lower productivity of the land in Yits'un.

TABLE 28

INVESTMENT AND PROFIT

(Per *Kung*, or ½ *Mow*)

	Cost of Production	Total Income	Profit	Land Value	Current Expenses	Rate of Profit (Percentage)
Dry land..................	$21.73	$29.20	$ 7.47	$ 50.00	$ 71.73	10.0
First-grade wheat-field......	31.64	49.60	17.96	120.00	151.64	11.8
Second-grade wheat-field....	30.56	33.20	2.64	70.00	100.56	2.6

On this poorer land the system of hired labor cannot be developed because the owner will get very little or nothing after paying out wages. The same situation is true of tenancy. After the tenant has paid out one-half of his product to the owner as rent, his income will be insufficient to pay the cost of production. If tenants rent land and work it themselves, they actually receive a much lower return from their labor than the current wage. (The real wage for tenants is computed by subtracting from total income the rent and other costs of production.) Take 1 *kung* of dry field as an example. After paying rent and other costs of living, the tenant will have an income of $3.18. But he has employed 16 units of male labor and 6 units of female labor. Therefore, the wage for each unit of male labor is only 16 cents and of female labor 9.6 cents. On high-grade wheat-field, following the same system of calculation, the wage for male labor is 37 cents and for female labor 22 cents. On the poor grade of wheat-field the total amount of money for wages is only 39 cents; so the tenants receive very little besides food. But current wages are 50 cents for a male and 30 cents for a female.

Thus the tenants, after working a year for themselves, receive actually less for their time than the hired laborers. But, on the other hand, there are few opportunities for hired labor. Moreover, the social status of a tenant is higher than that of a day laborer.

It is different in Luts'un. The tenants there, after paying their rent and other costs of production besides labor, have a surplus. If this amount of surplus is computed as wage in 1938 on the high-grade land, the male laborer got 24 cents, the female laborer 12 cents; on the medium-grade land 14 cents for the male laborer, 7 cents for the female laborer; and on the lower-grade land, 1.2 cents for the male and 0.6 cents for the female. The current wage at that time was 10 cents for male labor and 5 cents for female. Except for the lower-grade land the tenants will get more than the hired laborers. This is how some of the tenants in Luts'un can employ laborers on their farms and still enjoy a certain amount of profit, and it explains the development of hired labor and tenancy in Luts'un.

From this analysis of the income of the tenants it will follow that the system of tenancy will not be able to function in Yits'un. But in the following section we shall bring out the point that there is a group of aboriginal folk living around the village who have a much lower standard of living. They will accept a lower tenant income than is accepted by the native inhabitants of these villages.

From these cases we can throw some light on the theory of rent. When we say that certain land has reached the margin of cultivation, we are speaking from a certain fixed wage, which is included in the cost of production. But for those who work on the land themselves, the wage is not a real item of expenditure. It is a part of their standard of living. So, if they are willing to accept a lower standard, they can continue their work on the land even if the return on their labor is lower than the nominal wage in the market. Different standards exist in the community as to which land is worth something for cultivation. And we must recognize that the standard of living is elastic. For some classical economists, rent has been viewed as a result of the differential productivity of land; but we think it is clearer to say that it may be a result of differentiated standards of living. Instead of approaching the problem from the point of view which sees the land as possessed of inherent values, we suggest that it be viewed from the point of view of the farmer. Rent may be determined by the willingness of an individual to rent land even though, by so doing, he must accept a lower standard of living.

III. THE EXTENSION OF LANDHOLDING AND ITS LIMITATION

The land within the boundary of the village is limited, and that which can be cultivated has already been occupied. We have seen that the villagers have even tried cultivating worthless land, although later they gave up. This huge mountain of sandy stones is of no value for agriculture. The only means for further investment in land is to buy land from other villages. This is the one way out. Several miles around this village there is undeveloped land, inhabited mostly by aborigines. This land is cheap; and by moneylending the rich houses of Yits'un are gradually concentrating on the ownership of land around them, like a grasping hand, reaching out as far as 17 miles from the village.

The total amount of land owned by the villagers is 1,649.5 *kung*. In the village there are only 535.5 *kung*. This amount is 32.2 per cent of the total. The rest, nearly two-thirds of the land, lies outside the boundary of the village. From this we can see how far the villagers have spread out.

If we discuss separately the land inside and that lying outside the village, we find that the land used for rice cultivation in the village consists of 264 *kung* and that that for other crops amounts to 266.5 *kung*. But outside the village are 913.5 *kung* of rice fields and only 200.5 *kung* for other crops. That is to say, in the village, land is almost equally divided in its use between rice and other crops, while outside there is 4.4 times more land used for rice cultivation than used for other crops. Taking the rice fields only, we find that about 77.6 per cent of them lie outside the village. This extension of rice fields is due to the fact that the people have sufficient vegetables and other subsidiary crops in the village, but they need rice. In Table 29 we can see the distribution of types of land inside and outside of the village.

Among the lands outside the village there are 192 *kung* of wheat-field and 190 *kung* of dry field rented to outsiders—a total of 382 *kung*—equivalent to 41.8 per cent of the field outside the village or 32.5 per cent of the total fields. Although the villagers have spread out very far from the villages, there is a limit of extension. When land is too far away, the farmers cannot cultivate it by themselves but must rent it to outsiders. With existing difficulties of transportation it is not only hard for the owners themselves to work on this distant land but it is also difficult to rent it out. Thus, those who rent this distant land are mostly people who live nearby, and these are mainly aborigines. Since the owners cannot get people to go out so far, they must accept a lower rent and take local people. We know of a farm, of about 30 *kung* of land, which lies more than 10 miles from the village. It is rented to aborigines, and the rent is only 30 *piculs* of unhusked rice—only about 10 per cent of the rice produced on the land. If the owners should be unwilling to accept this low rent, they would not be able to rent it out at all, and the land would be deserted. Another farm, 7 miles away,

TABLE 29

LOCATION OF LAND

	WHEEL-FIELD		DRY FIELD		SANDY LAND		DRY LAND	
	Size (*Kung*)	Per Cent	Size (*Kung*)	Per Cent	Size (*Kung*)	Per Cent	Size (*Kung*)	Per Cent
Inside	182.0	27.0	82	16.0	137.0	50.2	129.5	65
Outside..........	490.5	73.0	423	84.0	84.0	135.5	70.0	35

gave a rent every year of 100 *piculs*. But a few years before, the tenants asked the owner to lend them, without interest, the seed for broad beans. This request was turned down. As a result, the tenant refused to continue on the farm and the place has not been cultivated for the last two years. This shows the limitation of extension.

The land in this village is poor and incapable of absorbing capital. There are limitations in extension to more distant land, which the owners are not able to manage and cultivate by themselves. When they rent it out, they have to accept lower rent, because of difficulties in finding tenants. So those who possess capital in the village have to find other outlets.

CHAPTER XV
STANDARDS OF LIVING
I. YIELD FROM THE LAND

ALTHOUGH the people of Yits'un live on poor land, they continue to try to make a living through agriculture. Their isolated position in the mountains makes them rely upon their own land for food. If every grain of rice had to be carried over the mountains, if would take all their labor merely for this transportation. Moreover, to get rice from outside they must produce something to exchange for it. Under these circumstances, it is hardly likely that the people of Yits'un will depend on outside supplies rather than attempt to provide for themselves. In order to get enough food, they have cultivated even the marginal lands. They spend a large amount of labor for a mere handful of produce. They have extended their lands outside so that two-thirds of their cultivated land is not within the boundaries of their own village. We have shown that there are limitations both in intensive and extensive farming. We should like to see whether the people have completely solved their food problem. Is the land which is now owned by the people sufficient to supply the needs of the people?

How much rice can the people reap each year on the village lands? In the foregoing chapters we estimated that the villagers possess 672.5 *kung* of wheat-field and 505 *kung* of dry field. Of this amount, 122 *kung* of wheat-field are rented out and 190 *kung* of dry field are rented. They themselves rent 20 *kung* of wheat-field. The high-grade wheat-field yields about 15 *piculs* per *kung* of unhusked rice, and the lower-grade wheat-field yields about 10 *piculs* per *kung*. The best dry field yields about 10 *piculs* per *kung*, and the worst yields about 6 or 7 *piculs*. On the average, the wheat-field yields 12 *piculs* and the dry field 8 *piculs*. The total amount of yield from the self-cultivated wheat-field is 5,760 *piculs;* from the dry field, 2,520 *piculs*. Taking the rent as half of the produce, the people will get 1,270 *piculs* from the rented wheat-fields and 760 *piculs* from the dry fields, making the total annual amount 10,310 *piculs*.

What will be the total amount of rice needed in a year for the whole village? There is a popular saying: "No hunger and no gorging with 30 *piculs*. Not too salty, not unseasoned, with 9 *chin* [12 pounds] of salt." This gives the local estimate of the annual consumption of rice and salt. Thirty *piculs* of unhusked rice are equivalent to about 6.6 *piculs* of husked rice; this gives 440 pounds in weight as the annual consumption. This amount is close to that we got in Luts'un through actual measurement—1.429 pounds for an adult (per day).

Since Yits'un has largely a farming population and since those who work in the fields eat more than others, we may estimate about 500 pounds as the amount of rice consumed annually by an adult. But the amounts consumed by male and female, old and young, are different. To calculate the total need of the village, we must convert the total number of population into the number of adults. We do not have data on the age of this population and can only assume that the age structure is the same as for Luts'un. We will base our estimate upon the modified Atwater system that we used in connection with Luts'un. The total population of 235 in Yits'un is, then, according to this system of conversion, equal to 177 adults, who require 6,030 *piculs* of unhusked rice, leaving a surplus of 4,280 *piculs*.

Is there sufficient surplus to exchange for daily necessities not locally produced? The general standard of living of the Chinese peasants allows 50 per cent of their budget for food. Of this 50 per cent, 80 per cent is rice. The expenditure on rice thus amounts to 40 per cent of the total budget. It appears that the people of this village need about 9,000 *piculs* to exchange for other daily necessities. For maintaining their standard of living up to the level of the ordinary Chinese peasant, there is an annual deficiency of about 5,000 *piculs* of rice. This shows that agriculture alone is not sufficient to sustain the people.

Their natural environment is so poor that agriculture cannot provide them with a livelihood. Moreover, we have been talking about the village as a whole. In fact, the distribution of wealth is not even. There are rich people who possess a larger share of the income from the land. Therefore, the actual deficiency for many of the households will be much larger than that given for the village as a whole.

II. POPULATION PRESSURE

The people of Yits'un all belong to the same clan. It is said that all the households now living in the village are descendants of the same ancestor. This ancestor is said to have come in from the market center in the southeast at a date no longer remembered but not very remote. This old man had four sons, and so there are four divisions of the clan, each of which originally started with the same amount of land. But, because of the difference in rate of increase in offspring in each group and the varying abilities of the members, in the course of years the divisions have become differentiated—some becoming rich, others poor.

Of these four divisions, Division A is the most populous, but Division C has the largest amount of land. Division B has a large number of members and enough land, but Division D has only one household and is very poor. It is said that the present household in Division D is descended from a man who married into the clan from another village, and the division is looked down upon on this account. All recognize that Division C is the richest. The people explained to us that the reason for this was that for several generations there had been only one son, so that the estate had not been divided. And we know that the richest household in this division has had only one son each generation for three generations. The grandfather in this household had no son of his own; so he bought a boy baby from another village. Division A, being the most populous division, is relatively poor because the estate has been divided more often. Division D, being neither rich nor populous, is considered unworthy of its ancestors. It has shrunk in both size and importance.

The population pressure is merciless. Even the children know this. They point to the tomb of their ancestor, saying: "Look at this tomb. It bursts every year, and we have to repair it. His descendants are expanding." The tomb symbolizes the original inheritance; and the expansion of the population, which cannot be contained in it, is represented by the yearly bursting. Every generation there is some increase in the population. People are not inclined to leave the village but crowd together in this small area.

All the houses, which are packed together like the holes in a dovecot, are filled. In each court live four or five families. The ancestral tomb can be repaired or built anew, but to build new houses is more than the people can afford. A few years ago, there was a big fire. When we came, the ruins were still there. Fires are frequent because of the difficulty in bringing water up from the river. The people attribute this to their misfortune in being surrounded by mountains, which, because of their red color, according to traditional belief, symbolize fire.

Still worse is the land situation. It is impossible to maintain the ideal of both wealth in sons and wealth in property at the same time. In several generations without division of the estate they become rich. But if in the next generation they have several sons, the wealth disappears.

The villagers told us that it is not good to leave the village, for a man who does so will not rise in the world. This seems to be really the case. We were told that about twenty years ago a man moved out to the northwest, about 7 miles from the village. This place was still inhabited by aborigines, and the land was cheap. The man brought with him some money and bought a sizable farm. But when he died, one son became a leper, and the other became a vagabond, selling everything his father left. There are several other cases of individuals who have left the village, but these are always cited by the people as examples of failure. One became a bandit and was shot by the soldiers in 1939. Several of them joined the army; but since no messages have been received from them, they are thought to have died. Two others went to stay in a neighboring village to work on making paper, but they earn enough merely to keep going. There is no hope for them to accumulate sufficient money to buy land. However, a few years ago one of the young men, the son of the richest family, left the village in order to study at a high school in a neighboring district. When he graduated, he came back and became a schoolmaster. He is one of the few examples of someone whose leaving the village turned out fortunately. His gain is prestige rather than money.

There are a few cases of young men who marry into other villages on a matrilocal basis. We know two such cases. Of these, one, after the death of his wife, came back to the village again and married there, because his father-in-law in the other village "refused to find another girl for him because he was too lazy." Examples of this sort all tend to substantiate the belief of the villagers that it is unlucky to leave the village. As they explain it, the village is surrounded by big mountains. You cannot even see the source or outlet of the river. This blocked vision symbolizes in the mystic belief of the people the blocked outlet to the fortune of the people. There is "no way out"; and they must be satisfied with their simple life, just barely managing to subsist. "It is not too bad—it cannot be very good." The stagnation of population increases the pressure on the land. Even if they had better land, there would be a limit to the amount available. What can they hope for, then, with the kind of poor soil they do have?

III. RICH AND POOR

The sons of the same ancestor differed both in ability and in luck. The unlucky and the incompetent have been forced to sell their land. To prevent their land from going into other hands, there is an established tradition that one can sell only to his own clan members. So the land circulates among clan members and is gradually concentrated in the hands of a few men. For example, in December, 1939, when we were in the village, a man of Division A, an opium-smoker, sold all his land and even his home to a member of the same division of the clan.

One of the members of Division C, who has the same habit of opium-smoking, has, during the last few years, been gradually selling off all his land and his house to another member of his own division. If a buyer cannot be found in the same division, however, men may sell to members of other divisions. Two brothers in Division A, needing money for the expenses of a funeral, sold a large part of their land to members of Division C, as well as a piece of land to their own division. Another case that we heard of was one in which a man from Division A, also an opium-smoker, sold a *kung* and a half of land to someone in Division C. In this way rich and poor are differentiated. For the rich folk not only have enough food from their own land and are able to buy all their necessities from their own purse, but they also have savings. In the preceding chapter we surveyed the total deficiency in earnings of the village as a whole. This deficiency is not equally distributed throughout the village but is borne on the shoulders of the poor. In Tables 30 and 31 we give the incomes from rice of the individual households, ranging from rich to poor, with a statement of their surpluses or deficiencies. Since the households are assigned to the respective divisions, we can see that most of the rich households are centered in Division C.

IV. NECESSITIES OF LIFE AND DEGREE OF SELF-SUFFICIENCY

From this table we can see that, if the people of the village depended on agriculture alone, there would be twenty-one households deficient in food. This is about two-fifths of the total. The number of households deficient in other necessities is forty-three—that is, four-fifths of the whole. The situation is really desperate. But we must still learn how many of their necessities can be self-supplied. If they can be self-supplied, rice will not be needed to exchange for them. In other words, a new source of income to make up for these deficiencies need

G

TABLE 30
Yield of Rice and Its Place in the Family Budget

Household Order in Wealth from Land	Division of the Clan	Number of People	Amount of Yield Estimated (in *Piculs*)	Surplus or Deficiency for Food Consumption	Surplus or Deficiency for Total Household Expenses
1	C	9	94.80	+	+
2	A	9	79.60	+	+
3	C	5	77.80	+	+
4	C	4	63.00	+	+
5	C	5	54.40	+	+
6	C	4	54.00	+	+
7	C	6	48.00	+	+
8	B	7	46.00	+	+
9	A	3	31.80	+	+
10	B	5	25.60	+	−
11	C	5	24.40	+	−
12	C	4	24.00	+	−
13	C	4	24.00	+	−
14	C	6	21.70	+	−
15	C	3	21.60	+	+
16	C	5	20.00	+	−
17	B	4	19.60	+	−
18	C	4	18.80	+	−
19	A	4	16.80	+	−
20	C	5	15.70	+	−
21	A	3	15.20	+	−
22	C	4	14.00	+	−
23	A	4	13.60	+	−
24	A	5	13.60	+	−
25	A	3	13.60	+	−
26	A	2	13.60	+	+
27	C	3	12.00	+	−
28	B	8	12.00	−	−
29	A	6	11.20	−	−
30	A	3	10.60	−	−
31	C	2	10.00	+	−
32	A	4	9.60	−	−
33	D	4	9.60	−	−
34	A	3	8.80	+	−
35	A	3	8.80	+	−
36	A	3	8.80	+	−
37	B	3	8.80	+	−
38	B	4	8.40	−	−
39	A	6	7.20	−	−
40	A	4	7.00	−	−
41	A	6	6.40	−	−
42	B	5	4.80	−	−
43	A	4	4.40	−	−
44	A	7	4.00	−	−
45	A	3	4.00	−	−
46	A	5	3.60	−	−
47	A	4	3.20	−	−
48	A	2	1.60	−	−
49	A	6	1.00	−	−
50	A	3	0.80	−	−
51	A	3	0.00	−	−
52	A	4	0.00	−	−
53	A	1	0.00	−	−
54	B	4	0.00	−	−

not be found. In this section we shall describe the source of the most important items in daily use.

One item among the comestibles which the people must have, besides rice, is salt. The people do not produce salt themselves but must buy it in the market centers. In December, 1939, salt cost 45 cents a pound. While we were in the village, we found that there was some cheaper salt, costing 36 cents a pound, which had been smuggled into the village. Each adult required 12 pounds; so the whole village will require about 2,700 pounds. This costs about $1,200 and is equivalent in value to 450 *piculs* of unhusked rice. The demand for opium is even more acute. There are far fewer opium-smokers than in former days, but the habit is still strong in some households. We know of three house-

TABLE 31
YIELD OF RICE FOR VILLAGE HOUSEHOLDS
(In *Piculs*)

Household Number and Division	Number of People	Amount of Rice Yield	Food Consumption	Surplus or Deficiency after Food Consumption	Other Expenses	Surplus or Deficiency for Household Expenses
1 (C)............	9	94.80	23.13	71.67	34.70	36.17
2 (A)............	9	79.60	23.13	56.47	34.70	21.77
3 (C)............	5	77.80	12.85	64.95	19.28	45.67
4 (C)............	4	63.00	10.28	52.72	15.42	....

holds (Nos. 52, 53, and 54) who sold their houses and lands because of this habit. Opium exhausts not only their wealth but also their strength. These opium addicts cannot do any really productive work, though the drug sometimes acts as a temporary stimulant.

There are five individuals from households Nos. 12, 18, 21, 22, and 44 who occasionally feel the need for opium. Among these five, householder No. 12 is rich enough to be able to indulge the habit. In another household there is conflict between father and son because the father smokes. The other three smokers are farmers who go to the market centers and use opium to stimulate themselves before leaving and on their return. Unfortunately, the habit serves to use up the results of their labors. Men with the opium habit can never hope to improve their standard of living. Yits'un does not grow opium, and so it has to be brought in from outside.

Vegetables grow on the village lands and can be self-supplied. Before we arrived the village was flooded, and vegetables had to be bought from distant markets; but this was not usual. Pigs, sheep, chickens, and eggs are self-supplied. For the New Year the well-to-do will slaughter a pig and invite their clan members to have a feast, salting and preserving the meat that is left. Twice a year—once in the spring and once in the autumn—the people go to their ancestral tombs and make sacrifices. Divisions A and C then slaughter pigs and distribute meat among their members. In ordinary times there are peddlers who come from outside to sell meat. There are several villages whose members occasionally engage in this business. Since the village of Yits'un is on the river, fish can be caught at times. Every spring, when it is warm, the fish come up to the surface of the water at night. Most of the children and a few adults go out with flaming bamboo torches and catch the fish in baskets. Tea is another article of diet of which the people make a great deal of use; it is bought from peddlers. Formerly sugar was produced in the village, but now it must be bought from the market. Tobacco is grown on the dry land, but insufficiently for the village consumption. Although the folk consume a good deal of wine, they do not brew their own. On the dry land a certain amount of cotton is grown, but too little to amount to much. Still, a few people make cotton thread for their own use or for sale.

The poverty of the people is most clearly shown in their clothing. Most of them wear clothing which is ragged or patched. The brother of the headman wore, every day, a ragged, Western-style overcoat; the children called him "the old soldier" because of this coat. The children are usually without trousers, even in the winter. The little daughter of our landlord was, at eight years of age, still wearing only a shirt. Very few of the garments have cotton linings; so when it is cold the folk prefer to squat around the fire all day. They told us that they needed only one suit a year. This suit, made of cotton, costs about $8.00. But the poorer folk have only one suit every two or three years. The total outlay for clothing in the village amounts to about $2,000, which is equivalent to 700 *piculs* of unhusked rice. The people have no mosquito netting, which is one reason that malaria is so widespread. We brought with us some quinine and in a few days distributed it all. This generosity of ours with regard to the medicine so needed in the village established good relations for us with the village folk.

The beds are bare platforms of boards, with only one cotton blanket as cover when it is cold. No clothing is worn when sleeping. The rich people may have a woolen pad under them, however. Most of the men have a cap which they wear all the time, but very few of the men have shoes or stockings. When they go to bed, they do not wash their feet, since water is very difficult to get. Women wrap long strips of cloth about their feet and ankles and have cloth shoes, made by themselves.

We have already mentioned that the houses are very crowded. Each household usually occupies only two rooms, one above the other. For each bedroom there are usually three individuals. Each house, built, as the custom is, around a court, consists of a number of households—up to as many as six. To build a house of six rooms (three on the ground floor and three above) costs $1,000. All the stone and brick masons and carpenters come from outside. The furniture for the rooms is very simple. In an ordinary room, used for sleeping and eating, there will generally be found a small, low table; a low, broad cupboard on which the incense-burner for sacrifices is placed; a few bed platforms; and a water bucket. Around the stove, sometimes not even separated from their bedroom, there is the covered rice-steamer, water-dipper, high cupboard, a few wooden stools, and a straw hassock. The richer folk will be likely to have some tables with drawers, also chairs in their living rooms. These wooden articles are bought from the market or are made on order by carpenters from the outside. Even coffins have to be imported here. All iron, bronze, and other metal work, as well as silver ornaments, are imported.

This shows conclusively that clothing, certain articles of the diet, house construction, and many articles in daily use are not self-produced but depend upon outside sources of supply. What have the people to exchange for these things? Their farm produce is not, in many cases, even sufficient to supply them with food. Therefore, they must find some other means to make up their deficiency.

CHAPTER XVI

SOURCES OF INCOME OTHER THAN INDUSTRY AND AGRICULTURE

I. DOMESTIC ANIMALS

IN CHAPTER XV we showed the uneven distribution of land in Yits'un. If the people depended upon their lands alone, about four-fifths of the households of the village would be on a very low level of subsistence. On the other hand, there are a few rich households that have accumulated considerable wealth from the land. This enables them not only to live but also to amass savings which may be invested as capital. There are two questions we can ask here. First, how do the poor find some productive work, besides agriculture, which does not take capital? In other words, how can they find an opportunity to sell their surplus labor? Second, how can the rich find an opportunity to invest their surplus capital in something besides agriculture? The chief solution of these two problems is found in local industry, which is the main subject under discussion in this part of the report. But the solutions to this problem are not confined to industry. Thus, before we come to our discussion of industry, we shall review briefly all other productive activities in the village.

The most common supplementary occupation of the villagers is the raising of pigs, sheep, and other domestic animals, such as oxen, buffaloes, horses, and mules. When we entered this little mountain village, we met in our path pigs rooting in the mud. The villagers could, without difficulty, pick out just which pigs belonged to whom; and they were never tired of talking of the personal history of each pig. At the time we were in the village, there were 62 pigs in all. Each household had one or two. Small pigs, costing about $20, are generally bought. At the end of a year a pig should weigh about 80 pounds. Or a somewhat larger pig may be bought, for $40; such a pig should weigh 100 pounds at the end of a year. Pork sold at 75 cents a pound at the time we were there. The pigs are fed corn, the husks of grain, and the plants and pods of broad bean, amounting in cost to about $60 a year if bought. If the pig should not be healthy, and increases to less than 50 pounds during the year, the owner will not get his money back. Pigs

166

are raised for one reason—because the food fed them would otherwise go chiefly to waste. It is not necessary to go to market to buy fodder. If bought in the market, the price of fodder will be high, since it is only bought by those who have an urgent need of it. The cost of fodder as $60 a year is calculated from the market price, however. These pigs supply some of the villagers with meat, but the poorer folk sell theirs.

Every household raises some chickens. The total number of chickens is at least two hundred. It is not necessary to pay much attention to the chickens, since they stray about during the daytime, finding their own food, and come back in the evening. These chickens are used as sacrifice to the ancestors or are eaten when guests are entertained or festivals are celebrated.

Sheep are raised also. At dusk the whole flock comes back from the mountains; and as they gather on the central public ground, their baaings break the silence of the village. Then come a group of children, carrying the young lambs to their mothers, who pick out their offspring by smelling them. From an economic point of view, raising sheep is very profitable. Most of the ewes give birth to a lamb each year or at least every other year. On the average, every 10 ewes have 6 lambs a year. With the castration of young sheep, in one year about 15 pounds of meat will be produced. Sheepskins are worth 50 cents to $1.00. So, if a household raises 30 ewes, at the end of a year they will have 18 lambs, which will be worth $126. The increase in weight of the mother sheep, which will be about 13 pounds each, will come to $150. Thus, even with paying a shepherd, which comes to $70 a year, the total profit will be about $200—about 70 per cent profit. If a family has a child who can act as shepherd, the profit will be still greater. But, in spite of this high profit, not many households keep sheep, because they have to have a special outbuilding (usually built onto the house). Also, there are no veterinarians; and when epidemic diseases attack the flock, they may all die. When we asked the people if their flocks had not increased during the year, they replied that the best they could hope for was just to keep what they had. There is enough wild land, and this country should be an ideal place for raising sheep. Lack of knowledge, rather than lack of grasslands, prevents people from raising sheep in quantities. The poorer peasants will not risk their capital in this sort of enterprise.

The domestic animals which are closely related to agriculture are the ox and the buffalo. Buffaloes are used for plowing. Each buffalo costs $120, so the poorer peasants cannot afford them. There are only

17 households that raise buffaloes, the total number being 31. There are 33 households whose members work on the land but have no buffaloes. They rent them for their plowing. In fact, these 31 buffaloes can provide enough animal labor for plowing. Each buffalo will work one month a year, and each day it can plow 3 *kung* of land. So the 31 buffaloes are able to cultivate 2,700 *kung* of land—far more land than is available. But those who raise buffaloes are not always willing to rent them out, since they fear the animals may be worn out. As a result, buffaloes are sometimes rented from other villages. The buffaloes are useful not only for their labor but for producing manure. There are 21 oxen, belonging to 5 households. Oxen are not usually used for plowing. For instance, the household which has 4 oxen rents a buffalo in order to plow the land. People prefer to sell their oxen for meat. Thirty-one mares, 1 colt, 1 young mule, and 13 horses are owned in the village. The mares are used chiefly for breeding but are also sometimes used for carrying straw and grain from the fields. The mule and horses are used for transporting goods; they also provide fertilizer for the fields. In one household, which owns 3 horses, the young man of the family is constantly engaged in transporting salt around the region. It takes six days for a round trip from the salt-producing center to the district town of Yenmen. Each horse carries 200 pounds of salt, and the pack driver gets $17 for each trip. Subtracting the cost of the food for the man and for 3 horses, the driver can make $27, or $4.50 a day. But the initial cost of horses which can be used for transportation is high, and those who manage them must be strong. Men who are without capital and also without strength cannot engage in this occupation. Moreover, horses, as well as buffalo and oxen, suffer from diseases. We were told that during June and July, 1939, 5 buffaloes, about 10 per cent of the total, died. The people looked upon this as quite normal. In talking to us once, an old man said of a certain village: "The people of that village are very bad people—their horses and cattle die very often. In our village it is much better. Sick cattle and horses sometimes recover. Because the people in our village are doing good things, the gods reward us." Besides getting security for their cattle by doing good deeds, there are also special gods for the oxen and buffalo. Every year the twenty-third day of the sixth moon is the time for gathering and sacrificing to the horse god. In the same way the twenty-fifth day of the seventh moon is the time for sacrificing to the ox and buffalo god. Every time that a new colt or calf is born, the owner of the animal must go to the village temple and make a sacrifice by burning incense,

kowtowing, and then killing a chicken as a sign of thanksgiving. We know that each cow or horse is worth $200. The folk consider the ceremony worth while as a form of insurance, but unfortunately the insurance does not always lead to actual security.

In conclusion, in a situation in which the economic unit is the family, with limited opportunities for using capital and labor, as well as a limitation on markets and pasture land, and where disease among animals is prevalent, each household can raise only a few domestic animals, according to their circumstances, to supplement the family income. There has been no real development along this line.

II. THE FERRY

The landscape of Yits'un is very picturesque. The red mountains, the compact village site, the river, and the thriving green bamboos make a traditional Chinese picture. Under the shade of the bamboos along the river, there are usually one or two small boats, which remind us of the poem:

> Wild and solitary the river-side,
> No man, the boat alone.

These few boats are not only picturesque; they also have an economic value. The villagers have a great deal of land across the river. During the busy farming season the peasants have to cross the stream in order to get to their work, and those who live on the opposite side of the river have to cross it in order to go to market. When the water is down, it can be crossed on foot. But in the spring, when the river floods, a boat must be used for getting across. At that time the current is strong, and it is dangerous to try to get across without a boat. We mentioned above that the people realize this danger.

There are five boats in the village—one publicly owned and four owned by private families. The publicly owned boat belongs to the two villages on either side of the stream. Anyone can take this boat without paying and can pole himself across. But at the time we were there, the publicly owned boat was worn out and could not be used. Of the four privately owned boats, only three were actually running. The boat-owners keep them not only for their own use but also to ferry passengers over. There is no fixed toll. If the water is running high, the toll charged is higher. We were told that during the flood of 1939 as much as 10 cents (one-fourth of the daily wage of a laborer) was charged, but ordinarily the toll is only a few cents. No charge is made to friends. The cost of building a boat, according to prices when we

G*

were there, was $14.00 for the wood, $4.00 for the labor, $3.00 for food, $8.00 for nails, totaling $30.00. Within three years this amount can be recovered from toll charges. Each boat can be used, however, only from ten to twenty years, with repairs occurring every five years. These boats give a certain amount of income to their owners, but they are not important to the economy of the village as a whole.

<h3 style="text-align:center">III. MARKETING</h3>

In the rural regions of Yunnan there are market centers. In these centers there is, normally every six days, a gathering of villagers for an exchange of goods. The four nearest market centers are Chwan K'ei (10 miles southeast), Lo-chwan (17 miles northwest), Yau-tsei (50 miles northeast), and Lufon (30 miles northeast). Except for the Lo-chwan market, which is held every five days, the markets are at six-day intervals. Yits'un has no market itself; and when the people wish to sell or buy, they usually go to the nearest market, which is at Chwan K'ei. They also sometimes go to Lufon and Lo-chwan. Market day at Lufon is held two days after that of Chwan K'ei. Thus, one morning they may go to Chwan K'ei and return to the village on the same day. In the afternoon of the following day they may start another journey to Lufon but will stop for the night en route. Before noon of the third day they will arrive at the Lufon market. They will stay there for the night and come back on the fourth day. We visited all these markets. There are three types of exchange activities. Barter, the exchange of goods between producers without the medium of money, is rare. But we know that every year before the harvest those poorer people of Yits'un who have not enough rice will bring with them to Lo-chwan, the rice-producing center, baskets to exchange for rice. There is a special type of basket which is used as a container for rice. Traditionally one basket of this sort will be exchanged for one *picul* of rice.

The second type is indirect exchange, or exchange between producers with money as a medium. For instance, the villagers of Yits'un carry their native products, such as baskets, bamboo sheaths, and paper, to market. They sell these products in the market and use the money then and there to buy vegetables, hardware, and cotton cloth. Since those who sell vegetables will not necessarily need baskets, there can be no direct exchange. Money, in this case, is used for meeting the supply and demand of different people. This type of exchange is common in the markets. Money circulates very rapidly between buyers and sellers. We often saw women go to market without money but with goods and come back without money but with goods of another sort.

The third type is exchange through a middleman. In these markets there are peddlers who sell cotton cloth, soap, matches, cigarettes, needles, and other manufactured articles. The peddlers buy these things from the city and bring them to the market for retailing. They make a business of buying and selling, moving about to the various markets. Occasionally the villagers also make a business of buying and selling, taking advantage of the different prices in the different markets or taking advantage of the fluctuation of market prices. For instance, our friend in Luts'un, Uncle Chang, who suggested this trip to us, comes once a year to Chwan K'ei to buy paper, which he sells in Luts'un. This type of "business" is one way of utilizing the slack period of labor and surplus capital and of helping out the family income. But the people in Yits'un are not very commercially minded, since, because of the secluded location of the village, it takes time and trouble to go to market.

The villagers of Yits'un go mainly to two markets, those of Chwan K'ei and Lufon. These three communities form an isosceles triangle, the distance between Lufon and Chwan K'ei being the same (30 miles) as between Lufon and Yits'un. The distance between Chwan K'ei and Yits'un is 10 miles. The people of Yits'un are not in a position to compete with those who live near the markets and who can watch the prices so as to take advantage of the differential in prices between the markets of the two centers, Lufon and Chwan K'ei. The cost of transportation will be greater for them than for villages on a more direct route. Nor are they in a position to buy goods at one time and to hold them for a rise in price, for they might have to come back with the goods several times, perhaps, and they are too far away to do this easily.

Because of their bad ecological location, the villagers of Yits'un can sell only their own products. At most, they may buy things in the village from their neighbors and sell them at the market centers. For instance, I knew a man in Yits'un who went to the market at Lufon, bringing with him 200 patches (28 folded sheets) of paper, which he employed a laborer from another village to carry. Along with these, he brought 8 pounds of bamboo sheathes. This paper was not his own product but was bought from a paper mill. The two days' trip gave him $5.00 profit.

There are not many in the village who go to market regularly. We were in the village during the slack period of farming. There should have been more time then than at other periods for going to market. We have a record of the three times when people went to market. The first time, about twenty—five women, three children, and the rest middle-aged men—went to Chwan K'ei. The next time, twelve— eight middle-aged men, three children, and one woman—went to Lufon. The third time, ten—five men and five children—went. The people said that for ten to twenty persons to go to market was normal except during festivals. This is only one-tenth of the whole population, while in Luts'un at least one went from each household each market day. We may estimate the total income gained from marketing activities. For ten persons who go to the two market centers every six days—allowing three days as the time spent and $1.50 as the profit realized per day—the village, as a whole, will get an income of $8,700 a year from trading. This sum is equivalent to 960 *piculs* of unhusked rice. This is not a large amount, and it is evident that their economic problems cannot be solved in this way but only through industry.

CHAPTER XVII

BASKETRY

WE HAVE seen above that two-thirds of the households in Yits'un cannot make their living solely from the land. We have also described other sources of income, such as domestic animals, the ferry, and trading in the markets, and reached the conclusion that, though these occupations help in the life of the people, the amount of help derived is small. Now we can proceed to the main subject of this part of our study: rural industry. We have spent nearly one-half of our discussion on agriculture and other occupations, because these are the basis from which the rural industries arise. We are trying to show the conditions under which the rural industry acquires its character in the rural economy. A fundamental character of the rural economy is the dense population, which cannot be supported by agriculture alone. It is obvious that, unless there are sources of income other than those mentioned above, there is insufficient support for a village of this size.

Agriculture cannot support the existing population, nor can it utilize the existing supply of labor. During the winter and spring, there are more than three or four months when there is actually nothing to be done on the farms. Labor cannot be saved; if it is not used, it will be wasted, meaning an economic loss to the people. Handicrafts are the ideal way for utilizing labor which is not needed in agriculture. Work of this sort can be carried on without regard to changes of temperature or weather, and work which requires only simple hand skill can be stopped at any time and taken up again at any time. It does not conflict with agriculture but supplements it.

An industry which is adapted to using the slack period of agriculture and to getting some supplementary income for the family must be one on a small scale. Nor is there likely to be, among poor folk, a large amount of capital available for investing in tools. Therefore, labor and skill are the main elements in this sort of industry. Moreover, it will not be able to use a large amount of material which has to be transported from afar. Thus, the types of articles produced in the industry must be limited to those made from local materials. In a place where clay is produced, pottery will develop. Where mulberry trees grow, the silk

173

industry will come into existence. In a flax-growing region, linen-weaving will be found. In Yits'un, basketry is an example of the same sort of development.

The raw material for basketry is bamboo, especially the one-year growth. Bamboo grows in abundance along both sides of the river in Yits'un. Nearly every household possesses several clumps at least. The tools and technique of basketry are very simple. A wedge-shaped knife is used to cut down the bamboo and to split the shoots into long strips in the field. The strips are rolled up and carried home. Frameworks for the different sorts of baskets are made of stronger bamboo sticks, and the strips are woven in. A scraper is used to smooth off the rough surface of the strips. In order to bend the bamboo sticks, they are either heated, close to the fire, or soaked in water for some time. The technique of basketmaking is so simple that it does not need any special instruction. The people say: "We learned just by looking at others."

A number of different types of baskets are made. In Table 32 we have listed the most important ones and have given the labor required, the cost of the materials if the bamboo is bought, and the profits from each. The cost of materials was based upon the quantity of bamboo shoots used. Each shoot weighs about 25 pounds and costs 40 cents. The prices of the articles listed are based upon the market prices in the village when we were there in December, 1939. Actually, the prices of baskets in different markets near the village vary but slightly.

We can see from Table 32 that the highest profit a basketmaker can get in one day is only $1.00 and that the lowest profit is as little as 30 cents. From our point of view, we might imagine that with such a wide range in profits the people would choose to make those articles which give the biggest profit. This is not the case, however. Why should they not produce mainly those articles which give the greatest return? The reason is that for such articles as the big rice-containers, which give the greatest profit, there is less demand. If the people make these large baskets and carry them to the market center, they may return without having disposed of them. Small articles, such as the scoop, are easily sold. These scoops were especially in demand during the building of the Burma Road.

The work of making baskets is not so hard as working in the fields, but the working hours are longer than in the fields. Farm work rarely exceeds eight hours a day; but in basketmaking, men may go on for more than twelve hours. As early as seven o'clock in the morning, when the fog still hangs over the valley, groups of villagers are already to be found at the public ground, settled down to their basketmaking. And when the sun drops down behind the western mountains and shadows fall on the village, these dark figures still sit in the twilight, hard at work. Sometimes they continue to work even in the moonlight or by the light of small oil lamps. Are they so busy because they are so anxious to earn money, or is it because they must do so in order to get the necessary supplementary income in order to survive?

Here we shall analyze the profits from basketmaking. We mentioned that the highest profit obtained from this handicraft is $1.00 a

TABLE 32

PROFITS ON BASKETMAKING

Article	Days Needed for Completing Article	Cost of Raw Material	Price of Each Article	Profit on Each Article	Profit for Each Day of Labor
Hampers...............	1	$0.20	$0.50	$0.30	$0.30
Pack basket.............	$\frac{1}{2}$	0.20	0.60	0.40	0.80
Rice-container:					
Large................	2	0.80	2.80	2.00	1.00
Medium	1	0.13	0.50	0.37	0.37
Small...............	$\frac{1}{2}$	0.10	0.30	0.20	0.40
Baskets on yoke	$\frac{1}{2}$	0.13	0.40	0.27	0.54
Basket carried on arm.....	1	0.10	0.40	0.30	0.30
Scoop.................	$\frac{1}{4}$	0.08	0.20	0.12	0.48
Threshing floor..........	7	4.00	9.80	5.80	0.83
Incense sticks, bundles of	$\frac{1}{10}$	0.04	0.10	0.06	0.60

day; the lowest, 30 cents. On the average, the profits are only 40 cents daily. But, added to this is the fact that one day will be expended in carrying the baskets to market and that on this day no baskets can be produced. However, since the raw material is usually self-supplied, the ordinary income from basketmaking will amount, on the average, to 60 cents a day. At the time of our study the price of rice was about $1.60–$1.80 for each 6.6 pounds (one local *shen*) of husked rice. This amount is sufficient to feed one man for six days, allowing for two meals a day. (Only two meals a day are eaten while the basketmaking is being carried on, but three meals a day are thought necessary when work is being done in the fields.) Including rice, vegetables, salt, and oil, the cost for food for each person is about 35 cents a day. So the actual income, after taking out food and when considering the raw materials as self-supplied, amounts to only 25 cents. People who work in the fields, however, will have their food provided; and, besides this, they will earn 50 cents for male labor or 30 cents for female labor. This shows that the basketmaking industry gives even less reward than does farm labor.

I have remarked several times that the opportunity for employment in agriculture is seasonal. There is a long period of slack in which the laborer cannot find any employment. Although basketmaking is less rewarding than farm work, it is better than idleness, and the people can to some extent control their employment. Moreover, we have seen that most of the villagers cannot be supported by agriculture alone; they have to find some income. That is why, even with such low rewards, the people continue this type of work.

There are about 33 persons who are constantly engaged in basketmaking—about 14 per cent of the total population; 24 of them are male, 9 female. Seven of them are old, 26 are middle-aged; 9 of them do not work in the fields, and 24 of them are engaged in farming as well.

These basketmakers go to the market centers frequently, because they have to sell their baskets. If they go to the nearer market, they will spend one day in six. If they go to the Lufon market, it will take them two days. If they go to both markets, it will take them one-third of their time. If it is assumed that there are six months of leisure time in agriculture and that two days in every six are spent in going to market, there will remain four months for making baskets. Assuming that the basketmaker will make an average of 60 cents a day, we find that he will get from this work an income of $72 a year. The total income of the 33 basketmakers will be $2,400 a year, which is equivalent to 850 *piculs* of unhusked rice.

The 33 basketmakers belong to 23 households—that is, 42.6 per cent of the total households. Among them are 22 households which have insufficient land, 11 of these households not having even sufficient income from their land to supply their own food. These facts explain the position of this household industry in the economy of the village. It arises, let us repeat, from the lack of opportunity for employment on land and serves to make up the deficiencies of the family budget.

CHAPTER XVIII

NATURE AND ORGANIZATION OF
THE PAPER INDUSTRY

I. THE NATURE OF THE PAPER INDUSTRY

WHILE we were in Luts'un, it was the paper industry which attracted us to the village of Yits'un. This industry continued to be the center of interest in our investigation. The villagers naturally thought that the reason for our making such an effort to come to them through the mountains must be to open up a new paper mill. Some of the people there urged us to buy up all the supply of bamboo and to start a modern factory which should produce foreign-style paper. Some of the paper-mill owners of Chwan K'ei had appeared quite willing to adopt new methods of manufacturing and had even proposed to us that we start a joint enterprise with them. Others in that region had asked us to use our influence in helping them to procure loans from the government. But in Yits'un there were a number of owners of paper mills who were frightened by our presence, believing we were going to compete with them and reduce their profits. They tried different ways of preventing our work and even started something like a boycott against us. These varied reactions made very clear the fact that the paper industry is, without question, the center of economic interest for this region. Those who have no chance to profit by the industry look at the flourishing bamboos and listen to the grinding of the millstones, while dreaming that someday they, too, may have a share in an enterprise of this sort. But those who own the mills hold tenaciously to their privileges and are sensitive to any threat of outside competition.

What attracted us, however, was not the profits to be realized from an enterprise of this sort but the fact that it represented a type of rural industry hitherto unexplored by us. The type of local industry represented by the paper mills is essentially different from that represented by household basketmaking, even though the two may be carried on side by side. In the previous chapter we explained the nature of the basketmaking industry. It arises from the fact that agriculture cannot provide full employment and is a type of industrial activity

177

having the function of supplementing the family income. It requires no large amount of capital. A knife, the one tool required, costs only a few dollars and will last for generations. The basketmaker can work anywhere—on the public grounds or in his bedroom or kitchen. He depends upon his own supply of materials, and a few clumps of bamboo are enough to keep him going. If he does not have enough raw material of his own, he can buy some for a few dollars. When the baskets are made, he can sell them within a short time and get his money back. Labor is the principal factor of production in this household type of industry. This is not true of the paper mills. To start a paper mill requires considerable capital. The poor cannot acquire the capital needed to set up the plant required. The industry is, therefore, limited to the rich. We call this type of industry, which is characterized by special and expensive equipment (see chap. xix, Sec. II), a "village mill." It is characterized also by the considerable amount of capital required and by the emphasis on labor, rather than on capital, in production.

In chapter xiv we analyzed the limits to investment in agriculture. In a community where land is limited and the population is large, agriculture cannot provide a livelihood for the people, on the one hand, and absorb the increasing capital, on the other. In Yits'un the distribution of land is uneven, and the rich families hold a large part of the land. But rich, as well as poor, suffer from the limitations of the land. The land cannot utilize the labor of the poor, nor can it utilize the capital of the rich. It is true that in the traditional rural economy the rich simply keep the accumulated earnings in money, often burying it in the ground. This, however, is as unproductive as unused labor. The title of this volume, *Earthbound China*, expresses the limitations which the land puts upon economic development. The village mill departs, to some degree, from the traditional basis of rural economy, which is the land. We may call this system "budding capitalism." In discussing Chinese rural industries we must not neglect the importance of this type of rural industry and the difference between its position in the rural economy and that of the household handicraft described above. In working out a plan for rural industrial development these two types of industry will require different treatment.

II. JOINT OWNERSHIP

The paper industry in the village is about thirty years old. The villagers told us that in the second or third years of the Republic (about

1913) immigrants from Szechwan came into the village and helped the villagers to start some paper mills which manufactured a different type of paper from that made today. The raw materials were steamed; and the paper was of a more refined type, was more expensive, and was used for writing. However, the manufacturers could not find a large enough market for this type of paper. In 1928–29 they began to make raw paper of a rough sort. This coarser paper is used chiefly for ceremonial paper money, for wrapping bundles of tobacco leaves, and for toilet paper. In 1934 the number of mills began to increase.

The people of Yits'un own nine mills, six of which are established in the village. Two of them are on the opposite bank of the the river, and one is located still farther away. By taking Yits'un as the center of the bamboo-producing area, there are, within a radius of 25 miles, twenty-three mills. In Yits'un is located more than one-fourth of the whole number, and these are owned by two-fifths of the village population.

The nine mills owned by the villagers of Yits'un belong to twenty households—seventeen of which live in the village, and three of which have recently moved to the other side of the river. These three are descendants of village people, and ceremonially and socially they are an integral part of Yits'un. Therefore, we decided to include their mills in our analysis.

Of the nine mills, four are owned by single households, two are owned jointly by two households, one by three households, one by four households, and one by five households. Table 33 shows the owners of the mills and the ties of relationship between them. From this table we may note the fact that, in every case, those who jointly own a mill belong to the same division and are brothers or the descendants of brothers. This is because each factory was established some years ago by a single household. When the sons grew up and the house divided, the mill came to be owned jointly by brothers. When some of the brothers died, it came to be owned by uncles and nephews.

In principle, the organization of the paper industry is the same as that of basketmaking—the single household is always the unit of production. But when the problem of succession arises, this principle is modified. In basketry, the capital goods are negligible, and so there is no problem of inheritance. But in the paper mills, the plant becomes a problem. According to the principle of equal inheritance among male siblings, each of the sons has an equal claim on the inheritance. But the plant is not like bamboo or land, which can be divided. Divided up, it would be worthless. To meet these difficulties, the principle of equal inheritance is retained, but in a modified form. The plant will not be owned by the inheritors, who pool together and form a company to operate the enterprise in the interests of all. Instead, each man will retain an equal claim to the use of the equipment, and the equipment will be used by one owner at one time and by another owner at another time. This joint ownership is not a partnership, because the management is separate and independent for each

TABLE 33

MILLOWNERSHIP

Mill	Owner	Relationship
I	Household No. 1 (C Division)	
II	Household No. 3 (C)	
III.......	Household No. 12 (C)	
IV.......	Household No. 14 (C)	
V........	Household No. 4 (C), No. 7 (C)	Uncle and nephew
VI.......	Household No. 5 (C), No. 6 (C)	Brothers.
VII......	Household No. 9 (A), No. 40 (A) Household No. 43 (A)	Brothers and nephew
VIII.....	Household No. 19 (A), No. 34 (A) Household No. 35 (A), No. 36 (A)	Brothers
IX.......	Household No. 2 (A), No. 23 (A) Household No. 24 (A), No. 25 (A) Household No. 26 (A)	Four brothers and one nephew

joint owner. Only the ownership of the plant is shared, and it varies somewhat in its organization. In some cases, the whole plant is held in common; in others, ownership is limited to part of the plant only. For example, the use of the grindstone, the tank, and the drying oven may be shared; but each joint owner has his own pool. This joint ownership has no influence on the management. From the gathering of raw material to the manufacturing and marketing, each household carries on separately. We found not a single case of a real partnership in enterprise. Each household owns its own bamboo clumps, employs its own workers, and has complete rights to the finished product. In management the unit of enterprise has never been more than one household. This is quite different from the modern partnership or joint-stock company. Since the plant is owned jointly but the management is separate, the problem might arise as to who is to use the plant first, how long each shall be permitted to work, and so on. The owners assured me: "Each man is free. There are no regulations, and no disputes arise on this account." This may be due, first, to the fact that the joint owners are regulated by kinship relations, which, in their turn, define certain traditional priorities and privileges, and thus no special written contract is needed. Second, under present circumstances, as we shall show presently, there are not sufficient raw materials to keep the mills fully employed. Therefore, every owner has time to use up his supply of raw material at some time during the year.

III. OWNERS AND WORKMEN

To establish a paper mill requires capital, and only those who possess capital can be owners. If we examine the financial condition of the owners of mills in Yits'un, we can see this clearly. From Table 34 we see that, of the twenty owners, eighteen possess enough land for their own consumption of food. Nine have enough land to maintain their families entirely. In saying this, we are taking account of rice production only; but, in fact, these households possess other lands besides rice fields. Thus, their real incomes must be even higher than shown in the table. The total income of these households is usually more than their expenditures, as is shown by the fact that seventeen households out of the twenty are moneylenders. The amount of bamboo owned is comparatively greater, and six of the group are considered the largest owners of bamboo.

Among the millowners, only three engage in basketmaking. These three are brothers. While their father was alive, they were prosperous, for he possessed lands and mills. But he had four sons; and when he died and the house was divided, each inherited a comparatively small amount of land, insufficient to support all the expenses of their households. The paper mill was jointly owned by the four brothers; but the youngest son, who was drafted, is thought to be dead, so that now only three share in the mill. These three make baskets and also take part in papermaking. They are a middle group between the rich and the poor.

Among the owners, some have greater resources than others. Those who have more raw materials can start their work earlier. The rich households can buy their raw materials from other villages or from other households in advance. If they possess more materials and prepare them earlier, they produce more paper. While we were in the village, there were five mills operating, while four were not in operation. The mills which were operating belong to households Nos. 1, 3, 4, 5, 6, 7, and 14. The first six households are the richest in the village. The owner of household No. 14 possesses a smaller amount of land than the others but was active the year before in transporting goods and in selling wine and so made some money, which he invested in paper making. The other thirteen owners were not operating, because of their lack of capital.

TABLE 34

ECONOMIC STATUS OF MILLOWNERS

Millowner	Food Supply from His Own Land	Land for Total Expenditure	Money-lending	Basketry	Large Supply of Bamboo
1 (C)	+	+	+	−	+
2 (A)	+	+	+	−	−
3 (C)	+	+	+	−	+
4 (C)	+	+	+	−	+
5 (C)	+	+	+	−	+
6 (C)	+	+	+	−	+
7 (C)	+	+	+	−	+
9 (A)	+	+	+	−	+
12 (C)	+	−	−	−	−
14 (C)	+	−	+	−	−
19 (C)	+	−	+	−	−
23 (A)	+	−	+	−	−
24 (A)	+	−	+	−	−
25 (A)	+	−	+	−	−
26 (A)	+	+	−	−	−
34 (A)	+	−	+	+	−
35 (A)	+	−	+	+	−
36 (A)	+	−	+	+	−
40 (A)	−	−	−	−	−
43 (A)	−	−	+	−	−

There are two sorts of skilled workmen in the paper industry. Those who work on the molding and dipping of the paper fibers form a team with those who dry the sheets on the oven. In making paper the co-operation of different types of workers is needed. Such co-operation is absent in a simple craft such as basketry.

In Yits'un there are ten men who know how to mold paper and twelve who know how to dry it. Sometimes the owners employ outsiders; but for the most part they depend on workmen from their own village and, even more, on their own household. Seven-ninths of the skilled labor is supplied by the village. And, of these men, seven molders and five driers work in mills belonging to their own households, but not exclusively in such mills. The supply of skilled labor is limited. To get men to work in the mills is a matter of personal relationship and personal obligations. When an employee has to make up his mind for whom he will work, he solves the problem by reference to the kinship relation. He will work first for his own household, then for his close kin, and only after that for others.

In the traditional types of industry in the villages of the interior the relation between employer and employee is one of intimacy before the economic relationship is established. This previous relation determines the association in the industry and the behavior after the association is established. It gives form to the organization and also limits its development.

The employment in the paper mill is short; it does not continue through the year. Within a year a workman may work for several millowners. For example, we know one molder who, after working first for his own household, went to work for seven other owners. Another drier worked for three owners in a year. On the other hand, the owners may employ several different workers in succession. For instance, household No. 7 employed two molders and three driers in one year, one after the other. This sort of arrangement is due to the nature of the work: it stops and starts again, according to the supply of raw material. An owner will not retain his workmen while there is nothing to be done. But to get workmen at the right time may be difficult unless the owner has them in his own household. Thus, the owner must adjust the time of beginning and ending work to the supply of workmen as well as to that of raw material. Moreover, these same workmen also manage their own farms and cannot be employed the whole year around. From their point of view, the paper industry simply affords a supplementary income—in this respect, resembling basketmaking. Time left over from farming is used in this extra work.

We can see now that, though the paper industry shows a tendency to break away from its bondage to the land, fundamentally it still has a close connection with agriculture. The raw materials come mainly from self-owned supplies; the ox which is used to turn the grindstone is also used for farming; and the workmen will operate the paper mill only in the slack season. It is clear that the paper mills have not yet become an independent and self-sustaining industry.

CHAPTER XIX

PAPERMAKING AND MARKETING OF PAPER

I. RAW MATERIALS

THE first step in papermaking is to collect the bamboo. The workers cut down bamboos with knives similar to those used in basketmaking. (Each mill possesses three or four knives of this sort—a total investment of about $8.00.) The men peel off the sheathes and carry the inner portions back to the village, where they cut them into pieces about 3 feet in length and then split them into strips about an inch wide. These strips are dried in the sun for two or three months, when they are ready to make into pulp. The bamboo used to make paper is a special variety, locally called *fung-we* (meaning "tail of a mythical bird"), which grows to a height of 20–30 feet and is about 3–4 inches in diameter. This variety is used because the inner part of the stem is thick. To cultivate bamboo requires no fertilizer. The sandy land around the river is the best place for bamboo. According to the villagers, every year that the river floods it carries in a layer of sand, and the next year the bamboo thrives.

In June, in the fifth moon, the new growth of bamboo is transplanted in the sand of the riverside, and the top is pruned off. The transplanted root produces young shoots—the first year usually only one shoot, but increasing numbers of them in following years. If the new shoots are not cut, the clump will increase to about one hundred shoots in eight or nine years. New shoots attain the same height as the old shoots in the period from spring to winter. The new shoot preserves its sheath and is distinguished from the old shoot by the silvery gray fuzz on the outside. If these new shoots are cut off with some of the stalk left on, new shoots may develop from the root. But the plant frequently dies. Two-year-old bamboos will sometimes also give off new shoots, but older plants cease producing. Only the one-year-old shoots are used for papermaking. These are cut down in the period from December to February. The people cut down only a part of the shoots, so as not to use up all the new shoots at one time. The way in which bamboo grows makes it difficult to increase the supply of raw materials quickly, since it takes years to build up a good crop.

We may ask here how much raw material is used every year in

papermaking. The villagers themselves have no idea. We employed several methods for estimating the amount. The first was to take each clump as a unit and to count the number of bamboo shoots. We then counted the number of clumps in the whole village, classified them into large and small, and from this enumeration were able to get a rough estimate of the number of bamboos. In classifying the clumps we were assisted by two villagers. Another method for estimating the quantity of bamboo available was to measure the extent of bamboo growth along the river and to count some sections. We then climbed to

TABLE 35

OWNERSHIP OF BAMBOO CLUMPS

Location	Number of Big Bamboos	Number of Small Bamboos	Residence of Owner
1.............	....	11,000	Owner resident of village
2.............	....	4,000	Same
3.............	20,000	10,000	Same
4.............	5,500	2,000	Same
5.............	....	18,000	Two-thirds belong to the owners of this village
6.............	52,000	8,000	Three-tenths belong to an owner of this village
7.............	15,000	5,000	Owner resident of another village
8.............	....	15,000	Same
Total....	92,500	73,000	
Amount belonging to Yits'un.....	41,100	41,400	

the top of the mountain and counted the number of large sections of bamboo along the river. There are eight stretches where bamboo grows.

Table 35 gives the approximate number of bamboos in each stretch. In this table we made a distinction between the big bamboos, weighing about 20 pounds, and the small ones, weighing 9 pounds.

Each ten bamboos will have only two young bamboos. Every year Yits'un produces approximately 8,000 large and 8,000 small bamboos. If half this amount is cut down to make paper, the total weight of raw material will be 120,000 pounds. (The local unit of weight used exclusively for bamboo is different from that used for other purposes. Each local unit is equal to 2 pounds, but in our discussion we shall use pounds instead of the local unit.)

Is there local material sufficient to supply the nine mills belonging to the village? For this problem we must see, first, how much raw material was prepared in the winter and spring of 1938–39. The following table (Table 36) gives the amount used by each paper-producer. The total amount the mills collected for that year was 287,200 pounds. The owners of the mills collected 237,600 pounds, and those who rented mills collected 49,600 pounds. But the total local supply was only 120,000 pounds. There was a deficiency of local material. Even

TABLE 36

BAMBOO FOR PAPERMAKING: ONE YEAR'S SUPPLY

Household Number	Amount of Bamboo (Pounds)	Operator of Mill	Household Number	Amount of Bamboo (Pounds)	Operator of Mill
1 (C)	20,000	Owner	25 (A)	6,000	Owner
2 (A)	40,000	Owner	26 (A)	6,000	Owner
3 (C)	20,000	Owner	27 (C)	3,000	Renter
4 (C)	20,000	Owner	28 (B)	2,000	Renter
5 (C)	20,000	Owner	29 (A)	2,000	Renter
6 (C)	20,000	Owner	30 (A)	2,600	Renter
7 (C)	16,000	Owner	32 (A)	2,000	Renter
9 (A)	4,000	Owner	34 (A)	3,000	Owner
10 (B)	2,000	Renter	35 (A)	3,000	Owner
11 (C)	4,000	Owner	36 (A)	3,000	Owner
12 (C)	16,000	Owner	38 (B)	2,000	Renter
13 (C)	10,000	Renter	40 (A)	3,000	Owner
14 (C)	14,000	Owner	41 (A)	8,000	Renter
16 (C)	2,000	Renter	43 (A)	4,000	Owner
17 (C)	2,000	Renter	44 (A)	2,000	Renter
19 (A)	3,000	Owner	46 (A)	3,000	Renter
20 (C)	3,000	Renter			
23 (A)	14,000	Owner	Total	287,200	
24 (A)	2,600	Owner			

taking into account the whole valley around the village, as can be seen in Table 35, the region supplied only 227,000 pounds. It is plain that bamboo must be imported from outside the valley. We mentioned that there are fourteen other mills in this region, within a radius of 15 miles. Raw material in this region is clearly limited. Moreover, the transportation of the bulky, heavy bamboo over these high mountains is very costly.

The rich houses pay in advance, in June or July, for the raw material purchased outside the village, for prices are lower then. The poorer owners have no capital until after their rice is harvested in the winter. By this time not only has the price of bamboo risen, but the supply, which is variable, may be scanty. The price for each 2,000 pounds of bamboo is $20. To import about 13,000 pounds of raw ma-

terial will cost $200, not including transportation. This is too expensive
for the ordinary houses.

Each mill has at least two pools—one for limewater and another for
clear water. These are about 30 feet long, 10 feet wide, and 15 feet
deep. The bottom and sides of the excavations for the pools are lined
with a type of cement, and the total cost is $50.

In preparing the pulp the workers put the dry bamboo strips into
the limewater pool. Stones are used to keep the strips submerged. The
fibers soak here for about three months, at which time they have become soft, when they are taken out and dried again. During the drying, which lasts two months, they are covered with a layer of straw.
They are then put into the pool of clear water to clean them off. The
total time needed for preparing the fibers is from eight to nine months.

Near Yits'un there are two lime quarries. One is located about 7
miles away; another, 15 miles. The more distant one has better lime,
but transportation costs are greater. As a result, the people usually depend on the nearer quarry. Each 1,000 pounds of bamboo require 680
pounds of lime. If the pool is new, it will require 50 per cent more lime.
It costs $8.00 for 680 pounds of lime and $4.60 for the transportation of
this amount by horse, or $4.00 if carried on a man's back. If the lime is
brought from a distant quarry, the cost of transportation is doubled.

When the bundles of bamboo strips are clean and dry, they are
ground into pulp. This is done in a special hut, which contains a large
grindstone, consisting of a stone base and a roller, worked by an ox.
Water is added to the pulp during the process of grinding. Each grindstone can in one day supply an amount of pulp sufficient for making
from 150 to 160 patches of paper. This amount of pulp will give work
to two molders and two driers for a day. After grinding, the pulp is
scooped up, put into a basket, and taken to the molder.

The simple hut used for the grinding process, built of wood and
thatched with straw, costs $100 or more. A better-built one may come
to $200. The grindstone is of granite, and the cost of bringing the stone
from the mountain and of making it is about $250. The ox costs $120.
The entire equipment for the grinding unit costs about $500.

Molding takes place in an open shed, which costs about $20 to
build. Inside the shed there is a basket for carrying the pulp and a
wooden bucket for holding the sticky matter which is added to the

ground fibers to make them adhere. There is a basket filter in the bucket to hold the cactus and the roots of a certain tree from which this "sticky matter" is produced. The cactus grows near the village and can easily be gathered, but the roots must be obtained from the mountains. Eighty pounds of roots, the amount needed for 300 patches of paper, cost $1.00 for transportation. The bucket, basket, and a wooden dipper cost $11.60 in all. The bucket containing the dissolved sticky matter stands by a wooden tank (5 feet long, 2½ feet wide, and 3 feet deep) which is used to hold the pulp and a solution of water, the sticky matter, and the pulp. This tank costs $24. The solution is stirred with a paddle. The molding apparatus consists of two parts—the frame and the sieve, the latter imported from outside—totaling $70.

The molder holds the molding frame with sieve in both hands and dips it twice into the tank solution. The pulp, which is spread out on the sieve, forms a sheet of paper. With the frame removed, the mold is turned and the sheet of paper is placed on a pile of other sheets on a press. The pile is heaped up to a height of 3 feet, when a wooden plate is placed on the top and the press tightened, in order to squeeze out the water. The height of the pile is reduced to about a foot and a half. This pile of sheets is then taken into the drying-room. The press costs $15, and the total cost of the equipment for molding is $140.

The drying process takes place in a special house with an oven inside. This is a well-constructed building costing $200. The oven is built out into the room in a rectangular form, with one end against the wall and going up to a chimney. At the other end it is open, for putting in the fuel, the heat passing beneath the whole length of the oven. The oven, which is built of sun-dried bricks, is 18 feet long, 5 feet high, and 1 foot in width. The two sides used for baking the paper are made smooth with lime.

For drying the wet paper, fuel must be burned. The wood for this purpose is floated down as logs from the upper part of the river. We once met four aborigines delivering wood to the village. They had long bamboo poles with hooks on the end, and they walked in the chilly water and pushed the logs when necessary. It takes three days for four persons to transport, in this way, one hundred logs for 7 miles. The men are provided with food by the buyer of the logs and are paid $6.00 additional. The cost of these one hundred logs will come to $50. If the water is lower, the cost of transportation will be doubled. So each log, which weighs about 360 pounds, costs about 20–30 cents each. Each oven, consuming two logs a day, will dry 70–80 patches of paper.

The drier puts the whole pile of wet sheets of paper, carried from the molder's shed, onto a small table. Taking a wooden pestle, he presses down the paper so that the corners stick up. He takes up 20–30 sheets at one time. Holding these sheets on his left arm, he walks to the oven and, with his lips and an intake of breath, catches hold of the corner of a sheet. With the head directed toward the oven wall, he simultaneously uses a small brush, which is held in the right hand, to whisk the sheet against the oven. The wet sheet sticks to the oven wall for about three minutes and is then dry, when it can be peeled off with the fingers. Each 28 sheets are folded, making one patch. Twenty-five patches are tied up into a bundle, ready for sale.

The oven costs $40. Two stands—one for wet paper and one for dried paper—cost $10. Two stools, for sitting on, cost $3.00. The brushes are made from pine-tree needles by the people themselves. The total cost of the drying equipment amounts to about $2.53. The minimum cost of a simple paper mill, using only one molder and having only one oven, was at least $1,000 in 1939.

IV. SKILL

Papermaking requires a certain specialized skill in molding and drying. We have already roughly described, in the above section, how the paper is made. Superficially the process seems very simple, but the molder has constantly to watch the density of the pulp. This cannot be discovered by any special test but must be learned simply from experience. To make paper of a regular thickness and evenness depends upon the proper movement of the hands. The drier, who has to stand by the heated oven, perspires all the time. He keeps busy with both hands and mouth. His skill depends on his peeling off the wet paper without tearing it. The co-ordination of mouth and brush can be acquired only through long experience.

We recorded the speed of this work. One molder can make 27 sheets of paper in five minutes; another can make 23 sheets in the same time. On the average, in an hour, a worker can make 300 sheets, or about 10 patches. He begins early in the morning, at about seven o'clock, and leaves off at six in the evening. However, he takes time off several times a day to smoke and to eat. The total number of hours of work will not be less than eight. A worker can mold about 80 folds of paper a day, and this will be dried on the following day. It takes about 12 seconds to mold each sheet of paper, and the same amount of time for drying.

The technique of papermaking requires instruction and practice, differing in this respect from basketry. The apprenticeship period for learning the molding of paper lasts a year. During that year the apprentice stays with his master in the owner's house. The owner of the mill provides him with food as well as with lodging. After the term of one year the apprentice has the obligation of making 3,000 patches of paper for his master and 2,000 for the owners. During the time in which he makes this amount of paper he asks no wage but simply gets his keep. In recent years the amount he must make has been increased to 6,000 patches for the master and 5,000 for the owner. After having fulfilled this obligation, he becomes a recognized worker and receives a wage. But he still has the obligation of working for the owner of the mill where he got his training. It is said that, if he wishes to change, he must find a substitute.

The term of instruction for the apprentice who dries the paper is the same as that for the molder, but his obligation is different. He need make only 1,000 patches for the owner, but he must pay $10 to his master (this was increased in 1939 to $30).

V. MARKETING

The paper made in this village is sold chiefly in Chwan K'ei; Lufon; Yits'un, north of Lufon; the salt-producing areas; and in Kwangtung across the river. Very little of this paper reaches Kunming. The pack driver who goes regularly to the markets told me that several years ago he carried some bundles of paper to Kunming but that it was difficult to find buyers, because it was said that the quality of the paper was too poor and the sticky matter bad. In our opinion, the native paper sold in Kunming is in no sense better; but, adding the cost of transportation, the paper produced in Yits'un could not compete in price with that produced locally. It is true, we did not find paper produced in this region sold in Kunming.

Every New Year's Day, at the time of the spring and fall festivals, when the tombs are visited, and on the seventh full moon, each household will burn paper money for the dead. The Szechwan immigrants, especially, observe this custom. Paper money is made from paper such as that produced in Yits'un. Sometimes a little yellow dye is added to the paper by the producers, especially for burning in temples. Much of the paper is used in this way for religious purposes.

The use next in importance is for wrapping the native tobacco. In the autumn, when the tobacco leaves come to the market, there is a great demand for wrapping paper.

We did not see the villagers use their own products very extensively. They burn paper money during their visit to the tombs and in their sacrifices in the temple and also use paper for the exercise books in the school. But the local paper is too coarse to be used for writing. The paper made in this village is used mainly for export. Shortly before the festivals a number of outsiders come into the village and buy paper in large quantities. Uncle Chang of Luts'un came once before the Ghost Festival in 1939. While we were in the village, we saw some people who came from Yimen to collect paper for making paper money. But most of the paper is transported by the villagers themselves to the market centers—sometimes by the owners, sometimes by the basket-makers, who, as middlemen, take the paper along with their baskets.

In the market a part of the paper goes into the hands of consumers; a part, to middlemen. We know of a number of cotton-cloth and also earthenware peddlers who buy paper in the market after selling their wares. If manpower is used for transport, each man can carry 100 patches. To employ him, supplying food in addition to a wage, costs $1.00 a day. Each patch will thus cost 1 cent for transportation for each day it is carried. If a horse is used, each horse can carry 150 patches. A horse costs $1.00 for food; but, in addition, each driver requires $1.00 a day for food and wage. If one man takes only one horse, the cost of each patch will be 1.3 cents. If he drives five horses, the cost will be less—only 0.8 cent. But there is no co-operation between those who are taking the paper to market, and usually only one or two horses are used.

Yits'un is located far from any market, and the people cannot stay in the market long enough to wait for individual buyers. Thus, they usually sell at wholesale. Sold this way, the paper brings a lower price, but time is saved and they do not run the risk of having to take the whole load back. If the villagers had some co-operative storerooms in the market, they would be better able to bargain. Under present conditions, however, each producer looks out only for himself. Thus, they suffer from disadvantages both in transportation and in bargaining. It appears to us that, if the principle of co-operation were to be introduced into this industry, the people would be in a better position than they are now.

CHAPTER XX

MANAGEMENT AND PROFIT IN THE PAPER INDUSTRY

I. THE OWNER-PRODUCER

NONE of the nine mills in Yits'un is operated all through the year. According to our estimate, a mill possessing one grindstone, two molders, and two driers and operating the year round would use up 144,000 pounds of raw material. A mill consisting of one molder and one drier would consume 72,000 pounds in a year. But among these nine mills the greatest consumption of raw materials amounts to only 68,000 pounds, while the smallest consumption is 10,000 pounds. Thus, none of the existing mills consumed as much as could have been consumed by the smallest-scale mill running through the entire year, and none consumed more than half the amount which could have been used by a medium-sized mill running through the year.

As we have seen, in order to set up a mill a considerable amount of capital must be invested. If the plant is run only for a short period, it is disadvantageous to the owner. As we shall show later, the rate of profit for a mill running 160 days out of the year is only 60 per cent; but if the mill could run the whole year, the rate would be increased to 88 per cent.

Although the profit would be greater, no one can operate a mill for the whole year. The principal reason is that the supply is not well organized. Each owner of large amounts of raw material thinks he will make money by establishing a new mill. But the whole supply of raw material in this village is only enough to keep two good-sized mills running the whole year. When these materials are scattered through nine mills, it is obvious that none of them will have sufficient raw material. On the other hand, to establish a mill costs about $1,000, but to maintain the work of a regular mill during the year takes $5,000 for current expenses. In Yits'un this industry has always been restricted to the household unit. No household has sufficient means to run a regular-sized mill all through the year. They can operate only for the period of time they can finance. They have raw materials for this limit-

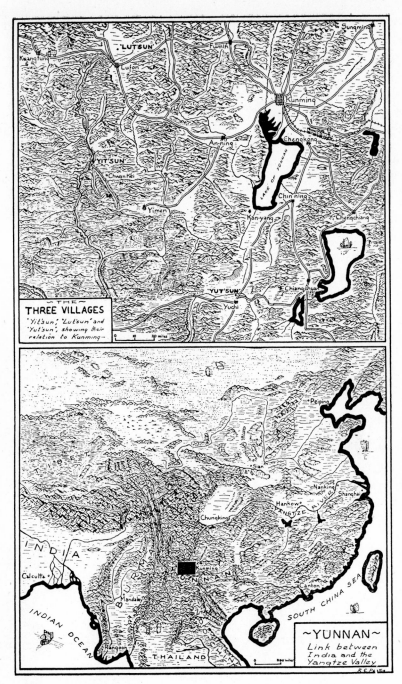

The Three Villages   Yunnan

Luts' un

Author Fei (center top, in Station Uniform); Landlord Wang (Household A) (front row, right of the old man);

At the Market. Village Head, Chao, in center

Funeral Procession

At the Cemetery

ed period but do not make as much profit from the industry as they otherwise might.

Industry in the villages of the interior is bound by family organization. It cannot be planned or managed in the most rational way. In the case of the paper industry in Yits'un, most of the mills remain inoperative for a long time. Since the owner cannot operate his mill the whole year, he rents it, either through friendship or for profit, to others who possess raw materials.

II. RENTERS

The villagers who possess raw materials but no mills can rent mills to produce their paper. They rent the whole plant—from the pool up to the drier. According to custom, they give the owner 10 per cent of their product. But if they provide their own sieve, they need give only 5 per cent. However, if they are bound to the owner either in close kinship or in close friendship, no rent will be charged. In the winter of 1938 we knew of fifteen households who rented mills to produce paper. They collected 49,600 pounds of raw materials, the biggest producer having 10,000 pounds and the smaller producer only 2,000 pounds. One-half of this was bought from others. These producers were not rich. Not one of them was a moneylender, which indicates that they did not have surplus capital. Eight of them had only sufficient land to produce their own food; seven of them had not even enough land for this. Eight of them were basketmakers, and five were skilled laborers in the paper industry. They had no capital to start a new mill but wished to gain some profits from the industry; so they tried to collect some bamboo and to rent mills.

They did not need to invest a large amount of capital in overhead expenses, nor did they need to bear the maintenance of the plant. All they were required to do was to pay out 10 per cent of their products to the millowner. As a result, their rate of profit was 40 per cent higher than that of the owner-producers. However, since they did not own the mills, they were dependent upon the owners' permission as to whether they might produce or not. Actually, they were unable to produce a large amount of paper.

Since the owners of the mills cannot operate their mills during the whole year, there are opportunities for others to rent them. Since profits are still higher for these renters, many people are anxious to engage in such enterprises. But only those who have a special relation to the owner can take advantage of this opportunity. Table 37 lists ten renters and gives their relation to the owners. From this table we can see a tendency for the closer kin (usually of the same division) to get the advantage of renting the mills. But there are four exceptions of men who do not belong to the same division as the owners. In one case, the owner and renter live in the same house; in another, the two parties became intimate through working together in the mill. From this we can see the importance of kinship in the rural economy.

TABLE 37*

RELATIONSHIP OF RENTERS OF MILLS TO OWNERS

Renter	Owner-Producer	Relationship
10 B.............	14 (C)	Clan uncle and nephew
11 C.............	1 (C) 6 (C)	Uncle and nephew Brothers
13 C.............	12 (C)	Brothers
16 C.............	1 (C)	Uncle and nephew (nephew usually works in mill as molder; does not pay rent)
20 C.............	14 (C)	Brothers
30 A.............	7 (C)	Clan uncle and nephew (uncle works for nephew in mill)
32 A.............	9 (A)	Uncle and nephew
41 A.............	7 (C)	Uncle and nephew
44 A.............	14 (C)	Granduncle and grandnephew (live in same house)
46 A.............	9 (A)	Uncle and nephew

* Another five families not included in this table had collected their bamboo but had not decided which mill to rent.

III. ESTIMATE OF PROFIT

The paper mills in this village operate only a part of the year. For the whole village they collect 7,200 pounds of bamboo (every 2,000 pounds produces 800 patches of paper). The total produced by this village is 114,880 patches—80 patches daily for each medium-sized mill. This amount of raw material can be worked up in the nine mills in 160 days. We may take this length of time as the normal period of operation for the mills and calculate the profit gained. If all the raw materials are bought and from them are produced 12,800 patches, the items of cost produced in 160 days will be as shown in Table 38. We did not include the rent for the oxen because we had already included the value of the oxen in our estimate of overhead expenses. These oxen are also used in plowing the fields; so only a part of their cost need be included under the paper industry.

Straw is used as fodder for the oxen, which are also pastured. The straw is produced on the farms. When an ox is sent out to pasture, a boy goes out to care for it, but this is usually a boy from the household. Moreover, each owner owns at least some part of the raw materials he uses, so that the actual cash expenses of the owner should be lower than those listed.

TABLE 38

COSTS OF PAPERMAKING

Items	Expenses	Remarks
Bamboo.................	$ 320.00	Weight of raw material, 32,000 pounds; every 2,000 pounds costs $20
Lime..................	128.00	11,100 pounds; each 690 pounds costs $8.00
Transportation of lime....	64.00	Transportation of 170 pounds costs $1.00
Fuel	96.00	320 logs; each log costs 30 cents
Sticky matter............	43.00	1 load for a man, sufficient for 300 folds of paper
Fodder.................	40.00	80 days fodder, 50 cents per day
Wage of herdboy for ox ...	40.00	50 cents per day, 80 days
Food of herdboy.........	40.00	50 cents per day, 80 days
Molder—wage...........	89.60	Every 100 folds, 70 cents wage
Molder—food...........	80.00	160 days, 50 cents per day
Drier—wage............	89.60	Every 100 folds, 70 cents wage
Drier—food............	80.00	160 days, 50 cents per day
Maintenance of plant.....	100.00	10 per cent of overhead
Total...............	$1,210.20	

The price of paper is $20 for 100 folds; this is the wholesale price. The value of the total production of a normal mill will be about $2,560. Thus, there is a surplus of $1,350. The total investment, which includes both the initial investment of capital and the current expenses, is about $2,200. The annual rate of profit will then be around 60 per cent.

This estimate is based upon operations lasting the ordinary length of time—160 days. If the mills were run all through the year, they would produce 28,800 patches of paper, which would sell at $5,760, wholesale. The total current expenses would come to $2,598, giving a surplus of $3,162. The rate of profit would be increased in this way to 88 per cent. If there were two sets of molders and driers who could share one grindstone, the rate of profit would be more than 90 per cent.

If the owner of the mill rents out his mill to someone else for a period

of 160 days, he will get a rent of 1,280 patches of paper—equivalent to
$256. If the renter has no ox, he will need to rent an ox from the mill-
owner and will pay $40 more—that is, $296. The profit to the millowner who has invested his capital in the plant and must, moreover,
maintain it, will be only at the rate of 27 per cent. But the renter has
to pay only 1,280 patches of paper as rent and still has 11,520 patches,
or $2,304. His expenditure will amount to $1,150 (he need not pay for
the depreciation of the mill but must add $40 for the rent of his ox).
Even so, he will have a surplus of $1,154. This means that he gets 100
per cent annually on his investment—a very profitable enterprise for
the renter. But the owners are unwilling to rent out their mills until
they have exhausted their own raw materials. Then they do so with a
feeling of doing good to others. Only close relatives or friends are permitted to enjoy these profits, and since none of the latter produce a
large amount of paper, though the profits are large, the income of the
renters remains low.

Those who do not own mills but have raw materials of their own
may find owners who are willing to rent them mills. Those who have
only a small amount of bamboo and have no money with which to
buy more cannot take part in the papermaking but must remain
jealous bystanders. Thus, it is capital which actually determines the
profits in this industry. We mentioned above that those mills which
were operating when we were there belonged to the few big houses—
the large landowners who acquire capital from their land, which they
can invest in the paper industry. The more capital a man has, the
earlier he can begin to buy raw materials. The more he gets, the longer
will be the period for operating the plant and the higher the profit.
Such a man becomes richer; and the richer he is, the better position
he has in running the industry. Here are the germs of capitalism.
Those who have no capital can do nothing but make baskets. For this
they will get even lower wages than those received by farm laborers.
Thus, as the rich become richer, the poor will continue on a bare subsistence level. In the economy of this type of village there is a sharp
line of demarcation between these two types of rural industry, basketry
and papermaking. It is no wonder that the paper mills have been the
center of economic interest, for this is the one real opportunity open
for getting rich. The rich guard what they possess jealously, while the
poor are helpless. Let us continue our analysis of what the different
consequences of these two types of rural industry are for rural economy in general.

CHAPTER XXI

CAPITAL AND LAND

I. ACCUMULATION AND UTILIZATION OF WEALTH

THE impoverished land surrounding Yits'un forces the people to struggle for new resources. We have seen that they engage in a number of productive enterprises besides agriculture, of which the most important are trading, the transport of goods, basketry, and papermaking. From these occupations they get as much income as they get from the land. The people should be able to maintain a standard of living above that of the average Chinese peasant. Is this true in fact?

In chapter xv we estimated that there are eleven households that possess a surplus yield of rice—2,200 *piculs* of unhusked rice besides that consumed by the household. There are forty-three households that have a deficiency of 6,960 *piculs* of unhusked rice if they depend upon their land only. In other words, if we take the villagers as a whole, they need, in order to maintain the average standard of living, 4,760 *piculs* of unhusked rice in addition to what they raise. If they had bought this amount of rice from the near-by market, according to the prices at that time, it would have cost them $13,328. The basket-making industry, as we showed in chapter xvii, gives the village an income of $2,400, making up about 18 per cent of the deficiency. These two occupations are engaged in by poor people. If we exclude the rich households, these two occupations—basketry and trading in the markets—make up about 33 per cent of the income of the poor. This indicates that, for poor folk, subsidiary activities are not enough to solve the problems of gaining a livelihood.

The paper industry gives a large amount of income to the village. During the course of a whole year the village produces 115,000 patches of paper, amounting to $23,000 wholesale. After paying $4,000 to other villages for necessary materials, such as lime, fuel, and so on, there will still be $19,000 coming to the village. This amount is enough to make up the entire deficiency of the village, with a surplus of $5,000.

Although the paper industry produces enough wealth to make up the whole deficiency of the village, this income comes into only a few hands. In Table 38, which gives the amount of raw materials possessed by the producers, we can see that there are only nine owners who support themselves entirely by the products of their land alone. These nine possess 160,000 pounds of raw material for paper—about 53 per cent of the total. In this industry, only about 47 per cent ($9,000) of the income is distributed among twenty-seven households. Adding the income derived from basketmaking and from trading, we get a total of $15,000 as the entire income of the poor people, while their deficiency in rice is 6,960 *piculs*, or $19,000. After working hard at a variety of occupations, they produce barely enough to live on. Moreover, we must add that the estimate we give here for the normal standard of living does not allow for the expenses of ceremonies or for accidents. In the next section we shall see that the poor are burdened with debt.

About $10,000 from the paper industry is shared by nine rich houses. The income of these people from land is already larger than they need. The surpluses gained from industry are not consumed. Therefore, the village possesses wealth which can be used as capital.

The best investment is the paper industry because it gives the largest profit. But there is a limitation to the expansion of this industry. Lack of raw material is the first limitation. I have mentioned that raw material produced in the village makes up only three-quarters of the total amount used. In other words, they already buy one-quarter of their material from outside the village. Even with this supply, the nine mills can operate about only one-half the year. The bamboo which grows in the sandy land around the river can be increased, but this will take time. If the people depend upon the supply of raw material from outside, they again meet the difficulties of transportation. Although there may be bamboo in distant regions, it costs too much to use in these mills. The high profit of 60 per cent is attractive, indeed; but the amount of capital which can be invested in the industry is limited. We mentioned above that we met a number of paper-mill owners who expressed their willingness to improve production and were ready to join in any plan for reform. This was not due to any specially modernized ideas but because they had accumulated some wealth in industry and wished to put it to use. To improve production would be to their interest; they would like to find some way for expansion in this industry, which at the present time is largely blocked.

II. MONEYLENDING

Further investments in the paper industry will not give great profits. As we have seen, there is no good reason for building new paper mills while some of those already built remain idle. So the money of the rich goes elsewhere. One way of dealing with surplus wealth is to lend money to others—to the poor who need money in order merely to live. There are three ways to lend money in Yits'un. The first method is to lend money and to collect the interest in terms of rice. The second method is to lend money and to collect the interest for it in money. The third method is to lend rice and to collect the interest in rice.

The first method of moneylending is the most common. While we were staying in the village, we frequently saw our landlord, of household No. 1, carrying bags of rice which he had brought in from outside the village. The people told me that most of this rice was interest paid for loans of money. We tried many different ways to find out the amount of money lent and the number of loans but were only partly successful.

In Yits'un rice production is insufficient; and, as a result, people ordinarily pay interest in terms of money rather than of rice. Information on such loans is difficult to get. But the money lent to people living outside the village, which is likely to have been more than that lent to the villagers themselves, is usually paid for in terms of rice. The moneylenders of the village collect, each year, 2,420 *piculs* of unhusked rice as interest, which points to loans of about $5,000. In Table 39 are listed loans made in terms of rice interest amounting to $200. We can see from the table that, except for the pack driver, all those who lent money were paper-mill owners, while those who borrowed money live mainly outside the village.

The common rate of interest in 1939 was 5 *piculs* of unhusked rice as interest on $10. There are variations on this rate. For instance, household No. 8 lent out $50. and got, as interest, 55 *piculs*, which is a higher rate than that quoted above. Household No. 3 lent out $100 and got, as interest, 150 *piculs*—a much higher rate. This same man lent out the same amount ($100) to another villager and got only 90 *piculs* of rice. Households Nos. 19, 34, 35, and 36 jointly lent out $500 and got 150 *piculs* as interest—a much lower rate, only 3 *piculs* per $10. But at that time each *picul* of unhusked rice cost $2.80, so that the highest interest on $10 came to $42 and the lowest to $8.40. The average rate of interest was $14 on $10. We should not, however, read this number at its face value, because in 1939 inflation had already affected the price of rice and it was rising continuously. In fact, the $10 borrowed the previous year was worth much more than its face value this year. When paying interest, people do not pay in terms of the present value. How much a loan is worth at the time the interest is paid is determined by the increase in the price level and on how the loan was used. According to the commonly recognized rate, interest is at about 40 per

TABLE 39

AMOUNT OF INTEREST PAID IN UNHUSKED RICE RECEIVED
BY YITS'UN MONEYLENDERS

MONEYLENDER	AMOUNT OF INTEREST RECEIVED (IN *Piculs*)		OCCUPATION
	From Outsiders	From Fellow-Villagers	
1 (C)............	81	10	Paper-mill owner
2 (A)............	20	....	Paper-mill owner
3 (C)............	24	....	Paper-mill owner
4 (C)............	8	....	Paper-mill owner
7 (C)............	29	....	Paper-mill owner
8 (B)............	10.5	....	Horse-driver
19 (A)			
34 (A)	15	....	Brothers, paper-mill owner
35 (A)			
36 (A)			
23 (A)............	20	....	Paper-mill owner
24 (A)............	20	....	Paper-mill owner
25 (A)............	5	....	Paper-mill owner
43 (A)............	10	....	Paper-mill owner
Total..........	2,425	10	

cent. Householder No. 43 in 1939 borrowed $10 from his uncle in the same division. The interest was $4.00. Householder No. 4 lent $10 to his cousin and demanded interest of $3.00. A moneylender of another village lent $20 to a villager of Yits'un and asked only $3.00 as interest. Another householder lent $200 to some person in the market center, and $40 interest was paid. We did not run into any loans where the interest charged was above the 40 per cent rate. It is said that, in borrowing rice and in paying in rice, the rate charged is also 40 per cent—that is, 10 *piculs* of rice are borrowed and 4 are received in return—but we do not know any cases of this sort. During inflation the method of borrowing money and paying rice as interest has led to confusion. The debtor feels that he is paying an interest which amounts to more than he borrowed. But the moneylender feels, on the other hand, that, if he had used the $10 he lent to buy food and resell it, he might have made much more than the interest. Under these circumstances the rate of interest on loans is constantly changing.

No borrower would be willing to pay 5 *piculs* of rice for a loan of $10. Toward the end of 1939 the interest rate was decreased to 3 *piculs* for $10, and there was a tendency to change to money interest altogether. We knew of a case in which a man borrowed $10 in September, 1938, and agreed to pay 10 *piculs* of rice as interest. In 1939, when the interest was due, the debtor felt that 10 *piculs* of rice was too high an interest and got the interest changed to $10 instead. Lender and debtor agreed on a rate of 30 per cent interest for later loans.

As we know, a large part of the money loaned goes outside the village; therefore, the total amount of money lent must be more than $5,000. We also know that the normal rate of interest on loans is 40 per cent, which is 20 per cent lower than the rate of profit in the paper industry.

III. CONCENTRATION OF LAND OWNERSHIP

Loans such as the above, of a few hundred or a few tens of dollars, are not often used for production. They are absorbed by the poverty of the people. Many villages around Yits'un are mountainous and even worse off economically than Yits'un itself. The inhabitants of these villages are largely aborigines, whose standard of living is still lower. When these people are touched by misfortune or need money for ceremonies, they have no savings but must borrow money. To do this, they give their land as security. But once the land is mortgaged, there is very little chance of getting it back. In the end they usually have to sell. The people of Yits'un who have accumulated wealth have become a strong financial power in this region and hold land for tens of miles around the village.

There is a limit to this expansion, however. Distant lands are not worth buying, as we have already made clear. So the rich houses turn back to their own village. The poor people of the village, although they have a certain amount of income which supplements what they get from farming and are better off than the aborigines, live at a bare subsistence level. They cannot stand any stroke of ill-fortune. Moreover, their children are growing up, and their already small estates will be divided. Some of those unfortunates who are bound by the habit of opium-smoking are still more helpless.

H*

It must be recognized that investing money in land is not what the rich folk are interested in. The profit on land is very small. Even for the best wheel-field, each *kung* of which is worth $30, the owner can ask as rent only about 7 *piculs* of rice. In 1939 this was worth $20— only a 15 per cent return on the investment. This rate is lower than that gained on moneylending and much lower than that gained from papermaking. Thus, the rich houses take over land only in the case of a default of interest. From the point of view of the utilization of capital, they accept a less profitable means of investment. The amount of capital which can be invested is also limited, however, because only in very distressed circumstances are the people willing to sell their land. Thus, if there is still surplus wealth, there is no way to use it, and it must simply be hoarded.

Isolated rural industry is different from urban industry. The former cannot be expanded in an unlimited way. The surplus from one industry cannot be turned into another industry as capital. Therefore, the wealth accumulated will go back into land. The more capital that goes into land, the more the price of land increases; and the cost of agriculture goes up. The profit in agriculture goes down, and the farmers have to lower their standard of living in order to reduce the labor costs of agriculture.

The poor farmers who live in an economy where this traditional mill industry is developing will find life more and more difficult. Therefore, we cannot make a generalization to the effect that rural industry always helps the life of the people. If we have made anything clear in this treatise, it should be that we should not consider rural industry as one entity. This term implies different types of activity. Each type has its own characteristics and exercises varying influences on the rural economy. We distinguished in Yits'un two types: the household handicrafts, represented by basketry, and the village mill, represented by papermaking. There must be still other types, with varying characteristics.

In the next part we shall see another, more developed type of industry, which affects the life of the peasants still more seriously.

PART III

YUTS'UN: COMMERCE AND THE LAND

FROM Luts'un, which represents a type of rural economy characterized by petty landowners who occupy their farms and manage them mainly by hired labor, we proceeded first to Yits'un, a village situated in a gorge along a river which frequently floods and where the land is poor. The villagers of Yits'un would be even worse off than they are if they depended only on their land. They make up their deficiencies of income by engaging in two rural industries: basketry and papermaking. Basketry is engaged in by the poor villagers who cannot find full employment or secure enough income from farming. Paper mills are owned by rich houses that possess enough capital to build the plants. From their investment they gain high profits; however, expansion of the industry is limited. The wealth accumulated in the paper industry is usually redirected into land. Conseqnently, the millowners become, at the same time, the holders of large amounts of land. Land miles away gradually comes into the hands of a few houses in the village. Here we find the germ of capitalism in industry and absenteeism in the land system. However, within Yits'un there are no tenants. The owners rent only that land which lies too far away for them to manage themselves. When the village alone is considered, it is found to be made up mainly of occupying owners. But what happens if industry and commerce develop more? With these problems in our mind, we went to Yuts'un in the spring of 1940.

Yuts'un is about 100 miles south of Kunming, close to a highway connecting Kunming and southern Yunnan. The highway was still under construction when we took up our investigation. The regular bus service ends at the walled town that is only fifteen minutes' walk from Yuts'un. But this walled town is a center on the old traffic route of central Yunnan. Caravans of pack horses, the traditional type of trading expeditions which are still very common in that region, start at this place. They follow the southward route to Indo-China and to Thailand, the westward route to Tali and to Burma, and the northward route to the Lake of Yunnan, on the north shore of which is Kunming. The road from Kunming to Yuchi, the district in which

Yuts'un is located, is level, although surrounded by mountains. The geographical location of this region has led to industrial and commercial development. It is known as the center of trade and of the textile industry in the province. The valley is several times as large as that of Lufon. In Luts'un one can see the complete circle of surrounding mountains; but in Yuts'un, except on the western side, the mountains lie on the far edge of the horizon. Since most of the mountainous land is uncultivated, the size of the valley is a direct indication of the richness of the region. Yuchi is one of the few well-populated regions in the province. Even a casual traveler will not fail to be impressed by the wealth of the inhabitants. They are better clothed and nourished than are the people elsewhere in the province. It is not an accident that the girls of this region have long been known for their physical beauty. In this valley we find large towns.

The growth of towns indicates the development of commerce and the concentration of wealth. The development of commerce in the traditional economy has different effects on the general population. On the one hand, it enlarges the opportunity for employment; but, on the other hand, it accelerates the concentration of landownership. The villages which are located near the town can enjoy better markets for their produce; also, they can raise cash crops. This changes the principle of land utilization. In Yits'un we saw that the villagers depend upon growing their own foodstuffs. They cannot depend on the rice produced in other localities. Moreover, if they grow more vegetables than they need, they cannot find a market for their produce— they are too far away. But those who live near towns where green vegetables are not grown can select the most profitable crops and grow them. Commercial development encourages a wide range of agricultural development. Owing to better transportation, rural industry can be developed not necessarily on the basis of locally produced raw materials. In Yits'un villagers make baskets and paper because they grow bamboo. In neighboring villages where bamboo is not grown, no one can make a profit from this industry. But in the trading centers raw materials can be imported and produce can be exported. Commercial development again widens the range of rural industry. Therefore, the people living near a town can be both better and more fully employed.

However, it is not necessarily true that the development of a town will improve the livelihood of all the villagers. Sometimes the town represents a threat to the poor peasant in the village. In Luts'un we have shown that in the traditional economy there is a strong force working for the decentralization of landholdings. It is the principle of equality in inheritance among the brothers. Landholdings will be divided up by the generations to come. It is true that, from time to time, poorer homes rise in the world; but few of them can hold on. On the whole, the tendency to sink down from big holdings to small holdings and from landed to landless is strong. This is the process that maintains the structure of petty owners and landless laborers. But the development of industry and commerce changes the outlook for the rich houses.

Opportunities for accumulating wealth in industry and commerce are much greater than in agriculture. We have shown that in Yits'un profits from the paper industry are several times that from farming. The low profits in agriculture keep the small owners from having any considerable amount of savings for investment. But, in developed industry and commerce, income may easily exceed daily living expenses. We have seen how the paper-mill owners worry about the lack of opportunity for further investment of their surplus capital. Once the capital gathered from commerce and industry moves to land, it not only prevents the large landowners from sinking down to lower levels but also tends to promote expansion. The land begins to concentrate in the hands of big owners.

We should keep in mind, however, the fact that there are different types of rural industry. Only those types which require considerable capital will give high profits. The poor peasants who cannot even maintain themselves are cut off from profitable industries and commerce. They may carry on some simple manufactures, such as basketmaking; but from this they get even less return than from hiring out on farms. It is all the more so as the handicraft industry develops into the put-out system. As we shall see in the following pages, weavers of cotton cloth receive very low wages. Profit from this industry goes entirely to the investors of capital. For the poor peasants the pressure of population on the land is by no means lifted through the development of industry. They have no easy way to expand their holdings. Therefore, there is no counterforce against the process of division of estates in inheritance. The small holders of land are drawn down, generation after generation. Any misfortune will force them to sell their land to the rich. The development of industry and commerce in the rural economy creates a sharp distinction between rich and poor, capital and labor, and those who are rising and those who are sinking. The split between these two classes eventually becomes more marked by the tendency to separate into town- and village-dwellers. The rich houses move to trading centers for economic advantage, material comfort, and social security. But once they move out from their villages, they cannot manage their farms by themselves. Tenancy develops, the tenants living in the village while the landlords live in town. This leads to the type of landholding represented by Kiangts'un, as described in *Peasant Life in China*. In Yunnan, absentee ownership of this extreme form does not exist; but in Yuts'un we can see the beginning of it. Yuts'un thus fills a gap between Luts'un, Yits'un, and Kiangts'un. These four types, put together, show the process of economic development going on in the rural China today.

CHAPTER XXII

FARMING AND TRUCK GARDENING

Y UTS'UN and Luts'un are villages which outwardly resemble each other. Both are located in the center of fertile valleys where the population is dense and arable land is limited. If we compare the two villages more closely, however, it can be seen that Yuts'un is even more populous and has even less land than Luts'un. There are 156 households and 777 individuals in Yuts'un. The total amount of land owned by private households is 665 *mow*. The average amount of land owned by each household is 4.3 *mow*, or 0.85 *mow* for each individual. In Luts'un there are 122 households and 611 individuals, who possess 690 *mow* of land, which is about 5.7 *mow* for each household, on the average, and 1.3 *mow* for each individual. As regards the area under cultivation, the average size of a farm in Luts'un is 9 *mow* and in Yuts'un 6 *mow*. If we compare how the land is used, the difference is even more striking. In Yuts'un a large amount of land is cultivated intensively as truck gardens, while in Luts'un we recall that some of the rich sandy land along the river is little cultivated and used simply to grow corn. The reason for this difference in the use of the land in the two villages is that Yuts'un is located near a market town where vegetables are in demand and has good transportation to other distant markets, while Luts'un is more isolated. We may start our discussion of Yuts'un, then, by a discussion of the use to which the land is put.

I. CROPS

Two kinds of land can be distinguished in Yuts'un—rice field and truck garden. The area used for truck gardening is located about one-sixth of a mile north of the village along the southern bank of the Yuchi River. This river, which runs from east to west, floods regularly; and as a result the sandy land along the river is very fertile. About 120 *mow* of this sandy land are cultivated by the villagers. On this land they grow from thirty to forty different kinds of vegetables, including cabbage, turnips, celtuce, leeks, squash, spinach, *lutze*, a snail-like tuber, and many others. All through the year something is grown; not a bit of land lies waste at any time.

Only a small part of these vegetables are consumed by the growers; the greater part of them are grown for sale. The village is near a large walled town in which on every other day a market is held. Or the villagers may go to other markets near by, as round trip to these more distant markets takes only half a day. With markets near at hand, they can select those crops to grow which bring the highest returns. They can grow less rice and other staple food crops for themselves because they are able to count upon buying them when needed in the market. Market gardening develops in response to these conditions.

South of the truck-garden land around the village are the rice fields. Two types of rice field are distinguished: the dry field and the wet field. The dry fields are on high ground. During the winter they can be drained, and broad beans, rape, "bitter grass" (grass used as fertilizer), barley, and wheat may be grown after the rice is harvested. The fields located on the lower ground are hard to drain; they stay wet all through the year and can only be used for growing rice.

There are several kinds of rice grown in the village, locally called "early white rice," "late white rice," and "red rice." The early white rice requires 170 days to mature and can be planted earlier than the other varieties. The other two varieties take 180 days to mature. Eighty-eight per cent of the rice field is used for growing the late white rice, 10 per cent for the red rice, and only 2 per cent for the early white rice. The late white rice can be grown on both wet and dry land and is said not to exhaust the fertility of the soil. Red rice may be grown on both wet and dry land but cannot be grown continuously. The early white rice can be grown only on dry land. The annual yield of the various varieties is different. The late white rice and the red rice yield, on the average, 16 *piculs* per *mow*. But the early white rice yields only 12–14 *piculs* per *mow*. Of the late white rice and the red rice, every 4 *piculs* of unhusked rice will give 1.9 *piculs* of husked rice. In the case of the early white rice, however, the same amount of unhusked rice will give 2.1 *piculs*. The early white rice also tastes better and thus fetches a higher price. The red rice is more nourishing, so that 5 pounds of rice will feed six people for one day, while the white rice will feed only five people for one day.

It appears that the rice yield is a little less per acre than in Luts'un. In Yuts'un every *mow* yields about 16 *piculs*, which amounts to about 100 *piculs* of unhusked rice, 52 *piculs* of husked rice, or about 3,450 pounds per acre. In Luts'un the average is 60 *piculs* per acre of husked rice—about 8 *piculs* higher per acre.

There are about 300 *mow* of dry land in the village. Seventy per cent of this is used for growing beans in the winter; 15 per cent of it, for "bitter grass"; 10 per cent for rape; and 15 per cent for barley and wheat. Broad beans, used on the table when green, are employed chiefly for feeding ducks, horses, and pigs. The stalks and pods, when dried and pulverized, are the principal food used for feeding pigs. "Bitter grass," when cut and plowed into the land, serves as fertilizer, 1 *mow* of grass serving to fertilize 3 or 4 *mow* of land. Rape produces a seed which can be pressed to produce an oil that is used both for cooking and for light. What is left of the seed after the oil has been pressed out is used for fertilizer. Wheat is used for food, and barley to make wine.

II. FARMING ACTIVITIES AND THE AGRICULTURAL CALENDAR

In the previous two parts we described in detail the growing of rice and beans and gave the calendar of agricultural work (p. 22). Since there are no essential differences either in the type of work done or in the periods at which the different types of work are started between Luts'un and this village, we shall not repeat this material here. In neither Luts'un nor in Yits'un did we describe the way in which other crops are grown, because in these villages subsidiary crops were unimportant in village economy. But here we shall give a detailed account of how eight important vegetables are grown, in order to give an idea of the art with which vegetable growing is carried on.

Cabbage is sown in the nursery bed in the middle of December. In the latter part of February the plants are transplanted into the main bed. From the beginning of June to the end of July, the cabbages may be gathered. Before sowing the seeds, the soil must be turned over and pulverized; and it then has liquid manure (human and animal) applied to it in quantity, twice in three days. After this the seeds are sown. Before transplanting the plants, the garden must be prepared. The young plants are put into the soil and then watered, in order to make the earth stick to the roots and also to wash the sand off the plants. On the two days following they are again watered, and again a few days later, in order to keep the soil moist. After four or five days the plants will be watered regularly once a day, and liquid manure applied once a week. Some cultivators apply "bitter grass" after the plants have been growing for a month. During this time there is very little rain.

Turnips are started in the latter part of September. They are sown rather thickly; but when the young plants start, they are thinned out, to leave only the best. They are watered every few days and have fertilizer applied to them after they are somewhat grown. In one hundred days they are ready to be pulled.

There are two kinds of celtuce. The first is sown at the beginning of September, and it may be sown even as late as the beginning of November. After it has grown a month, it is transplanted; and it can be used in March. Another, later type is sown in January or February and will be ready in April or May; it needs to be fertilized three or four times after it has been transplanted and must be watered.

In the winter, from November to January, the seeds of leeks are sown in the prepared nursery bed. They are covered with pure sand, watered, and kept well weeded. When they have grown 3 inches high, fertilizer is applied. In July or August clumps of four or five are taken up and transplanted into trenches; the plants are put in slantwise. They are watered every two or three days, and fertilizer is applied— first diluted and later more concentrated. In February they are cut off close to the ground, and fertilizer is applied again, to encourage the plant to grow upward. When the plants have grown about 2 inches high, about an inch of soil is heaped up around them, and the plants are then watered. After twenty days they are again cut and fertilizer applied. Every twenty-three or twenty-four days this process of cutting and applying fertilizer is continued, up to April, so that they are cut three or four times in a year. The cut shoots may be sold and are an important vegetable in the village. In June they begin to bud, and by August the buds may be picked every other day and sold. If the buds are left to develop flowers, the gardener will apply fertilizer every ten days. In the latter part of October the flower may be collected and salted to make a relish, and again ten days later. But by the middle of November frost comes, and the cutting must be discontinued. The leek plant is a perennial, and so this process of cutting may be repeated on the old growth from year to year (up to seven years). But market gardeners replant their leek after it has become four years old. Ordinary gardeners will wait a year more and then resow.

In growing *lutze* the old tubers are gathered at the end of December and are heeled in. By February, when the roots of the tubers have sprouted a little, they are divided and set out in the nursery bed—one in every 2-inch square. They must be well soaked with water every day. After ten days leaves appear. At the end of June the plant will have grown 1 foot high. The stalk is then cut down to the ground. An

8-inch piece of the stalk is cut with scissors; and the cutting is laid in a shallow trench in the main field, and soil is laid on top, so that only about 3 inches protrude. The soil is pressed with the foot, and it is well watered and then pressed down again. Next, trenches are covered with tree branches, so as to protect the cuttings from the strong rays of the sun. After ten days this cover is removed and liquid manure added. When the plant begins to flower, the top is picked off. This makes the plant spread out. Fertilizer is applied again. After forty days the whole plant is dug and the ground turned. Trenches are again prepared; and every 6–7 inches along them the plants are set, with soil heaped up around them so that only 3 inches protrude. The soil is pressed well with the foot and watered, and after three days liquid manure is applied. The plants are kept weeded and cultivated. In October manure, straw, and ashes are applied to the base of each plant; and the plants are watered weekly. The tubers are collected in December and January.

Squash is planted after the cabbage has been harvested, in the land in which the cabbage has grown. In May the cabbage is still growing, and the squash may be grown in the nursery bed. Squash requires little care and only a moderate amount of fertilizer. By August or September it may be gathered. It may also be planted in January or February, after the leeks, and harvested in June and July. Squash plants are placed about 10 feet apart and fertilizer applied, though not too near to the plant. Sand must be kept off the sprouts.

Chinese cabbage may be grown from July to November. It should be transplanted when one month old, and it takes two months more to develop. It may be planted in any vacant place. After sowing the seed a top layer of sand is applied, and the plant is watered. The seeds sprout in three days. In five or six days a dilute insecticide is applied. The plants need frequent watering until they are a month old, when they are transplanted into the main garden. After that they will require watering only every three or four days, unless it rains, in which case the sand must be washed off. Every two weeks fertilizer and insecticide are applied, and in about two months the crop is ready to sell.

One of the characteristics of the truck garden is the variety of its crops. Three motives are effective in the selection of crops. The first is the desire for personal consumption by the gardeners. For instance, our landlord, in answering our question as to why he grew potatoes, said: "I used to grow a few for my own use every year." When we discussed a kind of squash, he said again: "I grow that for my own household." However, this is only true of some minor crops. Most of the garden produce is grown solely for marketing. According to our rough estimate, about one-sixth of the garden produce is grown for the gardeners' own consumption, the rest being sold. In 1940 the total amount of income from vegetables of the whole village was about $180,000. Since the villagers grow vegetables mainly to sell, the kind of crop selected is determined largely by the profit to be gained. "We decide what our garden crops are to be according to the prices of the previous year," said our landlord. "For instance, last year I grew celery, but the price was low; so this year I have not grown any. Formerly, the village grew a great deal of squash, which was made into a kind of candy by adding honey and sugar to it and was a speciality of the district. But last year the price of sugar increased, less candy was made, and the price of squash was consequently low. This year less squash is being grown in the village." The third factor determining crops is the nature of the soil. Different crops require different soil. Some of them are particularly suited to the soil of this village, while others are not. The demand for bitter squash has increased during the last few years. Yuts'un gardeners were attracted by the high price for which it sold and tried to grow it. But when they found this type of squash did not grow very well in their gardens, they gave it up. Nevertheless, allowing for the limitations of the soil, the crops grown in truck gardens vary much more in their response to the market demand than those grown in the main fields. The truck gardens have been developed to meet the demands of commerce, while the rice fields are still governed mainly by the needs of self-sufficiency.

Another difference between the truck garden and the rice field is found in the elasticity of the farming schedule. On the whole, garden crops have a less rigid schedule than field crops such as rice, beans, wheat, and so on. For instance, rice cannot be sown before Yu Shui (February 5) or later than Ch'un Fen (March 21), and the other field crops have a definite time for sowing also. But in the truck gardens the celtuce may be started at almost any time from September to November. Squash grows in either summer or winter. Chinese cabbage may also be grown throughout both summer and autumn. The rigidity of the planting calendar comes from the need for a certain temperature and amount of moisture. In Yunnan, as we have seen in Part I, temperature changes are moderate, but rainfall changes are radical. The rice farms must have the rain which comes in the rainy season. But the

market gardeners are not dependent upon rainfall. They make irrigation ditches around their garden plots and water them constantly,
dipping out the water with long dippers.

In the agricultural calendar given on page 22 we show the periods
of time in which certain activities may be performed. But, actually,
the farmers confine themselves to still more limited periods of time
because other considerations enter in. For instance, throughout the entire village the late rice will be harvested in five days because the villagers say they wish to avoid the depredations of the birds who feed
on the ripened rice. Squash is usually sown in May, because then they
can use the field where the cabbage has been harvested. Plants sown
in January and February follow up the leek plants.

Owing to the seasonal character of farming activities on the rice
farm, there are big gaps in the work—at least one hundred and ninety
days during the winter and spring when there is no actual labor needed. But in the truck gardens, labor is much more evenly distributed
throughout the year. The work on the rice farm results in long periods
of idleness, when the villagers may go off and seek other employment;
but in gardening, constant care is needed. Practically every morning
the plots must be watered. There is no very hard work for long periods, but the gardeners are kept busy every day.

III. LABOR SUPPLY

We mentioned that in Yuts'un there are two types of rice fields. On
the double-cropped fields there are five different spring crops, and for
each crop the labor required is different. In Table 40 we show the
amount of labor required for 1 *mow* of land for the different crops.

In Luts'un on a farm of the same size, to grow rice requires 22.6
male units of labor and 18.2 units of female labor. To grow beans requires 1.3 units of male labor and 10 units of female labor. It appears
that less labor is spent on the rice field in Yuts'un. For instance, weeding is done only twice, and only 6 units of female labor per *mow* are
needed. But in Luts'un the farmers weed three times, using a total of
10.4 units of female labor. In addition to this, they use clippers to cut
down the weeds, which adds another unit of female labor for each
mow. These facts may indicate that in our third type of village, Yuts'un,
attention has been shifted from the rice field to the market garden. We
have already noted that production of field crops is less in Yuts'un than
in Luts'un.

But the market gardeners, as we have shown in the last section, are occupied with cultivation of their plots all the time. Each *mow* requires continuous care from one man. If the farmers transport their produce to market, they must employ someone to help them.

Now we may proceed to consideration of the labor supply in the village. Is there sufficient labor in the village to carry on the work both of the fields and of the garden plots? To answer this question we need to know the size of the farms. The total area under cultivation by the villagers is 126 *mow* of vegetable gardens and 788 *mow* of rice field; of the latter, 25 *mow* are used as nursery garden for young rice. Half of the rest is about equally divided between wet and dry field. In the dry field 266 *mow* are used for growing beans, 57 *mow* for "bitter grass," 42 *mow* for rape, and 8 *mow* each for barley and wheat.

TABLE 40

LABOR REQUIRED FOR FIELD CROPS ON 1 *Mow* OF LAND

(Labor Unit, 1 Person per Day)

	Wet-Field Rice	Rice	Beans	Dry-Field Rape	Bitter Grass	Wheat	Barley
Male	14.4	18.7	2	14	6.6	12	10
Female	6.0	10.0	6	2	15.0	....	2

Among the adult population from the age of sixteen to sixty there are 194 men and 201 women. (These figures include some who have temporarily left the village.) Assuming that 35 men and 35 women are engaged in the work of market gardening, there are 159 men and 166 women whose labor can be employed in the rice fields. We know that the busiest period for women in the rice fields is during the transplanting time. This work takes 40 days; and the total amount of labor required is 2,668 units, or the work of 66 women. If all the women available were to be used, the work could be completed in 16 days. The busiest time for male labor is during the harvest, which takes 30 days, or 4,346 units of labor. It will keep 145 laborers busy throughout the period, which is less than the supply of labor available in the village. We can see that the labor supply in the village should be self-sufficient.

Although Yuts'un should be able to supply all the labor needed in the village, it does not attempt to do so. Some people are absent. Others either do nothing, because they lack the necessary strength, or are engaged in other activities. The actual number of people who work in agriculture is 136 men and 59 women. This is not enough to care for both the garden plots and the field crops. The actual supply is thus smaller than the amount needed. Moreover, instead of spreading out the work so as to allow more time for each worker, the farmers cut down on the time for completing the work, which makes the shortage of labor all the more marked. For instance, harvest would not have to be completed for thirty days, but it is finished within a week. All the villagers start work at about the same time, so that they can harvest at the same time. To complete the harvest in this time they must have about 620 laborers daily and cannot depend entirely on their own supply of labor. The reason they are able to cut down their work to such a short period is that they have a large supply of labor outside the village. In the neighboring walled town and in several larger village around the town during the busy season there are labor markets. Thousands of laborers, most of them aborigines, come from different parts of the region and gather there to wait for calls. Those who are in need of laborers may go to the market and pick up the number of laborers they require. During transplanting time these laborers are all women; during the harvest, men.

The aborigines who live on the mountainsides around the valley are poorer than the villagers in the valley. A wage which is not sufficient for the Chinese of the valley will satisfy them. These people do not raise rice but live on corn and millet, which have a different farming season, and so are free for the busy season in the rice crop. They like to come and earn a sum of money to supplement their regular incomes. We do not know just how much labor can be supplied, but there has always been enough. During 1939, owing to the draft, many adult men in the valley left; and since only the same number of aborigines came as had come the previous year, there was a labor shortage. At that time it was necessary to ask the entire company of the home guard to come and help with the harvest. But the following year more aborigines came, and the supply again balanced the demand.

Employers in the village prefer to get laborers from the labor market rather than from among their neighbors, for in the latter case they cannot bargain about the wage to be paid. In the market there are no personal relations and no hurt feelings. Bargaining as to what the wage shall be takes place then and there, since there is no uniform wage and wages are adjusted to the supply of labor as well as to the strength and ability of the laborers.

Since Yuts'un is located near labor markets, the farmers of the village are always sure of getting enough labor if they have the money

to pay for it. As a result, they tend to depend upon a supply from outside, and they use in the rice fields only a small part of the labor which
might be available in their own village. There is, in fact, a popular
saying in the village that "if we had no aborigines, we could not manage our farms." In the village there is a public temple which is used
for giving lodging to laborers from outside, which indicates that the
practice of depending upon outside labor has been long practiced
and is a regular institution. The system is advantageous to the farm-
owners, since they do not need to provide for their laborers the year
through but have them only when they need them. As a result of this
situation, the system of hired labor has developed further in Yuts'un
than it has in Luts'un.

However, labor brought from the outside can only be used in the
rice fields. In the vegetable gardens the situation is different. They
require daily tending and cannot use the seasonal supply of labor.
Moreover, this type of gardening requires a high degree of skill. As we
have shown in our discussion, minute care of the plants is needed. An
inexperienced worker is of little use. Our landlord had a full-time employee, a man with a deformed hand, who was also rather stupid. This
man was not good at raising vegetables. Since aborigines could not be
employed for this purpose either, our landlord has been forced to tend
his own vegetable garden; and, because of his lack of energy, the garden is badly cared for. Thus, the labor for market gardening is always
supplied from the households of those who operate the plots.

IV. AGRICULTURAL PROFIT

In discussing the profits from agriculture we shall not give a detailed discussion and estimate of each item of cost because we have already given this information in foregoing sections. But in Table 41 the
money value of each item is given at the price level of the spring of
1940. During that time inflation had already affected the price level.
For instance, the price of rice was 25 cents for 7 pounds in 1938 in
Luts'un. This same amount cost $3.50 in 1940 in Yuts'un, the price
having risen fourteen times. But the rise varies as regards other items.
When we compare these prices with the estimates in the other sections,
we must keep this in mind.

Judging from the figures on net profits, the highest profit was gained
from rice and rape, the lowest from the single-cropped wet land. If we reduce this number fourteen times, the double-cropped land profited the
cultivators only a little less than the same type of land did in Luts'un.

TABLE 41

Cost and Yield of Field Crops on 1 *Mow* of Land
(Unit in Dollars, Chinese National Currency)

	WET FIELD SINGLE-CROPPED			DRY FIELD DOUBLE-CROPPED		
	Rice	Rice and Beans	Rice and Rape	Rice and Bitter Grass	Rice and Wheat	Rice and Barley
Cost						
Labor............	63.14	95.64	131.04	119.94	115.44	113.04
Tool depreciation..	20.00	20.00	20.00	20.00	20.00	20.00
Fertilizer.........	10.20	10.20	15.20	10.20	17.20	15.20
Seeds............	4.80	4.80	4.80	4.80	4.80	4.80
Rice						
Beans		9.00				
Rape..........			1.00			
Bitter grass.....				12.00		
Wheat.........					2.00	
Barley.........						2.00
Total........	98.14	134.84	72.04	156.94	159.44	155.04
Yield						
Rice	280.00 (16 *pic.*)	280.00	280.00	280.00	280.00	280.00
Straw (rice)....	7.00 (200 bundles)	7.00	7.00	7.00	7.00	7.00
Beans...........		57.50 (45 *pic.*)				
Fodder from beans		10.00 (10 *pic.*)				
Rape seed......			120.00 (3 *pic.*)			
Bitter grass.....				84.00		
Wheat..........					90.00 (4.5 *pic.*)	
Barley..........						80.00 (4 *pic.*)
Total........	287.00	364.50	407.00	371.00	377.00	367.00
Expenditure......	− 98.14	−134.84	−172.04	−156.94	−159.44	−155.04
Profit...........	188.86	229.66	235.96	214.06	217.56	211.96

The cost of 1 *mow* of the market garden for a year is, on the average, $500 for labor, $100 for fertilizer, $29 for seeds, and $19 for depreciation of tools, making a total of $748, which is much higher than for the field crops. It is difficult to estimate the income from these gardens because there is a big difference in the wholesale and retail prices of vegetables. If the producer carries his vegetables to market himself and sells directly to the consumers, he will get a better price. He may also bring his produce to market and sell to a middleman, but in this case he gets less. He may also sell the crop, as it stands, to a retailer who will carry it to market; but with this system of disposing of produce he gets least of all. Our landlord had 2 *mows* of garden land and always sold the produce in the last way. He told us that his total income from this land for the whole year is usually only $300–$400. But another householder of whose expenses we got a complete account and who owned 0.7 *mow* of garden land made $1,664 annually from his vegetables. He made $2,400 on 1 *mow*, and his net income amounted to about $1,500—about seven or eight times the income derived by our landlord from the same-sized garden. The gardener who made such a high profit took the produce to market himself and is, moreover, an expert in raising vegetables. He knows exactly the right time for watering and for fertilizing, and he is industrious in weeding and in getting rid of insect pests. In his garden, vegetables grow abundantly. He knows the conditions of the market very well; how to grow those crops which fetch the highest prices; and at what time to sell—when vegetables are scarce and the price is high. These two cases show the great variation in the yield from garden plots. On the average, each *mow* of garden land will produce 1 load (a load for a man's back) of vegetables every other day. There will be about 180 loads a year. Each load can be sold for about $10. The average income for 1 *mow* of vegetable-garden land will be $1,800, and the average profit $872. This is about four times the profit to be gained from the rice field; and it shows that, while intensive gardening takes more labor, it also gives a greater profit.

CHAPTER XXIII

LAND TENURE

FOR purposes of analysis, the households of the village have been grouped into four classes: rich, middle, poor, and landless. This classification is made on the basis of the variation in income derived from the land, since, with only a few exceptions, land-ownership determines not only social position but income as well. Those who are able to live on the proceeds from their land in the form of rent we have classified as "rich"; those who can live on the income from their land but only by managing their property themselves, as "middle"; those who cannot maintain themselves merely by working on their own land, as "poor"; and, finally, those who have no land and must always work for others rather than for themselves, the "landless." As a basis for comparison we had to set up a normal standard of living for an average household of five, which is equivalent in consumption to 3.7 adults. Every year such a household will require about 2,000 pounds of husked rice—worth, in 1940, $1,665. All other expenses will amount to one and one-half times the expenditure for rice; this is the usual allowance for rice in relation to other expenses in an ordinary Chinese household. Thus, each household needs approximately an income of $2,600 (on 1940 level) in order to maintain the standard of living of the ordinary Chinese peasant. Following this system of classification, we can proceed to see how the land in the village is distributed, who rents out land to whom, and what the sizes of the farms are in the various classes. We shall discuss these problems in the following section.

I. DISTRIBUTION OF LAND

The number of peasants who have insufficient land to maintain themselves is greater in the village of Yuts'un than in Luts'un, but less in Yuts'un than in Yits'un. In Yuts'un 77 per cent of the villagers have insufficient land, that is, less than 15 *kung*, or are landless; in Luts'un only 66 per cent are in this category; while in Yits'un about 90 per cent come under this head. In general, while each of these three villages has its own special character, they resemble one another in the fact that the majority of their inhabitants cannot make a living from their own land. The more concentrated the ownership of land, the more the people suffer from land hunger. This is because land is limited in quantity, so that whenever anyone acquires land he does so by making someone else give it up. In this village only 23 per cent of the households can maintain themselves on their own land, but this 23 per cent possesses 79 per cent of the rice field and 58 per cent of the vegetable-garden plots. In Luts'un 34 per cent of the households have sufficient land to maintain themselves, holding 79 per cent of the land. The concentration of land becomes clearer when we come to the average size of a landholding. In Yuts'un a rich household possesses, on the average, about 36 mow of rice field and 3.7 mow of vegetable plot, while in Luts'un the biggest total holding is only 25 mow.

As we have seen, the percentage of people who have insufficient land is higher in Yuts'un than in Luts'un. But in Yuts'un there are truck gardens where the land produces more per mow. In the preceding chapter we have shown that the profit on the truck gardens is more than four times that on the rice fields. In Luts'un, if a farm is very small, it is not worth cultivating. But here in Yuts'un the peasants do intensive gardening. The concentration of the poorer folk on truck gardening is shown in the distribution of garden plots. If we examine Table 42, we see that in the distribution of the two types of land—rice field and truck garden—the middle peasants possess more of the rice field and the poorer peasants more of the vegetable garden plots, although the average holding of the poor household is smaller than that of the middle household. This indicates that the concentration of garden land is less pronounced than that of rice field. In the preceding chapter we showed the difference in labor required for these two types of land. In the rice fields, work is on a bigger scale, and seasonal labor can be employed. But the vegetable plots demand daily skilled cultivation, and thus the amounts under cultivation cannot easily be expanded. The more attention put upon these truck gardens, the greater the yield. In the two cases discussed above, the difference in yield between the well-cared-for and the somewhat neglected plot amounted to seven to eight times as much profit for the former as for the latter. We shall presently show that the rent on rice fields and garden land is almost the same. As a result, the poorer peasants are attracted to the garden plots, and they tend to hold on to this type of land more tenaciously than to the rice field. There is a popular saying that "the rich folk like the rice fields, and the poor folk like the vegetable gardens."

The distribution of land can be discussed on the basis of operation.

Farmers may, through renting land and temporary transference of land, operate larger-sized farms than they own. On the whole, the rich class rent out both rice field and truck garden; the middle class rent rice field; and the poor and landless classes rent both truck garden and rice field, the former being more important. This indicates the tendency, noted above, for the poor folk to work the truck gardens.

In Table 42 may be found the amount of land under operation for each class. The rich class operate less land than they own, while the other classes work more land than they own. As a class, the poor rent the largest proportion of rice field, and the landless the next largest. By estimating by individual households, however, it is found that those in the middle class rent more than any of the other classes. But in the case of the truck gardens, the middle class, like the rich, rent out to others more than they rent for their own use.

However, the average size of holding for both rice field and vegetable garden remains larger for the rich, and there is a gradual decrease both in operation and in ownership from the middle to the poor and landless classes. The rich, as a class, still hold most of the land and operate it themselves, although they employ seasonal labor to do the work. We should ask, then, how the poorer classes can increase the size of their farms. If we compare the total of the land owned with the total under operation, we find that there is more land under operation than there is land owned. We must go into the matter of rented land and of land temporarily transferred on the basis of a loan.

II. TENANCY

The system of renting land in Yuts'un is similar to that in the two other villages discussed. The tenant does not need to pay a sum in advance to the owner as guaranty but must provide the personal guaranty of some middleman. According to custom, an owner cannot evict a tenant within three years after an agreement has been made. Nor can he increase the rent at will during that period. On the other hand, the tenant can return the land at any time. Recently some of the restrictions on owners are decreasing. It is said that an owner can now evict a tenant after two years if the latter does not pay his rent or if the owner wishes to operate the farm himself. However, the owner is still prevented from changing his tenant at will, while the tenant is free to find a substitute or even to sublet the rented land. The owner has no right to interfere with him if he continues to pay his rent.

TABLE 42

DISTRIBUTION OF LAND ACCORDING TO WEALTH

HOUSEHOLD			RICE FIELD							
			Owned			Rented				Temporarily Transferred
						Out (−)		From Others (+)		
Class	Number	Per Cent	Size (in *Mow*)	Per Cent	Average Size per Household (in *Mow*)	Size (in *Mow*)	Average Size per Household (in *Mow*)	Size (in *Mow*)	Average Size per Household (in *Mow*)	Out (−) (Size in *Mow*)	From Others (+) (Size in *Mow*)
Rich	6	4	215.2	38	35.9	34.9	5.8	20.4	3.4	43.9	1.3
Middle	31	19	226.4	41	7.3	14.4	0.46	132.4	4.3	8.4	7.2
Poor	75	49	114.3	21	1.5	10.3	.14	131.0	1.7	2.5	9.5
Landless	44	28	....	....	....	....	....	53.3	1.2	....	1.5
Total	156	....	555.9	....	....	59.7	....	337.1	....	54.8	19.5

TABLE 42—Continued

RICE FIELD—Continued			VEGETABLE GARDEN											
OPERATED			OWNED			RENTED				TEMPORARILY TRANSFERRED		OPERATED		
						Out (−)		From Others (+)		Out (−) (Size in Mow)	From Others (+) (Size in Mow)			
Size (in Mow)	Per Cent	Average Size per Household (in Mow)	Size (in Mow)	Per Cent	Average Size per Household (in Mow)	Size (in Mow)	Average Size per Household (in Mow)	Size (in Mow)	Average Size per Household (in Mow)			Size (in Mow)	Per Cent	Average Size per Household (in Mow)
158.1	19	26.3	22.4	21	3.7	10.1	1.7	1.4	0.23	3.9	2.3	12.1	9	2.0
343.2	43	11.1	42.4	37	1.4	3.7	0.12	1.9	0.06	2.7	8.7	46.6	33	1.3
242.0	31	3.2	44.1	42	0.6	3.7	0.05	13.5	0.18	1.5	4.1	56.5	41	0.8
54.8	7	1.2	.....	.....	.....	.....	.....	9.6	0.22	.....	13.9	23.5	17	0.4
798.1	.....	.....	108.9	.....	.....	17.5	.....	26.4	.....	8.1	29.0	138.7	.....	.....

The amount of rent is fixed by agreement, the average rent being 50 per cent of the rice produced. The tenant can ask for a reduction in the case of a bad harvest. But in some cases the owner will restore the higher rent the following year. Sometimes the system of sharecropping is also practiced; that is, the owner shares half the rice yield with the tenant. In this case, the entire spring crop goes to the tenant. This custom is practiced on poor land whose yield is uncertain. As a rule, rent is paid in grain; but in some cases it is converted into cash in terms of grain, usually at a lower price level. This practice has been stopped during inflation. The rent on truck gardens is paid either in cash or in grain, and the rent is lower than for the rice field. But the usual practice is that the tenants of truck gardens pay half the rent in advance.

After an owner rents out his land, he has no obligation to provide tools or capital to his tenant. The tenant manages the farm and bears the risk but has no other duty toward the owner except that of paying rent.

The total amount of land rented by the villagers of Yuts'un is 337.1 *mow* of rice field and 26.4 *mow* of vegetable garden. Only a small part of this rented land belongs to private owners in the village. The people of the village rent out to others 60 *mow* of rice field. Part of this land is too far away for them to operate themselves; or, since they cannot find tenants from their own village, they rent to people from outside. Thirty-five per cent of the land is rented out to the village members. Of the 26.4 *mow* of vegetable garden, all is rented by village members, although only 17.5 *mow* of this amount are owned by the villagers themselves. The farmers of the village rent from the collective owners of their own village 78 *mow* and from collective owners who live outside the village 71 *mow*. The remaining land—that is, 153 *mow* of rice field and 6.9 *mow* of vegetable garden—is rented from private owners who live outside the village. It can be seen from these figures that, among the owners who rent out land, the private owners from outside the village are the most important. We may recall that in Luts'un the total amount of land rented from owners outside the village amounts to only 10 per cent of the land under operation; but in Yuts'un the land from these sources amounts to 28 per cent, 19 per cent of this 28 being land rented from outside private owners. In Yits'un there is no case of land being rented from outside. This indicates that the development of the system of tenancy in Yuts'un has advanced. However, in the case of the vegetable plots, only a small amount is rented from outside. The holding of this type of land is more stable and the system of tenancy less developed here.

Local private owners.—Three out of six rich houses rent their land out to others. But only one of them rents all its land, the other two renting out only a portion. They all possess large holdings, so that they are able to live entirely on their rent and need not trouble to farm if they do not care to.

Of the thirty-one middle-class households, there are five who rent out land. One of them had no able-bodied man in the house; so this household gave up all its vegetable garden and kept only the rice field, which it operates with hired labor. The second household possessed rather extensive vegetable plots, which it found too large to be worked by its members exclusively; so it rents out a part. The third household is that of a widow, who rents out all of her vegetable plot and rents from others rice fields, for which she can hire labor. The other two households rent out all their fields to others. If they operated their land themselves, they would be prosperous; while by not doing so, they are badly off. The head of one of these households is a cripple and cannot do manual labor. He stays in the house and does nothing but recite Buddhistic classics and smoke opium. Having given up this world, he is looking forward to the next. He will not be able to hold his land very long and is rapidly sinking down to a lower social status. The head of the other household is a graduate of a middle school who does not know how to work on a farm and is, besides, inclined to be neurotic. The whole household is run by his wife, who is still young and occupied with caring for young children. In the middle class, opium and education appear to have an almost equally stultifying effect. Lack of manpower makes truck gardening impossible. But the rice field is not so dependent upon the labor of the household, since hired labor can be employed. In some certain special cases, such as that of the cripple, even the attempt to operate the rice fields is abandoned, however.

The poorer farmers suffer from land hunger, but nine out of the seventy-five households rent out land to others. Three of these households have, as their heads, widows with young children. Another has a widow with an adopted son, who has left the household. In another three households the men are still living but have gone off to engage in commerce. All these seven households rent out their land because of the lack of manpower. Of these seven, some own only small garden plots, others a small amount of rice field, and still others own both

I

types of land. Usually they retain their rice fields if possible. Of the others who rent out their land, the remaining two rent out a part of their land but rent a large amount of land from someone else. Their reason for doing this is not known.

Collective owners.—In Luts'un we indicated the importance of the collective owners in the village economy. The same thing is true in Yuts'un: there are the village lands, the clan lands, and the temple lands. The total amount of land owned collectively is 80 *mow* of rice field and 2 *mow* of garden land. Seventy-eight *mow* of rice field and all the garden land is rented out to the villagers. The rent on these lands is usually lower than that of the ordinary land. For example, the land of one clan was rented for only three-eighths of the rice produced, and only recently was the rent raised to the normal rate of one-half the produce. The clan rents this land to its own members, piece by piece. Clan lands are always rented to clan members and village lands to villagers. Since these lands are rented more with the idea of helping out clan members (or friends), the collection of rent is not very strict. The temple lands are sometimes rented to outsiders.

The collective land owned by outsiders is the school land, which is owned by the government. A part of the school land is rented out to villagers. The rent for this land, in terms of rice, is lower than the normal rent. Every year, after harvest, the district controller sends an agent to collect the rent. In the past the government refused to accept rice, because rice is difficult to hold over a period of time. Instead, money was accepted, at a lower rate than normal. In 1930, owing to the sudden change in price of rice, the government began to accept rice instead of money, but still at a low rate of rental. Because of the low rate, the people like to rent this land. As a result, the people with the most influence get most of the land—that is, people of the middle class, who have influence with the district officials. Besides this, middle-class folk are held to be more responsible than the poorer classes and less likely to default on their rent, so that they are given the first opportunities at it. As an example of this preference, we see that a house belonging to the middle class was able to rent 40 *mow* of this land.

From collective owners, both local and outside, the villagers rented 149 *mow*, amounting to 49 per cent of the land rented. Since we have discussed the nature of these collective owners in Part I, we shall not go into this again. It is sufficient to repeat here that, owing to the low rentals asked and the tolerance of default, renting land of this sort should not be confused with ordinary tenancy.

Outside private owners.—The most important source of rented land for the villagers comes from outside private owners. This land amounts to 45 per cent of the rice field and 39 per cent of the garden plots. The owners of this land live, for the most part, in the near-by walled town. We shall give several cases here to show the economic position of these owners. The first case is one where the owner has more than 20 *mow* of land, all rented out. In the second case the individual is the owner of a hotel in town and has more than 10 *mow* of land, which is rented out to the villagers of Yuts'un. The third case is that of a merchant of salt and cotton, who has more than 20 *mow* of land, half of which is rented out and half operated by the man himself. The fourth case is that of a man who owned a grocery but later, becoming a cotton-cloth merchant, acquired a great deal of money and bought more than 400 *mow* of land near Yuts'un. He rents out about 20 *mow* and operates the rest with the help of hired labor. The fifth case is that of a man who started as a gold merchant, became a part owner of a bus line running from Kunming to Yuchi, and is now a cloth merchant. This man owns more than 400 *mow*, more than 10 of which are located near Yuts'un and are rented out to the villagers. The first four cases all represent villagers who moved to town. Some of them moved because they had begun to engage in commerce; others, because their houses were burned in a bandit attack on the village. After the latter disaster many people moved out; some of them were poor peasants, who sold their land at this time. Others among the small farmers, whose land was hardly worth coming back to, rented out their land. But, more important than these are the rich folk who move to the city and, since they cannot take their farms with them, become large absentee landlords. In the fourth and fifth cases, we can see the effects of commerce on the concentration of land. This is only a small part of the whole picture. From this glimpse we can get some notion of the effects which the accumulation of capital through commerce has on land ownership. This problem will be discussed in more detail at the end of this part.

III. TEMPORARY TRANSFERENCE OF LAND

Temporary transference of land, briefly mentioned in Part I, is a common institution in China. This institution is called in Chinese *dien*, which has no equivalent in any Western language because there is no similar institution in the West. In legal terms, "*dien* is the right to use an immovable of another person and to collect fruits therefrom by paying a price and taking possession of the immovable."[1] The *dien*-maker is, therefore, entitled to redeem his land after the duration of the *dien*.[2]

Temporary transference of land is an arrangement between the creditor and the debtor of a loan. Instead of giving interest, the debtor offers the creditor a piece of land for temporary but not permanent use. The debtor is to have the land back after a term of years, when the loan has been cleared. This arrangement is different from ordinary mortgage loans, where the debtor gives a deed to the land to his creditor, the deed being held as security so that, in case the debtor cannot pay back the loan, the land may be sold to clear the debt. In this latter case the debtor continues to use the land and merely pays interest on the loan. But in the case of a temporary transference, the debtor gives up the right to use the land for a certain period.

This system developed in the peculiar agrarian situation in China. As we have repeatedly shown, Chinese peasants do not like to sell their land. They regard their land not merely as a commodity to be handled for profit but, since land is mostly inherited from their fathers, as a symbol of kinship solidarity. Restrictions on the selling of land are found both in individual attitudes and in clan regulations. Therefore, when a person needs money and has no other resource than his land, he will secure loans either by mortgaging the land or by temporarily transferring the right of use of the land to his creditor. In this case, since the property right is retained, clan members cannot interfere with the action. On the other hand, those who do not have sufficient land may get more land for their own use under this system. To them the advantage is that they need only pay a part of the land value to acquire the right of use. It is similar to renting land; but, by advancing a sum of money, they do not need to pay annual rent. In other words, they pay the rent by foregoing the use of the money loaned. The cost to the borrower is sometimes lower than the ordinary interest rate, as we shall show later. If the lender makes this arrangement with his own money, it gives him an opportunity for investment. Even if he has no money of his own, but gets it from borrowing from someone else, he can pay the interest of the loan out of the money gained from the land. In this case, he is, in fact, paying a lower rent for the land that he temporarily possesses. It is, therefore, quite common for poor peasants, who may have a little savings or have the opportunity for borrowing money, to arrange a temporary transference of land from middle or

[1] *Civil Code of the Republic of China*, art. 911. [2] *Ibid.*, art. 923.

rich peasants who are in need of money. As we have seen in Luts'un, this arrangement is also used by the rich peasant to help his poor relatives, since it serves as a way of giving them some land to use for a limited period.

How much land is to be transferred for how much money is an individual arrangement, no definite amount being established by custom. We know that in 1929 a man of the village arranged a loan for $3,000 and gave his creditor 20 *mow* of land for temporary use. This piece of land was worth $5,000 at the time, so that the amount of money received was only 60 per cent of the value of the land. In 1940 another villager got a loan of $1,700 by transferring 2.6 *mow* of land to the creditor. But this land was worth $2,600, so that the money loaned amounted to 65 per cent of the value of the land. My landlord told me that, in 1940, 5 *mow* of land could secure $2,500— about 48 per cent of the value of the land. Thus it appears that the rate varies.

Let us take 50 per cent of land value as the average amount that the temporary possessor has to pay to the landowner in order to get the right of use—about $500 for 1 *mow* in 1940. He will get about $200 of profit from the land if he operates it himself. The rate of interest on that loan is about 40 per cent, which is higher than an ordinary loan. If the landowner rents the land out, he will receive about $140 of rent in that year, or 14 per cent of the land value. By sacrificing the rent in order to get a loan of $500 by this arrangement, he is, in fact, paying interest at a rate of 28 per cent, which is a little higher than the ordinary rate of interest of about 20 per cent.

There are twenty-one houses of the different classes in the village which have acquired land under this system. Of the four classes, the poor class got the most rice field, and the middle class came second. The landless got the most garden land. In the case of both types of land the rich got the least, since they are not interested in getting land for use only.

As to the sources of transferred lands, the largest amounts of rice field came from outside private owners, the next largest from local private owners, and the least from the local collective owners. The garden land was transferred mainly by local private owners. Among the private owners who have given up their land by this system are eight houses of all classes who own land, the larger proportion coming from the rich. The rice fields are usually transferred to outsiders; the garden lands, to villagers. We shall give cases of each type.

In the last section we have shown that there are a number of rich people who live outside the village and rent their land to poor villagers. The system of temporary transference of land may be used by the poor instead of renting. A cloth merchant in the town transferred 3 *mow* of rice field and 1 *mow* of garden land to a landless man of the village. In another case a salt merchant of the town, who had become quite rich and then lost everything through trying to run a bus company, gave up some of his land, of which 1½ *mow* went to a man of the poor class. There are cases, also, in which poor villagers who have left the village but who still think they may come back, employ this system instead of selling their land. One case of this sort is that of a man who went to a mining center to do truck gardening. He transferred 1 *mow* of garden land to a landless man. Another case was that of a man accused of theft, who was driven out by the villagers and went to another district and became a carpenter. He transferred his land, 1 *mow* of rice field and ½ *mow* of garden land, to poor peasants. In still another case a man who left the village after the bandit attack and started a duck hatchery in the town transferred his land. A man who went to another district to be married did the same. Among all those who transferred land to villagers, the majority were originally members of the village, and only two of them were comparatively rich. The system is an emergency one. Many who suffered from the bandit raid and left the village on this account needed money to start them off again. Since tradition tells them it is bad to sell their land, they prefer to use the system of temporary transference.

There are eight houses of the local private owners who transferred land for temporary use. One of those eight belonged to the rich class. The man of the family lived very luxuriously; and, since both husband and wife were opium-smokers, they had no savings. In 1929 the marriage of their son took place, and the father at this time got a loan of $3,000 from a relative, with a temporary transference of 20 *mow* of land. Another household of the rich class was similar to this one, living luxuriously and smoking opium. In 1931 the grandfather of the household died, and his son gave up the use of a part of his land in order to pay funeral expenses. In 1936 the latter's daughter married, and her father got another loan for the expenses of the wedding. In 1940 the price of opium was very high, and the head of the house again obtained a loan by transferring land. In all, he has transferred 7 *mow* of rice field and 4 *mow* of garden land.

Among the middle class there are three houses which have resorted to this kind of loan. One was a naturally prudent individual who in 1923–24, when someone was promoting the silk industry in the village, learned how to raise silkworms. He wanted to reel silk, and he made his own machine for this purpose. But the machine did not work; and, as a result, he became indebted and was forced to transfer some of his land. The second case was that of a widow who wished to educate her son by sending him to high school. She had no one to work her garden land and also needed money for her son's expenses. In order to raise funds, she transferred part of her garden land and rented out the rest. Then she rented a rice field from someone else and managed this with the help of hired labor. In the third case the household also transferred part of their garden land and rented a rice field from others. The three houses from the poor class who transferred land all did so because of special financial emergencies.

Collective owners tend to rent out their land, not to transfer it, because the causes which lead to temporary transference are usually absent in their case. The expenditures of the collective owners are generally decided beforehand, according to the regular income they can count upon. There are not likely to be unusual expenditures; so there is no urgent need for acquiring money. On the other hand, if they do need to spend money in some emergency, they usually sell the land, because their chance of paying back the loan is slight. The two cases of collective owners who transferred their land to others are those of clan and of village owners. During a bandit attack the clan temple and the village temple burned, and money was needed to rebuild them. For this purpose they got loans on the basis of temporary transference of land.

We shall now see who the people are who get land through this system. Some are outsiders of the village, who are usually rich folk. We know of two cases of this sort. One was an old resident of the village who went to Kunming and started a teahouse and became very rich. Another was that of the vice-manager of the ammunition factory in Kunming, who got land from his wife's uncle in the village in this way. The rich who get land in this manner do not operate it themselves but rent it out.

Most of the people who get land by this system, however, are villagers. A householder of the rich class made a loan to his clan for rebuilding the temple. Five houses of the middle class got land under this system. In the first case the man, who was something of a miser, was engaged in the opium business. It was said that he was secretly hiding a store of silver coin, as a result of which he had money to lend out on the basis of land transference as well as simply at interest. But the people were suspicious of him and did not wish to transfer land to him, because, they said, his was "dirty money." As a result, he usually loaned money to outsiders rather than to the villagers. In another case the household had land amounting to 13 *mow* of rice field and 1 *mow* of garden land and rented an additional 40 *mow* of rice field. The head of this household possessed savings and so became a money-lender. Although he did not have a large amount of land of his own, he was rich, as evidenced by the fact that when he died in 1940 his funeral was arranged without the borrowing of money. In a third case the head of the house possessed 4 *mow* of garden land. He made money and gradually acquired land—4 *mow* of rice field by transference. A fourth case was that of a widow who got 7 *mow* of land on this basis. Most of these people were those who had savings and wished to ac-quire land.

Of ten householders of the poor class who got land by this system, five rented land and garden plots for their own use. Three of these five got a considerable income from their farms, but the other two did not have sufficient income to maintain their households from their own land. The other five of the ten did not rent land to use. If these households did not rent land or engage in other occupations, they would not be able to put aside any savings. For people of this class, the money for making loans must be acquired not from land but from other sources. Of the landless householders who acquired land by this system, most are truck gardeners who have accumulated some money through other sources and are anxious to get more land to cultivate, especially garden land. Both the poor and landless classes have a strong land hunger. The system of temporary transference of land in payment for a loan costs them less than buying the land outright. If people can get 1 *mow* of garden land for about $500 through this sys-tem, they can make, normally, $800–$900 a year. Thus, it is worth while for them even to borrow money for this purpose. The rich and middle classes are not interested in getting garden land because of the great amount of labor required to cultivate it.

IV. PROFIT IN DIFFERENT TYPES OF MANAGEMENT

In the last chapter we studied farm profits. Now we shall see how the different types of management differ as to profits gained. The price of land in the spring of 1940 was $1,000 for 1 *mow* of rice field and $940 for 1 *mow* of garden land. Table 43 shows the rate of profit on different types of land when it is operated by the owner himself, using hired labor.

A landowner of Yuts'un who operates the land by hired labor can derive a profit of about 20 per cent from the rice fields and more than 50 per cent from the garden land. These figures are much higher than those we obtained in Luts'un, which gave only 13 per cent profit for the rice field. This is because in Yuts'un the price of land is much lower than in Luts'un. If we reduce the price fourteen times, to take account of inflation, we get about $85 per *mow* in 1938 as the price of rice field, while the same amount of high-grade land in Luts'un

TABLE 43

RATE OF PROFIT FROM LAND, ACCORDING TO CROP AND TO TYPE OF ARRANGEMENT (IN PERCENTAGE)

Crop	Occupying Owners; Managed by Hired Labor	Tenant	Temporary Transfer; Run by Creditors Themselves	Owners Rent Out; Absentee	Temporary Transfer; Rented Out
Rice field:					
Wet (single crop).......	17	50	27	14	23
Dry (double crop):					
Rice and bean........	20	67	31	14	23
Rice and rape........	21	60	31	14	23
Rice and bitter grass..	19	54	29	14	23
Rice and wheat.......	20	55	30	14	23
Rice and barley......	19	51	29	14	23
Garden land............	52	97	66	16	27

would cost about $200 per *mow:* $130 for the middle-grade land and $85 for the low-grade. This difference in price does not seem proportionate to the yield from the land, although in Yuts'un the land is less productive than in Luts'un. It may be due to the fact that there is more opportunity for investment in Yuts'un. Even the high profits from garden land do not raise its price, since the demand for garden land is limited by the fact that only those who can put their own labor into it all the year round can do well with it.

On rented land the tenant does not need to invest a large sum of money but has only to pay the annual rent. On each *mow* of land, about $140 worth of rice is paid as rent annually, and $150 cash for the garden land. Since the tenant has invested less money than the owner and only needs to pay current expenses, he has a higher rate of profit—about 50 per cent for the high-grade land. Those who have only a small amount of money actually can make more profit by renting land than by buying a small piece. The highest rate of profit is on the rented garden land. Normally, one who rents this land can get the same amount out of it as he invested. This encourages poor people to put their money into renting garden land rather than rice field.

Under the system of temporary transfer, the creditor who acquires the land does not need to pay rent. But he has invested the sum of money which he gave out as a loan. This loan usually amounts to about 60 per cent of the value of the land. Here the rate of profit is higher than for the occupying owner. The absentee owner who receives only rent from his land makes the least profit on his investment. The man who receives land by temporary transference in payment of a loan may rent it out and live on this rent. Since he has invested less than the actual owner, he gets a higher rate of profit than the latter.

It is clear that it is disadvantageous for a poor farmer to try to own land. It is open to question whether the policy which is advocated by the government of lending money to tenant farmers in order that they may buy land is a practical one. If they pay interest on their loan— interest which, because of the present situation, cannot be lower than 15 per cent and almost always is higher than this—and pay back the capital in instalments to the government, they will be paying more than they do at the present time by renting. For instance, a *mow* of land worth $1,000 will be rented for $140. Twenty per cent interest on this $1,000 amounts to $200; and $30 as a part payment on the capital investment over a period of thirty years will bring it to a total of $230, which is much higher than the rent of $140. In order to pay this $230, it means that standards of living, already very low, must be reduced still more. For relieving the hard-pressed peasant it is more urgent to approach the problem by reducing rents. Unless the government can provide loans with a low rate of interest, sustain the loan over a very long period, and prevent the increase in land values, the policy that "those who cultivate the land should own the land" cannot easily be carried out.

Although the rate of profit is higher for those who rent the land than for occupying owners, we should not think the latter are in a worse condition than their tenants. The important thing, after all, is not the rate of profit but the actual income. With the same amount of investment, a higher rate of profit yields a higher income. But the different types of management absorb different amounts of capital. On rented land, less capital needs to be invested. Therefore, on limited land the income will be less. For instance, in 1 *mow* of rice field the tenant can invest only $98. At a 50 per cent rate of interest he gets a total income of $49. The occupying owner can invest $1,098 in a year. On the same piece of land with 17 per cent as the rate of interest, he receives an income of $189.

In the above example the occupying owner who operates the land himself receives an income about four times as large as that of the tenant. In other words, to get the same amount of income, the tenant has to run a farm four times as big as the occupying owner. It is clear that tenants must actually work much harder than owners. The amount of land which can be managed by a household is limited, although they can get seasonal labor for the rice field in the labor markets. But, even if a tenant can rent 100 *mow* of rice field, his maximum income will be only $5,000; the occupying owner, however, will get $19,000 on the same amount of land. When there is a limit on the scale on which farming can be done, the tenant is in a worse position than the owner.

We do not actually know what the limit to the size of a farm under one household is. At the time we were in the village the largest farm was one of only 58 *mow*. Since the limits on expansion are more marked in case of the rented land, because the tenants can only rent land the owners do not wish to work themselves, the total amount of rented land was only about 340 *mow*. There is no hope that the tenants may be able to extend their scale of farming. But the absentee landlords who do not operate their own farms are not limited in expansion. Therefore, concentration of ownership is theoretically unlimited. We see that in coastal China a few families may own the land of a whole village. Among the town-dwellers in the Yuts'un region, as we have mentioned, a rich man recently bought 500 *mow* of land from different villages. From this land he can get a rent of $70,000 a year.

The rate of interest on garden land is high for those who actually work on it, but the limitations on size are even greater than for the rice field. A household of five has, on the average, three adult gardeners. Each adult can care for 2 *mow* of garden. The limit is therefore 6 *mow* of garden land, one-tenth that of the rice farms. In actual fact, the largest truck garden in Yuts'un is only 4.8 *mow*. From a truck garden of this size the household can get a yearly income of $4,000, while on the largest farm of wet rice land (58 *mow*) the household can get an income of $10,000, or about two and a half times the income from truck gardening.

CHAPTER XXIV

SUPPLEMENTARY OCCUPATIONS

I. DUCK RAISING

BESIDES agriculture, the people of Yuts'un have some other important economic activities. One of these is the raising of ducks in large flocks. This is supposed to be a somewhat discreditable occupation, carried on only by the poor. The villagers say: "These people are rotten rascals, dead dogs." The ducks harm the crops, and for this reason those who raise them are always abused. "Only those who don't care about face can engage in this occupation," it is said. But is this true? Let us examine the matter in a little detail. There are nineteen households that raise ducks—about 12 per cent of the total number. Five of these nineteen are in the middle class; twelve of them are in the poor class; and two are from among the landless people. They are, it appears, mostly from the lower middle class. But of the five households of the middle class, the average income from the land amounts yearly to $3,650, which is higher than the average of their class. For the twelve households of the poor class, the average annual income from land is $1,400, which is also higher than the average. Of the two from the landless class, one does not rent land. Another rents land and has an annual income of about $900, which is better than the average income of his class. The rich folk do not like to raise ducks, and the poor who have no capital cannot do so. So we find that the people who engage in this occupation are mostly those who have a little money and also those who don't mind carrying on an occupation that is considered somewhat disreputable. Thus, duck raising is engaged in mainly by those who are somewhat more prosperous among the poorer class.

Those who raise ducks have also the most populous households. The average number of individuals in a household among the duck raisers is 5.4, which can be compared with the average of 4.6 members per household in the village. One reason for this is that the houses who have more members have a larger supply of labor and can more easily spare someone to take care of the flock. Moreover, their land is usually insufficient for their needs, and they are forced to get some income even if public opinion is against them. For this occupation there are two requirements: a certain amount of capital and spare labor. From among nineteen households, only eleven continued the work in 1940, the remaining eight having stopped. When we inquired of these people why they had stopped, they offered two reasons: "We have not sufficient hands. We have not enough money." We know that three of them stopped because the householders were growing old and other house members had either died or gone away. Two of the other households had enough spare hands but did not make enough money from their land the year before to enable them to take up the work. Another householder had enough money but his son died, and this brought his venture to an end.

In the eleven households which continued duck raising, the average number of members of the household is six. Of these households, two are well-to-do and get a surplus income from their land. Only two or three of them are in straitened circumstances. These men borrowed money to finance their work and could not have started if they had not got this money. It is clear that duck raising is not really a poor man's occupation.

There are three parts to duck culture, each of which may be carried on by different people. First, there is the hatching; second, the rearing; and third, the production of eggs. Among the nineteen duck raisers, only one opened up a hatchery, and he did not continue the business for long. Another produced eggs for sale. The rest confined themselves to raising ducks for sale. We shall discuss here only the last occupation.

The duck raisers arrange to buy small ducklings from the hatchery. In general, the orders for ducklings are put in in advance, and the price for them is decided at that time. Those who do not order in advance can only take those which are left; and, if there are only a few, the price will be higher. The ducklings begin to hatch at the end of June; and every five days thereafter a new batch is hatched, until a total of thirteen batches, up to the beginning of September, has been hatched. Each batch is given a name to distinguish it. The three batches hatched before Li Ch'iu (August 8) and the three batches hatched immediately after this date bring the highest price. In 1940 ducklings hatched at this time of the year brought a price of $70 per hundred. The first batch hatched cost only $35; the second, $42; and the third, $50. The reason for the extra high price for the batches of ducklings hatched in the middle of the summer is that the young ducks hatched at this time of the year can take specially good advantage of foraging in the fields after the rice harvest. The others, which are either too early or too late, cannot profit so much from running wild in this way.

After a purchaser has acquired his ducklings, he lets them out every morning into the fields, where they feed upon weeds, worms, and insects. A duckherd keeps them in a flock and prevents them from going outside the village boundaries. Each person could care for from 700 to 800 ducks; but, owing to limitations upon capital investments, the duck raiser of Yuts'un rarely keeps more than 200 to 300. Since it is not worth while for one man to devote his full time to such a small number, different households often combine their flocks and care for them in rotation. The ducklings are not allowed to go outside the village boundaries to graze on the land of others, and only those who are residents of the village can graze their ducks in the village fields. Formerly the village head asked a certain sum of money from the duck raisers. The latter got together and divided up what was owed, in proportion to the number of ducks they were raising—about 1.8 per cent of the income derived from the ducks. After they had paid this amount, they could let the ducks wander freely. If any controversies arose as to damage done, they could appeal to the village head for arbitration. But this custom was abandoned about twenty years ago. For, after paying their due, the keepers of the ducks became careless, and much damage to the crops resulted. As a result, the people decided that it would be better not to collect any money from the duck raisers, so that they would not feel they had any rights with regard to grazing. Since the interests of the duck raisers still conflict, to a large extent, with those of the general public, they are called "rascals" by the people.

Toward evening the duckherds bring the ducks to the open ground near the field and herd them into a movable inclosure. Here they are fed on soaked beans cut into small pieces, and then are counted, put into a big basket, and carried home. When grown, they are driven rather than carried. After fifty to sixty days the ducks are ready to be sold to the restaurants in the town. Merchants also come to buy them, in order to export them to other districts. The duck raisers like to sell their ducks before they are too old, since older ducks require more food and also do not bring so good a price.

The cost of raising ducks consists in, first, the ducklings; second, the feed; and third, the labor. The average price of ducklings is $50 per hundred. The cost of feed varies. If the ducklings can get more from the fields, they do not need so many beans, and in harvest time they need not be given any beans in the evening. The average feed for 100 ducklings for fifty to sixty days is 110 pounds of beans, amounting to $120. The cost of the labor depends upon how big the flock is. If someone is employed, he gets $2.00 a day as wage and $1.00 for food, amounting to $195 for sixty-five days. If we take an average flock as 350 ducks, the labor costs are $56, and the total cost $226.

Mortality in the flock is about 10 per cent, so that for every 100 ducklings, there will, with luck, be 90 full-grown ducks. Each of these should sell for $3.00, making a total of $270. Thus, each 100 ducklings gives a profit of $44. In 1940 the village raised 6,300 ducks, getting a total profit of about $2,800. Including wages and food, the money involved in duck raising came to $6,300. This sum, divided among eleven households, gives each one $570, or a net profit of $250.

Although the enterprise of duck raising is helpful to a few individual households, it is rather unimportant for the village as a whole, since it yields only one-sixtieth of the total income gained from agriculture. The life of the people is still mainly supported by the cultivation of the land. The development of duck raising on a large scale is limited by the amount of food available for the ducks to pick up for themselves in the fields. Food of this sort is to be had only in the summer and autumn, when the rice is growing. When the bean crop is growing, real harm can be done by letting the ducks wander loose. Raising ducks is too expensive if they must be fed entirely on beans, and space is limited for raising them on a very large scale. Moreover, since it is difficult to transport live ducks, the ducks are mostly used in the district, so that the quantities which can be sold are also limited. Roast duckling is one of the special delicacies of this region.

II. WEAVING

Besides duck raising, the weaving industry is important in Yuts'un and throughout the district. Luts'un and Yits'un do not weave but buy their cloth, for the most part, from this district. The work is limited to women, no men working on the loom. In Yuts'un, out of 157 households, there are 112 in which weaving is done. The clack of the wooden machines can be heard all over the village from morning to night. Among the households in which weaving is done, 2 are those of rich farmers, 22 are from among the middle class, 60 from the poor, and 28 from the landless. The percentage of each to the total number of each class is 33 per cent for the rich, 71 per cent for the middle, 80 per cent for the poor, and 64 per cent for the landless. In other words, the women of the poor farmer class, and next to them those of the middle class, are those who engage most in this occupation.

Women of the rich farming class who engage in weaving have incomes below the average level of their class. The average income from land for the rich farmers is $7,300 annually. But the average income of the household in which weaving is done in this class is only about $6,300. In the middle class the average annual income from land is about $2,700. But among the households in which weaving is done, the average income a year from land is $2,500—a very slight difference from the general average. Among the poor farmers the average yearly income from land is $1,130, while for the weaving households the average income from land is $1,170—a little higher than the general average. Among the households of landless farmers, 27 rent land and get as an average income from farming $550 a year. The 22 households of this 26 who weave get, as an average annual income from land, $620. From these figures we can see that among the rich and middle classes there is a tendency for the poorer people of the class to take up this industry. But among the poor and landless, it is rather the opposite: those who are somewhat better off engage in this work. In other words, the weaving industry is centered in the middle class. Rich folk do not like to carry on this work. Among the rich, the men do not go into the fields and the women do not weave. The poor people, on the other hand, often do not have enough money to buy thread. Only those who have a certain amount of leisure and also some capital can take part in weaving. As a result, most of the weaving is done in the lower middle and upper poor households. Most of those who weave work periodically, stopping when they have other work on hand. We know of only three households—one from the middle class and two from the poor—who actually keep on weaving throughout the year. In general, weaving is only a subsidiary occupation in the household. The women make as much money as they can out of it without considering it of vital importance.

The girls of a household learn how to weave, from their mothers or other older women, at a very early age. Each girl traditionally has a loom as part of her dowry when she marries. Although nearly all know how to weave, as has been pointed out above, few of the rich bother with it. Poor women sometimes do not have the necessary materials. And among the middle-class women, some are tied up with household cares, such as cooking and rearing of children, and also with working on the farms, so that they have no time to weave. The total number of women in the village who work at the loom is 151, out of 201 adult women. This includes some girls as young as twelve and some old women of sixty to seventy years of age; but, for the most part, the weavers are middle-aged.

Weaving is not a simple process. From the cotton thread to the woven piece of cloth, several stages must be gone through. Especially complicated is the setting-up of the loom. To prepare the warp, first the hanks of cotton thread must be cleaned; and then they are boiled in a paste made from rice flour, to which sometimes some white clay is added in order to increase the weight. This is used to make the thread smoother and tougher, so as to avoid breakage. Then, with a wheel, worked by hand, the thread is wound up onto the bobbin. This work is usually done by young girls. A number of bobbins are prepared, corresponding to the number of threads required for the warp of the loom. The preparation of the warp of the loom is usually done in the street. The thread is unwound the length of the loom and coiled with even tension on a beam. The beam is placed on the loom, and with a hook the thread is passed through the heald and the reed and is fixed on the other end of the loom. The weft is prepared on a bobbin and put into the shuttle. Each day one girl can prepare enough bobbins for the warp for a loom or the weft for two days' work. Looms used are of two types, both hand operated. The older type is one in which the shuttle is thrown across from hand to hand; and the newer is a modification of the old one, in which the shuttle is moved by drawing a cord hanging from the top.

The cloth made is natural color. Each piece, which is 8 inches wide by 22 feet long, weighs approximately 1⅓ pounds. This kind of cloth is used, to a large extent, for village clothing; but, since the people do not wear the natural color, they must send the material to be dyed. After it has been dyed, the women make clothes for the household. Since the villagers use mostly home-woven materials, they tend to be much better clothed than the people in other rural parts of the province. It is said that some years ago the people of this district raised the cotton, produced their own plant dyes, and spun their own thread, so that their clothing was entirely self-produced. But later they came to use imported cotton thread exclusively; and when better dyes were introduced from outside, the local dye disappeared. Self-sufficiency in clothing is now limited to weaving and tailoring.

If a woman produces more cloth than she needs for her own household, she may carry it, on the morning of a market day, to one of the drygoods stores to exchange for thread. Most of these stores are open only on the market days. The cloth that is bought by these stores is used mainly for export, since people of the district ordinarily do not buy cloth of this sort. The cloth woven by various households is not standardized but differs somewhat in size and in quality. It cannot be sold to townsfolk but only the peasants; and, as better machine-woven cloth is coming in, the market for the home-woven materials is shrinking.

The exchange rate for cotton cloth and thread is not uniform. Some weavers obtain more thread than the weight of the cloth; others, an equal amount in weight or even less than the weight of their cloth. The storekeeper is a good judge of the quality of the cloth and of the weight added by the paste and will decrease the amount of thread given in exchange if the quality of the cloth is bad or if there is too much weighting. The amount of thread given also depends upon the demands at the moment for cloth for export. Each piece of cloth weighing about 1⅓ pounds contains, as a rule, about 0.8 ounce of paste. If the exchange of thread for cloth is equal by weight, the weaver gets only 0.8 ounce more thread. At the best rate of exchange the weaver will get 1.3 ounce more thread. The weavers try to add more weight so as to get more thread, but the stores cut down the rate of exchange in such a way that actually the weaver usually get only 1 ounce more thread at best. Each lot of 10.5 pounds of cotton thread cost $80 in 1940, so that each pound costs $7.50 and each ounce 46 cents. As a result, the average income from each piece of cloth amounted to 50 cents.

We need to subtract the cost in paste and in fuel from this 50 cents in order to get the actual wage. Each loom, as set up, has about 400 feet of warp thread, which, when woven, can be cut into 18 pieces, 22 feet long. Two reels of cotton are required for this; and for this amount of thread 3.3 pounds of rice flour, costing $2.00, are required. To boil the thread takes 20 pounds of wood for fuel, costing 75 cents. The cost of fuel and paste for each piece of cloth is then 15 cents, which makes the actual income from one piece of cloth only 35 cents. To prepare the warp thread for 18 pieces of cloth requires 3 units of labor, and 6 units are required for the weaving. In one day one woman, working all day, can weave 2 pieces of cloth. Her actual daily wage will be, then, 70 cents, which is not sufficient to pay for her food. If the women devoted all their time to this work, they would not earn sufficient for subsistence.

The low profit from this industry is clear to the weavers. The situation at the present time is growing worse. People like to talk about the old days. Thirty years ago, they told us, before the importation of Western manufactured thread, when the weavers of the district produced their own cotton, spun their own thread, and made their own cloth, they got much more income than they do at present. Since that time, things have been getting steadily worse. On the one hand, manufactured thread has entirely taken the place of native thread, so that the spinning is entirely wiped out. The price of manufactured thread fluctuates very much and is in the hands of big merchants. It is not like the old-type thread, the supply and demand for which was much more stable and the price of which did not fluctuate. Now, every time the cotton market rises or declines, it directly affects the weaving industry in the village. From this fluctuation the big merchants take advantage at the expense of the weavers. On the other hand, manufactured clothes have reached the markets of the interior. They are better in quality and not much higher in price than the home woven. To compete with them the native cloth has to lower its price, and a limit is put on the price of the native cloth. So the price of the hand-woven cloth is not determined by the actual cost of production but by the price level set by the machine-made cloth and by the price of the cotton thread. The price of the thread sets the lower limit on the price of the cotton cloth. The weavers are squeezed on both sides. The only thing they can adjust is their own wage. As a result, the wage received for weaving goes down when the price of cotton thread increases to such a degree that it does not even pay the upkeep of the workers.

The reason that the weavers continue to work under these very adverse conditions lies in the situation under which they work and live in the village. Most of the weavers are wives in farmers' households and take up weaving simply as a side line. During May, June, and July there is work to be done on the farm, and the women are busy. If they work in the fields each day, they can get a wage of from $0.70 to $1.00, with food provided. If we count the food as coming to about $1.00, the wage is about $1.70–$2.00 a day. This is much higher than they can get from weaving; so those who can work in the fields leave the looms at this time. But when the farming season is over, from August to April, there is a long period when the women cannot find regular employment on the farm. If they don't work at the loom, they will not be gainfully employed.

Each loom costs $20 (it is usually included as part of the dowry), and two lots of thread cost $160. Those who have this amount of capital are able to weave. The women who weave do not count much upon the actual income from their activity, nor do they depend upon it for their living; so they can accept a low wage. This is the difference between rural and urban industries. Urban industry must provide income at least for the food of its workers. In the rural communities, agriculture has, so to speak, subsidized the developing industries. This is even truer of weaving, which is the work of those members of the household who are traditionally provided for. In this way, a primitive industry can still persist for some time even under the strong pressure of modern industrialism.

If we compare duck raising and weaving, we find that the former gives a greater profit. Each family in which weaving is done gets, on the average, only $94, which, compared with the $570 from duck raising, means that the latter occupation is about six times as profitable as the former. Moreover, the weavers spend about a hundred days a year on their work; the duck raisers, only two months. As a result of this higher profit, the villagers are attracted to duck raising in spite of the constant scolding of the other members of the village.

On the other hand, it is true that weaving does supplement the income from agriculture. Since there are 151 women who work at the looms on the average of one hundred days a year, with a wage of 70 cents daily, they produce an income amounting to approximately $10,600. Divided between 121 households, this amounts roughly to $90 a family. This helps the individual family considerably. However, it is far behind agriculture in providing the family livelihood. Although this industry may not appear so important in the family economy, it is very significant in providing a basis for capitalistic enterprise in the towns.

CHAPTER XXV

HOUSEHOLD CONSUMPTION

I. CONTRAST BETWEEN RICH AND POOR

WHEN we first visited Yuts'un, we entered the south gate of the village, following a path to the north. Both sides of the street were lined with dilapidated huts. Some of them were partly demolished; some of them still bore traces of fire, with charred wood and beams lying in the corners; and still others were roofless and deserted. We felt distressed, walking through these gloomy streets of a village which seemed to be struggling in the shadow of misfortunes. Presently, however, we came to a well-built house with whitewashed walls—an impressive sight in these surroundings. Our guide led us into this house and introduced us to a well-dressed middle-aged gentleman, who courteously invited us to come and be seated in the central hall and ordered tea to be served to us at once. This house became our lodging place. Our host showed us over his house and pointed out a room which we might occupy. This room, on the second floor in the left wing, was a storage-room in which beans and other produce were being stored; but it was clean and light, with big windows on the court and with room for two beds. Our host apologized for not moving out his harvested crops. But when we had opened our bedrolls and our host had brought us a light, in the form of a glass kerosene lamp, we felt more comfortable and happy than we had felt at any time during our last few years of field work in the villages.

The house in which we stayed was a typical home of a wealthy villager. It consisted of ten rooms, including storerooms, on two floors and was built around a courtyard. The heavy street gate opened onto a small antechamber, which led to the courtyard. On one side of the courtyard, leading off the antechamber, was the kitchen; on the other side, a stable or storeroom—a room in which the loom is often kept. Standing in the gateway, one could look through the courtyard to the central hall, where the portraits of the ancestors were kept over the altar. Here were also the red-lacquered ceremonial table and the chairs which were used for specially honored visitors, as well as a small, low table for the use of the family, a washstand with a mirror over it, and a stand for clothing—all lacquered and beautifully decorated—literary decorations on the wall, an embroidered picture over the altar, beautiful vases, and incense-burners. Two small rooms which were partitioned off from this hall served for the grandmother and grown son. On the second floor were the rooms for the parents and younger children, as well as the storerooms, above the kitchen and stable, one of which we occupied. When later we visited the homes of other well-to-do men of Yuts'un, we realized that the home of our landlord, though somewhat larger than those of some of his friends, was not an exception but, rather, was typical, even as to its decorations, of the houses of the rich villagers.

Our landlord's house was not the best in the village. One day we visited a man who was called by the people the "Fifth Lord." His house, which was entered by a large carved gate, leading into a courtyard in which flowers and trees were growing, consisted of at least forty rooms, built around five connecting courtyards, each with its gardens. The rooms here were large and well furnished; there were carved wooden window frames and glass in the windows, painted and decorated beams, and in certain of the rooms not only Western-type decorations but a Western-style sofa.

Later on, when we had settled down, we began to visit the poor people. Each day, as soon as we had gone past the pigsty of our landlord, we came to the houses of the poor. Looking inside the doorway of one such house, we could see just one dark, smoky room, with no window but with a simple hole in the wall to let out smoke, and near the door a ladder leading up to the attic. Even the casual observer could not help but be impressed by the great contrast here between rich and poor. For some time we had no opportunity to enter one of the poor houses, since their owners evidently felt shy because of poverty. But one afternoon we were invited by a lean, undernourished villager to come into his house. When we entered the dark room, he asked us to sit on the wooden bed platform to the left, since he had no chair but only a straw hassock. From the door came a dim light, allowing us to see the shape of the small, damp low room with its dirt floor. The bed on which we sat occupied a quarter of the whole room. On the bed was a ragged dirty cotton cover; and beside it was an old black table on which a stand for a lamp, consisting of a wick stuck in a saucer of oil, a teapot and several cups, some bottles of oil, and cooking utensils were all spread out in a disorderly fashion. Even in the dim light we were aware of the griminess of dust over all. Opposite the door, against the wall, was an open hearth with a hole in the wall above it, by which some of the smoke went out; and pots and utensils lay near by. Scattered around on the floor were straw and baskets, holding beans and rice. Our friend told us that, months ago, his wife had died suddenly. Something twisted in our hearts at his ghastly, hopeless face—at this life helplessly dragging on. When we came out, we drew a deep breath. Back in our room, we felt that we had been in another world. Later on we had more opportunities to visit the poor and found some of them not so badly off as this. Some have as many as four rooms, two upstairs and two down; and their homes are better kept. However, if we compare the conditions under which these people live with the life of the wealthy, we find a great difference.

The contrast we saw in the housing is also true of other aspects of life, such as in clothing and food. The "lord" wears long silk gowns, which are soft and light. He need not walk, because he has a ricksha. He keeps a cow to give milk; takes ginseng root and the tip of a deer's horn, which give vitality; and smokes opium. The women in the house dress in long robes made of silk or fine cotton materials. The young men wear foreign-style student uniforms. Besides their regular meals, they have an extra one at midnight; and in a year they consume 650 pounds of meat as well as several dozen chickens and ducks. When the family wish to, they go to Kunming, simply for diversion. In a year they spend about $20,000. This is the outstandingly wealthy home in the village.

In the ordinary well-to-do household, such as that of our landlord, the things used by the master of the house for himself are not so different from those used by the ordinary villager. He smokes native tobacco and wears homemade clothes and a Chinese cap; and, though he has shoes and one pair of cloth socks, he rarely wears them. His mother, wife, and daughter-in-law also work industriously and wear clothes made of native cloth, thus still preserving the aspect of an ordinary peasant family. But the younger generation, especially the boys, have a different appearance. The sons of the family wear student uniforms and rubber-soled shoes with foreign-style socks. The third son, who is the eldest son left in the family, has a foreign-style felt hat and leather shoes. The family's food is mainly vegetables, but they have some meat. Life here is not luxurious, but it is comfortable.

Chang, the carpenter, representative of the poor people, wears clothes somewhat similar to my landlord's; but his children all wear clothing made of native cloth. When compared with the children of the landlord, the difference is striking. This family lives mainly on vegetables, rarely eating meat. Chang is an example of the upper level of the poor villagers. Still poorer families sometimes live on corn rather than on rice, corn being much cheaper and considered inferior; and their clothes are usually very worn. On the whole, clothing in Yuts'un is better than in other villages, however, because the inhabitants produce their own cloth.

II. SAMPLES OF FAMILY BUDGETS

The contrast between the living conditions of the rich and those of the poor can also be seen from the family budgets. We collected materials from five households. The first household from which we got materials was that of the "lord." These materials were supplied by our landlord, who for many years had kept the accounts for that house. Since the "lord" still consulted with him on money matters, he knew the conditions in the house very well. The second house was that of our landlord, who gave me the materials personally. It is true that it is difficult to get information on economic matters from anyone directly, because it is not considered polite to talk on such matters. But my landlord was different. He understood the purpose of our investigation, and we had gained his confidence and friendship through our long association; so he willingly assisted us in our work and consulted us on, all his family affairs. The third house for which we got information was that of the old headman of the village. He kept accounts, and we were able to get these from the ninth day of the eighth month of 1933 to the same day in the following year. Since very few of the villagers keep accounts, this was rare and valuable material. Only three days' accounts were lacking, and this only because some of the pages had been lost. One difficulty which arose in dealing with this material was the comparison of money values, since at the time the accounts were kept old provincial currency was still being used. The exchange rate of that currency with the national currency was, in 1940, ten to one. But the actual value of the currency, that is, the actual purchasing power of the provincial currency, during 1933 was just about the same as that of the national currency in 1940. We checked this and found that 7 pounds of rice in 1933 cost $4.00 in old provincial currency and that the same amount cost $4.00 in national currency in 1940; so we were able to take the values of the currency as given. However, in the accounts there are items for productive purposes which we had to deduct. Also, items which appear in the accounts are limited to things bought in the market. Since in the peasants' household most of the goods consumed are self-supplied and thus would not appear in the account book, we had to add these items. The usefulness of these accounts in studying the rural economy is, therefore, limited.

The materials for the fourth and fifth households were gathered by direct questioning. My landlord helped jog up the memories of these householders. The information may not be complete, but it is sufficient to show the general situation.

In selecting these five households we not only considered the practical ease with which materials might be obtained but tried to represent the different classes. The first house, that of the exceptionally rich man, serves to show the wide range of expenditure even in village life. The second household belonged to the rich farmers, the third to the upper part of the middle class, the fourth to the poor class, and the fifth to the landless. In Table 44 we give a brief description of the conditions existing in each household.

The total annual living expenses of household No. 1, excluding the cost of opium, was $11,424; of the second, $6,049; of the third, $4,776; of the fourth, $2,581; and of the fifth, $1,611. The average expenditure for an adult in each of these houses is, then, in the first, $1,705; in the second, $903; in the third, $853; in the fourth, $717; and in the fifth, $488. The expenditures for each individual in the first house can support 1.9 persons of the second house; 2 of the third; 2.2 of the fourth; and 3.5 of the fifth. Table 45 shows the percentage of income spent on food and other items.

There is a regular decrease in the percentage for food and a regular increase in the miscellaneous items according to the increase in financial standing of the families. Fuel and light do not vary much, and this variation does not seem to have much significance. The percentage for housing is not very different for the first three families. The houses used by the peasants are their own; there are no rented houses. So an increase in annual income does not make them move into a better house unless they have saved enough money to permit them either to rebuild the old house or to build a new one. The "lord" inherited his house all complete and needed only to maintain it. The second and third householders are still improving their newly built houses, and thus spend more in proportion to their income. The building of a new house is not done all at once but continues with gradual additions. The last two families do not spend more than a little money on their houses, being satisfied to live in their poor huts without attempting to make improvements on them.

TABLE 44
HOUSEHOLDS FOR WHICH SAMPLE BUDGETS WERE MADE OUT

FIRST HOUSEHOLD

Member	Age (in Years)	Occupation and Expense
The "lord"	65	Gentry, leisure class, owner of farm. Opium-smoker
His wife.................	55	Does not work on farm. Smokes opium
Second son..............	22	Clerk in district high school. Lives at home
Wife of second son.........	23	Does not work on farm
Third son................	17	Studying in high school. Lives at home
Wife of third son..........	17	Does not work on farm
Granddaughter...........	5	
Granddaughter...........	3	
Granddaughter...........	2	
Grandson................	1	

Total number, 10; equivalent to 6.7 adults

Member	Age	Occupation and Expense
Maid....................	17	Household worker, not paid wages
Maid....................	15	Household worker, not paid wages
		Expenditures for maids included in miscellaneous
Laborer.................	30	Works on farm and pulls ricksha. Yearly wage, $300; $287 for food
		One-third of $587 is included in miscellaneous; rest put under expenses of production
Laborer.................	35	Works on farm only. Expenses on his account not included
Boy.....................	13	Takes care of cows, oxen, buffaloes

Land	Owned	Held by Temporary Trans-ference	Temporarily Trans-ferred	Rented Out	Total Self-managed
Rice field...........	80.09 *mow*	1.3 *mow*	20 *mow*	11.7 *mow*	49.69 *mow*
Garden.............	2.58	....	....	1.5	1.08

Gross income from land.........	$17,411

SECOND HOUSEHOLD—OUR LANDLORD'S

Member	Age (in Years)	Occupation and Expense
Our landlord.............	54	Occasionally works on farm
His mother..............	73	Invalid
His wife.................	52	Household work occasionally; weaves
Second son..............	29	White-collar worker. Lives outside
		His expenditures not included in budget
Wife of second son	24	Lives with husband
Third son................	26	Lives at military academy

TABLE 44—*Continued*

SECOND HOUSEHOLD—OUR LANDLORD'S—*Continued*

Member	Age (in Years)	Occupation and Expense
Fourth son...............	15	At military medical school. Expenses not included
Fifth son.................	12	In middle school. Lives at home
Sixth son.................	9	Primary school
Seventh son..............	3	
Widow of first son........	32	Takes care of household and weaves
Grandson................	5	
Grandson................	3	
Grandson................	2	

Total number living in house, 11; equivalent to 6.7 adults

Laborer..................	24	$400 for wage and food

Land	Owned	Rented	Total Managed
Rice field..................	20.05 *mow*	13.65 *mow*	33.70 *mow*
Garden....................	0.75	1.42	2.17

Gross income from land	$10,389

THIRD HOUSEHOLD

Number	Age (in Years)	Occupation and Expense
Head of house (female).....	55	Household work; weaves occasionally
First son.................	32	Headman of village; works on farm occasionally
Second son...............	13	Primary school
Third son................	11	Primary school
Wife of headman	28	Household work; weaves occasionally
Daughter of head of household	8	
Grandson................	5	
Grandson................	3	
Grandson................	1	

Total number, 9; equivalent to 5.6 adults

Laborer..................	24	Works on farm only. Total wage and food, $500. Excluded from budget
Boy......................	12	Cares for buffalo. Wage $300. Not included in budget

TABLE 44—*Continued*

Land	Owned	Rented	Held by Temporary Transference	Total Managed
Rice field.........	10.00 *mow*	40.00 *mow*	2.00 *mow*	52.00 *mow*
Garden............	0.50	....	....	0.50
Gross income from land (estimated).........		$8,186		

FOURTH HOUSEHOLD

Member	Age (in Years)	Occupation and Expense
Head of household........	53	Works on farm
His wife................	48	Household work and weaver
Second son.............	11	Middle-school student
Wife of second son........	13	Works on farm and weaves
Daughter of family.......	9	

Total number, 5; equivalent to 3.6 adults

Land	Owned	Rented	Held by Temporary Transference	Total Managed
Rice field...........	2.0 *mow*	14.9 *mow*	4.1 *mow*	21.0 *mow*
Garden............	0.52	....	0.15	1.02
Gross income from land.........		$5,253		

FIFTH HOUSEHOLD

Member	Age (in Years)	Occupation and Expense
Head of house (widow)....	50	Hires out as farm laborer; weaves
Son....................	31	Hires out for farm work; carpenter and mason
Wife...................	21	Household work and weaving
Grandson...............	3	
Grandson...............	1	

Total number, 5; equivalent to 3.3 adults

No income from land

According to Engel's law, an increase in the percentage of income spent for food indicates a lowering of the standard of living. According to Buck, the average percentage of income spent on food by the Chinese peasant families is 58.9.[1] The first three houses expend less of their income than this on food, and by this standard are above the general level of the ordinary Chinese peasant. The fourth and fifth houses are lower, according to this standard. But it must be added that this general principle may not always apply to conditions in China. The Chinese have a tendency to increase the money spent on food if they are able, not merely for actual nourishment but as a luxury.

TABLE 45

PERCENTAGE DISTRIBUTION OF EXPENDITURE IN FIVE BUDGETS

	HOUSEHOLD NUMBER				
	1	2	3	4	5
Food....................	43.6	49.5	53.4	63.0	68.8
Clothing................	10.5	12.0	8.4	10.2	10.1
Housing................	8.7	11.5	12.5	3.9	3.1
Fuel and light...........	9.3	12.5	12.7	10.4	9.5
Miscellaneous...........	27.9	14.4	13.0	12.5	8.7

And it is difficult to distinguish in the budget between these two uses of food. We mentioned that the household of the "lord" regularly had an extra meal at midnight. This meal is simply a luxury and should be included under "miscellaneous." We did not attempt to make this distinction, however.

III. SPECIAL EXPENSES

In dealing with the family budgets of rural Chinese families we found another difficulty, in that there are expenses, such as those for ceremonies, which occur only from time to time. Buck, in his *Chinese Farm Economy*, divided the budget into nine items: "food," "clothing," "shelter" (or rent), "fuel and light," "advancement" (social obligations, education, religion, charity, and recreation), "furnishings," "health," "personal" (tobacco, ornaments, gambling, and liquor), and "unclassified" (funerals, weddings, lawsuits, servants, and other expenses). He considers the first four items as physical necessities and groups the last five items into one called "others," which corresponds to our "miscellaneous."[2] It may be questioned whether we should in-

---

[1] *Chinese Farm Economy*, p. 386.   [2] *Ibid.*, chap. xi.

clude the expenses of opium, gambling, interest on loans, funerals, weddings, litigation, and servants among the miscellaneous items. If we include opium in "miscellaneous," the percentage of income for miscellaneous items will, in some cases, be greatly increased while the percentage for other items is lowered. In case we should have two households which appear to be very similar but one of them indulges in opium and the other not, then, if opium is included among the miscellaneous items, the relative percentage of the budget spent on food will be much lowered for the opium-smoking household. Is it fair to say, then, that the standard of living of the household which does not use opium is much lower than that of the household which does? However, if we include opium with food, the opium-smoking household then appears to have a very low standard of living. To avoid these difficulties, we think it better to omit this item entirely in a comparative study of nominal expenditures.

Expenses of funerals and marriages are necessary and inevitable, but they do not occur regularly. Over a long period, each household will have more or less the same expenses; but over a short period of time, the variation in expenditures of this kind may be great. If we include them in "miscellaneous," then a household which happens to have a girl who is getting married will appear to have a very high standard of living. However, these expenses should not be entirely excluded, since in the case of the expenditures for marriage, at least, they actually constitute, in large part, a renewal of the household furnishings. It will be best to give these expenditures in a separate table.

Litigation does not necessarily occur in every household but only occasionally in a few households. Nevertheless, when Chinese peasants are involved in legal disputes, which are usually for the sake of "saving face," they may become so involved as eventually to ruin their families. Expenditures of this sort will usually lead to a lowering of the standard of living generally. It would be misleading to include them in "Miscellaneous."

The items for gambling, interest on loans, and servants should also be treated separately rather than in a general discussion of the family budget. Gambling is considered as a speculative enterprise as well as a diversion. To indulge in gambling does not necessarily mean that a man has reserve capital, however, for men may sell their property in order to speculate with it in this way. A heavy burden of interest on loans indicates the poverty of the household. It is not like other miscellaneous items, in that it is rigid and cannot be easily reduced, as in the case of the other more elastic items included here. As to servants, Buck says: "Only a few well-to-do farm families have servants. Nine-tenths of one per cent have such expenditures."[3] He does not explain what a "servant" means, however. We know that some of the rich families in Yuts'un employ laborers all through the year. Their job is to work in the fields, but they also sometimes help in the work of the household. Thus, it is hard to say whether we should include them under "consumption" or under "production expenses." We think that it is better to treat them separately, excluding them from the items of the budget which are to be analyzed comparatively according to Engel's law.

IV. OPIUM

The consumption of opium is a special kind of expense. For those who are addicts, it is a fixed expense, because they feel they cannot live without it. It is not like food or clothing, the expenditures for which can be somewhat reduced. Those who have the habit may even risk their lives to satisfy their craving. Since the government has adopted a drastic policy in prohibiting the growing of opium and made its use illegal, addicts depend mainly on smuggled goods, the price of which is exorbitant. If an addict cannot force himself to give up the habit, there is a continuous heavy drain upon the family fortunes. Among the rich, surplus income is completely expended. For example, the "lord" should accumulate thousands of dollars as savings every year, but he uses all his money up in smoking opium. We know that his expenditures for this item amount to one-third of his daily household expenses. During the last few years his estate has not expanded. Among the poorer people, the habit of opium-smoking affects their standard of living directly, lowering it very quickly. There are cases, which we shall mention later, in which households have sold their property, the family becoming entirely disorganized and even dying off as a result of this habit. At the present time, opium is still an active factor in disturbing the rural economy and accelerating the change of property from hand to hand. As we mentioned in Part I, if in Luts'un the price of opium continues to rise as it has been doing, the whole surplus rice production of the village will be just enough to exchange for opium. Thus, opium-smoking is still a serious problem in rural China. In Yuts'un the situation is a little better. There are sixteen households, or one-tenth of the whole number, in which there are opium-smokers. Under the pressure

[3] *Ibid.*, p. 418.

of the rise in price they have tried to cut down the amount smoked to about 1 ounce a day (which seems to be the minimum); but in one year the total expenditure for this one item in the village amounted to $14,000, which is equal to the total income derived from duck raising and from weaving.

V. MARRIAGE

Although marriages do not take place frequently in the individual households, they must be counted upon to occur in each generation. If twenty years is taken as constituting one generation, the probability is that from twenty households there will be at least one marriage every year. In marriage ceremonies the peasants usually spend as much as possible, since these expenditures are bound up with social prestige. Marriage in the folk society is an important occasion, in that social status is here reaffirmed and maintained. This changes the psychology of consumption. As we explained in Part I, the people follow a set of standards in this situation that are different from those followed in ordinary daily life. Although they are usually very frugal, at such times as these they spend extravagantly and enjoy doing so. Previous to a marriage, they prepare for a long time, accumulating what money they can. This is a form of savings. Part of the savings will be spent on the ceremonies and entertainment, and part of it on a renewal of household furniture and clothing. In the daily expenses we ordinarily have a rather low figure for clothing, but actually most of the women's clothes are supplied in their dowry. Girls will work for years, preparing this clothing. At this time, gifts of clothing to family members will also be made before the ceremony. The furniture of the household comes mostly through the dowry of the bride and presents of the bridegroom's family. Guests make offerings of money while their hosts entertain them with a feast. There is, in some sense, an exchange, so that the money spent on the ceremony is not used merely for a display of wealth but brings returns of both a social and a material nature. We hope to discuss in a future treatise the psychology of consumption in general and the concept of exchange economics in particular.

Table 46 shows the expenditures by the houses of both the bride and the bridegroom on a marriage in 1940. (We shall not go into the details of the marriage ceremony here but simply that part of it which involves economic transactions.)

The marriage arrangements start with the people of the boy's house asking a matchmaker to go to the girl's house. With the consent of the girl's house, the matchmaker gets information on the time of birth of the girl (the eight characters indicating the year, month, day of the month, and time of day of birth). Then the boy's house goes to a fortuneteller to see whether the birth times of the young pair are in conflict or not. If the birth times are right, the matchmaker goes again to the girl's house. Now begins an exchange of gifts. The first time, the boy's house sends $50 in cash to the girl's house, and the girl's house then returns 10 per cent of this. A few days or even a few months later, the boy's house sends another, larger gift, amounting to $200; and the girl's house again returns 10 per cent of this. The third gift will amount to $600 and will be sent with five cards of the head of the household. Of

TABLE 46

EXPENDITURE AND RECEIPT IN MARRIAGE CEREMONY

(In Dollars)

	BRIDEGROOM'S HOUSE		BRIDE'S HOUSE	
	Expenditure	Receipt	Expenditure	Receipt
Negotiation....................	50	5	5	50
Agreement.....................	200	20	20	200
Engagement....................	600	60	60	600
Informing of wedding date........	1,600	160	160	1,600
Dowry.........................	250	4,250	4,250	250
Wedding feast..................	3,000	....	2,400	....
Total.....................	5,700	4,495	6,895	2,700
Net expenditure................	1,205	....	4,195	....

the cards, three will be sent to the girl's family elders—the father, grandfather, and greatgrandfather—one to the whole household, while the last bears the eight characters of both the boy and the girl. The girl's family again returns 10 per cent of the gift and the cards of the three generations. This means that the engagement is fixed. The fourth gift, costing $1,600, is offered, and 10 per cent is given back. This is to fix the date of the marriage. On the first day of the marriage ceremony, the boy's family again sends a gift, amounting to about $250, and sends people to fetch the bride. The bride's family offers a big feast to this party and other guests. The girl is then brought to the bridegroom's house, and the wedding ceremony is performed. A big feast is offered to all the invited guests. On the second day the newly married couple sacrifice to the ancestors and are introduced to the kin members in the boy's house. This is followed by another feast. After sacrificing to the ancestors on the third day, the newly wedded couple go to

K

the bride's house and are introduced there to the relatives on the girl's side. This is followed by a feast. The couple then return to the bridegroom's house and sacrifice to the ancestors and offer another feast to the guests. On the fourth day the guests leave. On the day of the marriage, before the bride comes over, the dowry is brought over. In a case that we actually knew of among the middle class in Yuts'un, the value of the dowry was $4,250; and the total expenses for the feasts for the bridegroom, with fifty tables, came to $3,000. The bride's family offered forty tables, costing $2,400.

The total expenses for the boy's house is $5,700, but they get the dowry worth $4,000. The traditional dowry consists of two big chests of drawers and one small chest of drawers, a dressing table, a round table and a square one, four chairs, four stools, a small child's chair, a washstand, two leather suitcases, one washbasin, a soap-container, four cups and a teapot, two mirrors, a bronze charcoal brazier, dresses, bedding, pillows, and nearly everything that the young couple will need in their daily life. This equipment is to last their lifetime. The girl's family receives gifts amounting to $2,700 from the boy's house and sends nearly $6,900 worth of gifts and dowry, so that their net expenses amount to about $4,000. However, they also have some gifts from their guests.

According to the patrilocal system, it appears that a family who marry off their girl not only lose her but must provide a substantial dowry. From the point of view of the newly established couple, we can see that they receive unequal contributions from the two sides. However, since the boy's family have gained a member who will work for them, it appears that the girl's family has suffered a loss. This reinforces the prestige of the male.

The estimate for expenditures was made on the basis of a middleclass family. For the most part, people try to keep up to this standard not only for their own prestige but to establish the prestige of their daughter in her husband's family. To keep up to this standard, the may even sell land or borrow money. In 1939 we knew of one household of rich farmers who sold 20 *mow* of land in order to celebrate the marriage of the son of the house. Another house in 1937 borrowed money by temporarily transferring a piece of vegetable garden land to a man who was able to lend him money. In 1940 another household of the middle class was trying to borrow money in order to get a daughter-in-law. This shows that the expenses of marriage are somewhat fixed, rather than varying according to the means.

Although it is true that the custom of making large expenditures at
the time of a marriage is well established and that the older generation
feel that marriage is an important occasion for reinforcing social status,
among the younger generation this attitude is changing. They are beginning to feel that such extravagant expenses are unnecessary. During a discussion with our landlord on marriage expenses, he suddenly
added: "My son hates this sort of thing. He maintains that we should
make it easier. He says it is unnecessary to follow the custom entirely,
and we do not need to spend such an amount of money." This son is
studying now in the military medical school. He has broken the engagement which his parents made for him. His father continued: "Let
them do what they like—so-called 'free love' if they want. Anyway, it's
no longer the parents' business." It is true that, generally speaking, in
the villages the younger generation, educated in the modern schools,
refuses to follow the old marriage customs. A change in customs will
naturally lead to a change in expenditure. Thus ceremonial expenses
become more elastic.

On the other hand, the spending of a large amount of money in
marriage ceremonies is limited to those who can more or less afford it.
If people are really poor, even if they would like to do something, they
are not able to. A villager of the landless class once discussed his problem with me, as follows: "I am looking forward in the autumn to
marrying a widow of a near-by village. I need only pay $100 to the
widow's house and $80 to the matchmaker. Four pounds of meat and
some sugar will be enough for a gift. Since I have no money, I can do
only this [give the food]." We also encountered a case of simplified
marriage in a family of the poor class that married out a daughter.
This girl was engaged to a boy belonging to a man in a neighboring
village. Her fiancé was in the army and thus away from home. But the
mother of the boy came in a sedan chair, bearing a hen as a present, to
fetch the girl to her home. In this case no money had to be spent; the
marriage was considered to be concluded; and, in case the husband
came back, the affair was all settled. This kind of marriage, which
takes advantage of the absence of the husband, is a recognized form
but is used only by poor people. We tried to follow up this case. Some,
who knew the whole story, told us: "Nothing has been heard from this
boy for a long time. But his mother knew the girl was very capable
and wanted to get her into the household. If the boy should turn out to
be really dead, the mother will marry her daughter-in-law off to the
younger son." In such a case the household will do no more than burn

some paper money before the ancestors at the end of the year. Instead of a community affair, the marriage has become a family arrangement, and in this way there are no real expenses.

So far, we have discussed patrilocal marriage. In this village, as in other parts of Yunnan, matrilocal marriage is sometimes practiced. A boy from a poor household that is not able to afford the marriage ceremonies can go out and get married to a girl and stay in her household. A brother of one of the men in a poor household we knew married a girl of the poor class and lived in her household in this way. In another case a man of the same class married out into another village. In Yuts'un there are more cases of village girls taking in outsiders than of boys from the village going out to live elsewhere. Of these cases, there was one from among the rich farmers, two from the middle class, seven from the poor, and four from the landless. But it is always considered something of a disgrace. In all these cases except one, this custom was followed because of lack of funds. Almost all the boys who married in this way were poor, and most of them were wandering laborers. The houses which took in boys in this way are also mostly from the poor and landless classes in Yuts'un. Marriage in this way is much less expensive than the usual marriage ceremony. In the exceptional case of the rich farmer, the only child was a girl. If this girl had married out, the property would have gone to the clan members. So the father actually persuaded the boy to marry his daughter and live in his household. In ordinary cases, rich boys refuse to marry in this way. The situation is somewhat different from that in Luts'un. As we explained in Part I, in Luts'un there are more cases in which the better-class farmers follow the matrilocal system of marriage. This may be due to the fact that in Luts'un the women take greater part in the farm management, so that for the continuity of the family enterprise there is greater interest in trying to retain the elder able girls in the house. Thus, there may be resort to this type of marriage. But in Yuts'-un, where the women weave, the woman's role in agriculture is much less important.

There is another, less expensive, way to arrange a marriage. This is to adopt a young girl and then marry her to the son of the family when she grows up. In this case the whole series of gifts is unnecessary.

In this village in nearly every year some household celebrates a wedding. In 1939 there were eight households who married off their daughters and one household which took in a daughter-in-law (a case of levirate). In about one in twenty households a marriage took place.

In that year there were two marriages among the rich houses, one in the middle, four in the poor, and two in the landless classes. The costs of each ceremony (in 1939) were about $3,000 for the rich household, $1,000 for the middle class, $500 for the poor, and $200 for the landless. The levirate marriage in the middle class cost $300. The total spent for marriage ceremonies in 1939 was about $10,000. (In 1940 the expenses had risen to about four times this amount.)

VI. FUNERALS

On the third day of the seventh moon in 1940 the father of the headman of Yuts'un died. That afternoon the neighbors of the headman gathered in his house and assisted in buying the coffin and the cotton materials needed to make the mourning clothes. On the morning of the next day the corpse was put into the coffin, which was in the central hall; and the coffin was sealed by painting it with lacquer. The geomancer was then summoned to decide the site for the tomb. The headman himself went to the market to sell the rice and wine he had stored, in order to get money for the funeral expenses. On the fourth day of the next month the funeral ceremonies were offered.

At the time of the funeral ceremonies the women members of the household gathered around the coffin and lamented. When visitors came, the relatives mourned in chorus. These visitors were on that day offered a feast. Guests stayed the whole day, and some stayed overnight in the house. For each meal thirty tables (each one seating from six to eight guests) were set, for about two hundred guests. On the next day, which was the burial day, other feasts were offered before the procession took place. The guests walked in a long procession from the house to the burying ground, lamenting as they went and setting off firecrackers. Even those who were not invited came to watch the procession. In the evening the guests returned to the house and were offered another feast, and on the third day they left.

A few days after this funeral the mother of a landless householder died. Her son went to the community relief center in the walled town and got a free coffin, worth about $30. Then he went to some of the rich houses and asked for donations. He got about $20 in this way. He put the corpse in the coffin and on the second day asked some neighbors to assist him in carrying the coffin to bury it. The man, in mourning clothes, walked in front of the coffin, and his wife followed behind. Very few came out even to watch them go by. The still air was unstirred by the silent removal of the poor old woman.

The contrast between these two funerals was quite marked. Both were villagers; but the former possessed property, and the latter had none. In the case of the poor son, he not only had no land but he did not even rent any, living only upon wages. He knew, of course, that it was quite disgraceful to bury his mother in this way; but he could do nothing but get a coffin, some very coarse burial garments, burn a little paper money, incense, and a candle, and provide food for the neighbors who helped him. Even this, which cost him $100, he could not afford; so he had to ask for help from the rich. In contrast, the village head of the first funeral, having about 10 *mow* of land and renting 40 more, beside 2 *mow* which he had temporary possession of as security for a loan, operated a farm of more than 50 *mow* and had, besides, ½ *mow* of garden land. Every year he had saved a little, so that when his father died he could have an extravagant funeral. In view of his social status in the village he was obliged to do so, even though exhausting his resources. He spent $3,000 at this time. His father's coffin, of cedar, cost $1,000 alone. The headman was much dissatisfied with this coffin, however, because he said it should be better; and he came to consult with my landlord, whom he knew had wood of a quality better suited for coffins. According to my landlord, this wood had been bought many years ago for several hundred silver dollars in the south of Yunnan, near the Burma border. It was said that the tree from which the wood was taken had been sunk in water more than a thousand years and had not rotted through. It was thought that the heart would never rot, and thus it was considered the very best quality of wood for a coffin. In 1940 this wood was already worth more than $5,000, and my landlord was keeping it for his mother. He naturally refused to sell. This incident brought clearly to our minds how important these matters are in the eyes of the villagers. To secure a good coffin and a good tomb for the last resting place of their relatives, they are prepared to pay any price.

Besides the price of the coffin, the headman spent about $1,000 for the funeral feasts, which amounted to one-third of the total expenses. He received from his guests gifts of about $270. The custom is to give every close relative a long piece of white cloth and to the more distant relatives a square of white about the size of a large handkerchief. If the headman had distributed this cloth according to custom, it would have cost him about $500 in addition. But he did not do so; and, as a result, the relatives were rather displeased.

Comparing the marriage ceremony with the funeral ceremony for the same class, we find that $3,000 was spent on the funeral and nearly $12,000 for the marriage, including the expenses of both houses. The marriage was considerably more expensive; but about $4,000 of the money spent was used for the dowry, which serves the useful purpose of establishing the young couple rather than merely being put in the ground, as was the coffin. Preparations for financing a marriage are often made many years ahead. In the case of funerals, old men usually prepare their own coffins if they have money. But not all make these preparations. It tends to be something of an emergency expense. We saw that even the village headman had to sell his reserve of rice and wine. From selling his rice he got $780; from the wine, $600; from selling five loads of vegetables, nearly $50; from collecting on old loans, $520; and from gifts he got $270—a total of $2,200. But even this was not enough, and he was obliged to pay for the coffin on the instalment plan. So we see that, even in a household like that of the village headman, there were not enough savings to meet this emergency. Although not every household will have a death in it every year, there are always some households suffering in this way. In 1939, in the village as a whole, thirty-one persons died, not including infants. These deaths occurred in twenty-six households—about 4 per cent of the village and 16.6 per cent of the households. They included one adult from among the rich farmers; three children and one adult from three middle-class farmers; five children, seven adults, and five aged persons from fourteen poor peasants' households; and two children, one adult, and six aged persons from eight landless households. The total expenses for funerals came to about $13,000.

VII. ACCUMULATION OF WEALTH

Now we can make a summary of the last few chapters on production and consumption by giving a table to show the average income for the different classes. From Table 47 we can see that, for the first three classes, income comes mainly from agriculture. The income from labor and from miscellaneous items, such as small crafts and trading, gradually increases, however; and in the fourth class the income from these miscellaneous items becomes as important as that from agriculture, and the income from labor exceeds the income from management or rent.

From the sample budgets we discussed, we reached the conclusion that an adult in the first class spends, on the average, $1,705 a year; in the second class, $903; in the third class, $853; in the fourth class,

$717; and in the fifth class, $498. The first two budgets belong to the rich, the third to the middle, the fourth to the poor, and the fifth to the landless class. If we compare these figures with the average incomes of the various classes, we can see that, although the second household spent less than the average income for his class, all the rest spent a little more than average. These houses have a little higher standard of living than the average, but the difference is not very great and indicates that they represent fairly well the conditions in their respective classes.

TABLE 47

AVERAGE INCOME ON CLASS BASIS

INCOME	CLASS			
	Rich	Middle	Poor	Landless
Number of households........	6	31	75	44
Number of persons...........	67	176	349	193
Number of adults...........	50.1	127.1	251.0	146.5
Agricultural yield...........	$43,782	$ 83,080	$ 84,450	$14,916
Garden labor...............	$ 4,927	$ 20,013	$ 30,107	$ 6,802
Rice-field labor.............	$ 250	$ 5,850	$ 15,210	$ 8,020
Fertilizer..................	$ 1,308	$ 3,317	$ 6,551	$ 3,824
Weaving...................	$ 188	$ 2,068	$ 5,640	$ 2,632
Duck raising...............		$ 2,864	$ 2,291	$ 1,145
Miscellaneous income........	$ 6,750	$ 9,000	$ 26,250	$25,500
Total.................	$57,205	$126,192	$170,419	$62,839
Average income for each adult.	$ 1,142	$ 992	$ 679	$ 429

The fifth household spends about $488 a year, of which $287, or 54 per cent, are spent on rice. There is only about $200 left to spend on other items. The standard of living represented here is quite low, and it will not be easy to make further reductions in it. Since these people have reached the minimum level of subsistence, they must develop new sources of income in order to find money to live on. So they are willing to work for quite low wages, and the members of their family may scatter in order to seek better opportunities for a livelihood elsewhere. There are many who remain single. To get a bare living, they have to sacrifice family life and personal enjoyment. In other words, they are trying to adjust their income to a relatively fixed amount of consumption. The rich people live far differently. The first household is very rich, with an income double the average income of others of their class. Their expenditures are also double the amount spent by other rich peasants. If we include the expenditures for opium, then the average annual expenditure for an adult in this household is $2,630, which is higher than their regular income per adult. To meet this deficiency, they try, therefore, to cut down upon those items which they think are not essential. They refuse to pay taxes and accept graft. They may also seize ducks which come into their fields. The "lord" can do this because of his powerful position in the community and his connection with the officials in the town. His way of life is, in general, due to the struggle he is making to maintain a luxurious way of life, including smoking opium.

The second household represents a case where income and expenditures are well balanced. Our landlord was very economical on his own account; but for others he was more extravagant—for example, he bought his mother a $5,000 coffin and allowed his sons to wear good leather shoes and expensive hats. He constantly subsidized the son who was a schoolmaster. By careful management of his affairs, he was able to make both ends meet, however. In the third household, representing the middle class, in order to maintain a standard of living a little above the average Chinese in the rural areas, the father of the family was obliged to rent additional land and work it himself in order to increase his income. He has a little more income than he spends, but he must be very careful in his expenditures. In the fourth case the head of the household works very hard; but, in spite of the fact that his average income is a little above that of his class, his income is like that of the landless—a little less than his expenditures. The general economic condition of most of the peasants is one in which they subsist on such a low level of income that it is very difficult to make savings.

CHAPTER XXVI

POPULATION MOVEMENTS

I. THE UNSTABLE POOR

THE main income of the villagers comes from the land; but because the land is limited and unevenly distributed, there are many villagers who have very little land or none at all. Those who have no land or an insufficient amount may continue farming by renting land. But the opportunities for renting land are also limited. Thus, there are poor villagers who are unable to acquire land either by renting it or in any other way. If they still persist in trying to make a living from agriculture, they must become hired laborers. In Yuts'un, however, there are many seasonal laborers who come from different parts and who are mainly aborigines with a very low standard of living. To compete with these men, the villagers must accept a very low wage. But, even when the villagers get employment, it is usually limited to three or four months in the year, and they cannot live a whole year on the wages they receive in this short period. Thus the outlook for them within agriculture is very bad. In Yuts'un there are some supplementary occupations, such as duck raising for the men and weaving for the women. However, in order to take up these occupations, the people must have a certain amount of capital. Moreover, the yearly income from these occupations is very low. People with no better prospects in the village than these must go somewhere else in order to find opportunities to earn more. In the preceding chapter we saw that the income these landless people receive from their own village amounts to 59 per cent of their total earnings. This means that about one-half of their income must be sought outside. Only one-fourth of their total income comes from agriculture in the village. It appears that really indigent folk are not rooted to the land of the village but float, as it were, on the surface. In the foregoing chapter we mentioned twelve households that moved into the village. Some of them had been there as long as six years, the most recent one coming two years ago. But few of them had gained any land—had even rented; and those who had gained land had acquired so little that it was negligible. Thus they have no real bond with the village.

Households similar to these leave the village, going forth, one by one, like scraps of paper blowing away. Only once, in 1922, at the time of the bandit raid, did we hear of the poor people moving out in a body. This catastrophe is still clearly remembered. One evening our landlord and the headman of the village told us at length of how the village guard fought with the bandits and then retreated, of how the bandits came into the village and looted it, and of how the villagers watched the fire which burned nearly half the houses in the village. Of more than one hundred and fifty households, eighty-six became homeless. The present headman described in a low voice how his grandmother was killed by being caught under the ruins, of how they took the children out from the demolished houses, and of how later he and his family lived in the ruins. Twenty years later one sees the ruined houses still standing there, since only part of the people have rebuilt their homes.

Those who were not rooted to the soil had nothing to hold them in the village after the bandits had destroyed their homes and property. After the great fire, eleven poor households moved out of the village and sought their living elsewhere. Nine of them went to the near-by town. Of these nine, two became shoemakers, two became cotton merchants in a small way; one acquired a sedan chair for marriage ceremonies, which he rents out, as well as his services as carrier; one started a rice store; one is an odd-job man; one became a tax-collector; and the last rented some land and became a tenant farmer. Of the other two households, one went to Kunming and, after making a beginning by teaching the local folk-drama, started a small grocery; the other disappeared. Nine out of eleven are seen to be struggling to make their way in lines other than agriculture.

There are always a few poor people who move out from the village from time to time. People remember, from the period directly before the fire, four families who left, two of them going to near-by towns. One household head became a butcher; another, a cloth merchant; a third went to the next district and became a gardener there; and the fourth went to Kunming. Some time after, fifteen other families moved out. One householder had a sister in Kunming, married to the owner of a theater. He went there to sell noodles in the theater. Another went to a distant village and became a fortuneteller. Still another began to travel around as a peddler of rapeseed oil. Three others became gardeners in a market center. The seventh went to Kunming and got a job in a drygoods store. The eighth went into the business of making sugar from sugar cane in the near-by town. The ninth became a tenant farmer. The tenth became a carpenter in the town. The eleventh became a purser on a steamer. The twelfth became a general laborer in the mining center. The thirteenth became a carpenter in the next district. The fourteenth came to Lufon to be a gardener. The fifteenth became a farmer in a distant district.

There are seven householders who moved out during the last two years. The first of these moved to a neighboring district and became a gardener. The second and third became gardeners in the mining center. The fourth went to be a gardener some distance away. The fifth one raises chickens in the near-by town. The sixth became a porter

TABLE 48

EMIGRATION FROM THE VILLAGE AND OCCUPATIONS TAKEN UP

	No. of House-holds That Moved Out	Destination		Occupations			
		Same District	Outside District	Agri-culture	Trade	Crafts	Others
Before 1922.....	4	2	2	1	1	0	2
1922...........	10	9	1	2	4	2	2
1923–37.	16	4	12	7	3	2	3
1938–40........	7	2	5	6	0	1	1
Total......	37	17	20	16	8	5	8

in Kunming. And the seventh became a farmer in another village. These seven householders, who, as recent residents, are well remembered in the village, all belonged to the landless class. Some of them moved out to avoid military conscription. Table 48 summarizes the foregoing facts. The data are not necessarily exhaustive, since they are simply as given from the memory of the people.

II. THE ASCENDING RICH

Those who move out are not only the poor people but also the rich. The motives for moving out are different, however, in the two groups. The poor move out because they are driven forth by the hardships of life. The rich, on the other hand, are impelled by the craving for greater comfort and prosperity. We may take the year 1922, the time of the big fire, as a point of reference. Before the fire, eight rich householders had moved into the near-by town, four of them renting out all their land to others and living upon their income from rent only.

Of the remaining four, one household rented out part of their land and operated part themselves. Another householder rented out all his land and engaged in old-style banking and also in selling cotton thread. The third rented out his land and started a hotel. The fourth rented out only part of his land and started a grocery.

Shortly after the great fire, twelve rich householders moved out, nine of them to the walled town. Of these nine, four live on income from rent alone; three still manage their own land; one became a minor official in the government and also continues to operate his own land; and one became a merchant. The other three moved to more distant places: two went to the next district, where one started a grocery and the other a shop for candy and sweetcakes, and the third went to Shanghai, where he worked in a hospital. The total number of rich householders that moved out was twenty, seventeen remaining in the same district and three leaving entirely. All of them, without exception, moved to towns or cities. The attraction of the town is that it provides security and also opportunities for economic development. The rich householders in the village still fear a recurrence of the bandit raid. They try to organize the village guard but remember that in the catastrophe of 1922 this guard was not very effective. So, if they can, they prefer to move to town, where they can live together in a place inclosed by a wall and where they can organize and pay for better guard protection.

Moreover, in the town there is better opportunity to get rich. As regards the twenty householders who moved to town from the village, six of them engaged in trade, selling such things as drygoods, groceries, candy, salt, and medicines. The scale on which business is carried on is comparatively large and can be carried on only in a town. Remaining in the village, they would not have had opportunities of this sort. Thus, among this class, the movement is not from village to village but from village to town.

The rich households tend to stay closer to home, however, than do the poor. Among the thirty-seven poor peasants, twenty of them went outside the district. But among the twenty rich householders who moved out, only three went outside the district; the rest all settled in the near-by town. Although they had moved out, most of them still kept their ownership of land. In order to collect the rent, they must not move too far away. The poorer peasants have less to keep them near at hand, and so they go wherever they find the best opportunity for a livelihood. They can often find better jobs if they go farther away.

For instance, the skilled gardeners have less competition in the mining center or some of the other more distant places. The rich, unlike the poor, do not really sever connections with the village. But the rich who move into the town gradually give up the management of their own land. Among the twenty households mentioned above, thirteen have become absentee landlords. The rest still manage their own land, but with difficulty. If they succeed in making enough money in the town, they will be likely to rent out their land also.

III. INDIVIDUAL EMIGRANTS

Up to this point we have discussed emigrants who moved out as families. There are also individual emigrants. From among the original 785 villagers, we know that 75 (about 1 out of every 10 persons) left the village, since the village record still keeps their names. From almost every other household an individual had left. This is a very striking phenomenon. Among the 75 who left, 11 were drafted into the army, and 9 left the village in order to escape the draft. These 9 may have gone to distant places or may have joined the government service, which gives draft deferment. One-third of the group, thus, are seen to have been those who left because of the war. According to the draft law of that time, students, schoolteachers, and public servants were deferred. The boys of the rich houses could easily get deferment on these grounds, but the poor who had no educational opportunities could not get out of being drafted in this way. If the latter did not wish to be soldiers, they could only run away. Of the 11 drafted soldiers, 10 are from the poor and landless classes and only 1 from the middle class. The effect of the draft is very serious for the poor peasant households, since they depend upon their own members for their supply of farm labor. There is no allowance for soldiers' dependents. We know of a case in which a wife, whose husband was drafted, was unable to carry on the farm work herself. She brought her two young sons to Kunming and engaged in making bamboo hats. The draft completely disrupted the traditional family organization. Not only has it taken away many of the young men but, as an accompanying effect, it has increased the rate of emigration.

The number of drafted men is small, but there are more who leave in order to escape being drafted. These men belong to the poor and landless classes, and they endeavor to avoid the draft not only to save their own skins but also for the sake of their families. Since they cannot gain deferment and have no money to employ labor to take their place on the farm, they resort to running away. The security of the family depends on the individual members rather than on the community; so the draft scores a direct hit on the family unit. The conflict of loyalty to the nation and to their own families is very great among the Chinese peasants.

However, it is not easy for the peasants really to get away. To escape the draft, a man must go very far away. In order to look out for his family, he must find a good job, so that he can send money back. For those who have no experience in the outside world, this is not easily accomplished. My landlord told me that he had a relative living in a district farther west, where the people are isolated and rustic. When these people go out from their homes, they lose their bearings; and, since they know no one outside, they cannot find jobs except close at home. Therefore, they have no hope of escaping the draft but just sit in their village and wait. When the order comes, they go. The same thing is true, my landlord told me, of the aborigines scattered over the mountainsides. But in Yuts'un it is different. Because the people of the village are less cut off, they have become used to traveling and know something of the outside world. As we have shown, it is not unusual for them to leave their native place. Even before the war, many families, as well as individuals, were constantly moving out. The war has merely accelerated the process. However, those affected by the draft are only a minority, since but one-third of the folk who moved out did so for this reason.

The 75 individuals who moved out were mainly young men and boys, except for 2 women, 2 children, and a few middle-aged men. Each age class takes up different occupations in the world outside the village. The young boys usually go as apprentices to learn trades or go to the mining centers as child labor. The young men mainly enter the military academies or else learn to be chauffeurs or do factory work. The older people become janitors, peddlers, or craftsmen. Most of the people mentioned went to distant places. We had no opportunity to talk to them and to find out what their real motives and aspirations were. But from the condition of their families who were left in the village we got some idea of the motivating force behind their movement.

Besides the 11 who were drafted, there were 64 individuals who left, of whom 10 belonged to rich families, 9 to middle, 3 to poor, and 21 to landless households. The percentage according to the numbers in the respective classes was 15 per cent for the rich, 5.1 per cent for the middle, 6.6 per cent for the poor, and 11.4 per cent for the landless. This distribution shows that, comparatively speaking, it is the rich and the landless classes which tend to leave the village rather than the middle and poor, both for family units and for individuals The very poor must find jobs, and opportunities to get them are limited in the village. Sometimes families break up entirely in this way. We knew of one case in which the father hired out as a laborer and the mother did weaving, but still their income was insufficient. So, for $10 they contracted to have their boy of thirteen work in the mines. The advantage of this to the parents was not so much to increase their income as to reduce their expenses in raising the child. Life for this boy in the dark mines has become that of a beast of burden, and it is doubtful whether he will last very long at it.

The pressure of life which drives the poor men from the village is very great. But not all who leave the village are like this poor boy who gave up his freedom. There is always a chance of improving one's lot in life. In 1911 our landlord was rather badly off. His father, who was still living, had about 10 *mow* of land but had transferred about half of this amount to others in order to get loans. Our landlord worked on the remaining land and hired out to others when the work on his own family's farm was finished. For all this hard work, he had accumulated about $20 as his wages for the year. Then his foot became infected while working on the farm, and he was unable to continue. Because of the lack of his labor in the fields, things went from bad to worse in the household. One day he happened to go to the house of his wife's family and met his father-in-law, who had just came back from a neighboring district, where he had gone with a friend to sell pigs. This man had started out with $80 capital and, in a trip lasting only twenty-five days, had made $30. Our landlord was much attracted by the opportunity for profit which he saw here. The profit was not very great, but he saw a better chance to get ahead in that way than in staying and working on his father's small farm. So he decided to go out with his father-in-law and sell pigs. Although our landlord was not landless, the pressure of life was strong enough to make him wish to take a chance, to go against the traditional warning against "turning his back on his native land and leaving his own well."

The psychology of taking a chance is not limited to the poor, however. Although the rich may not necessarily be worrying about their daily bread, the pressure of growing generations is strong. Unless they can expand, their family will descend in the social scale, and expansion can be achieved only with difficulty if they remain in their own village.

To get rich, one must go outside of agriculture. To improve one's social position, one must go outside the village—this is well established. Those who have prestige in traditional Chinese society are not those who work on the land but those who are scholars, working with books. For example, in Yuts'un the man who got his wealth from illegal smuggling and from hoarding silver is, in fact, as rich as the "lord," but his social status is far below that of the latter. The miser is illiterate; but the "lord" understands classical literature and his ancestors received decorations, and so he is in a special class above all others. The traditional idea which exalts the scholar class has been summarized in the epigrammatic sentence which is the first thing a boy learns in starting his classical studies: "Everything is low, only the learning of books is high." This traditional idea still exists in the minds of the villagers. To be a scholar is a way to enter the government and become socially important and also to become rich. We shall discuss this in the next chapters. It is sufficient here to say that parents will try their best to send their children to school with the hope that one day the children will reach a higher social status than that of their parents. There are more than ten young men from the rich houses who have received a middle-school education. None of them are satisfied to carry on the work of their parents on the farm. They do not like to stay in the village but tend to go out to seek their fortunes.

The school is like a bridge, over which the young men of the rich houses enter the outside world and go into occupations other than farming. By spending a few years in school, even if they get nothing else, they get a strong reaction against farming. Everyone of this group we met, without exception, despised his parents' occupation. The second son of our landlord, after leaving middle school, entered the Chemical Corps and then, not satisfied, changed to the Land-Survey Corps. Still not satisfied, in 1940 he came home in despair, giving, as an excuse, that of illness.

We often talked with the schoolmasters in the near-by town and became well acquainted. We were deeply impressed by their discouragement and sense of frustration. One day, we came to the problem of their prospects in the future. They expressed the feeling that they could no longer stay on in their own homes because they no longer fitted in with the life of their families. To teach in a primary school is both difficult and poorly paid, they said. The second son of our landlord joined the conversation and said: "One's native town is the place that kills the ambition of a young man. We must go away and live!" A few days later he left to enter a military academy in Kunming. The "bridge of learning" is a long one. From the primary school to the upper grades of the middle school takes nine years. And during these nine years parents must pay not only for the food but also for the other expenses of their children, which amount to about $3,000 per child. Moreover, while the children are in school, they cannot help on the family farm. This means that only the rich can afford to send their children to school. The young men of the poorer houses have no chance to pass over this bridge; so they must find another way out. None of those from the middle, poor, and landless classes who left the village had had a middle-school education. Among the ten persons who went out from the rich houses of the village, seven of them had received a middle-school education.

The work taken up outside the village differs for rich and poor. Poor folk work at mining, as peddlers, in crafts, are apprenticed to learn trades, do odd jobs, or become policemen or soldiers. There is much variety in the jobs they perform, and very few of them require special training. So they are able to change easily from one job to another, seeking out whichever is more profitable. They can even come back and take up agricultural work again if they have bad luck outside. But the young men from the rich houses have a more restricted choice. They do not like to take "low-class" jobs of the sort mentioned above; but they are not prepared for really good jobs, since a middle-school education is not enough to enable one to enter a really good profession. Young men of this sort are not satisfied with the low and cannot attain the high; so they hang between the two. They may accept the job of a low-ranking civil servant or of teacher in the primary school. Or, after training for a short period in a military academy or the Military Medical Service, they may become petty officers in the army. These positions can hardly satisfy them, however, because the salaries are low and they cannot maintain the standard of living they are used to. They are even worse off economically than if they remained in agriculture. As we shall show in the next chapter, they have completely changed their standards of living, adopting a standard which cannot be supported by their own earnings. As a result, they still depend upon the support of their families and become a burden to their parents. The only satisfaction they get is from the improvement in their social status, and for this they pay a very high price. In changing China this class of young men has become an unstable group, uprooted from the traditional occupations of their families and not yet fixed in the new structure. They go back and forth, from village to town, and move from one job to another with dissatisfaction and discouragement.

IV. POPULATION MOVEMENTS AND FARM MANAGEMENT

Regardless of whether an individual is rich or poor, when he leaves the village he is separated from his farm and cannot continue to manage it. So he usually disposes of his land by temporary transfer or by renting or selling it. The households from which some of the young men have recently left are beginning to suffer from a shortage of labor. For instance, in our landlord's family, only his eldest son, who died, had been willing to remain on the farm and help his father. None of the other sons, who received a middle-school education, was willing to do so. As a result, our landlord was forced to keep a hired man, who not only was inefficient but also was always threatening to quit. One day our landlord heaved a sigh and said: "Since the death of my eldest son, our farm has gone from bad to worse."

Our landlord was himself a very competent farmer; and even with lack of help, he was able still to keep the farm running. But with those who are inexperienced farmers or are too old to carry on farm work, the situation is even worse. For example, the "lord," who is a scholar and who passed the first-grade imperial examinations, has never gone down to his field and worked himself; he knows nothing of agriculture and has no son who is willing to take up the management of his estate. He comes to our landlord for advice, but his hired laborers are so lazy and pay so little attention to their work that his whole farm is in a bad state. Our landlord once pointed it out to me, saying: "It looks terrible."

In the above two cases the farms are still being managed by their own households because the older generation are still alive. But this cannot continue indefinitely. When the fathers of these families die, there will be no one to continue this work, so that inevitably the land must be rented out. Since every rich household is trying to send their sons out into the world, the knowledge of agriculture, which is usually transmitted through personal contact and experience, is no longer being handed on. And when, as frequently happens, the sons, after unfortunate adventures in the outside world, return, they are unable to work on the farm if they did wish to. Thus, on the one hand, absentee ownership is encouraged, by the renting of land, and, on the other, the concentration of ownership, by its sale. However, sometimes those who go out do have a chance to become rich. This will be discussed in the next chapter.

CHAPTER XXVII

THE ACQUISITION OF WEALTH

I. PUBLIC OFFICE

IN A village where the farms are small and wealth is accumulated slowly, there are very few chances for a landless man to become a landowner or for a petty owner to become a large landowner. It takes generations to climb the ladder of success simply by frugality; and during these long years the prospect of periodic upsets, from natural sources such as famine or from personal misfortunes such as illness and death, must always be faced. Even in ordinary circumstances, resources will constantly be drained by the expenses of ceremonies, marriages, and so on. It is not going too far to say that in agriculture there is no way really to get ahead. We made this point clear in the previous parts, but it may be repeated here. In Yuts'un none of the rich families has gained its wealth through agriculture. To become rich one must leave agriculture—this is generally true throughout rural China. For Yuts'un we have described how the people work on the land and how they raise ducks and engage in weaving. None of these occupations carries a promise of wealth for the people. Here in this village there is nothing like the papermaking industry of Yits'un. If the people of Yuts'un wish to become rich, the only thing for them to do is to leave the village. Outside there are certain opportunities open to them.

In the traditional economy, before the introduction of modern industry, opportunities outside the village were quite limited. Conditions in this village were, on the whole, similar to those in Luts'un. Almost the only way to climb from the lower to the higher levels was to get into the bureaucracy as an official. However, since this village is located on the traditional trading routes, there was another way—commerce, including smuggling.

It is, indeed, not true that every official becomes rich, but there are officials who regard their positions as a way to get money. There is a deeply rooted traditional idea that to be an official leads to wealth; and there are clear cases in the village which show that this idea is not merely a belief.

The ancestors of the "lord" were only ordinary persons until his great-grandfather became a military officer in the Tsing Dynasty. The officer acquired at this time more than 100 *mow* of land. His son, grandfather of the "lord," became a military commander in Hunan, acquired more than 300 *mow* of land, and built a large temple and also the large house now occupied by the family in the village. No one knows, at present, how the grandfather, as a simple military officer, was able to accumulate such wealth; but the big estate is evidence of his success and reinforces the traditional idea of how wealth is acquired in the village. However, although it is believed that getting rich in this way is a common occurrence, not all are able to do it. During the last forty years there must have been a number of people who attempted to do so. Of numerous young men who recently have passed through the middle school, graduated from a military academy, entered a military medical school, joined the Chemical Corps, or become civil servants or regimental commanders, none has as yet attained the high success of their heroes of the past, although it is true they are looking in this direction. Since the village economy is closed, it is quite natural that ambitious young men should struggle to get ahead in the world in this way, following traditional ideas. It is true that there is an ideal type of good official who retires from office with only "two sleeves of cold wind," meaning that he has gained nothing but the love of the people. But, on the other hand, the mores also encourage a man to build up security for his descendants. The sense of personal obligation to one's family is often strong enough to make the ideal of the good official seem an impractical one for ordinary life.

Although the traditional situation has changed in China, expectation of economic gain as a result of holding the position of an official still remains in rural areas. But, even if we accept the proposition that there are still possibilities of acquiring wealth in official life, it is not so easy for the villagers to become officials. Formerly, if the parents could afford to do without the work of their son on the farm and could allow him to attend a private school for ten years or so, and if he were then able to pass the examinations by displaying good calligraphy and his knowledge of some of the standard classical verses, he might automatically become an official. But when this traditional system was abolished and the modern school took its place, to complete a college course (the minimum requirement for a high official) came to take sixteen years. Formerly, little need be spent on equipment; and books need not be bought, since the old ones could be used. Formerly, also, the students could live in the village as they worked and studied. Now, for higher education they must go to the urban centers and must wear better student clothing, which costs much more than that generally worn in the villages. We have mentioned the second son of our landlord, who was a middle-school graduate. We do not know what he gained from school except his costume, which is the student uniform with leather shoes and a felt hat. His standards in clothing are much higher than those of others of the same age in the village. But the expenses of education are not only those of tuition, equipment, and clothing. This new education changes not only outward appearance but the whole outlook upon life of the individual, so that traditional ways of life are no longer acceptable to him. The well-to-do families cannot afford to send their children to a university. Even to give them a middle-school education means that they must strain to the limit. But a middle-school graduate finds it almost impossible to get a good position in the government or in any public service. So there is a tendency for the young men to enter military academies. After a short period of training they become commissioned officers in the army and, if lucky enough, may be promoted to the higher ranks.

The motive of private gain is scarcely a good motive for efficient public service. But since the traditional conception lingers on, lack of success in attaining wealth through public office leads to a sense of frustration among those brought up with this idea, as well as to their whole clan, who stand behind them. As we have said in Part I, an efficient modern government can be established only when the basis of rural economy is changed, so that there are other outlets for ambitious young men, such as industry. Then, at last, corruption may be eliminated.

II. ILLEGAL TRAFFIC

The traditional rural economy even forces people into criminal action. It is quite reasonable for a young man to be dissatisfied with the closed economic system. Opportunities which are open to him are very limited and sometimes require excessive expense and preparation. A man who starts from one of the poorer peasant families must work on the farm when young. Only a few can enter school or the military academy. But the dream of rising in the world exists in every mind. Although, as has been shown in Part I, Chinese culture has done its best to support this limited economy by emphasizing the attitude of contentment, even in the past this doctrine probably failed to satisfy everyone fully. Today, in the rapidly changing world which surrounds us, we may say that it has become less and less effective. Desperately poor peasants are led into illegal adventures. These may take the form of political revolution or widespread banditry. In this part of the country the smuggling of opium becomes a lamentable means of getting ahead.

In the first days of the Republic the government adopted strict measures toward the vicious habit of opium-smoking. But since the importation of this drug, a large body of the population has developed the habit, for which, unfortunately, there is no easy cure. The result of the prohibition of opium was the rise of a black market in opium and the encouragement of smuggling. Both Burma and the western part of Yunnan, where Chinese political power was not yet firmly rooted, became centers of opium culture, and the neighboring districts discovered the profit in opium-smuggling. Since the district in which Yuts'un lies is in the center of a traditional trading route, it has both profited and suffered from this traffic.

We know of a villager in Yuts'un who engaged in this sort of smuggling. He was very poor and had no prospect of bettering himself on his farm. In an effort to make a livelihood, he followed his father-in-law to the western part of Yunnan to sell pigs. They followed the same route as that taken by the opium traffic. Seeing the far greater profit to be made in this way, the villager changed and became an opium-smuggler. He gathered $500 from his clan members and went, not to Burma, but just a few districts west, to get opium. Every year he made several trips, lasting about a month. In six years he made a fortune of $30,000; but this, except for $500, all went to the clan members who had financed his trips. With this $500 as capital, he then started his own venture. In two years he had made another fortune of $30,000. He then incorporated again, collected money, got 1,000 ounces of opium (each ounce costing $300), and transported it to Keichow. There were four men who organized this expedition, and they carried the opium in a kerosene can. After running many risks, including going through suspicious customs offices on the boundary of the provinces, he at last arrived at his destination and sold his opium, at a 300 per cent profit, or $300,000. Then he became a smuggler in a big way, organized several large expeditions into Burma, and each time got several thousand dollars' profit. He bought more than 20 *mow* of land, built a new house, and rose from near the bottom to be one of the rich. Long ago he withdrew from this sort of business and became a farmer—and a very good one!

Another villager was very rich but had to hide his wealth. About thirty years ago he was a poor peasant with three brothers; and there were only 5 *mow* of land in the family, an amount insufficient for their subsistence. This man, needing to do something besides farming, engaged in transporting vegetables to another district, hired himself out in the mining district, and also engaged in carrying fish from the lake districts. In that period he was running here and there, trying to find a living. In 1915 he joined with the smuggler mentioned above and for two years was paid by him to carry a weapon and protect him. In this way he accumulated $200 of his own. Then he became very daring and started his own smuggling project. He bought horses and started to smuggle opium. One rich man gave him $700. With that and his own money, he had about $1,000, with which he bought opium. A number of smugglers joined together for mutual protection on the journey, but on their way they had an encounter with some soldiers. In the confusion which resulted, the others ran away, but this man hid in a ditch. When the soldiers were gone, he discovered beside him two horses with a load of 3,000 ounces of opium. He took this load and hid it in a friend's house and sold it gradually, after telling those who had given him money that he had lost everything. From this he got a fortune of tens of thousands of dollars and became one of the very rich. But he cannot display his wealth.

To smuggle opium, one has to keep out of the hands of the army as well as of bandits. The smuggler must be daring and, in addition, very shrewd and experienced. There is no surety of success. Sometimes the whole fortune hangs by a thread. We knew a case of a failure. In 1910 a man became a servant to an officer in Szechwan. From this trip he got experience in traveling; and when in 1915, he came back to the village, some friends asked him to smuggle some opium for them into Szechwan. But when he arrived in Chungking he was searched, the opium was discovered, and he lost everything. He is still a poor villager, and his dream of worldly success has not been realized. There are a number of other people who have failed in this way. It is often very difficult to recover after a loss of this sort, in which ambition is killed.

The first smuggler described here enjoyed telling me of all the risks and adventures he had passed through. Once, all by himself, he had driven a horse, loaded with opium, over a wild mountainous path and had lost his way. It was already late and nearly dark. Suddenly he saw a man coming up. He sensed that something was wrong, but he had no weapon. Although very nervous, he saw that there was no way for him to retreat. The man, as he came nearer, showed himself to be armed with a club and looked as if he were going to attack; but our friend calmly put his hand under his robe and pretended that he had a pistol. The man passed by. That evening our friend reached a little inn and told the innkeeper about his encounter. The innkeeper was greatly astounded, saying: "That must have been the well-known killer, Li. He is one who kills people without a blink of the eye. I know that many of my customers have been killed. How could you escape?"

Another time, when he had put his opium in a kerosene can, he and his friends arrived at the customs office at the boundary of the province It was early in the morning, and they thought they were not seen. After they had gone a few miles, however, the customs officers appeared, armed with knives. Our friend got out his pistol and managed to escape.

Gradually, individual smuggling is organized into expeditions. The following is a case of this sort. This expedition took place at the end of March, 1917; its destination was Rangoon, in Burma. It consisted of the head of the expedition, a lieutenant, a business manager, and twenty-four bands, each band made up of ten or more people. The members of the various bands all knew each other well, being either friends or relatives. Each band carried a stove, and all the members camped together. Before the journey started, they prepared all the things necessary for the trip and drew lots for the order of the procession. Sometimes the head led the way; sometimes he watched the rear. For the whole procession there were twenty-six scouts, who were decided upon by the drawing of lots. These men went on about 10 miles ahead, disguised as small traders. Their business was to find out if the road were clear and, if necessary, to clear it. It was the business of the head to decide whether they should fight or hide. When camping, each band camped separately, ranging themselves in two rows, with guards on watch at night. They carried three days' food in reserve and got supplies on the way. The amount of money carried by each band for buying opium was reported to, and registered by, the business manager. The scouts were paid expenses and a special salary besides, in proportion to the amount of money or opium carried. Arms also were portioned out according to the amount of money or opium carried. If anyone was killed, compensation, up to $200, was given by the common treasurer. Any loss was shared equally, according to the proportionate amount of money carried. There was a most detailed code as to the order of march, and those who did not follow the orders were fined $5.00. They were not allowed to seize property by force, and anyone so doing was fined $5.00. In buying opium there had to be collective bargaining. Anyone buying opium individually was fined. This code was strictly enforced. The whole expedition carried with it $400,000, which in Burma would be enough to purchase about 150,000 ounces of opium. There were about 200 members and 160 horses when they started; but on the way they met another band, which they incorporated into their own, and so the band increased to 300 people and 200 horses, with 170 rifles and pistols. It took 172 days to make the round trip. The group stayed in Rangoon for 42 days and camped 47 times on the way. The money for this was financed by a number of persons who did not go along; so the actual number of persons involved was much greater than the number who made the trip. All the members of the expedition were young and strong; and the head was a well-experienced smuggler, a very able man from a poor peasant family. On the way the group engaged in fighting several times but came through safely and returned home with a fortune.

Incidents and accounts such as these can be multiplied, but we have given enough examples to show that in this wild frontier country force was often stronger than law. Adventures such as these constituted romance for the young folk and also furnished an outlet to the closed economy. Owing to the better government of the province, such big-scale smuggling disappeared some time ago. But the results of such traffic can still be traced in the present distribution of wealth.

III. COMMERCE

Illegal adventures are risky under any circumstances, but with an increase of political power they can no longer be carried on. The money acquired in the sort of expedition described above eventually comes back to the village, where it is used to buy land. The large landowners no longer wish to take risks. But, once involved in the rural economy, they are likely, as we pointed out in Part I, to sink down again in the course of generations. Enterprises of this sort are thus not a stable basis for establishing a family estate. The situation changes when commercial enterprise develops. We may take as examples a number of individuals whom we came to know in the walled town near Yuts'un: the cloth merchant, the gold merchant, the owner of a general store, the lumber merchant, and the mineowners—individuals whose property amounts to more than a million dollars in value. If we compare agriculture with commerce, we can see how in commerce, unlike in agriculture, wealth can easily be accumulated. As we can see in this one district, there are a number of merchants who have become very rich in one generation.

There are a number of large-scale commercial houses in the town, which, being the center of a distributing system for a wide area, lends itself to large-scale commercial development. The type of enterprise carried on by these houses is not like that carried on by the peddlers or small retailers. Because of the scarcity of towns in the region, these houses are able to concentrate on, and monopolize, trade in certain articles. This kind of business is, by its nature, emancipated from the restrictions that we found in agriculture—emancipated by the scale of enterprise, the amount of investment, the rapid turnover of capital, and the efficiency of management. In this town we find modern organizations, such as partnerships and corporations, which enable individuals to pool their resources. For instance, the salt store, started by one of the Yuts'un villagers, was a case of partnership; and the bus company was organized on the principle of a modern corporation. In Yits'un we saw how the growth of capitalism is checked because of the lack of a good system of transportation. In Yuts'un, where transportation is better, capitalism develops.

In this interior, rural area, where modern commerce is just beginning to appear, large monopolies, controlled by a few people, spring up more easily than elsewhere. But only a few people have the qualifications necessary for becoming rich merchants, and these qualifications may be those of a personal or an accidental nature. The lumber merchant mentioned above is the head of the aboriginal population in the region. Having come into contact with the Chinese, he came, in time, to know Chinese as well as his native tongue. In time he came to serve as a go-between for the two groups—the Chinese and aborigines. In this strategic position he began to engage in the lumber business. He collected wood which was owned and cut by the mountain-dwelling aborogines and sold it to the Chinese. In neither group was there anyone in a position to compete with him, and so he maintained a monopoly. The cigarette merchant accidentally became acquainted with a representative of a foreign tobacco company and secured the monopoly for cigarettes. Another example is that of one of the cotton merchants. In the late Tsing Dynasty, before 1910, he was a peddler selling bandages for bound feet in Kunming. He also bought cotton thread in Kunming and sold it to the villagers. In 1911 there was a

Cantonese who started a cotton store, selling cotton thread imported from Hong Kong. His store was large, but in the beginning he had very few customers. At New Year's time our friend the peddler brought some packages of firecrackers to this storekeeper to wish him a Happy New Year. Since this is supposed to bring luck, the owner of the store was very pleased by this attention. When the peddler asked to buy cotton thread, the gratified storekeeper said he would not bargain with him but would sell the thread for whatever the peddler thought fit to pay. The peddler, however, paid the market price for the thread and in this way established his reputation as a reliable individual with the storekeeper. Later on, therefore, he was enabled to get supplies on credit. The store-owner and the peddler becoming at length very good friends, the former advised the peddler and kept him informed as to conditions in the market in Shanghai and Hong Kong. As a result, when the price of thread was about to rise, the peddler bought quantities of thread; and before the price had gone down, he sold it. In this way he gradually became rich and started his own store. In 1930 he had already accumulated a fortune of more than $1,000,000. From these cases we can see that the commodities on which these fortunes were based were goods new to this part of the country, which tapped new markets. In this situation, those who get in at the start can easily monopolize the field. With vast markets behind them to exploit, they can make fortunes. A sudden rise in family fortunes of this sort is impossible in agriculture.

The most important big business in this district is the selling of cotton cloth. It has not had a long history, since it started only about thirty-five years ago. At that time, Western machine-made cotton thread began to be imported to that region. In a short time, owing to its better quality and relatively low price, it superseded the native-spun thread. The weavers who formerly supplied themselves with their own thread began to rely entirely on imported thread.

The most important business in Yuts'un is the weaving industry, which here is a traditional occupation. In the past the people raised their own cotton, spun it and wove it, and supplied cloth to the neighboring districts. Around 1910, with the introduction of modern machine-produced cotton thread, the nature of this industry changed. The weavers began to depend on imported raw materials, and native spinning ceased entirely. For the production of the machine-made thread takes place in faraway Western countries, the thread being imported through Shanghai and Hong Kong. A group of middlemen, who import the thread and sell it in that area, sprang up. This gave a new impetus to the weaving industry, which was thus tied up to the international world of commerce. But there developed the system, described above, of the exchange of cotton thread for completed pieces of cotton cloth. The storekeepers collect the cloth and distribute it. In this way the process of distribution also comes into the hands of the importers. The producer has, more and more, lost his independence in this industry because he cannot sell his goods in the market independently. So this industry has gradually become concentrated in the hands of a few businessmen.

The amount of business involved in the weaving industry is very large, and we can only estimate it. There are about 270 villages in this district, with about 25,000 households. If we take 70 per cent of these households as containing weavers, there are about 11,000 households where weaving is done. Every household produces about 200 pieces of cloth a year. The total production amounts to about 4,000,000 pieces of cloth, which take about 380,000 lots of thread. The businessmen in the walled town also control the weaving in the neighboring districts, where there should be about the same number of weavers as in this district. According to this estimate, cotton thread valued at $60,800,-000 must be imported. About 50 per cent of the cloth produced is used by the weavers' households. After subtracting the amount used by the people in their own homes, we have about 3,000,000 pieces of cloth, which were disposed of in the market and sold to other districts; these were valued at about $30,000,000. The whole business of buying and selling cloth involves $100,000,000. If the merchants get 10 per cent, their income will be $10,000,000, which is far and away more than the income derived from agriculture. Moreover, this income is concentrated in the hands of a few.

The concentration of wealth so quickly and in such large amounts creates a strong financial power in the town and stimulates the development of other trades. The cloth from this district is transported to the east and south of the province. In return, tea, hogs, opium, Chinese medicine, and hides are brought back to the town, which is the commercial center, and from there redistributed; some of these goods are even exported through Shanghai. So the town is a real center of commercial activity. We mentioned before the ecological advantages which the district possesses. The walled town is only about 130 km. from Kunming and is connected with it by daily bus service; and, besides this, there are trucks to carry out the goods. Part of the transportation can be done on Lake Yunnan, since it is only one day's journey on horseback to the shores of the lake, which can itself be traversed in one night. The route is not mountainous but level. On the southeastern side of this district is the mining center. From this center one can go on to Kwangsi or to Indo-China. To the south, on the Yuan River, one can reach the border of Indo-China or Thailand. Beyond the border of this region lies the opium-producing area. To the west, through the aboriginal region, is the old trade route to Burma. To the northwest is Tali and the valley region of the Salween River, the big tea- and rice-producing area. Also, this latter region is in contact with the Tibetan border, from which come hides and Chinese medicine. With the building of the Burma Road, Kunming became a center of distribution for the area to the north and east and also west. It is clear that with the elaborate system of roads which exists transportation is easy and commerce is likely to develop.

As commerce grows, modern hotels and the traditional inns, restaurants, foodshops, stables, department stores, cakeshops, hat and cigarette stores, large salt stores, and dyeing establishments spring up. These stores may be started by one family or in partnership. For the most part, they keep old-style accounts, but some of them have begun to use modern bookkeeping. In 1940 the bus company mentioned above was organized on the basis of a modern corporation, having shares, stockholders' meeting, trustees, and a manager. Each share cost $100, and there were one hundred and fifty shares. My landlord bought one share, and the "lord" bought two. The shareholders were paid regular interest and were also given bonuses. In addition, the corporation had a written constitution. In one year the company made $7,000 profit, and in three years it grew from three or four busses to ten. But as the war gradually came closer, the busses were taken over by the government for use in transporting soldiers and the company was suspended. The people of this district went to Kunming and started a combination bus and steamer company, which was to run around the lake. These attempts indicate that the people of the town are moving toward the development of modern commerce.

Another place for the investment for capital is in the mines. A man who was originally a native of Yuts'un moved to the town and started a department store; later he opened up grocery, salt, and cotton shops and became very rich. He bought from the aborigines a mountain where iron ore had been found. He invested only $1,000 and operates his mine in the old style; so we do not know, yet, how far he will go in exploiting his resources. Another man was, during the Tsing Dynasty, a counterfeiter and became rich thereby. When the Yunnan Indo-China Railway was built, he stopped his illegal enterprise and, with his brother, went into the cotton business. He also bought a mountain containing iron ore, where iron is still produced. These men made about $1,000,000, and their descendants still continue working the mine.

We have mentioned in this chapter that opium-smuggling was one of the old ways of attaining wealth. Usually, these smugglers had been poor villagers. They ran risks but were connected with big merchants who supplied them with capital. These merchants gave the money to the smugglers so that they could get opium in distant parts. Even when the merchants did not finance the expeditions, they might buy the opium from the smugglers, store it, and later sell it to others. In this way the merchants did not risk their lives but made more profit than the actual smugglers. Since there was still a limited field for investments, opium has always, in the past, been something to speculate with. Formerly, opium and cotton were closely linked, because, as the cotton cloth was sold to the people of the interior on the western borders, the only valuable item the people had for exchange was opium. So opium and cotton became a balance of trade in the inter-district commerce. For example, one very rich man, whose ancestor was a resident of Yuts'un, moved into town and started a small grocery shop. Later one of his family married the daughter of a cotton merchant. The maternal uncle of the man we speak of engaged in transporting cotton cloth to the west. One day a man came in who had been engaged in transporting a number of pigs from the west country. On the way the pigs had contracted an epidemic disease and had died. This man had lost everything and had no money to buy cloth. The cotton merchant gave him cloth on credit, and the man sold the whole stock of cloth and bought opium in exchange. He acquired 100,000 ounces of opium and brought this back. He took part of the opium to pay back the money which had been loaned him. The uncle to whom the opium was thus given sold it to his nephew. In two months' time 100 ounces of opium rose in price from 11 *liang* (ounces) of silver to 25 *liang*. So in two months the nephew got 14,000 *liang* of silver. After this he started a cloth store and became very rich. In the above case we can see that in one transaction millions of dollars were involved. These profits are realized in a very short time, purely through speculation. Nothing like this could be dreamed of in agriculture. What is more striking is that this man started his cotton business from the money he got from opium. But the money he made from cotton cloth he put back into opium. This is different from the man we mentioned who got rich from opium but remained in the village, merely hoarding his wealth. The latter became only a wealthy farmer, but the man who continued to speculate became one of the big merchants. One of the great differences between agriculture and commerce is that agriculture never helps a man to expand his wealth quickly but acts rather as a stabilizing factor in rural economics.

The development of commerce again stimulates the financial system. A type of credit society, also, is found in this region; but there is more variation, and the organization is bigger here than in the places described previously. Throughout most of China these organizations have limited members, usually ten to twenty people, who are friends and relatives. The money pooled together amounts only to from $100 to $1,000, and each year the whole sum is given to one of the members. But here, in the town near Yuts'un, appears a kind of large-scale society. There is no fixed sum of money decided on beforehand; and, though there is only one head, the number of contributors varies from two hundred to seven hundred. Each participant subscribes from $5.00 to $10.00 for each term. At the end of each term a number of subscribers will get money by applying to the organizer, who sets a definite amount of interest (usually a 12 per cent rate) for the monthly loan. In fact, the organizer almost becomes a banker. He decides for each term who and how many people are to get the money. Each term several thousand dollars, up to as much as $10,000, are collected; and the total amount collected in twenty terms, which is the usual period for which a society is organized, may amount to more than $100,000. The heads of these societies are usually big merchants. For example, organizers whom we knew were a cotton merchant, the owner of a grocery and of a dyeing establishment, and a hotel-owner. We do not have the complete details of the organization of this type of credit society; but from the general description we can see that the organizer, who has the power to determine which man is to get money at the end of each term, actually controls the finances of the region. When he needs money, he can always get it; or if he has too much, he can lend it out. We know that the merchant who organizes this kind of society does so with this advantage in mind. In this way he is enabled to get money easily when he needs it. Under ordinary conditions the members keep depositing money. Then, when one of them needs money urgently, he

L

can apply and get, on short notice, even more money than he has contributed—that is, an advance on what he is going to contribute. We know that in Yuts'un the wealthy households are all members of different credit societies.

Besides the credit societies, the merchants also accept deposits, serving as bankers. For instance, a certain merchant receives each year more than $20,000 from different depositors. The depositors are mostly absentee landlords. If they do not wish to lend out money to individuals because these debts are sometimes difficult to collect and if they are not engaged in business for themselves, they may deposit their money with the big merchants and get interest on it. This interest rarely exceeds 10 per cent.

Merchants gather money from their own business, from the credit societies, and from deposits made by others. They may invest this capital in their own enterprises or lend it out. The interest on the loans is paid in two ways—either in money or in rice. Before 1940, for a $100 loan the lender asked an amount of rice worth about $20—that is, about 20 per cent interest. But, because of the inflationary rise in the price of rice, interest paid in rice has gradually disappeared. When we were in the village, practically all the loans were paid in money, at a rate of 24 per cent yearly. Sometimes, however, the rate was as low as 18 per cent. If we compare these rates of interest with those found in Luts'un, they are seen to be much lower, which indicates the relative abundance of capital on the market in and around Yuts'un.

Owing to the importance of the merchant class in financial circles, the absentee landlords and rich farmers in the village have become less important in moneylending and other financial activities. In Yuts'un we knew of only two houses which made loans to others. Those villagers who need money usually go to the cotton merchants in town. Thus, financial power has been transferred from the villagers to the financiers of the town. And there are few opportunities for the rich farmers in the village to take advantage of moneylending, which is always important in accumulating wealth.

CHAPTER XXVIII

THE EFFECTS OF COMMERCE ON VILLAGE HOUSEHOLDS

THE continuous rise of the big merchant class is contributed to by large numbers of villagers. The large cotton merchants are supported by thousands of weavers. The sudden rise to wealth of the opium-traders was due to the fact that so many houses in the village had been ruined by opium-smoking. On the other hand, the money collected by the rich merchants in the form of loans is constantly being sent back to the villages to finance ceremonies and agricultural production. It also opens wider employment to the villagers in local industries, such as weaving. The gathering of nonagricultural people in the town creates a need for farm and garden produce. Therefore, the character of the agriculture carried on in the village has been gradually changing—to cash crops rather than to subsistence crops. It is evident that the development of commerce cannot be considered apart from rural economy. In conclusion, we may mention two essential consequences of the development of town commerce: first, making the villagers become real wage-earners and, second, making the villagers into tenant farmers. We shall discuss these two sides of the general process separately.

I. ENSLAVED WEAVERS

Since the importation of modern machine-made thread the weavers in the village do not supply thread spun by themselves but depend entirely on that supplied by the merchants. Thus they have no control over the price of the thread. The weavers buy a certain amount of this thread and weave it into pieces of cloth; then exchange the cloth, not for money, but for thread supplied by the merchants. This is a continuous process of exchange. As the price of thread fluctuates, the price fetched by the cotton cloth fluctuates also. This price instability is beyond the comprehension of the weavers. Nor can they wait for a better price. The continuation of their work depends upon selling the pieces of cloth they have just completed. This system of exchanging cotton thread for woven cotton cloth gives the merchants control over the profits made from weaving. The weavers, in fact, are at their mercy. Their position is even worse than that of regular laborers because they share the risk involved but do not share equally in the returns. As a result, as we showed in chapter xxiv, the weavers get even less wage than the cost of the food they consume.

The merchants control both the supply of raw material and the collection of the woven piece goods. They consider their own profits first and then adjust prices. There is always a very small margin for bargaining for the weavers. When the market is dropping, a smaller share of profits is given to the weavers than when the market is better. Unfortunately, the market for this kind of native weaving is shrinking, since the modern machine-made cloth has come to compete with it and sets a limit on the price of native woven cloth. Thus, the very small profits in weaving are constantly diminishing, with the merchants' taking the lion's share of the profits; what remains is insufficient even to maintain the livelihood of the actual producers. These weavers may seem to maintain the position of independent producers with their own materials and their own tools, but actually this supposed independence does not exist. In fact, the weavers are, to some degree, slaves of the merchants.

In recent years one of the cotton merchants has carried this process on still further by providing better looms, supplying the thread, the warp, and paying the weavers a varying amount for completed cloth. In this way the amount of wage received is fixed absolutely by the merchants, and the producers have no protection.

With such low rewards, why do the weavers continue to work and to be exploited by the merchants in the town? We spent all the first chapters of this book answering this question. The answer is this: With the limited supply of land, which is not sufficient to provide for the livelihood of the peasants, they must accept some subsidiary occupations. This weakness of the rural economy gives rise to the exploitation of the villagers by the town merchants.

II. CONCENTRATION OF LANDOWNERSHIP

We have shown that a rapid accumulation of land is not possible through agriculture; also, that the subsidiary occupations may aid the people but do not enable them to accumulate wealth. In agriculture there seldom arises the problem of surplus capital, which comes either from the rent of big estates or from other enterprises, such as rural industry, commerce, mining, and illegal activities. If the capital accumulated in these ways can be reinvested elsewhere, it will not go into agriculture. But in interior China the opportunities for continuous expansion in industry and commerce are usually restricted, as is illustrated in Yits'un. When the limits of expansion are reached, the accumulation of capital becomes mere hoarding unless it is attracted to the land. Then it affects land distribution and the land system in the villages.

There are some attractions in the land itself. First, landholding gives more security than the holding of other sorts of property. During the bandit attack in 1922, houses were burned and property was looted. The "lord" had opium worth 10,000 ounces of silver, which was all lost in one day. Almost the only thing of value that was left after the fracas was the land. An insecure social situation, in which the memory of social disturbances lingers on, emphasizes the value of land as a security for life. Second, land gives a constant income. Even if the owner does not work upon it, he can rent it and live on the rent. There are few risks in renting land to tenants, because, if the tenant is unable to pay what he owes, he can be put off the land. This is not like moneylending, in which there is danger of default. Third, to own land gives a better social position than not to own land. As we have shown in Part I, the landless people are in some ways not really accepted in the community life. They even live on the outskirts of the village. To acquire land is the most important way to establish one's influence in community life. Fourth, owing to the fact that the land will be divided by inheritance, to maintain the social position of a household the estate must gradually be extended. It is traditional to believe that the father has the obligation to see that his children are well provided for with a secure source of income—that is, with land. All these factors direct the wealth accumulated from different sources back to the land.

Nevertheless, it must be understood that to buy land does not necessarily mean an investment in agriculture. The buying and selling of land affects the ownership and distribution of land. The money used in the transaction may or may not be directed into farming production. A piece of land passing from one hand to another will not change in productivity unless the buyer can use more labor, more fertilizer, or better tools in working it. But that is usually not the case. The one who sells the land usually gets the money to meet a financial crisis and, as we have shown above, will use the money for ceremonial or other purposes of consumption. So the amount of money involved in the transaction does not improve farming at all. We call it an investment because the buyer of the land, when he has spent the money, can get an annual rent from the land. But in view of the productivity of the land, it is not an exercise of capital for increasing production.

The strong incentives for acquiring land make the owner equally reluctant to sell his land. Actually, throughout China there is no open market for farm land. Rather, it is considered disgraceful to sell property of this sort, as we explained in Part I. It is improper to ask others if they have land to sell. A middleman is needed to arrange the transaction, and the validity of the business rests on the consent of the brothers and uncles of the seller. Without their signature the transaction is customarily invalid. So the capital which is ready to be put into land must be held until the chance to invest it comes. The amount of land purchased at one time cannot be large. We tried to find out, from the memory of the villagers, how much land had been bought and sold in the ten years prior to 1940, where one or both of the partners to the bargain belonged to the village. According to their accounts, the total amounted to 140 *mow* of rice field and 80 *mow* of garden land, and, according to this, the average amount of land which changed hands in each year amounted to only 2 per cent of the total land owned by the village. More detailed data on land transactions are available for 1942–43. In 1942, 16.10 *mow* of rice field and 3.85 *mow* of garden land changed hands, 12.9 *mow* of rice field being sold by the villagers to the buyers in town and 3.15 *mow* of garden land by townspeople to the villagers. In 1943 before October, 5.9 *mow* of rice field and 1.7 *mow* of garden land were affected, 4.8 *mow* of rice field going into the hands of the town-dwellers. These amounts are small. But, according to the villagers' memory, during the ten years prior to 1940 there were only about 45 *mow* of land taken by town-dwellers. The rate seems to be increasing, since in 1943 and a part of 1944 nearly 20 *mow* of land left the hands of the villagers.

There are many causes which lead to the selling of land. For instance, part of the village land was sold because the temple had to be rebuilt after the bandit raid; and another part of it was sold, by order of the government, to the agricultural school. Of the privately owned land, some was sold to meet emergencies. For instance, one man was drafted and sold land to get money to employ a substitute. Some sold their land because they left the village; others sold land to finance ceremonies, especially funerals. As described in Part I, the sons of the house who are unable to finance the funeral ceremony may sell the land to outsiders; it is considered quite proper to sell the parents' land for this purpose.

Another cause of selling land is the poverty caused by opium-smoking. This is a very common cause. We know a number of households which, forty years ago, descended from the same ancestor. This man had 400 *mow* of land, which he divided among his sons, who were opium-smokers. The whole family is now poor. In forty years they have lost most of their land. Another villager in 1911 still possessed 100 *mow* of land; but he had three sons, all of whom smoked opium. In 1919 they sold most of their land. Another man told me personally that his household became very poor just because his father had been an opium-smoker. Similar cases can be multiplied for all those Chinese villages where opium affects the people. We must list the introduction of opium into the Chinese village as one of the strongest factors in accelerating the process of concentration of landownership into a few hands. But these factors are only one aspect of the whole situation. More fundamental is the vulnerability in the position of the rural families. These earthbound folk have no margin for savings, no way to sustain any misfortune or to allow themselves any indulgences whatever. A little slip from normal, and they are caught and forced to sell their land. There exists, as Tawney says, "districts in which the position of the rural population is that of a man standing permanently up to the neck in water, so that even a ripple is sufficient to drown him.[1]

However, there are a few who go outside of agriculture and become rich. If these men remain attached to the village, they may build up their homes and create an air of prosperity. Such a one was the ancestor of the "lord," who returned to the village and built a big house. But this prosperity has not been derived from agriculture; it does not mean an actual change of the structure. However, so long as the *nouveaux riches* come back to the village, ownership of the land remains within the village at least. When commerce develops in the town, the situation changes. Land acquired by these commercial people is much more likely to be kept from the hands of the villagers permanently. The forces which so easily affect the entire fortune of a villager are rather weak when they attack the big commercial houses. Marriages, funerals, opium-smoking—none of these things will cause them to sell their land, because their economic base is much larger and stronger. Only when they become bankrupt will they sell their land; but then it is usually sold to other merchants and is not likely to return to the hands of the villagers. This establishes absenteeism on a firm basis.

It is true that the development of industry and commerce offers some

[1] *Land and Labour in China*, p. 77.

opportunities to the villagers. But under present circumstances it is also true that the more the town develops, the poorer are the peasants. The development of absenteeism, which means the concentration of landownership in the hands of the town-dwellers and the constant flow of village wealth to town in terms of rent, actually impoverishes the rural population. This we cannot deny. In the last twelve years or so, Yuts'un has lost more than 65 *mow* of land to the merchants in the town. We know, too, that these merchants have acquired huge amounts of land in the region roundabout. For instance, in the last ten years one cotton merchant got 400 *mow* of land; another, 500 *mow*. A mineowner acquired 300 *mow;* a gold-trader, the same amount; and the aboriginal lumber merchant got 500 *mow*. The estate of each of these men is more than the total amount possessed by the village as a whole. But this is only the beginning of the process of land concentration. We have seen in the villages of coastal China, as described in *Peasant Life in China*, that nearly 80 per cent of the land in the villages is owned by absentee landlords. It is obvious that this same process which has made petty owners into tenants elsewhere is now active in the interior of China, especially in the vicinity of the commercially developing towns. Unless there is an effective land policy to check this process, it does not necessarily follow that the development of industry in China will bring a good life to the people.

CONCLUSION

AGRICULTURE AND INDUSTRY

SOCIOLOGICAL field work begins with a hypothesis and ends with a hypothesis. The conclusions we have reached in the preceding study may serve as a working guide for future studies and be corrected by new evidence. Generalizations made in each stage of inquiry are a redefinition of the situation. Social action is organized by the situation as conceived. A definition of the situation is a revision of the direction of social action. Therefore, the validity of the definition is tested in the action which follows subsequently. To us, it is legitimate and even essential to link up scientific studies with practical policies. In a certain sense, we are the plaintiff for the Chinese peasants. Having set forth their cause and submitted evidence, we shall then appeal for certain actions, to improve their way of life. At the end of our pleading we shall summarize the essential facts and argue for an appropriate policy. However, as scientists, we are ready to accept suggestions for further inquiry and to revise our views accordingly.

I. BASIC FACTS IN CHINA'S AGRARIAN SITUATION

The basic problem of the present study is simple: How do the villagers in interior China live on the land? To explore this basic problem, we must inquire into the following specific questions: How much land have they? How do they use it? How much do they get from it? Is their income from land sufficient to maintain their present standard of living? If not, how do they make up their deficiencies? What happens if these deficiencies cannot be made up by additional income? How does this financial situation affect land distribution? How are property rights split and transferred? What kind of land system results from such a process?

The figures in Table 49 provide the answers to these questions. We shall include, in our comparison, a village near Lake Tai, in the Lower Yangtse Valley, called by us Kiangts'un.[1] In order to summarize complex phenomena in a table, we must use averages or approximate estimates. It is needless to say that in this way we oversimplify the situation purely for convenience in presentation.

[1] See *Peasant Life in China.*

TABLE 49

Average Means of Subsistence

	Luts'un	Yits'un	Yuts'un	Kiangts'un
Size of family holding (in *mow*, with acre in parenthesis; 6.5 *mow* equal 1 acre).........	5.7 (0.87)	15.2 (2.31)	4.3 (0.65)	3.8 (0.59)
Size of farm under operation (in *mow* and acres):				
Rice farm...............	8.8 (1.33)	7.5 (1.14)	5.1 (0.77)	8.5 (1.29)
Garden land..............	*	4.4 (0.66)	0.9 (0.14)	*
Total size of farm.....	....	11.9 (1.80)	6.0 (0.91)	....
Main crops (C indicates consumption; S, sale; and M, manufacture):				
Rice farm................	Rice (C, S), beans (mainly S)	Rice (C), beans (C, S)	Rice (C, S), beans (mainly S)	Rice (C, S), wheat, rape (C, S)
Garden land	Corn, vegetables (C, S)	Bamboo (M), vegetables (C)	Vegetables (mainly S)	Mulberry trees (M), vegetables (C)
Average rice yield per acre (in *piculs*)....................	60	36	52	40
Rice yield per household from the farm under operation (in *piculs*)....................	79.8	41.0	40.0	51.6
Other crops on main farm in terms of rice (in *piculs*).....	15	5	17	10(?)
Total income from main farm in terms of rice (in *piculs*)...	94.8	46.0	57.0	61.6
Population:				
Individuals...............	694	236	777	1,458
Households..............	122	54	156	360
Average size of household ..	5.7	4.4	5.0	4.1
Equivalent to number of adult males in food consumption (3.5 *piculs* of rice for a household of five)..............	3.8	3.1	3.5	2.9
Rice required for household consumption (7 *piculs* for one adult male a year).........	24.6	21.7	24.5	20.3
Size of rented land (difference between family holding and farm under operation) in acres....................	− 0.56	+ 0.51	− 0.26	− 0.7
Rent (half of annual rice yield) (in *piculs*)	− 33.6	+ 18.3	− 13.5	− 28.0

* Insignificant and unestimated.

TABLE 49—*Continued*

	Luts'un	Yits'un	Yuts'un	Kiangts'un
Rice remaining after consumption and rent (paid or received) (in *piculs*)	36.6	42.6	20.0	13.3
Surplus or deficiency for other expenditures (same amount as rice consumption).......	+ 12.0	+ 20.9	− 4.5	− 7.0

From Table 49 it is clear that in Luts'un and Yits'un an average household which depends on its rice field alone, after paying or receiving rent and making daily expenditures, will have only a small amount of surplus for other expenses. In Yuts'un and Kiangts'un the average household will already be in debt. But the average household is an ideal, not an actuality. The above statement does not mean that most of the households in these villages are in this condition, for the land is not evenly distributed. Table 50 gives the percentage of different classes in the four villages (definition of these classes given in Part III). In all four villages the number of poor and landless, that is, of people who cannot depend on their own land entirely for providing a living, is around 70 per cent, or more than two-thirds of the population. So conditions are actually much worse than those described above.

We may therefore conclude that most of the villagers in the communities we have studied must seek an income from other sources besides that derived from the main rice field. The first possibility for opening up a new source of income is, instead of cultivating rice and beans (or other field crops), to go in for intensive cultivation of better-paying crops—in other words, to gain new income by changing the use to which the land is put. This means of procuring additional income is employed in Yuts'un, where truck gardens have developed. Large amounts of labor and daily attendance are necessary to carry on this type of cultivation; but, by so doing, the gardeners get a profit about four times as large as that obtained from rice cultivation. But garden produce of this sort must be grown as cash crops and therefore requires a near-by market. In most rural communities, such markets are very small or practically nonexistent, because the farmers usually grow their own vegetables. The opportunity for intensive gardening is limited to villages near the urban centers. This is especially true with the present lack of transportation facilities.

The second common way for opening up a new source of income is to develop an industry with raw material produced by agriculture. This type of rural industry, which is very common in China, may be seen both in Yits'un and in Kiangts'un—in the former consisting in basketry and papermaking and in the latter, of silk production. It has been observed in Kwangsi that, "because in this region population is too dense and land limited, the produce of the land cannot support the life of the people. They must take up some kind of handicraft besides farming. It is common that in certain villages the whole population is engaged in certain crafts, and then the villages are known by their specialities."[2] Another investigator, in Shansi, reports a similar situation: "In Shen-ko Ts'un the villagers engage in one or more crafts besides farming. This is especially true for the small owners. It is necessary to supplement the income from the farm."[3]

TABLE 50

DISTRIBUTION OF POPULATION IN ECONOMIC CLASSES

	Luts'un	Yits'un	Yuts'un	Kiangts'un
Rich	15	13	4	6.2
Middle	19	15	20	18.0
Poor	35	65	50⎱	75.8
Landless............	31	7	29⎰	

China is commonly regarded as an agricultural country. This is certainly true if it refers only to the fact that agriculture is the main occupation of the Chinese. But it should not be taken to mean that China lacks manufacturing industries or that only a few Chinese engage in manufacture. The backwardness of Chinese industry is in its technology, not in the number of people engaged in it. In fact, most of the farmers of China are, at the same time, craftsmen. Through widespread rural industries, China was self-sufficient in manufacturing goods prior to her contact with the West. Rightly, our Emperor Ch'ien Lung wrote to King George III of England: "Our Celestial Empire possesses all things in prolific abundance, and lacks no product within its own borders; there is no need to import the manufactures of outside barbarians." The manufactured goods, which were abundant, were produced not in big industrial centers but in thousands of villages

[2] P. N. Wu and Others, *Economic Survey in Kwangsi* (Academia Sinica), p. 154 (in Chinese).

[3] Y. Y. Li, "Economic Organization in a Shansi Village" (unpublished M.A. thesis, Yenching University).

like Yits'un and Kiangts'un. Chinese traditional industry is a diffused industry—diffused among millions of homesteads. It is diffused not for convenience but by necessity. The necessity, as seen from our analysis, is that the people in the villages cannot live entirely on what their land produces.

Another important factor for the development of such diffused industry is seen in the peculiar character of labor utilization in agriculture. Agriculture requires seasonal labor. With present techniques of field cultivation the amount of labor needed during the busy period is enormous, while during the rest of the year practically no labor is needed on the farm. We have shown that the maximum size during the busy season for a couple to work by themselves is about 10 *kung*, or ½ acre. Even if couples take advantage of working on the farms of others who enjoy a somewhat different climate, the amount of land worked cannot be more than 1 acre. This fundamental fact everywhere holds down the man-land ratio. The tragedy of unemployment is implicit in agriculture on this level of technological development. Therefore, it is necessary that the farmers should take up some sort of subsidiary work to occupy their idle time. The result is that most of the industries that can be diffused have been diffused.

Now let us turn to the dynamic side of the agrarian situation. Land remains the most important and stable source of income in the rural community. It is the only real source of security. However, with only a limited supply of land available, any attempt to enlarge one's own farm holding will mean dispossessing others. The peasants' tenacity in holding land and their reluctance to give it up is expressed very well in the fact that they prefer to borrow money at exorbitant rates of interest rather than to sell their land. As a result, land transactions are far from being a matter of merely marketing a commodity, but rather represent a struggle for survival.

Yet there is an everlasting threat to landholding—division through inheritance. According to custom, all the sons have an equal right of inheritance; and, as the estate is divided through generations, each division means a reduction of the size of the individual farm. The question is often asked: How can such a custom, which works against the principles of efficient farm management, persist? Let us consider the alternative in a situation where few independent professions are open. Without other means of making a living, dispossession from the land is the worst fate conceivable, since it may lead to a family's extinction, as seen in many cases in Part I. With the strong sentiment of kinship that exists, it is inconceivable that a brother's family should be allowed to perish in such a way. But, so long as the customary principle of equal inheritance among siblings exists, time is a strong disintegrative force in landholding. Even the owners of sizable farms must be on the watch for any opportunity to enlarge their holdings, in order to insure the future of their descendants.

The question thus arises: How can the peasants accumulate enough wealth for the acquisition of land? Following our analysis above, it is clear that, for an average farmer, it is already difficult to win subsistence from the land. If there is a certain surplus, it will easily be exhausted in periodical ceremonies. Moreover, there are famines, bandits, and personal misfortunes. That land breeds no land is all too true. Those who seek for security look beyond agriculture. Ambitious people leave the village to find fortunes either by obtaining a position in the government, by risking their lives by joining the army, or by engaging in even more dangerous adventures in illegal traffic. If one is shocked by hearing of this unhappy choice of ways of attaining wealth, he should remember that in the traditional economy the concentration of wealth usually takes place outside of industry and agriculture. "Through power to wealth" is the general formula in a precapitalistic society. The basic truth is that enrichment through the exploitation of land, using the traditional technology, is not a practical method for accumulating wealth.

Opportunity in industry acquires, therefore, a new significance in an agarian situation. This significance resides in the fact that the concentration of wealth through violence or power does not lead to further accumulation of wealth and thus is maintained with difficulty. An official may become rich; but, unless he can invest his wealth in getting more power and becoming richer, he will gradually begin to sink when he retires to the village and becomes a landowner. But industry is different. Through it, wealth can be accumulated continuously. When the wealth obtained from industry is used to buy land, the owner can continue to buy, and the disintegrating force of division through inheritance is no longer effective. The landowning class thus becomes more or less permanent.

II. INDUSTRY AND COMMERCE IN RURAL ECONOMY

The analysis of rural industry in Part II is significant at this point in the discussion. Rural industry has two bases: one the necessity for finding employment on the part of the farmers, and the other the striving for profit on the part of the rich. The second type of rural industry emerges when a larger amount of capital is needed to set up mills and factories. As technology develops, capital becomes more important than labor in the process of production. Mills and factories cannot be established in small huts and carried on by poor peasants who have nothing but labor to sell. Moreover, such industry, organized on a capitalistic basis, finds its limits in interior China, where transportation is difficult and markets restricted. When the margin of expansion is reached, the profits gained cannot be invested in the same enterprise. This capital then goes back to the land again and begins to concentrate land in the hands of big owners.

Most of the rural industry in traditional China is developed from a local supply of raw material and is only a process of refining agricultural products. But in those places where communication is improved and raw material can be brought in from outside through commerce, new forms of industry are growing up, as we have seen in Part III, in regard to Yuts'un. In Yits'un the two types of rural industry—the one giving employment to the laboring class and the other giving opportunity for investment—are separate. But in Yuts'un these two functions are combined in the cotton industry. Here capitalists distribute raw material and collect industrial products from the laboring class, who carry on the manufacturing process. This is a put-out system of handicraft, in which the function of the capitalist is more commercial and financial than industrial. The development of commerce has thus quickened the process of the concentration of wealth. And, owing to the improvement of transportation and the expansion of markets, the limitations on the reinvestment of capital are partly removed. But in Yuts'un, and even more so in Kiangts'un, financially distressed peasants compte with other outlets for capital by offering higher and higher interest in order that they may gain a short intermission between the claims of their creditors. Thus, the process of concentration of land continues in a form even more unfavorable to the peasants.

Because of the fact that the poor peasants are barred from sharing the profits of industry and commerce organized on a capitalistic basis, the development of industry and commerce brings them disastrous consequences. It is interesting to note that, where commerce is developed in China, tenancy follows suit and that, in the area where commerce is underdeveloped, we find more occupying owners. In Yunnan the exchange of goods among villagers takes place largely in periodic markets, temporary gatherings in which producers and consumers meet. In this system of exchange the profits from trade are diffused throughout the general population. There is only a limited scope for the commercial activities of the middleman. Here the tenant is in the minority. In northern China, where the periodic marketing system is common, a similar situation in regard to land is found. But in the coastal regions, like the Yangtse and Canton deltas, where from 80 to 90 per cent of the farmers are tenants, big towns, where middlemen sell produce in stores, are in existence.

A more significant fact in the development of commerce in the rural areas is that it prepares the way for the intrusion of foreign goods, which are gradually wiping out traditional industry. As the latter disappears, the peasants lose a source of income and are the more impoverished. The chances of losing their land are increased. Contact with Western industry is the most important factor in the present agrarian situation in China. Let us examine the process more closely.

We may begin with the basketmaking in Yits'un. The basketmaker uses his own material, works by himself, and sells by himself. He gets a sum in return which includes the value of the raw material, wage, transportation fee, and selling profit. In Yuts'un, in the former days, the work of the weavers was similar to that of the Yits'un basketmakers. They grew the cotton, made the dye, spun the cotton thread, wove it into clothes, and sold it to the buyers. But as a result of the development of commerce, they now receive cotton thread from, and return the woven piece goods to, the shops. The money received amounts to wages only. They have lost their position as producers of raw material, spinners, and sellers. Thus the profits derived from this product are shared with a number of other persons. If the techniques of production were to be improved, the total profits might be increased; and if these profits were distributed equally among the participators in the process, the weavers might gain an even larger return than by carrying on the entire process by themselves alone with primitive techniques. But this is not true. The lion's share of profit goes to the those who supply the capital. The poor weavers have no power in bargaining. They have to accept any terms, since they must take up some subsidiary work, as dictated by their agricultural situation. The amount allotted to the weaver is, at the present time, insufficient to maintain bare existence. Even so, the weavers have no choice but to continue to work; otherwise they will lose more through total unemployment.

In the case of the Yuts'un weaving industry, we can already see that the development of modern industry and commerce has wiped out certain occupations of the Chinese villagers. In this case, the villagers have given up spinning entirely because the thread made from the local process is costly and lower in quality than that made in Lancashire and Manchester. Very soon even the cotton piece goods woven in Yuts'un will lose its market when, with the improvement in transportation, the machine-woven clothes from modern industrial centers flow into the interior. The same situation is seen even more clearly in Kiangts'un, where the native silk industry is declining rapidly in the face of the competition of the better silk made by machine in Japan and of the rayon industry in America.

Now let us once more remind the reader of two fundamental facts in Chinese rural economy: the first is that traditional Chinese industry is diffused among villages, and the second is that the farmers depend on it for subsistence. The industrial revolution in the West at last threatens the peasants in the Chinese villages in their capacity as industrialists. It is a hopeless struggle for the unorganized mass of petty owner-workers. However skilful they may be, they are fighting a losing battle against the machine. But they must keep on fighting, because otherwise they cannot live. The result is that China is gradually being reduced to an agrarian country, pure and simple; and an agrarian China is inevitably a starved China.

The desperation of this situation is felt by every household where income is declining. Any stroke of misfortune will force the peasant owner to sell his land. We have emphasized the fact that Chinese peasants do not sell their land for profit but only when they are in real distress. In the interior, where Western industrial and commercial influences are less strong and the traditional order is still maintained, the system of mutual help and fortitude with regard to material adversity helps to tide them over their financial crises. So long as they can find any other means to get out of their financial difficulties, they will hold onto their land. As a result, the rate at which land is becoming concentrated in the hands of a few is slow. Even in Yuts'un, in the last twelve years, only about 65 *mow* of land has left the hands of the villagers. It would take seventy years under the present rate to attain the status of Kiangts'un, where nearly half of the land is in the hands of absentee landlords. But when rural industrial workers face a direct attack from Western machine industry, it appears to take only a short period to sink most of the petty owners to the status of tenant. This is the reason, we believe, why at present in the coastal provinces a very high percentage of tenancy is found. Of course, the hypothesis which we are stating will require further research before its full validity is established. But the present study clearly supports this conclusion.

With this background some of the conclusions given by Tawney become illuminating:

> What appears to be occurring, in some regions at least, is the emergence, side by side with small landlords who live in their villages and are partners with their tenants in the business of farming, of a class of absentee owners whose connection with agriculture is purely financial.[4]

It seems to us that financial depression in rural areas, as a result of the decline of rural industry in competition with Western machine industry, is the essential condition for the concentration of land in the hands of a few, usually townsmen. The fertility of soil, specially mentioned by Tawney in explaining the development of tenancy, is only a secondary and contributing, although an important, factor in the situation. Soil fertility makes tenancy possible but is not sufficient in itself to bring it about. In other words, this explanation, which is a restatement of the classical theory of rent, though true by itself, does not suffice to give a complete understanding of the total situation, as we have attempted to give in the present study.

III. DEVELOPMENT OF CO-OPERATIVE RURAL INDUSTRY
AS A SOLUTION TO THE LAND PROBLEM

Since a definition of a social situation is a preliminary step toward action, if the agrarian situation is defined in technological terms only, the actions followed will be limited to technological improvements. It is essential, however, for us to recognize that the situation is much more complicated. We do not deny the importance of technological improvement, but we must also understand its limitations. The present study—far from conclusive—at least indicates that the Chinese treatment of rural economic problems merely as problems of agriculture is one-sided. We should like to emphasize our conclusion that the land problem is aggravated by the problem of rural industry. If we are correct, then the ultimate solution of the land problem is closely allied to the problem of Chinese industrialism.

In the matter of technological improvements, enough attention is already being paid by experts in that field. Marked success in the improvement of crops and of soil and insect control has been attained where scientific knowledge has been applied. We need discuss this

[4] *Land and Labour in China*, pp. 67–68.

side of the question no further. However, with regard to problems such as the mechanization of farm tools and the enlargement of the size of farms—problems in which the social situation is generally involved—no effective reforms have been achieved. It is unfair to blame the government on that score. Policies for reform are not lacking; but when they are applied, difficulties arise which make ineffective all efforts. The crux of the matter is that, unless we can stop the constant decline in the standard of living of the peasant by increasing his income considerably, every measure adopted will be one of temporary relief rather than of cure. An increase in agricultural productivity, for instance, is helpful, indeed; but, by employing all scientific means available, it is estimated that the possible increase can be only about 20 per cent above present productivity. Such an increase is dwarfed in comparison with the rapid decline in price of rural industrial products, such as silk, for example.

Again, take the measure for the equalization of holdings. It is indeed essential, in view of the present unequal distribution of land. But we must remember that, if the government were to pass measures entirely reallotting all available land to the peasants, the size of a farm would be still under 5 acres, this figure including much which is uncultivable. In Yunnan the maximum size, not including mountainous country, would be about 1 acre. One acre of farm land, even with all possible scientific improvement of crops, gives a yield permitting a standard of living no better than the average at present. This policy, if it can be carried out, will make for an equitable distribution but will not effect great improvement in the economic status of the average villager.

There are two ways to enlarge the size of farms: one is the extension of land under cultivation, and the other is reduction in population. Manchuria and northwestern China may offer some relief for land hunger; but how much population can be moved to these parts is still unknown, and the prospect of extension is uncertain. Reduction in population has been the most common solution to the Chinese agrarian situation throughout her history. Periods of prosperity are usually followed by periods of disturbance, in which large numbers of people are wiped out by civil war and famine. Such catastrophes, of course, must not be allowed to occur again. With an improvement in public health, even if measures for decreasing the birth rate are introduced simultaneously, there will not be a quick reduction in population. Therefore, a practical solution cannot be sought along that line either.

The remaining alternative is to move the agricultural population out into other occupations. This certainly sounds like a promising solution. We are told that in 1870 the percentage of rural population in the United States was as high as 73.8, but by 1930 it was reduced to 43.8. American experience shows definitely the possibility of a reduction of rural population by the development of industry in urban centers. However, these figures do not hold any real promise for China. Stated realistically, we may say that, even if China can achieve as rapid an industrial development as the United States did in the last sixty years, we can only reduce by 30 per cent the population in the rural areas, giving a possibility of enlarging our individual farms less than ½ acre per owner.

It seems unreasonable to hope that in the near future the Chinese peasant can live entirely on agriculture. This does not mean that China is born to be poor forever. Her economic potentiality is large, in view of her abundance of manpower and resources. It means only that we must not hope that agriculture alone will save China and give a higher standard of living to the people. If we recognize this fact, the way open to us is one similar to that which has been employed for centuries—the supplementing of agriculture with diffused industry.

We must make our position very clear in this connection. We are not concerned here with the ideal type of industry or the most efficient industrial organization but with a practical type of industry that will fit into the situation of the masses of the peasantry, a situation which is constantly deteriorating. It is perhaps important to bear in mind that, given the opportunity, China will inevitably be industrialized; but whether or not this new industrialization will be beneficial to the peasants is the problem. The answer depends upon the form taken by this new industry. If it develops according to the pattern of European and American industry of the last few centuries—that is, if it is concentrated in urban areas and in the hands of a few capitalists—it will only aggravate the distress of the rural population, because it will take away from the village all its homestead industries and thus further decrease the income of the peasants. This process has already been taking place during the last few decades. The further industrialization of China in this way would simply mean that the wealth concentrated in industry will be in the hands not merely of foreign but also of Chinese industrialists—a difference which will not alter the economic condition of the peasants. It is true that the government might tax the industrial profits of the Chinese industrialist for the benefit of the peasants. But this, again, is merely an alleviation. What we are seeking is rather a way to avoid the evil in the first place.

It should also be pointed out, at this point, that, if the mass of peasants cannot share in the profits of industry but only suffer from its effects in decreasing their livelihood, the growth of newly developing industry in China will be checked by a shrinkage of its markets. An all-round planning of industry should consider not only how much can be produced and how much profit can be gained but also how much can be sold. The impoverished masses, though too weak to challenge the power and privileges of the industrialists, will block the way simply by their inability to buy industrial goods. Therefore, for the success of industrial development in any form, we should try to work out a solution to these problems in terms of its ability to lift the standard of living of the common people, among whom the peasant is by far the most numerous. From this point of view, we can then lay down the principle that the future form of China's industrial organization must be such that the peasants can share in its profit in order to raise their standard of living, since agriculture alone is unable to do so. In order to achieve this, some part of industry must be decentralized and established in villages or in centers near villages, so that the profits of the industry can be widely distributed among the peasants.

To return to the traditional principle of supplementing the family income of the peasants by industry does not mean to retain the old industrial technology. To argue for retention of traditional industrial practices in the village is impractical. The handicraft technology must be improved by introducing machinery. What we should retain is the fundamental principle underlying the traditional form of this industry—that of a diffused industry suited to the agrarian situation in China. For, in the immediate future, it does not seem likely that conditions in the rural areas will be radically altered. The traditional principle is a practical solution to the problem gained through years of experience. Let us not be blind to the teachings of the past. However the question which now arises is whether it is possible to have technological improvement under the traditional principle of diffused industry.

Historically, it is true that the industrial revolution was achieved through the concentration of machine equipment and of population. The improvement in technology has been, so far, largely parallel with the development of urban centers. However, this was mainly due to the employment of steam power at the first stage of industrial development. When electric power was introduced, the trend toward concentration of industry changed. Charles Abrams said:

> The use of steam power was the first major step in the development of a modern system, and it made for concentration of manufacturing operation within a small area, since it could be generated economically only in large plants and could be transmitted only by belt or shaft, and then only over short distances. Factories and related activities were thus confined to a relatively compact center, from which the manufactured products were transported to the more distant markets now made accessible by steam transportation.
>
> But with the development of electric power which can be transmitted economically over relatively long distances, a counter trend became discernible. The pattern now broadened out, and a net work of smaller plants spread over a larger area, replacing, to some extent, the huge establishments of Victorian days. The barriers of distance dwindled with the perfection of communication devices and the sweeping improvements in transportation technique, so that the ever widening influence of the city came gradually to embrace huge metropolitan areas, in which purely local matters became less and less important.[5]

It is, therefore, clear that decentralization of manufacturing plants is not a regression in industrial development but a general tendency in modern industry. Ought China, as a latecomer in the modern industrial world, start with the old pattern and only later move to reorganize? The economic history of the West is a warning against such a policy. The cost involved in such reorganization is great and explains why the decentralized pattern, although it has been proved to be more economical, is slow in being adopted in the West. Large investments in old-style industrial plants prevent a quick adjustment to new technological advances. China thus may have an advantage in starting from the industrial front instead from the rear. Therefore, it appears that the decentralized industrial pattern is to be recommended, in view both of the traditional background and of modern technology.

As we have emphasized repeatedly, China's modern industry should be organized in such a way that the profits brought by improved methods be distributed as widely as possible. Assuming this to be our aim, we recommend the decentralized system. However, mere decentralization of industry is not sufficient. As we have seen in the papermaking mills in Yits'un, the effect of such industrial development, rudimentary as it is, is bad, so far as the poor villagers who have no opportunity to participate are concerned. It is, therefore, essential to widen the industrial opportunities of the masses. This consideration makes us advocate the principle of the co-operative in economic or-

[5] *Revolution in Land* (New York and London: Harper & Bros., 1939), p. 79.

ganization. The co-operative movement in China is already developing rapidly. Both the government and private individuals have been
active in promoting it. There is no need for us to stress again the merit
of this system, which appears to be the form of modern industry best
adopted to China. However, the success of small-scale rural co-operative factories depends as much upon their external relations with other
similar factories and with the markets as upon their internal organization. In *Peasant Life in China* an analysis of the silk factory is given to
show the weakness of such an establishment. A large organization,
which will co-ordinate the small manufacturing units, is necessary for
the new rural industry of China.

Given a co-ordinating organization, manufacturing centers scattered through the villages can work on machine parts or on a specific
part in a manufacturing process. They can pool together their products, to be assembled later in a central plant. Thus the advantage of
large-scale production is preserved while the concentration of population in urban centers is done away with. For the central co-ordinating
management we will look to the government for aid.

A decentralized pattern for China's new industry is suggested mainly in order to improve the people's livelihood. We have shown the
necessity for industrial employment in the village and the possibility
of introducing modern technology into such an organization. But, at
the end of our discussion, we must point out that such industry must
be confined to the manufacturing of consumers' goods. For heavy industry a concentrated plant is necessary. Therefore, another problem
arises. What kind of industry, heavy or light, should be emphasized in
China in the immediate years after the war? If we concentrate our
efforts on heavy industry first, as Russia did after World War I, it
seems that there will be no alternative but to follow the Western pattern. Moreover, if development of transportation lags behind, manufacturing industries will naturally be located near heavy industries.
The result will be a rapid concentration in urban centers and the deterioration of the rural areas as pictured above. Thus the sequence in
which the various types of industry develop will determine their location.

We can offer no choice as to this sequence because it depends upon
another factor, which is not settled at present—that is, the international order. In China there is today an unprecedented enthusiasm for
industrialization. This is due to the plain fact that we have suffered so
much in this war because of our industrial backwardness. That enemy

planes have been able to fly over our cities and villages and drop their bombs at will without any opposition has been a profoundly painful experience. To protect our wives and children, it is natural that we should feel that we must have our own planes and tanks. If there are no international guaranties of security, every sane Chinese will be willing to go to any length in order to prevent a recurrence of such disasters in the future. In other words, if the postwar world is again to be governed by power alone, China will have no alternative but to give first place to heavy industry and armaments. It is needless to add that such tactics will be disastrous to China as well as to the world. Defense industries are costly, and the capital thus invested does not profit the investor. Since the standard of living in China is already on a bare subsistence level, any further decline will mean starvation and death. If the international order is such that the Chinese government, in view of the national safety, must prepare for another war—or at least must arm, to maintain an effective neutrality in the coming world struggle for power—it will be obliged to adopt extremely strong measures in order to squeeze the last pennies from the people. This, in turn, will inevitably block the development of democratic institutions in China. Let our friends in the West who are worrying about political trends in the East keep in mind the fact that China has been ever ready to trust international tribunals and that the ideal of T'ien Hsia, the global community, is deeply rooted in her tradition. It is for the coming world order to prove that such an ideal can be realized and to offer guaranties of security and prosperity to all peace-loving peoples. China cannot achieve this by herself alone.

Given a co-operative world order, China will have no reason to devote herself to economically unprofitable armaments. If she is allowed to rehabilitate her national economy in a stable world order, she can take advantage of industrial organization in the West and make plans for her own industry on the basis of real consumers' needs and a wide distribution of profit in the form of small rural co-operatives. It cannot be denied that, for some time after the present war, foreign aid will be necessary for China's industrial development. In view of the rapid increase in production by America during the war, it will also be to the interest of the American people to export their industrial goods. It is essential for investors to see that their capital can be employed in productive enterprises. The mutual benefit of such financial relations can be realized only when the standard of living of the investees will be improved by such investment.

We need not apologize for concluding our scientific study with a practical appeal, because we firmly believe that scientific knowledge should be helpful in promoting the good of the people and serving as a guide for our actions in the future. The need for an awakened conscience among social scientists has been cogently expressed by Professor Karl Mannheim:

> There will be no effective Democracy until the man in the street adopts the concepts and results of rational social analysis instead of the magical formulae which still dominate his thinking on human affairs. Nor can we have a Democracy unless the scholars and scientists do not occasionally break through the self-established barriers imposed by intraprofessional fears and conventions which prevent them from applying their systematized knowledge to the practical problems of the day.[6]

Let us recognize that we are now at a crossroads. The fate of innocent Chinese peasants is in the hands of those who will decide the pattern of China's industry in the future. No one nation can decide the issue, however; the choice of what sort of a world we are to live in must come with the wide co-operation of the citizens of the world, whose opinion will ultimately decide the case. If the present work, as an analysis of the conditions existing in the rural China, can contribute to a right choice for the future, we shall feel that our efforts have not been in vain.

[6] *Diagnosis of Our Time* (London: K. Paul, Trench, Trubner & Co., Ltd., 1943), p. v.

INDEX

Aborigines, xi, 9, 11, 113, 145, 155–56, 160, 188, 201, 215, 266, 271, 284, 287

Absentee ownership, 4, 6, 17–18, 19, 76, 203, 206, 227, 233–35, 269, 276, 290, 293–96, 305–6

Agriculture, 1–2, 5, 289, 291, 292; and industry, 300–313; *see also* Crops, Landownership, Rice, Tenancy, *etc.*

Ancestor worship, xi, 9, 56, 89, 91, 164, 167, 190, 257–58, 260, 262

Animals; *see* Livestock

Anthropology, 13–16

Apprenticeship, 190, 271

Army, 129–30, 302

Bamboo, 133, 135, 137–40, 169, 174–76, 179–80, 182, 184–87, 194–96, 198, 204; sheaths of, 170, 171, 184

Banditry, 160, 227, 230, 231, 267, 269, 280, 293, 294, 302

Banking, 123, 290

Barley, 138, 139, 208, 214, 217

Basketry, 134, 139, 174–78, 179, 181–83, 193, 196, 197, 198, 202, 203, 205, 300, 304

Baskets, 170

Bean curds, 45, 106

Beans: broad, 21–24, 30, 33, 34–37, 39, 61, 91, 105, 138, 141–42, 146, 151–52, 208–9, 213–14, 217, 298; consumption of, 87–88; for feed, 49, 166, 238, 299; green, 70; oil, 46; yield of, 70–71, 85; *see also* Bean curds, Soybeans

Bilateral inheritance, 112

Birth, 102–3, 128

Birth rate, 62, 307

"Bitter grass," 208–9, 217

Blacksmiths, 45

Bronzework, 165

Budgets; *see* Family, the

Buffaloes, 72, 73, 105, 150–52, 166, 167–68

Burials; *see* Funerals

Burma, 280, 281, 282

Burma Road, 8, 10, 63, 99–100, 287

Bus service, 284, 286, 287

Butchers, 45

Cabbage, 207–8, 211, 212, 213

Cactus, 188

Cakeshops, 287

Calendar, farming, 27–28; *see also* Crops

Candy, 88, 212, 269

Capital, 6, 96–97, 150–53, 155, 178, 181–82, 186, 192–93, 195–96, 198, 202–3, 205–6, 224, 227, 234, 237, 240, 244, 266, 280, 284, 287, 289, 292–94, 303

Capitalism, 196, 284, 308

Carpenters, 45–46

Celery, 212

Celtuce, 207–8

Ceremonies, 100–103, 119, 121, 128, 167–69, 179, 190–91, 198, 201, 253–54, 256–63, 277, 291, 293, 302

Charcoal, 88, 106

Chia, 29

Chickens, 48, 49, 105, 167, 245

Christianity, 89, 93

Cigarettes, 46, 171, 287

Cities, 8–9, 269

Civil service; *see* Government service

Civil war, 307

Clans, xi, 3, 11, 53–56, 77, 85, 109, 121, 125, 130, 133, 148, 158, 161–62, 226, 228, 231, 260, 280

Climate, 21–24, 61, 135, 138, 212

Clothing, 47, 87, 91, 92, 93, 94–96, 106, 164–65, 241, 243, 247–49, 253, 256, 265, 279

Clubs, 54, 55–56

Coffins, 165, 261–62, 265

Collective ownership; *see* Landownership

Commerce, 17, 47–48, 50, 129, 171, 197, 198, 203–6, 227, 268, 269, 277, 283–90, 292, 295, 303

Conscription, 63–64, 99, 268, 270

Contentment, 82, 279

Co-operatives, 123–24, 129, 191, 306–13

Corn, 21, 23, 87, 138, 141–42, 149, 215, 248, 299

Corporations, 284, 287

Cotton, 137–38, 141–42, 147, 149, 164, 242, 247, 284–85, 288, 291, 303

Cotton cloth, 170–71, 205, 241–43, 247–48, 285–86, 288, 291, 304–5

Cotton thread, 164, 240–44

Cotton trees, 137–38

Counterfeiting, 288

The International Library of
SOCIOLOGY AND SOCIAL RECONSTRUCTION

Editor: KARL MANNHEIM
Late Professor of Education in the University of London

PLAN OF THE LIBRARY
Sections

ROUTLEDGE & KEGAN PAUL LTD.
68-74 Carter Lane, London, E.C.4

SOCIOLOGY OF EDUCATION

Education after School
by C. STIMSON   *15s.*

The Problem of Punishment in Education
by EWALD BOHM   *In preparation. About 21s.*

Mission of the University
by ORTEGA Y GASSET. Translated and introduced by HOWARD LEE
NOSTRAND   *7s. 6d.*

Total Education: A Plea for Synthesis
by M. L. JACKS, Director, Department of Education, Oxford University
                                        Second Impression. 10s. 6d.

Education in Transition
A Sociological Analysis of the Impact of the War on English Education
by H. C. DENT   *Fifth Impression. 12s. 6d.*

The Reform of Secondary Education
by H. C. DENT   *About 15s.*

Education for Adults: A Study in Transition
by T. MACKAY MURE   *About 10s. 6d.*

**Who Shall Be Educated? The Challenge of Unequal
Opportunities**
by W. LLOYD WARNER, Prof. of Anthropology and Sociology, Member
of Comm. on Human Development, Univ. of Chicago; ROBERT J.
HAVIGHURST, Prof. of Education, Member of Comm. on Human
Development, Univ. of Chicago; MARTIN B. LOEB Inst. of Child
Welfare, Univ. of California, at Berkeley   *10s. 6d.*

**The Social Psychology of Education: A Sociological
Study**
by C. M. FLEMING, Ed.B., Ph.D., University of London Institute of
Education   *Fifth Impression 7s. 6d.*

German Youth: Bond or Free
by HOWARD BECKER, Professor of Sociology, University of Wisconsin
                                              Illustrated. 18s.

2

Education and Society in Modern Germany

by R. H. SAMUEL of the Department of Germanic Languages, Melbourne University and R. HINTON THOMAS   *In preparation.*   *About 15s.*

The Museum: Its History and Its Tasks in Education

by ALMA S. WITTLIN, Dr. Phil.   *Illustrated. About 21s.*

Comparative Education

A Study of Educational Facts and Traditions.

NICHOLAS HANS, Lecturer in Comparative Education at the University of London, King's College   *About 21s. net*

SOCIOLOGY OF RELIGION

Sociology of Religion

by JOACHIM WACH   *30s.*

The Economic Order and Religion

by FRANK KNIGHT, Prof. of Social Sciences, University of Chicago, and THORNTON W. MERRIAM, Director of U.S.O. Training, Nat. Council of the Y.M.C.A.   *15s.*

SOCIOLOGY OF ART AND LITERATURE

Sociology of the Renaissance

by ALFRED VON MARTIN, translated by W. L. LUETKENS
Second Impression. 8s. 6d.

Theatre, Drama and Audience in Goethe's Germany

by W. H. BRUFORD, M.A., Professor of German, University of Edinburgh   *In Preparation. About 25s.*

Chekhov and His Russia: A Sociological Study

by W. H. BRUFORD, M.A., Professor of German in the University of Edinburgh   *16s.*

The Sociology of Literary Taste

by LEVIN L. SCHÜCKING, Dr. Phil.   *Second Impression 7s. 6d.*

Men of Letters and the English Public in the 18th Century, 1660-1744. Dryden, Addison, Pope

by ALEXANDRE BELJAME. Edited with an Introduction and Notes by Prof. BONAMY DOBREE. Translated by E. O. LORIMER   *25s.*

SOCIOLOGICAL APPROACH TO THE STUDY OF HISTORY

The Aftermath of the Napoleonic Wars: The Concert of Europe—An Experiment
by H. G. SCHENK, D.Phil. (Oxon) *Illustrated. 16s.*

Progress and Disenchantment: A Study of European Romanticism
by H. G. SCHENK, D.Phil. (Oxon) *Illustrated. About 21s.*

SOCIOLOGY OF LAW

The Sociology of Law
by GEORGES GURVITCH, Ph.D., LL.D., Prof. of Sociology, University of Strassbourg, France. With an Introduction by ROSCOE POUND, Prof. of Jurisprudence, late Dean of the Faculty of Law, Harvard University
18s.

The Institutions of Private Law and Their Social Functions
by KARL RENNER, President of the Austrian Republic. Edited with an Introduction and Notes by O. KAHN-FREUND, Ll.M., Dr. Jur., Lecturer in Law, University of London *About 10s. 6d.*

Legal Aid
by ROBERT EGERTON, Hon. Sec. Legal Sub-committee Cambridge House, Solicitor of the Supreme Court. With an Introduction by D. L. GOODHART, K.C., D.C.L., Ll.D., Prof. of Jurisprudence, Oxford
2nd Impression. 10s. 6d.

Soviet Legal Theory: Its Social Background and Development
by RUDOLF SCHLESINGER, Ph.D., London *2nd Impression. 16s.*

CRIMINOLOGY AND THE SOCIAL SERVICES

Theory and Practice of a Family Court

by CARL BIRNBAUM, formerly Professor of Psychiatry, Berlin University, and John Otto Reinemann, Dr. Jur., formerly Municipal Councillor in Berlin *About 12s. 6d.*

Juvenile Delinquency in an English Middletown

by HERMANN MANNHEIM, Lecturer in Criminology in the University of London *12s. 6d.*

Mental Health in a Rural Area

by Dr. MAYER GROSS *In preparation. About 15s.*

Criminal Justice and Social Reconstruction

by HERMANN MANNHEIM, Dr. Jur., Lecturer in Criminology in the University of London *Second Impression. 15s.*

The Psycho-Analytical Approach to Juvenile Delinquency: Theory, Case Studies, Treatment

by KATE FRIEDLANDER, M.D., L.R.C.P. (Edin.), D.P.M. (Lond.), Hon. Psychiatrist, Inst. for the Scientific Treatment of Delinquency; Clinical Dir., W. Sussex Child Guidance Service *18s.*

Voluntary Social Services since 1918

by HENRY A. MESS, late Reader in Social Science in the University of London in collaboration with Constance Braithwaite, Violet Creech-Jones, Hilda Jennings, Pearl Jephcott, Harold King, Nora Milnes, John Morgan, Gertrude Williams and W. E. Williams. Edited by GERTRUDE WILLIAMS, Lecturer in Economics, University of London *21s.*

A Textbook of Penology

by HERMANN MANNHEIM *In preparation. About 25s.*

A Textbook of Criminology

by HERMANN MANNHEIM *In preparation. About 25s.*

SOCIOLOGY AND POLITICS

Social-Economic Movements: A Handbook to the Understanding of the Modern Political Scene

by H. W. LAIDLER *In preparation. About 30s.*

The Analysis of Political Behaviour: An Empirical Approach
by HAROLD D. LASSWELL, Professor of Law, Yale University
School of Law   21s.

Dictatorship and Political Police
The Technique of Control by Fear by E. K. BRAMSTEDT, Ph.D. (London)
15s.

Nationality in History and Politics
by FREDERICK HERTZ, Author of "Race and Civilisation"
Second Impression. 25s.

FOREIGN AFFAIRS, THEIR SOCIAL, POLITICAL AND ECONOMIC FOUNDATIONS

Patterns of Peacemaking
by DAVID THOMSON, Ph.D., Cantab., Research Fellow of Sidney
Sussex Coll., Cambridge; E. MEYER, Dr. rer. pol., and A. BRIGGS,
B.A., Cantab.   21s.

French Canada in Transition
by EVERETT C. HUGHES, Professor of Sociology, University of Chicago
15s.

State and Economics in the Middle East
by A. BONNE, Dr. œc. publ., Director, Economic Research Institute
of Palestine   30s.

Economic Development of the Middle East
An Outline of Planned Reconstruction by A. BONNE, Dr. œc. publ.,
Director, Economic Research Institute of Palestine
Second Impression. 12s. 6d.

Federalism in Central and Eastern Europe
by RUDOLF SCHLESINGER, Ph.D., London   30s.

The Danube Basin and the German Economic Sphere
by ANTONIN BASCH, Dr. Phil., Columbia University   18s.

The Regions of Germany
by R. E. DICKINSON, Reader in Geography, University College, London
Second Impression. 10s. 6d.

French Political Thought from the Revolution to the Fourth Republic
by J. P. MEYER   *In preparation. About 12s. 6d.*

MIGRATION AND RE-SETTLEMENT

Settlement in Underpopulated Areas
by JULIUS ISAAC, Ph.D. (London).   *In preparation.   About 18s.*

Economics of Migration
by JULIUS ISAAC, Ph.D., London. With an Introduction by Sir ALEXANDER CARR-SAUNDERS, Director of the London School of Economics   *18s.*

Co-operative Communities at Work
by HENRIK INFIELD, Director, Rural Settlement Inst., New York

15s.

ECONOMIC PLANNING

Retail Trade Associations
A New Form of Monopolist Organisation in Britain, by HERMANN LEVY, Author of "The New Industrial System"   *Second Impression.   15s.*

The Shops of Britain: A Study in Retail Trade Distribution
by HERMANN LEVY   *21s.*

The Price of Social Security—The Problem of Labour Mobility
by GERTRUDE WILLIAMS, Lecturer in Economics, University of London
Second Impression.   12s. 6d.

SOCIOLOGY OF THE FAMILY AND ALLIED TOPICS

The Family and Democratic Society
by J. K. FOLSOM, Professor of Sociology, Vassar College

About 30s.

Nation and Family
The Swedish Experiment in Democratic Family and Population Policy
by ALVA MYRDAL   *2nd Impression.   21s.*

The Sociology of Women's Work
by GERTRUDE WILLIAMS, Lecturer in Economics, University of London
About 15s.

Adolescence
Its Social Psychology : With an Introduction to recent findings from the fields of Anthropology, Physiology, Medicine, Psychometrics and Sociometry
by C. M. FLEMING, Ed.B., Ph.D., University of London Institute of Education
16s.

TOWN AND COUNTRY PLANNING. HUMAN ECOLOGY

The Social Background of a Plan : A Study of Middlesbrough
Edited by RUTH GLASS. Illustrated with Maps and Plans
42s.

City, Region and Regionalism
by ROBERT E. DICKINSON, Reader in Geography, University College, London. With Maps and Plans
21s.

The West European City: A Study in Urban Geography
by ROBERT E. DICKINSON, Reader in Geography, University College, London. Illustrated, with Maps and Plans. *In preparation. About 21s.*

Creative Demobilisation
Vol. I. Principles of National Planning
By E. A. GUTKIND, D.Ing.
Vol. 2. Case Studies in National Planning
Edited by E. A. GUTKIND, D.Ing.
Second Impression. 21s. each

Revolution of Environment
by E. A. GUTKIND, D.Ing.
Illustrated. 30s.

The Journey to Work
by K. LIEPMANN, Ph.D., London. With an Introduction by Sir Alexander Carr-Saunders, Director of the London School of Economics
Second Impression. 15s.

SOCIOLOGICAL STUDIES OF MODERN COMMUNITIES

Negroes in Britain
A study of Racial Relations in English Society
by K. L. LITTLE, Ph.D., London   25s.

Co-operative Living in Palestine
by HENRIK F. INFIELD, Director, Rural Settlement Inst., New York
Illustrated. 7s. 6d.

ANTHROPOLOGY AND COLONIAL POLICY

The Sociology of Colonies: An Introduction to the Study of Race Contact
by RENÉ MAUNIER. Translated from the French by E. O. Lorimer
In preparation. About 42s.

Malay Fishermen: Their Peasant Economy
by RAYMOND FIRTH, Prof. of Anthropology, University of London
Illustrated. 25s.

Peasant Life in China
by HSIAO T'UNG FEI, Ph.D., London   *Fourth Impression. Illustrated.* 15s.

A Chinese Village: Taitou, Shantung Province
by MARTIN C. YANG   18s.

Hsinlung Hsiang
A Field Study of Peasant Life in the Red Basin, West China
by ISABEL CROOK and YU HSI-CHI   *About 21s.*

A Japanese Village: Suye Mura
by JOHN P. EMBREE, Visiting Assoc. Prof. of Anthropology, University of Chicago. With an Introduction by A. R. RADCLIFFE-BROWN, Professor of Social Anthropology, Oxford University. *Illustrated.* 18s.

The Golden Wing: A Sociological Study of Chinese Familism
by LIN HUEH-HWA, with an Introduction by RAYMOND FIRTH
16s.

Earthbound China: A Study of Rural Economy in Yunnan
by HSIAO -TUNG FEI and CHIH-I CHANG   *Illustrated. About 18s.*

SOCIOLOGY AND PSYCHOLOGY OF THE PRESENT CRISIS

War, Love or Money: A Psychological Study of European Culture Patterns
by H. V. DICKS, M.D., M.R.C.P.   *In preparation.   About 21s.*

Diagnosis of Our Time
by KARL MANNHEIM   *Fourth Impression.   10s. 6d.*

Farewell to European History or the Conquest of Nihilism
by ALFRED WEBER   *16s.*

The Fear of Freedom
by Dr. ERICH FROMM   *Fourth Impression.   15s.*

SOCIAL PSYCHOLOGY AND PSYCHO-ANALYSIS

Psychology and the Social Pattern
by JULIAN BLACKBURN, Ph.D., B.Sc. (Econ.), Lecturer on Social Psychology, London School of Economics   *Third Impression.   10s. 6d.*

The Framework of Human Behaviour
by JULIAN BLACKBURN, Ph.D., B.Sc. (Econ.), Lecturer on Social Psychology, London School of Economics   *12s. 6d.*

Individual Development in Society
by JULIAN BLACKBURN, Ph.D., B.Sc. (Econ.), Lecturer on Social Psychology, London School of Economics   *About 10s. 6d.*
(Three independent volumes supplementing each other)

A Handbook of Social Psychology
by KIMBALL YOUNG, Professor of Sociology, Queens College, New York   *Second Impression.   21s.*

Sigmund Freud—An Introduction
A Presentation of his Theories and a discussion of the Relationship between Psycho-analysis and Sociology by WALTER HOLLITSCHER, Dr. Phil.   *8s. 6d.*

The Social Problems of an Industrial Civilization
by ELTON MAYO, Professor of Industrial Research.
In preparation.   About 12s. 6d. net

Social Learning and Imitation
by NEAL E. MILLER and JOHN DOLLARD of the Institute of Human
Relations, Yale University   *15s.*

APPROACHES TO THE PROBLEM
OF PERSONALITY

The Cultural Background of Personality
by RALPH LINTON, Professor of Anthropology, Columbia University
                                                                     10s. 6d.

The Feminine Character. History of an Ideology
by VIOLA KLEIN, Ph.D., London. With an Introduction by KARL
MANNHEIM.   *12s. 6d.*

The History of Autobiography in Antiquity
by GEORG MISCH. Translated by E. W. DICKES   *About 21s.*

Personality and Problems of Adjustment
by KIMBALL YOUNG   *35s.*

PHILOSOPHICAL AND SOCIAL FOUNDATIONS
OF THOUGHT

Homo Ludens: A Study of the Play Element in Culture
by Professor J. HUIZINGA   *About 21s.*

The Ideal Foundations of Economic Thought
by W. STARK, Dr. rer. pol., Dr. Jur.   *Third Impression*   *15s.*

The History of Economics in Its Relation to Social
Development
by W. STARK, Dr. rer. pol., Dr. Jur.   *Second Impression.*   *7s. 6d.*

America: Ideal and Reality
The United States of 1776 in Contemporary European Philosophy by
W. STARK, Dr. rer. pol., Dr. Jur.   *10s. 6d.*

The Decline of Liberalism as an Ideology
by J. H. HALLOWELL   *12s. 6d.*

Society and Nature: A Sociological Inquiry
by HANS KELSEN, Formerly Prof. of Law, Vienna and Geneva, Department of Political Science, University of California   *21s.*

Demographic Material Appearing in the Transactions of the Royal Society in the 17th and 18th Centuries

Edited by Dr. R. R. KUCZYNSKI   *In preparation. About 15s.*

Population Controversies of the Eighteenth Century

Edited by DAVID GLASS, Ph.D.   *In preparation. About 15s.*

GENERAL SOCIOLOGY

A Handbook of Sociology

by W. F. OGBURN, Professor of Sociology, University of Chicago, and M. F. NIMKOFF, Professor of Sociology, Bucknell University.   *25s.*

FOREIGN CLASSICS OF SOCIOLOGY

Wilhelm Dilthey: Selected Readings from his Works and an Introduction to his Sociological and Philosophical Work

by H. A. HODGES, Prof. of Philosophy, University of Reading

Second Impression. 10s. 6d.

From Max Weber: Essays in Sociology

Translated, edited, and with an Introduction by H. H. GERTH and C. W. MILLS   *21s.*

DOCUMENTARY

Changing Attitudes in Soviet Russia

Documents and Readings concerning the *Family*
Edited by R. SCHLESINGER, Ph.D., London   *About 21s.*

Changing Attitudes in Soviet Russia

Documents and Readings concerning *National Autonomy and Experiments in Administrative Devolution*
Edited by R. SCHLESINGER, Ph.D., London   *About 21s.*

Changing Attitudes in Soviet Russia

Documents and Readings concerning *Foreign Policy*
Edited by R. SCHLESINGER, Ph.D., London   *About 21s.*

All prices are net

THE WESTMINSTER PRESS, LONDON, W.9